MARY BAKER EDDY: CHRISTIAN HEALER
Amplified Edition

Many historical records related to Mary Baker Eddy's life, including those used in this biography, are held at The Mary Baker Eddy Library in Boston, Massachusetts. The Library's collections are available for public research.

Yvonne Caché von Fettweis
and
Robert Townsend Warneck

Amplification by Robert Townsend Warneck

The Christian Science Publishing Society
Boston, Massachusetts, USA

ISBN: 978-0-87510-479-9

G750B50692EN

Several abbreviations appear in credits and copyright notices throughout this book:
CSPS–The Christian Science Publishing Society
TMBEC–The Mary Baker Eddy Collection
TMBEL–The Mary Baker Eddy Library

Cover image:
Kimball Studio. P00101. Courtesy of The Mary Baker Eddy Collection

Printed in USA
6th printing

Mary Baker Eddy: Christian Healer
Amplified Edition

*God has not given us vast learning to solve all
the problems, or unfailing wisdom to direct all the
wanderings of our brothers' lives; but He has given to
every one of us the power to be spiritual, and by our
spirituality to lift and enlarge and enlighten the lives
we touch.*

— Phillips Brooks

"The secret of my life is in the above."[1]

— Mary Baker Eddy

Contents

Preface

𝒲HEN MARY BAKER EDDY'S NAME is mentioned today, she is sometimes thought of as the founder of a Christian denomination that takes seriously Christ Jesus' command to "heal the sick." Others know her as the author of a book on spiritual healing. Besides that, the public in general knows little about her. Yet in her day, at the dawn of the twentieth century, Mrs. Eddy was one of the most well-known women in America. She was often in the news because her Church and Cause were flourishing—to the alarm of many theologians and medical authorities. The key to her success lay in her love for God and His Christ, and in her conviction that this love needs to be demonstrated tangibly through the spiritual healing of sickness and sin.

Her book *Science and Health with Key to the Scriptures* was recognized in 1992 by the Women's National Book Association in the United States as one of the 75 books by women whose words have changed the world. And Mrs. Eddy was inducted into the US National Women's Hall of Fame in 1995 because she had made "an indelible mark on society, religion, and journalism."

At the turn of the twentieth century, the age was demanding logical, "scientific" solutions to problems, and students of Mrs. Eddy's textbook on Christian Science rose to meet that demand through Christian healing grounded in an understanding of God and His divine laws. According to Mrs. Eddy's own description, *Science and Health* "maintains primitive Christianity, shows how to demonstrate it, and throughout is logical in premise and in conclusion."[1]

After her discovery of Christian Science in 1866, which was directly related to her own healing of injuries from an accident that was assumed to be fatal, Mrs. Eddy immersed herself in study of the Bible:

> For three years after my discovery, I sought the solution
> of this problem of Mind-healing, searched the Scriptures
> and read little else, kept aloof from society, and devoted
> time and energies to discovering a positive rule. . . . I
> knew the Principle of all harmonious Mind-action to be
> God, and that cures were produced in primitive Christian
> healing by holy, uplifting faith; but I must know the
> Science of this healing, and I won my way to absolute
> conclusions through divine revelation, reason, and
> demonstration.[2]

The demonstration she refers to was her public practice of Christian healing. But her ability to heal through prayer preceded her discovery of Christian Science. It began in her childhood and grew steadily through adulthood. Eventually, however, Mrs. Eddy announced that she was no longer accepting requests for treatment. She focused, instead, on teaching others her method of healing and, later, became fully occupied as Church founder and leader. But the historical record shows that her healing work didn't stop with this announcement. It continued undiminished.

This biography, which focuses on Mary Baker Eddy as a Christian healer, offers the first comprehensive record of her healing works and shows how essential her own practice of Christian healing was to her, compared with the many other roles she filled—as teacher, writer, and founder. Beginning in 1992, a concerted effort was made to find every reference to her healing work in the historical collections of The First Church of Christ, Scientist, in Boston, Massachusetts. The better part of five years was spent identifying, evaluating, and assembling chronologically hundreds of healing accounts from Mrs. Eddy's published writings, from her unpublished letters and articles (more than 28,000), from the reminiscences of her students and others who knew her personally, and from Church historical documents. Research conducted by former Church archivists was included as well. Placing all the accounts of this work into two-inch-thick (8½ x 11) binders filled eleven binders.

The next step was to read through all of Mrs. Eddy's correspondence and her other unpublished writings chronologically in order to glean the evolution of her thought. The result documented a lifetime of healing spanning almost ninety years. Initially, this material was used as the basis of an eighteen-part series of articles titled "Mary Baker Eddy: A Lifetime of Healing," which appeared as a series in *The Christian Science Journal* between January 1995 and December 1996.

That series of articles, somewhat expanded, forms the first

part of this book. The second part consists of additional healing accounts quoted directly from the original sources. In addition, Appendix B—a biographical glossary—provides information about individuals mentioned or quoted in the book. Work on this "amplification" of *Mary Baker Eddy: Christian Healer* was begun in 2006. The result of that work is the inclusion of more healing accounts, a Prelude about Mrs. Eddy's Puritan heritage, an Interlude with her advice to students concerning healing, and an appendix containing additional letters with her instructions to students regarding healing.

In the early chapters of the book, readers will notice that most of the healings related are Mrs. Eddy's firsthand accounts, given in her autobiography *Retrospection and Introspection* and in communications to her students. A number of these accounts are corroborated by other witnesses in the later chapters of the book, particularly in some of the new material in this edition. Also, it should be noted that throughout the book, Mrs. Eddy's name appears as it was at the time of her marriages, i.e., Glover, Patterson, Eddy. Furthermore, minor changes to original documents' spelling and punctuation have been made for clarity.

Following the example of Christ Jesus and his apostles, Mary Baker Eddy saw Christian healing as vital to humanity's salvation. Her study of the Bible convinced her that this type of healing existed even before the days of Jesus of Nazareth, and that the Christ, the healing and saving power of God, had always been present, as Jesus himself indicated when he said, "Before Abraham was, I am."[3] She was convinced that the ability to heal quickly and completely, through prayer alone, as Jesus did, grows out of a life grounded in Christ—a pure and loving consciousness that scientifically understands and completely relies on God as the divine Father-Mother to fully care for all Her creation.

The purpose of this biography is to make Mary Baker Eddy's healing work more widely known and, more significantly, to illuminate the standard for contemporary Christian healing set by her work—a standard she believed to be within reach of "any sincere seeker of Truth."[4] In February 1900, she wrote:

> I can look back and see that at the time of the accident [in 1866] although I had no faith in medicine and did not take it, I had faith that God could raise me up. Hence the effect of the Scripture that I read which strengthened my faith and its results in my recovery. And afterwards was seen in the illumination of the spiritual meaning of the Scriptures as given in my books and teachings. All of which is in accord with our Master's precious promise, "If ye have faith as a grain of mustard seed, ye shall say unto this mountain, Remove hence to yonder place; and it shall remove; and nothing shall be impossible unto you." [Matthew 17:20] My experience of the effects of faith was no miracle and nothing impossible to all who have that faith which is followed by spiritual understanding and is equal to avail itself of Christ's promise, not to a select number, but to all who exercise it.[5]

Part One

A Lifetime
of
Healing

Prelude

MARY BAKER EDDY'S PURITAN HERITAGE

"*F*ROM PURITAN PARENTS, THE DISCOVERER of Christian Science early received her religious education."[1] This statement in Mary Baker Eddy's primary work, *Science and Health with Key to the Scriptures*, might be thought of as one of the foundation stones in building an accurate understanding of this unique woman who founded a religious denomination with adherents around the world. The strong Puritan influence that lay behind her upbringing in the Congregational church explains much about how she thought and lived, how she sought, drew near to, and understood God. This Puritan approach to God was a motivating force behind both her private and public life.

To comprehend the Puritan effect on Mrs. Eddy, stereotypes of these believers as rigid extremists must be discarded. Instead, "practicality" gives a clearer, more precise picture of the Puritan, for whom fulfilling one's duty to God was the whole purpose of existence. Nothing was more important. Every detail in one's life could be dealt with correctly only through discernment of the divine will, and this discernment was not to be determined intellectually, but received directly from God Himself through spiritual communion. The Puritan sought to hear God's commands consciously, moment by moment. Obedience to God brought blessings. Disobedience was sin, which necessarily brought suffering. But the Puritan found good in the suffering because it made him turn back to God more strongly than before.

Every detail in one's life, no matter how seemingly trivial, was endowed with importance for the Puritan, because God was the fabric of his or her existence. And Christianity was the only way to deal with the details. Religion for these believers was not a cerebral exercise; it had to be practical and tangibly felt.

Richard Sibbes, a notable Puritan preacher active in the first half of seventeenth-century England, counseled: "Religion is not a matter of word, nor stands upon words, . . . but . . . of Power, it makes a man able. . . . [It] is an Art, not of great men, nor of mighty men; but of holy men: it is an Art, and Trade: a Trade is not learned by words, but by experience: and a man hath learned a Trade, not when he can talk of it, but when he can work according to his Trade."[2] It would be hard to find a better description than this of Mary Baker Eddy's expectation for Christian Science and its adherents.

One of the chief aids in the Puritans' "Art, and Trade" was spiritualization of thought. The state of their consciousness was one of their main concerns. Continual introspection kept them alert to prevent the affairs of this world from taking over their lives, which had to be devoted to spiritual striving, to the rooting out of sin in thought and action. Along these very lines, Mrs. Eddy writes: "Watch, and pray daily that evil suggestions, in whatever guise, take no root in your thought nor bear fruit. Ofttimes examine yourselves, and see if there be found anywhere a deterrent of Truth and Love, and 'hold fast that which is good.'"[3]

The Puritan code was outlined not by behavioral prohibitions but by an unselfed love for God and man. Puritans trusted that if they put God first in their thoughts and days, God would in turn supply them with whatever they needed—food, shelter, clothing, friends, and so on—to support their fulfillment of divine obligations. Being a Puritan was a way of life much more than a doctrine of belief. It was not a monastic life but an active living that engaged the world in order to lead others to God through word and deed.

For most seventeenth- and eighteenth-century Puritans, however, this daily searching for God's direction was filtered through John Calvin's doctrine of predestination, with its belief in God's election of some mortals to be saved from their sinful nature and the remainder to be damned for eternity. As a result, Puritans were constantly searching for indications of their election. A persevering faith in Christ Jesus' power and willingness to save and redeem was one sign. Others included a yearning love of God and the Bible, and a desire to be and do good. One of the most meaningful signs—because it was so tangible—was a hatred of evil. If men or women felt within themselves a genuine loathing of sin, this was a sure sign that God had chosen them to be saved. This, however, did not mean they weren't going to sin. Quite to the contrary, they accepted that, because of mortals' basically depraved nature, they would continue to do wrong in the eyes of their Lord, but their saving grace was that they hated doing so and consequently would strive to sin less. For Puritans, life was a continual warfare with the flesh, the world, and the devil. The desire to remain at war was their proof of God's election. They fought with confidence because they believed the outcome of the conflict was predestined salvation. All those not "chosen" were condemned to hell. From childhood, Mrs. Eddy rejected this concept of a wrathful Deity selecting some and damning the rest. Her mother and the Bible had taught her that "God is love,"[4] and that divine Love provides salvation for all.

Mrs. Eddy was not alone in her rejection of predestination. Almost from the beginning of the Puritan experience, some disagreed with this doctrine. Calvin himself was in part responsible for this. He sent men back to the Bible, especially to Paul and his letters, for confirmation and explanation. Puritan preachers encouraged searching the Scriptures, too. There, the seeker for salvation found this in the first epistle to the Thessalonians: "We give thanks to God always for you all, . . . knowing, brethren beloved, your election of God."[5] And in Romans, the Puritan found these words: "And we know that all things work together for good to them that love God, to them who are the called according to his purpose. For whom he did foreknow, he also did predestinate to be conformed to the image of his Son, that he might be the firstborn among many brethren."[6] But once in the Bible, those hungering and thirsting after righteousness invariably turned to the Gospels, where they found a less exclusive road to salvation in Jesus' declarations: "He that believeth and is baptized shall be saved"[7] and "He that heareth my word, and believeth on him that sent me, hath everlasting life, and shall not come into condemnation."[8] Even Paul answered one who had asked, "...what must I do to be saved?" by saying, "Believe on the Lord Jesus Christ, and thou shalt be saved, and thy house."[9]

It's not hard to see why so many Christians today have faith that their "belief" in Jesus Christ as their personal savior is in and of itself their salvation. Mary Baker Eddy was too much of a Puritan, however, to put her faith in a less-than-informed trust in God and His Son. In *Science and Health*, she gave this spiritual definition of *believing*: "Firmness and constancy; not a faltering nor a blind faith, but the perception of spiritual Truth."[10] And in another reference linking believing to firmness and constancy, she added, "This certainly applies to Truth and Love understood and practised."[11]

While the Puritans strove to understand not so much God but the path to salvation, and to practice Christian virtues, their insistence on thinking for themselves—using the Scriptures as their only authority, without an intermediary—inevitably led to differing opinions about how one could obtain heaven. One thing they did agree on, however, was that salvation from mortality is linked to a demanding discipline of Christian thought and action. In his book *The Rise of Puritanism*, William Haller points out: "The persuasive strength of the doctrine of predestination, as the Puritan preachers presented it, sprang not from its metaphysical but its moral validity. . . . It supplied a basis both practical and ideal for decision. It suggested an attitude and a line of conduct. Put to the test of experience, it applied and it worked."[12]

This is extremely significant in considering the life and thought of Mary Baker Eddy. Though she completely rejected the "horrible decree," as Calvin himself referred to his doctrine, as having any part in God, her Puritan nature still demanded a theology that was "both practical and ideal," that provided "an attitude and a line of conduct," and most important, that when "put to the test of experience, it applied and it worked." This practical idealism is essential to the theology of Christian Science.

Mrs. Eddy recognized many of the same footsteps for salvation as the Puritans, even though she defined salvation differently.[13] Significantly, she considered these footsteps possible for all, not just a few: overpowering love of God; unshakable belief in the Christ as God's Son; deep devotion to the Bible; daily striving to live a Christian life; and, of course, abhorrence of wickedness. Her writings teach that if we feel a genuine loathing for iniquity, and are daily striving to rule sin out of ourselves, this is practical, sure evidence that we are walking in the strait and narrow way Christ Jesus pointed out.[14]

Like the first Puritans, Mrs. Eddy meant her theology to be applied directly to the eradication of sin. She writes, "The emphatic purpose of Christian Science is the healing of sin ... ."[15] And she amplifies this in the third tenet of her Church: "We acknowledge God's forgiveness of sin in the destruction of sin and the spiritual understanding that casts out evil as unreal. But the belief in sin is punished so long as the belief lasts."[16]

In much of today's world, referring to something as a "sin" has become socially unacceptable and politically incorrect. People have become afraid to use this word, lest they be thought judgmental, insensitive, ignorant or,—heaven forbid—a devout Christian! But as Mrs. Eddy pointed out repeatedly, sinful behavior makes us feel separate from God, which in turn leads us to neglect and then forget our duty to our divine Father-Mother. To help prevent this, she gave this daily prayer—one could even describe it as a Puritan prayer—to her followers: "'Thy kingdom come;' let the reign of divine Truth, Life, and Love be established in me, and rule out of me all sin; and may Thy Word enrich the affections of all mankind, and govern them!"[17]

True to her Puritan roots, Mary Baker Eddy knew that sin must be faced—clearly seen for what it is—and dealt with head-on. She writes: "Expose and denounce the claims of evil and disease in all their forms, but realize no reality in them. A sinner is not reformed merely by assuring him that he cannot be a sinner because there is no sin. To put down the claim of sin, you must detect it, remove the mask, point out the illusion, and thus get the victory over sin and so prove its unreality."[18]

The "victory over sin" is as essential for Christian Scientists as it was for the early Puritans. For both, day-to-day triumph over evil in human thinking is inseparably linked to spiritual advancement. Mrs. Eddy knew that such triumphs are vital to one's ability to demonstrate God, divine Love, in daily life and to prove His omnipotence by healing sickness, a ministry she considered essential to Christianity.

Congregationalism was one of the most significant denominations to come out of the Puritan experience, especially in terms of United States history. Separatists, or Independents as they were also known, came over on the *Mayflower* and settled the Plymouth colony, while Puritans, who had hoped to reform the Church of England, settled the Massachusetts Bay colony, whose center would become Boston. The two groups eventually joined together, and out of that consolidation was born the Congregational church of New England. Their form of worship was unpretentious: hymn singing, readings from the Bible, prayer, and a sermon delivered without ceremony or ritual.

Speaking of her upbringing, Mary Baker Eddy wrote that it was the Congregational church "where my parents first offered me to Christ in infant baptism."[19] In her teens, she joined the Trinitarian Congregational Church at Sanbornton Bridge (later named Tilton) in New Hampshire in the summer of 1838, and she remained a member there for thirty-seven years.

Mrs. Eddy withdrew her membership from the Congregational church just a few months before her textbook on Christian healing, *Science and Health*, was to be published. A number of years later, in 1884, she wrote a minister:

> When a child of about 13 years,[20] I united with the Congregationalist church, and never left it until I had one built on its foundations. The only difference being the spiritual element taking the place of the material in its forms and doctrines....[21]

> ...We believe only in the baptism of Spirit. Our sacrament is a silent communion with our dear Lord and Christ. We repeat the Lord's prayer audibly and offer man's prayer silently.

The first tenet of our Church is—"We take the
Scriptures as our guide to life eternal." [The third tenet:]
"We covenant to faithfully obey the Ten Commandments, to deal justly, love 'mercy and walk humbly with
our God,'" etc.

We are essentially an Evangelical order, the life and
teachings of Jesus as contained in the four Gospels are
our basis. We believe that healing the sick is essential to
Christianity. We have *no doubt* of the inspiration of the
Scriptures....[22]

Mary Baker Eddy's insistence that "healing the sick is
essential to Christianity" was based on Christ Jesus' command
to his followers to "heal the sick."[23] However, the healing of
physical ailments through prayer was not foreign to Puritan
thought either. In John Bunyan's autobiography of his spiritual
life, *Grace Abounding* (1666), he relates two such healings. The
first was of his wife during pregnancy: "... before her full time
was come, her pangs, as of a woman in travail, were fierce and
strong upon her, even as she would have immediately fallen into
labor and been delivered of an untimely birth." The effect of his
prayer was immediate: "I had no sooner said it in my heart but
her pangs were taken from her, and she was cast into a deep sleep
and so continued till morning. At this I greatly marveled...."[24]
The second healing was of Bunyan himself, when he was "very
ill and weak." After he had pondered one of Jesus' parables,
a verse from the Bible suddenly came to thought: "At this I
became both well in body and mind at once, for my sickness
did presently vanish, and I walked comfortably in my work for
God again."[25]

Perhaps these healings account, in part, for the assertion a dozen years later in Bunyan's *Pilgrim's Progress* (1678) that "the soul of religion is the practic[al] part."[26] Like most Christians of her day, Mrs. Eddy was very familiar with this book. Its imagery and concepts permeated New England culture, and one hears echoes of them in her writings. Furthermore, viewing practicality as "the soul of religion" expresses the very nature of Christian Science. While Mrs. Eddy grounded her understanding and practice of spiritual healing in the Gospels, works like Bunyan's certainly bolstered her conviction that healing is a natural—and necessary—outcome of true Christianity.[27]

For Mrs. Eddy, the ability to heal in the manner of Jesus was proof of one's closeness to God because the life of a Christian healer must be permeated with Christliness—holiness—an unselfed love of God and man, genuine humility, scrupulous honesty, moral courage, and radical purity of thought. Mrs. Eddy explained this in her textbook: "By the truthful arguments you employ, and especially by the spirit of Truth and Love which you entertain, you will heal the sick."[28] She also wrote, "If you fail to succeed in any case, it is because you have not demonstrated the life of Christ, Truth, more in your own life,—because you have not obeyed the rule and proved the Principle of divine Science."[29] Living in accord with divine Principle in daily life, the healer is a transparency for Christ, Truth—reflecting God, who is the only healing power.

As Christian Scientists see it, Jesus healed by reflection. He said, "The Son can do nothing of himself, but what he seeth the Father do" and "...the Father that dwelleth in me, he doeth the works."[30] Mrs. Eddy echoed this idea: "All I have ever accomplished has been done by getting Mary out of the way, and letting God be reflected. When I would reach this tone, the sick would be healed without a word."[31] The only way to "reach this tone," Mrs. Eddy argued, is to live in the manner of the Puritan—letting God be the prevailing force in every detail of one's daily life.

Some credit John Milton, the great Puritan poet of *Paradise Lost*, with being able "to express for later generations the most vital thing in the whole Puritan movement, the belief, namely, in the transcending importance of spiritual values and responsibilities and the sanctity of individual spiritual life."[32] This would have resonated with Mrs. Eddy. She, too, strove to convey a similar message of "transcending importance," for it is only out of living in accord with one's spiritual values and fulfilling one's spiritual responsibilities that sickness can be healed and sin destroyed.

Though, like a true Puritan, Mrs. Eddy considered destroying sin more important than healing sickness, she neither minimized nor neglected the latter. Healing the sick is essential in Christian Science, not only because Jesus commanded his followers to do so, but also because doing so requires that one follow Jesus. One must strive to be a genuine Christian in thought and deed—relying on God alone—in order to heal after the manner of the Master. Mrs. Eddy made this connection between Christian purity and health when she told her household staff in 1908, "The healthiest person is the one who loathes sin the most."[33] In striving to be a true Christian, and in the emphasis she places on loathing sin, the Puritan influence in Mary Baker Eddy's character shines through most clearly. This Puritan, Christian character was absolutely essential to the appearance of God's revelation of Christian Science.

Raised as a Puritan by her parents, by the Bible, and by the Congregational church, Mary Baker Eddy never discarded the spiritual foundation and values of her childhood. Her adult life proved true the proverb, "Train up a child in the way he should go: and when he is old, he will not depart from it."[34] She never did.

Chapter 1

THE GIFTS OF CHILDHOOD
(1821–1843)

*E*VEN AS A CHILD, MARY Baker yearned for the tender, loving God who is Love. She leaned on God as a matter of simple, strong faith and witnessed His grace and care for herself and others when she prayed. From an early age, her reflection of, affection for, and trust in divine Love resulted in numerous experiences which affirmed that God's love does indeed heal.

Mary Baker's childhood household was large by today's standards, but typical both in size and religious fervor for that period in the United States. At the time of her birth on July 16, 1821, the family consisted of Mary's parents, Mark and Abigail, her grandmother Maryann Baker, three brothers, and two sisters. Samuel was the oldest at thirteen, followed by Albert (eleven), George (eight), Abigail (five), and Martha (two). Much of the boys' time was spent in helping with chores on the farm. It was a lively home, often welcoming visitors and thoughtful discussions on both sacred and secular matters, but it was also one that was run on strict Christian principles. Mark was an orthodox

Calvinist and Abigail was just as religious, though a good deal more expressive in her understanding of God as Love. However, Mary Baker Eddy's story really begins before she was born.

In the early months of 1821, the small New Hampshire town of Bow would likely still have been in the cold embrace of a New England winter. March winds would have blown across the hills, dipping into the valley and gaining momentum as they crossed the icy river and made their way up the hills on the other side. On the crest of one of these hills, a modest farmhouse sat quiet to the world. A pregnant Abigail Baker was in the attic gathering wool to spin into yarn. "Suddenly [she] was overwhelmed by the thought that she was filled with the Holy Ghost, and had dominion over the whole earth. At that moment she felt the quickening of the babe, and then she thought 'what a sin I am guilty of—the sin of presumption!'"[1]

The newest member of the family was some months away from making an appearance, and Mrs. Baker wondered what would become of this child, whose conception had been unexpected.[2] Mrs. Baker's concern arose from the fact that her consciousness had been flooded with thoughts that greatly challenged the theology of her Puritan upbringing—thoughts of the child's special purpose and spiritual promise. As lovely as these thoughts were to her, they were nothing short of profane in the world of Calvinism, into which Mary Baker was soon to be born.

Mrs. Baker would often share her experiences with Sarah Gault, a close friend and neighbor. Mrs. Eddy, recounting

The Bow Home This etching was drawn by Rufus Baker, a cousin of Mary Baker Eddy's, after talks with her about her childhood home.

this particular incident to members of her household in later years, told them, "[Sarah Gault] was calling on my mother one afternoon and they were praying together." Afterward her mother spoke to Sarah of the thoughts that had been coming to her about this child's spiritual purpose and promise. Mrs. Eddy continued, "My mother said, 'I don't know what I shall do to stop such blasphemy.'" Sarah reminded her that the Bible said God made man in His own image, and made him to have dominion.[3] Mrs. Baker found comfort in this.

With thoughts of her mother and of her own upbringing, Mrs. Eddy instructed her editor to write an article for *The Christian Science Journal* in 1889. Titled "Christian Science and its Revelator," it includes this passage:

> To-day Truth has come through the person of a New
> England girl, born of God-fearing parents, in the middle

walks of life; . . . gifted with the fullness of spiritual
life, and giving from the cradle indications of a divine
mission and power, that caused *her* mother to "ponder
them in her heart."[4]

A decade later, referring to these indications of spiritual
discernment and healing ability that marked her from childhood,
Mrs. Eddy wrote in a letter:

I can discern in the human mind, thoughts, motives and
purpose; . . . it is the gift of God. And this phenomenon
appeared in my childhood; it is associated with my
earliest memories, and has increased with years.[5]

In the second edition of the pamphlet in which this letter
was published, she elaborated on this gift of discernment:

It is a consciousness wherewith good is done and no
evil can be done . . . and has increased with my spiritual
increase. It has aided me in healing the sick, and subordi-
nating the human to the Divine.

Beginning in childhood, Mary's natural affection for and
trust in divine Love resulted in physical healings, in practical
proofs of God's grace and care for herself and others. Linked
to her natural outpouring of love for those who needed love
most, the healings were simple yet profound, happening at home,
among her relatives, and in the schoolyard.

Mary loved the animals on her farm. In later years Mrs.
Eddy told a member of her household, Irving Tomlinson, that as

a girl, she would nurse baby lambs and chicks, and sing hymns to animals in discomfort during the night. Mary's healing love was so evident that her father, finding a weakling in the flock, would say, "Here is another invalid for Mary." Tomlinson noted, "Then Mary would tenderly take her mild-eyed charge and nurse the fleecy little patient to health and strength."[6] Recalling those years, Mrs. Eddy said, "I would take the little chicks, that seemed sickly or perhaps dying, into the bosom of my dress and hold them until I heard a fluttering sound and found the chicken active and strong and eager to run away, when I would put it down and away it would run."[7]

Mark Baker recognized his youngest child's healing abilities, so it is not surprising to learn that when Mary's brother George severely injured his leg with an ax and was bleeding badly, her frightened father called on his five-year-old daughter to help. He put her hand on the wound and George stopped crying. Not long after, the doctor arrived and found the bleeding had completely stopped and the wound had already begun to heal. He remarked that he had never seen such an injury heal so rapidly. Although Mark Baker acknowledged Mary's ability to heal (and in this case sought her help), this ability ran contrary to his understanding of God, so when asked in later years what her father thought of it, Mrs. Eddy said it disturbed him and he would pray for her.[8]

Mrs. Eddy one time recounted to her household at the supper table a visit she had made to Bow in the 1870s with one of her early students, Miranda Rice. There they had met Mrs. Eddy's cousin, Nancy Baker, who joined them as they walked about the old farm. There was almost a generation between the cousins, and as in many families, the older woman, Mrs. Baker, was addressed as "Aunt." Mrs. Eddy remembered the experience this way:

> Mrs. Rice thinking to interest my aunt in Christian
> Science told her of many remarkable cases of healing
> wrought through me in Lynn, Mass. Mrs. Baker did not
> express surprise, in fact she seemed so calm that Mrs.
> Rice . . . [pressed my aunt to explain her bland] remark.
> [Mrs. Baker said,] "These things do not surprise me
> concerning Mary. They are no more wonderful than I had
> seen her accomplish before she went away from this farm
> a girl of thirteen."[9]

One of those healings was that of George Baker's injured leg. Another healing Nancy Baker herself experienced. As Mrs. Eddy told it, her aunt had come to visit her and was suffering from a severe headache. She asked Mary to pray for her, was healed, and "went home perfectly well."[10]

Evidences of Christian regeneration and healing in Mary's early days followed her to school. Irving Tomlinson recounts in his *Twelve Years with Mary Baker Eddy* that Mary once stood up to a girl who was terrorizing the other children, and the girl's nature was transformed: "The teacher confessed to me that I had done what whipping had failed to do, for I had completely changed her character."[11]

Sybil Wilbur's biography *Life of Mary Baker Eddy* tells of the time a teenage Mary calmed an insane man who appeared at school one day. In relating this incident to Mr. Tomlinson, Mrs. Eddy added that this same man forced his way into their home one morning when the family was at prayer. He rushed up to her father, who was reading from the Bible, and took it away from him. Handing it to Mary he said, "Here! You are the one to read from God's word."[12]

"Many peculiar circumstances and events connected with my childhood throng the chambers of memory," Mrs. Eddy wrote in her autobiographical *Retrospection and Introspection.* With that comment, she introduced her account of hearing her name called, Samuel-like, repeatedly until she answered, "'Speak, Lord; for Thy servant heareth.'"[13] Mary's religious upbringing had taught her that all men are God's servants, but her own unique experiences taught her that there was more to serving than what John Calvin had seen. She was learning that *divine service* meant daily deeds in service to a loving God.[14] That these deeds must include healing the sick was a vital part of her discovery of Christian Science.

Mary Baker did not break free of Calvin's iron grasp without a fearful struggle, however. Later on in life she recalled asking her mother if Calvin's teaching regarding eternal punishment was true. Mrs. Eddy said, "She paused, then with a deep sigh answered, 'Mary, I suppose *it is.*' What, said I, if we repent and tell God 'we are sorry and will not do so again.' Will God punish us then? Then he is not as good as my mother and he will find me a hard case."[15]

Mrs. Eddy as a child was so troubled by the doctrine of predestination that at one point it caused her to become feverishly ill. God had been gently showing Mary, through experience, that He is ever-present Love, but the theology of her parents' church was trying to teach her something quite different:

My father's relentless theology emphasized belief in a
final judgment-day, in the danger of endless punishment,
and in a Jehovah merciless towards unbelievers; and
of these things he now spoke, hoping to win me from
dreaded heresy.

My mother, as she bathed my burning temples,
bade me lean on God's love, which would give me rest,
if I went to Him in prayer, as I was wont to do, seeking
His guidance. I prayed; and a soft glow of ineffable joy
came over me. The fever was gone, and I rose and dressed
myself, in a normal condition of health. Mother saw this,
and was glad. The physician marvelled; and the "horrible
decree" of predestination—as John Calvin rightly called
his own tenet—forever lost its power over me.[16]

Mary Baker was able to join the Congregational church
a few years later without compromising her conscience. At her
examination for membership, she said she was willing to trust
her spiritual safety to God, as she understood Him, rather than
assent to the doctrine of predestination, even if doing so left her
outside the church. When questioned further, she humbly held
her ground:

The minister then wished me to tell him when I had
experienced a change of heart; but tearfully I had to
respond that I could not designate any precise time.
Nevertheless, he persisted in the assertion that I *had* been
truly regenerated, and asked me to say how I felt when
the new light dawned within me. I replied that I could
only answer him in the words of the Psalmist: "Search

me, O God, and know my heart: try me, and know my thoughts: and see if there be any wicked way in me, and lead me in the way everlasting."[17]

The minister was so touched by the earnestness of her reply that he accepted her into the church in spite of her protest against predestination.

Even as a child, Mary seemed willing and even eager to lay herself open to God, following wherever He would guide her, and this would become her fundamental standard for a lifetime to come.

Chapter 2

God's
GRACIOUS PREPARATION
(1843–1860)

*I*N JANUARY 1843 MARY BAKER attended a series of "revival" meetings that were held alternately at the Methodist and Congregational churches in Sanbornton Bridge, New Hampshire, over a period of five weeks. In a letter to her friend Augusta Swasey, she wrote, "the meetings were so very interesting . . . almost all of your acquaintances are now rejoicing in the hope set before them of higher aims and nobler joys." She went on to report a large number "who have experienced a change," including her married sister, Abigail Tilton:

> Would that you were here to witness with me this
> changed scene! tho I *fear* for *some*, I rejoice with *many*,
> whom I doubt not possess the "pearl" which is priceless.
> And do you not also rejoice with me if it were but for
> *one* sinner that hath repented? Doubtless as you feared,
> there are some who have deceived *themselves* by "zeal
> without knowledge"—But methinks we have less to fear

from fanaticism, than from stoicism; when a question is to be decided that involves our weal, or woe for *time* and *eternity*.[1]

It is quite possible that Charles Finney's ideas of "Christian Perfection" were preached at these meetings. A Presbyterian minister who had forsaken traditional Calvinist doctrine, the Rev. Finney is considered by some to be the Father of American Revivalism. He was preaching in New England at this time, though there is nothing to confirm his presence at the Sanbornton Bridge revival meetings. He defined Christian Perfectionism as

> perfect obedience to the law of God. . . . Christianity requires that we should do neither more nor less than the law of God prescribes. Nothing short of this is Christian perfection. This is being moral, just as perfect as God. . . . And he has created us moral beings in his own image, capable of conforming to the same rule with himself. This rule requires us to have the same character with him, to love as impartially, with as perfect love—to seek the good of others with as single an eye as he does. This, and nothing less than this, is Christian Perfection.[2]

Eleven months after attending these revival meetings, on December 10, 1843, Mary Baker became Mrs. George Washington Glover. She had been betrothed to Major Glover for two years.[3] On December 25 they sailed from New England to South Carolina to begin their married life together. The arduous experiences this young New Hampshire woman was soon to encounter would, in later years, be seen by her as "earth's shadows."

She would write of them, "The heavenly intent of earth's shadows is to chasten the affections, to rebuke human consciousness and turn it gladly from a material, false sense of life and happiness, to spiritual joy and true estimate of being."[4] And so it was in this way, she became convinced God had prepared her to receive His revelation of Christian Science.

The ship the Glovers were sailing on was in the hands of divine Providence as it tossed perilously on the waves, with the winds shrieking through its masts. A violent storm had descended on the vessel just as it was to pass several sandbars and enter the harbor at Charleston, South Carolina. Below in their stateroom, the young couple knelt in fervent prayer. The captain had just left them. He had never seen such a storm and had no hope that the ship could be saved.

The frightened bride and bridegroom had been full of hope and expectation when they departed New England on Christmas Day. The bride's mother had given them a letter to read during their voyage, and to comfort his new wife George Glover read it to her during the storm. It included a poem, entitled "The Mother's Injunction" by Lydia Sigourney, part of which reads:

> When judgment wakes in terror wild,
> By all thy treasured hopes of Heaven,
> Deal gently with my darling child.

Many years later, Mary Baker Eddy told Irving Tomlinson:

> ... When the reading was finished, [George] kissed me

and took me in his arms for it seemed that the staunch
ship would soon sink beneath the waves.

Within fifteen minutes thereafter a most
remarkable phenomenon occurred. The storm subsided
and the waves grew calm and the ship passed [the sand]
bars in perfect safety. The captain said that in all his long
experience he had never seen anything so wonderful.
Thus many a time has God miraculously preserved me.[5]

Seven months later the young bride returned sadly to her
family in New England a widow and mother-to-be; George
Glover had been stricken with yellow fever and passed away.
Mary characteristically turned in prayer to God to sustain her
through this trial. Some thirty years later she would write in the
first edition of *Science and Health,* in the chapter "Marriage," that
"sundering ties of flesh, unites us to God, where Love supports
the struggling heart."[6] Life would continue to be a struggle for
Mrs. Glover for many years to come, but with each ordeal she
would lean on that divine support through her prayers.

In order to gain some semblance of financial independence
from her family for herself and her newborn son George, Mary
taught in the local academies when her health permitted. On
one occasion she had to keep a persistently misbehaving boy
after school. Writing of this incident in later years, Mrs. Eddy
tells of taking his hand and saying, "I love you, but I must make
you suffer for bad conduct and its influence on my pupils." He
asked to be punished quickly so he could go. She told him to
kneel beside her and she would pray for him. He said it would
do no good. Mrs. Eddy then recounts:

I persisted and he at last dropped on his knees beside me, then I prayed. Soon he was sobbing and jumped up, imploring me to whip him and forgive him. I answered, "the whipping would do you no good . . . but my prayer will help you." Then I opened the door and he quickly disappeared.

Two days later the boy's mother came to see her. Mrs. Eddy goes on to recount:

> . . . mid smiles and tears she sobbed, "what have [you] done to my Willie . . . he's another child. He prayed last night and read the Bible, something I never could get him to do." That year the dear boy joined the Congregational Church of which his mother and myself were members.[7]

Children were always dear to Mrs. Eddy's heart throughout her life, and her own son, George, of course, was especially so. As he grew from an infant into childhood, Mary's family became concerned that he was too much for her to cope with alone, considering her delicate health. She would later write of this in *Retrospection and Introspection*: "... my little son, about four years of age, was sent away from me, and put under the care of our family nurse,.... The night before my child was taken from me, I knelt by his side throughout the dark hours, hoping for a vision of relief from this trial."[8] Two years after this separation, she accepted a proposal of marriage from Daniel Patterson. He promised that her son would be restored to her, and they were married on the twenty-first of

June 1853. After moving into their new home, however, he became unwilling to take George in.

In *Retrospection and Introspection* Mrs. Eddy says, "A plot was consummated"[9] to keep her and George apart, and the family caring for him soon moved to Minnesota. The loss of her child caused Mary's fragile health to give way. She became bedridden for months at a time. At this point in her experience, she was literally alone in the wilderness—in her home in the secluded woodlands of North Groton, New Hampshire—far from family and friends. Her only steady companion was a blind teenage girl who served as housekeeper, since Daniel Patterson was often absent for long periods because of his work as a traveling dentist.

While Daniel clearly had his weaknesses, he and Mary loved each other, and she missed him when he was gone. Even his refusal to let her son join them was in part well intended: he was afraid of the effect on her health of having to care for George. Daniel was kind to Mary and tried to be solicitous of her needs, though he never truly understood them. He would prescribe homeopathic remedies, which would help for a time, but her suffering would always return.

The remedies were familiar ones to Mary. Homeopathic treatment had come "like blessed relief" to her about 1848, when she was in her late twenties. She was introduced to this form of treatment by Dr. Alpheus Morrill, a cousin by marriage.[10] A system for treating disease with minute doses of drugs that in larger amounts would produce symptoms similar to those manifested by the disease, homeopathy was a popular method of that day.

From her late twenties, she studied textbooks on homeopathy, and after her return from the South she was not only prescribing remedies for herself but also doing so for others.[11]

One very special case took place during the period between widowhood and the first years of her marriage to Dr. Patterson. Mrs. Eddy would later write of it in detail in *Science and Health with Key to the Scriptures*. It was that of a woman with dropsy.[12] The previous physician had given the patient up. Both allopathic and homeopathic methods had been tried and had failed to bring any relief. Mary took the case and prescribed according to her understanding of homeopathy. There was soon noticeable improvement. At this point she learned that the former doctor had prescribed exactly the same remedy, and she became concerned about overdosing. The patient, however, would not give up the medicine that brought her relief. Without telling the woman, Mrs. Glover administered unmedicated pills instead. Even so, the improvement continued and the case was cured.

Six decades later Mrs. Eddy would speak of that cure as "a falling apple to me—it made plain to me that mind governed the whole question of her recovery. I was always praying to be kept from sin, and I waited and prayed for God to direct me."[13] Mrs. Eddy also told Irving Tomlinson that this had been "the falling apple," explaining it as "the enlightenment of the human understanding." She contrasted this with her discovery of Christian Science in 1866, which she described as "the revelation from the divine Mind."[14]

Two facts had become clear as a result of this cure of dropsy: first, the same remedy that had been impotent when

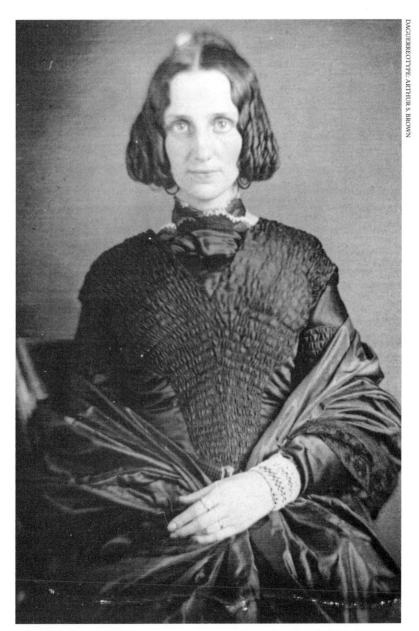

Mrs. Eddy around 1853

administered by the physician became effective when *she* prescribed and administered it; second, the unmedicated pills were as effective as the medicated ones. She saw that both the thought of the physician and the thought of the patient were the determining factors in the case, to the exclusion of matter. After receiving the full revelation of Christian Science, Mrs. Eddy would write:

> The physician must know himself and understand the mental state of his patient. . . . "Cast the beam out of thine own eye." Learn what in thine own mentality is unlike "the anointed," and cast it out; then thou wilt discern the error in thy patient's mind that makes his body sick, and remove it, and rest like the dove from the deluge. [15]

And so the revelation of Christian Science would move her far beyond material methods as having anything to do with the healing process. Ultimately, she would conclude that the laws of healing rested in divine Mind as the sole physician in every case.

During her years of invalidism in North Groton, Mary made a promise to God "that if He restored her to health, she would devote her remaining years to helping sick and suffering humanity."[16] Looking back on this promise, decades later, Mrs. Eddy felt that it marked the beginning of a new period in her life. Soon she was given the opportunity to begin her fulfillment of that sacred vow.

Shortly after Mrs. Patterson moved to Rumney, New Hampshire, in March 1860, a mother brought her sick baby to

Mary, who in later years recounted:

> Mrs. Smith, of Rumney, N.H., came to me with her
> infant, whose eyes were diseased, a mass of inflam-
> mation, neither pupil nor iris discernable. I gave the
> infant no drugs,—held her in my arms a few moments
> while lifting my thoughts to God, then returned the

The North Groton house where Mrs. Eddy lived from 1855–1860

babe to her mother healed. In grateful memory thereof Mrs. Smith named her babe "Mary," and embroidered a petticoat for me.[17]

Lifting her thought to God was more natural to Mary than walking. From a child she had been taught the centrality of God to everyday life. She knew Him through her daily prayers, and she "love[d] him, because he first loved [her]."[18] She also knew Him through the Bible, which was her constant companion and daily guide. In 1846, the year she identified as marking the beginning of her search "to trace all physical effects to a mental cause,"[19] she wrote a poem about the Holy Scriptures, expressing her awe of God's communion with man through its sacred pages:

THE BIBLE
Word of God! What condescension,
Infinite with finite mind,
To commune, sublime conception
Canst thou fathom love divine?
Oracle of God-like wonder,
Frame-work of His mighty plan,
Chart and compass for the wanderer,
Safe obeying thy command.
By Omniscience veiled in glory,
'Neath the Omnipresent eye—
Kingdoms, empires, bow before thee,
Sceptic, truth immortal see!
Spare O then the querist's cavil,
Search in faith—obey, adore!
Ponder, pause, believe and "marvel
Not, I say," forevermore.[20]

For this "wanderer" in the wilderness, the Bible was indeed her "chart and compass." She spent much of her time reading it during those lonely years when she was mostly confined to her bed (1856–1862). Once when Daniel was asked why she had not come to church, he replied, "O, she is at home reading her Bible."[21] Mrs. Patterson was not just reading, she was pondering deeply the Word of God, both studying and imbibing its healing message. "As early as 1862 she began to write down and give to friends the results of her Scriptural study, for the Bible was her sole teacher;... ."[22] She described herself then as "a child in the newly discovered world of Spirit"[23]—a world she would spend the rest of her life exploring and introducing to others.

Chapter 3

WAITING AND WATCHING...
THE DAYSTAR APPEARS
(1861–1866)

*I*N THE LATE 1850s IN the United States, the thunderclouds of war were gathering. The country was wrestling with itself over an issue of morality. The North thought it was a matter of the indissolubility of the Union. The South felt it was the irrevocability of states' rights. At the bottom of it all, however, was the immorality of slavery.

Mary Patterson knew all too well about a different kind of slavery—the slavery of a material body bound in the chains of chronic illness, under the lash of pain. But unlike the weapons soon to be unleashed on the battlefields of the American Civil War, "the weapons of [her] warfare [were] not carnal, but mighty through God to the pulling down of strong holds."[1]

When the Civil War between the North and South began in 1861, Mary was living in Rumney, New Hampshire, fighting against invalidism. The Bible and prayer were her only weapons.

Her neighbors had grown to know her as a devout Christian and would seek her counsel in time of trouble. Remembering one such incident, Mary Baker Eddy wrote in later years:

> ...a mother whose only son was drafted to enter the army, came to [me] in tears, told of her trouble and her deep concern for her son's moral welfare. At that time [my] husband was confined in Libby Military prison and [my] only son was in a military hospital.... But [I] took almost [my] last dollar and bought a Bible for the woman's son, wrote a scriptural text on the fly leaf and gave it to him. He was shot in battle, but the bullet struck the Bible and his life was saved. After his return home he united with the Methodist Church. He always said that Bible and the text written on the fly leaf were the cause of his conversion.[2]

Mrs. Eddy told Irving Tomlinson that this soldier came to see her after the war to show her the Bible she had given him: "Embedded between its covers was a leaden bullet. Said the soldier, 'That rifle ball was meant for my heart, and I have come many miles to show you that your goodness saved my life.'"[3]

Mary's only son, George, was a soldier in the Union (Northern) Army. At one point during the war, in the latter half of 1862, Mary was struck with the very strong feeling that something terrible had happened to her son. True to her nature, she prayed at once for his safety and well-being. Soon thereafter she received a message that George had been shot in the neck. At first the doctors thought the wound was fatal, but quite suddenly the danger passed, and his recovery began.[4]

When Mary learned that her husband, Daniel, had been taken prisoner of war, she went to see his family in Maine. While there, she studied the Scriptures and helped the family through healing. Frances Thompson Hill relates in her reminiscence, "During the time that her husband was in Libby prison, Mrs. [Patterson] visited the [Patterson] home, spending several weeks there. [Daniel's niece] said that she had been told by her father that Mrs. [Patterson] wrote a great deal and kept quietly to her room, but that her loving thought had healed one of their livestock."[5]

Mary's concern for her husband is quite evident in a poem she wrote during this period. The last two verses of "To a Bird Flying Southward" read:

> Oh! to the *captive's* cell I'd sing
> A song of hope—and *freedom* bring—
> An olive leaf I'd quick let fall,
> And lift our country's blackened pall;
> Then homeward seek my frigid zone,
> More chilling to the heart *alone.*
> Lone as a solitary star,
> Lone as a vacant sepulchre,
> Yet not alone! my Father's call—
> Who marks the sparrow in her fall—
> Attunes my ear to joys elate,
> The joys I'll sing at Heaven's gate.[6]

Several months before he left the South, Daniel Patterson had received a circular from a doctor in Portland, Maine, who gave no medicine but effected cures by talking to the patient. Daniel wrote to this doctor, Phineas P. Quimby, in the hope that he would come to treat Mary. Dr. Quimby could not come, so Mary went to him in October 1862, full of hope and expectation. His treatment consisted of explaining the "psychological" origin of her illness and then, after first dipping his hands in water, rubbing her head vigorously. "At first my case improved wonderfully under his treatment,"[7] Mrs. Eddy would later write. So great was the improvement that she felt it must be of God. Her Puritan upbringing and natural inclination toward the Divine were so strong that she could not conceive of any other source for something that had such a remarkable effect on her. But being made well, as marvelous as that was, was not enough for Mary; she must know *how* the healing was done. Dr. Quimby, however, could not tell her. He did not know himself.

Over the next three years, Mrs. Patterson made a number of visits to Portland. To her disappointment, she had found that Dr. Quimby's treatments never provided a permanent cure, so further visits were necessary. Another motivation for these trips lay in the hope of gaining an understanding of the cause behind the powerful effect. She would have long conversations with Dr. Quimby and afterward write of the insights that came to her from their discussions. Her writings, naturally, were permeated with references to God and lessons from her Bible study. Mary did not realize at the time that Dr. Quimby was a mesmerist and not at all inclined toward religion. In talking with patients, he simply found it most effective to speak in terms of whatever subjects interested them, not caring whether it was religion, spiritualism, or even witchcraft, as long as he could hold their attention.[8]

During her visits to Portland, Mary healed several people, some of whom had sought treatment from Dr. Quimby. Later in life, she told her personal secretary, Calvin Frye, of healing a man, in Dr. Quimby's absence, who was in leg braces and suffering greatly:

> . . . a man was brought to the International Hotel who had met with an accident which had injured . . . his spine and had broken both his legs above the knees. Dr. Quimby had treated the case twice, but one day the patient was suffering intensely, and Dr. Quimby was away. The landlord came to Mrs. Eddy (then Mrs. Patterson) and asked her if she would not go and see the patient. She was surprised at his request & asked his reason for the strange request of her. He said that Dr. Quimby had told him many wonderful things about her, and he was curious to have her go and see what she could do for the case. She went and stood inside the door of the sick room & said to the patient, "Why don't you get up?" He turned his head and looked at her surprised, then turned his head and looked up. She said again, "Get up." He got up and walked about the room, the wooden splints on his limbs clattering at every step and he came to the door and bowed her out.[9]

When [Dr. Quimby] returned and found this case so changed, he was quite aroused over it and told Mrs. Eddy never to do anything for another of his patients unless he asked her to.[10]

In describing this healing to her household in 1902, Mrs.

Eddy told them that when she was first asked to help she didn't think she could, but then the thought came to her, "God can do it. I went to his bed side and lifted my thought silently to God." One of the household asked, "This was not your only case of healing while with Dr. Quimby, was it?" She answered:

> No indeed, there was a young woman whom he had
> given up to die with consumption. . . . I visited her, called
> upon God to help her, and when [Quimby] visited
> her two days later, he declared that she no more had
> consumption than he did.

One of her listeners asked, "How was the healing wrought, not in the way that Dr. Quimby practiced?" Mrs. Eddy replied, "No, not at all. I used no material means whatever. I could not tell how the healing was done. I only know that God did it."[11]

Another case brought to Dr. Quimby was that of a man who had been run over by a train. Mrs. Eddy recounted, "Both limbs were shattered and his condition was so pitiable that Quimby would not stay in the room with him, but he said to me, 'Mrs. [Patterson] you go and see if you can't help him.' I went to the door, lifted my eyes to heaven, breathed a prayer, and the man rose up healed."[12]

Early in 1864, during one of her visits to Portland, Mary met Sarah Crosby and Mary Ann Jarvis, patients of Dr. Quimby. In the spring of that year, she stayed two months with Miss Jarvis in her home in Warren, Maine. During this visit, Mary healed Miss Jarvis of consumption and the suffering brought on by "east winds." She later described this healing in her book *Science and Health*:

A woman, whom I cured of consumption, always breathed with great difficulty when the wind was from the east. I sat silently by her side a few moments. Her breath came gently. The inspirations were deep and natural. I then requested her to look at the weather-vane. She looked and saw that it pointed due east. The wind had not changed, but her thought of it had and so her difficulty in breathing had gone. The wind had not produced the difficulty. My metaphysical treatment changed the action of her belief on the lungs, and she never suffered again from east winds, but was restored to health.[13]

In late summer and early autumn, Mary spent about three months with Mrs. Crosby in her home in Albion, Maine. During that visit Sarah was taking down a bottle of vitriolic acid from a high shelf when the bottle broke and the acid spilled on her face. A doctor was called, but he could do nothing for her. In fact, he thought she might die. Sarah then put herself in the hands of her guest, who told her to go lie down. She went to sleep while Mary prayed. Two hours later she woke to find the pain gone and her face showing no signs of the accident.[14] Sometime after Mary went home, Sarah wrote her about a problem she was having with one of her eyes. Another letter soon followed:

Since the accident to my eye, it has been so exceedingly sensitive to the light, I have shaded it, unable to do any writing or sewing of any note. The Sunday I mailed you a letter I suffered a great deal with it; Monday it was painful until towards night, when it felt better; Tuesday it was *well*, and I have not worn my shade over it since a week

Mrs. Eddy circa 1863

ago Monday, and I have read, sewed, and written, and still
all is well. . . . I told a friend the other day you had cured
my eye, or perhaps my fear of my eye, and it is so; . . .[15]

By this time, Mary was living in Lynn, Massachusetts,
where Dr. Patterson had set up his practice after his escape from
military prison. On occasion, she accompanied her husband to
his office and prayerfully assisted his patients when they were
in pain.[16] Then, in the autumn of 1865, the couple moved to the
neighboring town of Swampscott, and together they joined the
Good Templars, back in Lynn. Mary soon became the presiding
officer of the women's branch of that temperance association.

On a bitterly cold night, the first day of February 1866, Mary walked with friends to a temperance meeting. She slipped on the ice-covered street and fell with such force as to injure herself severely. Rendered insensible by the fall, Mary was carried to a nearby house and a doctor was called. His examination showed her to be suffering from a concussion and internal injuries, including possible spinal dislocation. The next day, at her request, she was moved to her home in Swampscott, in what the newspapers described as a very critical condition. The doctor left her some homeopathic medicine, which she did not take, having learned years before that material remedies had no real curative power. Instead, her healing rested in "that consciousness which God bestows."[17]

On the third morning after the accident, a Sunday, Mary's pastor visited her. She asked him to return in the afternoon. He said he would, even though he didn't expect her to live that long. When he had gone, she asked those attending to leave her for a while. Mary felt totally alone, bereft of all human aid. Her husband was absent, away on a trip to New Hampshire. There was no *person* left to whom she could turn for help. But Mary knew God to be "a very present help in trouble,"[18] so she turned to her Bible. In early editions of *Science and Health*, Mrs. Eddy stated that she read from the third chapter of Mark:

> ... where our Master healed the withered hand on the Sabbath day. As we read, the change passed over us; the limbs that were immovable, cold, and without feeling, warmed; the internal agony ceased, our strength came instantaneously, and we rose from our bed and stood upon our feet, well.[19]

23 Paradise Road, Swampscott, Massachusetts, where Mrs. Eddy lived when she was healed in 1866.

Mary dressed and walked into the next room to the utter astonishment of those who had given up hope of her recovery. When she greeted her pastor at the door that afternoon, he thought he was seeing an apparition. The doctor was sent for, but he could only express his incredulity at her improvement. When she told him she had not taken any of the medicine he had left, his disbelief seemed to strike at her, and she felt suddenly weakened and could no longer stand. She described this in an interview she gave many years later:

He said, "How was this done?" I said, "I cannot tell you

in any wise whatever, except it seemed to me all a thing or state of my mental consciousness." It didn't seem to belong to the body, or material condition. When I awakened to this sense of change, I was there, that is all I know. It came to me in a bit of Scripture, that is now absent from my thought, and I immediately arose from my bed, and before that, my feet were dead, and they kept something to heat them, for fear they would be stiff utterly, and it seemed to me as I talked to him that I was a little weakened, and finally there was another one came in, and it seemed that while I was talking with him that I was more weakened, and he said, "It is impossible that that could have been. It must have been the medicine." I said, "Your medicine is every bit in the drawer, go and look." There it was in my drawer, and I had not taken one bit of it. When I showed him that, he said, "This is impossible," and immediately I felt I was back again, and I staggered. He caught me and set me in a chair, and he said, "There, I will go out. If you have done that much, you can again." My limbs crippled under me just like that. . . . When I found myself back again, I felt more discouraged than ever.[20]

After the doctor left, Mary again turned to her Bible. From the ninth chapter of Matthew—the healing of the palsied man confined to his bed—Jesus' words "Arise, and walk" spoke to her across the centuries. Again she arose in strength, and the relapse ended.

Mrs. Eddy's recovery from her fall on the ice was especially significant because of what it revealed to her about the spiritual nature of life. She glimpsed "…Life in and of Spirit; this Life being the sole reality of existence."[21] She later described her recovery as "the revelation from the divine Mind."[22] This revelation was both the discovery of divine Truth and the fulfillment of Biblical prophecy of the Comforter promised by Jesus.[23]

As Christian Scientists see it, their religion came to humanity from God through the window of Christ-healing. They believe that Mary Baker Eddy was the "transparency for Truth"[24] through which this healing light of divine Love shone. From birth, they feel, God had been preparing her for this mission, nurturing her growth "into such a fitness for it…."[25] As her understanding of the divine revelation increased, Mrs. Eddy became increasingly convinced that the discovery of the divine Truth that had been revealed to her through Christ-healing could only be sustained in this world *by* such healing. God's assignment for her, she believed, was to share with mankind the "science" behind her healing. In the divine light of this revelation, the Bible she knew so well became a new book to her, a textbook that needed to be studied and then put into practice through the type of spiritual healing Christ Jesus had practiced two thousand years earlier.

Chapter 4

THE PIONEER ALONE:
A MISSION REVEALED
(1866–1868)

*O*NE MORNING, JUST A FEW months after her revelatory healing, Mary's husband told her, "You need not expect me home to dinner. I have some business and I may be gone for several days." That day Daniel Patterson eloped with another woman, one of his dental patients. The woman's husband pursued them and brought his wife home. Some days after, this woman turned up at Mary's door looking pale and very haggard. In recounting this episode to Irving Tomlinson years later, Mrs. Eddy said she asked the woman:

> For what . . . have you come to me? You, who have robbed me of my good husband and desolated my happy home. You, who have disgraced yourself and your family. Why *have* you come to me? She replied, "I come to you because of what your husband has told me of you. I knew you must be a good woman and I felt you would help me." I asked her what I could do for her. She said, "My

husband has locked me in a room and only gives me each day a crust [of bread] and cold water, and I know he means to kill me. Today with the help of the servants, I escaped through a window to come to you and ask you to go to my husband and ask him to forgive me." I told her that I would do all that I could for her.

The following day I went to her husband's factory, for he was a wealthy man, and the family was one of the leading families in the social circles of Lynn. I did not find him in and was told that he had gone on business to Boston. On returning home I wrote him a letter. That night he called at my house. I met him at the door. He said, "I received your letter and I desire to ask if you have really forgiven your husband and can you forgive my wife her cruelty to you." I answered, "I forgive them both and I ask you to forgive them." Then he left me and my heart went with him. I do not know but that I went to God in prayer for that husband and his home. Soon after, I heard that his wife was at the table, for the cruelly wronged husband had forgiven her and their home was again a happy one.[1]

Unfortunately, the same could not be said of Mary's home. Though she accepted Daniel back, he deserted her again a few months later. When he tried to return once more, she told him he could not.

For a period of time Daniel sent her money to pay part of her living expenses, but eventually it stopped. Though she had no choice at the time, living off the benevolence of friends was very difficult for Mary Patterson. She had been raised to believe that "…the noblest charity is to prevent a man from accepting charity."[2] In 1866 alone, she would change her residence ten times. This period of her life was certainly illustrative of Jesus' words to the man who promised to follow him wherever he went: "Foxes have holes, and birds of the air have nests; but the Son of man hath not where to lay his head."[3]

To follow faithfully the daystar of Christian healing places extraordinary demands on those who would walk in the way Christ points out, who would gain a practical understanding of divine healing. Mary, however, had learned from Jesus' teachings that "…no man, having put his hand to the plough, and looking back, is fit for the kingdom of God."[4] And just as her Way-shower, Christ Jesus, was tempted in the wilderness, so did temptation come her way. Abigail, her elder sister, wrote with an offer to provide a home and income, but added, "There is only one thing I ask of you, Mary, that you give up these ideas which have lately occupied you, that you attend our church and give over your theory of divine healing." Once before Mary had been told she had to give up what she cherished most—her own son. That time she had had neither the strength nor understanding to resist. This time, with the divine revelation firmly in thought and the babe of Christian healing[5] in her grasp, she replied, "I must do the work God has called me to."[6] For with the light of this revelation had also come a recognition of her divinely appointed mission. Not only did she feel God-impelled to gain a demonstrable understanding of what had been revealed; it was also imperative that she impart this understanding to others.

For most of her adult life, Mary had been searching for

an understanding of how to heal physical ailments—she sought not just improvement but complete cure. From her study of homeopathy and of Phineas Quimby's human mind methods, she had become convinced that all ailments have a mental nature and that their treatment rests solely in the mind. Now, with the divine revelation she had received through her own healing of a life-threatening condition, she came to believe that the Mind one needed in treating disease was the divine Mind, God, and no other. She glimpsed as well that what made divine healing superior to all other methods was that it not only cured the illness but renewed the patient as well.

The divine revelation of the Science of God had not only healed the internal injuries resulting from Mary's fall but also completely transformed her health. During childhood Mary had struggled with physical ailments and, for much of her adult life, she had contended with chronic illness that caused semi-invalidism. Now, with this revelation from God, all that had changed. In her own words, "... and ever after [I] was in better health than I had before enjoyed."[7]

The first edition of her textbook on Christian Science includes a description of severe suffering from dyspepsia. Though not written in the first person singular, it tells of Mary's own experience and shows how radically her health was transformed through spiritual revelation and healing:

> ... When quite a child we adopted the Graham system
> for dyspepsia, ate only bread and vegetables, and drank
> water, following this diet for years; we became more
> dyspeptic, however, and, of course, thought we must

diet more rigidly; so we partook of but one meal in twenty-four hours, and this consisted of a thin slice of bread, about three inches square, without water; our physician not allowing us with this ample meal, to wet our parched lips for many hours thereafter; whenever we drank, it produced violent retchings. . . . After years of suffering, when we made up our mind to die, our doctors kindly assuring us this was our only alternative, our eyes were suddenly opened, and we learned suffering is self-imposed, a belief, and not Truth. . . . and [we] recovered strength and flesh rapidly, enjoying health and harmony that we never before had done.[8]

In the third edition of *Science and Health*, Mrs. Eddy concludes her third-person account of this same healing with a clear assessment of what cured her: "Here metaphysical science came in and saved her, and she is now in perfect health, without a vestige of the old complaints . . . ."[9]

Friends and acquaintances found it difficult to have Mrs. Patterson live with them for any length of time. While they loved the sweetness of her healing work, digesting the revolutionary ideas she eagerly shared with them was difficult for the less spiritually minded. Due to her Puritan roots, even she herself wrestled with the question "[H]ow can sinful mortals prove that a divine Principle heals the sick, as well as governs the universe, time, space, immortality, man?"[10] To answer this question, she spent most of her time from the summer of 1866 through the winter of 1869–70 in hour after hour of Bible study and in writing down, from the perspective of her revelation, what she was learning.[11]

Initially, Mary was almost overwhelmed by the immensity of the task before her. She would later say of her thought at this time,

> ...it looked as if centuries of spiritual growth were
> requisite to enable me to elucidate or to demonstrate
> what I had discovered: but an unlooked-for, imperative
> call for help impelled me to begin this stupendous work
> at once, and teach the first student in Christian Science.[12]

Mrs. Eddy's first "call for help" following her discovery came in the form of a child with an inflamed, infected finger:

> [Dorr Phillips] had a bone felon which kept him awake
> at night and out of school during the day. Mrs. Patterson
> had not been to the Phillips' house for several days, and
> when she did go and found the boy in agony walking the
> floor, she gently and sympathetically questioned him.
>
> "Dorr, will you let me heal that felon?"
>
> "Yes, indeed, Mrs. Patterson, if you can do it,"
> replied the lad.
>
> "Will you promise not to do anything for it or let
> any one else, if I undertake to cure it?"
>
> "Yes, I promise, and I will keep my word," said
> Dorr Phillips. He had heard his father and their friend
> discuss divine healing many times, and had a boy's
> healthy curiosity to see what would happen if all this talk
> was actually tried on a wicked, tormenting, festering felon

that was making him fairly roar with rage one minute and cry . . . the next.

That night the boy stopped at his sister Susie's house. "How is your finger?" she asked solicitously.

"Nothing the matter with my finger; it hasn't hurt all day. Mrs. Patterson is treating it."

"What is she doing to it? Let me look at it."

"No, you'll spoil the cure. I promised not to look at it or think about it, nor let any one else touch it or talk about it. And I won't."

The brother and sister looked at each other with half smiles. They were struggling with skepticism.

"Honest, Dorr, doesn't it hurt?"

"No."

"Tell me what she did."

"I don't know what she did, don't know anything about this business, but I'm going to play fair and keep my word."

The boy actually forgot the felon, and when his attention was called to the finger it was found to be well. This strange result made an impression on the family. No one quite knew what to say, and they were scarcely ready to accept the healing of a sore finger as a miracle.

"But it is not a miracle," said Mary Baker. "Nor would it be if it had been a broken wrist or a withered arm. It is natural, divinely natural. All life rightly understood is so."[13]

Radical, uncompromised reliance on God's healing grace had become her standard, and it would be the basis for what she taught others as the only standard for Christian healing.

In later years, Mrs. Eddy told her students, "for the first four years [after the discovery of Christian Science] my healing work was not acknowledged although I healed constantly."[14] Another of Mrs. Eddy's healing works during this time also involved a child. Margaret E. Harding recounted what the child's mother told her:

> Sometime during 1865 or 1866, Mrs. Norton drove her young son, George, to Lynn Beach for a day's outing. At the time George was about seven years of age and had been carried on a pillow since birth, having been born with a deformity commonly known as club-feet, both feet being turned backward, and consequently he had never walked.
>
> Mrs. Norton laid the child upon the pillow on the sand and left him alone while she hitched the horse and went for water. On her return shortly the child had disappeared and the mother searched bewilderedly about, only to find him down by the water and walking, with a woman holding his hands, which she released a moment later and George stood alone. Later he took a few steps and from that time was able to walk. The strange woman and the mother both looked into each other's eyes, wept a little and thanked God for this seemingly miraculous healing... .

At the time of the incident, the boy told his mother that the strange lady was walking by, and seeing him stretched upon the pillow with his feet covered, asked why he was not playing with the other children there. He told her he had never walked, and she lifted the shawl and saw why. She put her hands under his arms, and while he protested his inability to do so, told him to stand, and when he was lifted to an upright position, she guided his feet with her own, supporting him the while he took his first feeble steps into freedom.

I need not add that the strange lady was Mrs. Mary B. Glover, who afterwards became Mrs. Eddy, and the founder of Christian Science.[15]

There is a record of three other healings that were accomplished by Mrs. Eddy during the last half of 1866: Dorr Phillips's mother, Hannah, who had dislocated her hip;[16] a young man delirious with fever;[17] and Mr. J. Wheeler who, like Dorr, suffered from a finger felon. Mrs. Eddy wrote about Mr. Wheeler's healing in later years: "The day that his physician, an M.D., had proposed to amputate his finger I asked to be allowed to treat him. My request was granted. With one mental treatment the finger was healed. . . ."[18] She shared details of this healing with Irving Tomlinson:

[Mr. Wheeler] was antagonistic to Science, but his wife was friendly. . . . His wife had already told me of his agony and had asked me to help him. He had his hat on waiting to take the carriage to visit the surgeon.

I said to him, "Will you allow me to stand here a few minutes before you go and think about your finger?" He replied, "If you will be quick, I will." I stood in thought for perhaps five minutes when he said, "There is not a bit of pain or soreness in my finger." I said, "Take the cloth off and leave it unbandaged." He did so and in a half hour, after rubbing his finger and saying, "It doesn't hurt a particle," he went out, got in his carriage and went about his business, never feeling any inconvenience from the finger thereafter.[19]

In the fall of that year, Mrs. Patterson met Hiram Crafts and his wife at a boarding house where she was staying in Lynn. In Hiram, she found her first student. She moved to his home in East Stoughton in order to teach him. While she still had her notes made years earlier from her discussions with Dr. Quimby, they were not what she used to teach Hiram. She turned instead to the Bible, writing out an explication of chapters 14 through 17 of Matthew's Gospel. For example, of Matthew 15:2, where the Pharisees ask Jesus why his disciples break tradition by eating without first washing their hands, she commented,

> An enquiry of Error why Truth hath left the traditions of elders, in that it takes no matter form in healing the sick.

For Matthew 15:24, where Jesus tells his disciples that he is sent to Israel's lost sheep, her notes read,

> Then the truth answered, "I am sent by wisdom to save

those ideas so misguided as to be lost in error, for such science has come to save."[20]

As early as 1867, Mary Baker Eddy began work on a class-book that would become the centerpiece for teaching Christian Science for all time. Over the next few years it would

Mrs. Eddy around 1867

evolve into "The Science of Man, by which the sick are healed. Embracing Questions and Answers in Moral Science." This is the pamphlet she refers to on page ix of *Science and Health with Key to the Scriptures*. It would eventually be incorporated into the third edition of *Science and Health* as the chapter "Recapitulation."

While in East Stoughton with Hiram Crafts and his wife, Mrs. Patterson healed James Ingham of consumption. His testimony appeared in the first edition of *Science and Health*:

> I was suffering from pulmonary difficulties, pains in the chest, a hard and unremitting cough, hectic fever, and all those fearful symptoms that made my case alarming. When I first saw Mrs. Glover, I was reduced to such a state of debility as to be unable to walk any distance, or to sit up but a portion of the day; to walk upstairs gave me great suffering from breath. I had no appetite, and seemed surely going down the victim of consumption. I had not received her attention but a short time, when my bad symptoms disappeared, and I regained health. During this time, I rode out in storms to visit her, and found the damp weather had no effect on me. From my personal experience I am led to believe the science by which she not only heals the sick but explains the way to keep well, is deserving the earnest attention of [the] community; her cures are not the result of medicine, mediumship, or mesmerism, but the application of a Principle that she understands.[21]

In the spring of 1867, the Crafts and Mrs. Patterson moved

95 J.W.   CRAFTS, HIRAM STAFF

Hebron N H Feb 23. 1902

Mr C. A. Frye

Dear Sir

I have had all of the manuscript
recopied. I think it is all right.
I sincerely hope it will stand
inspection. will mail it monday.
I sent the Negatives by Exp?
I began study with Mrs Eddy
in aug 1866. and finished my
studies aug 1867.

Mrs Patterson never
called on Mrs Eddy while she
was with me. she had some
corespondence with him. of
what nature I did not know.
I should say that she was, pretty
well deserted in 1866,

1902 letter from Hiram Crafts to Calvin Frye

CRAFTS, HIRAM S. 6/7/72

about rubing the head &c.
Mrs Eddy never instructed
me to rub the head. or body.
or manipulate in any forme.
But when I was a Spiritualist.
I used to use water and rub the
head. limbs and body.
So. sometimes when I was
studying with her I would
try it. but I did not say
anything to her about it.
Be wise as a Serpent. and harmless
as a Dove.
We used nothing outside
of the New testament. she
had no manuscripts of any kind
until after I had been studying
six months

Fraternally your
Hiram S Crafts

to Taunton, Massachusetts. There, Hiram advertised his services as a healer in the local newspapers. In later years, he wrote of Mrs. Eddy's teaching:

> ...Mrs. Eddy never instructed me to rub the head,
> or body, or manipulate in any form. But when I was a
> Spiritualist, I used to use water and rub the head, limbs
> and body. So, sometimes when I was studying with her, I
> would try it, but I did not say anything to her about it....
>
> We used nothing outside of the New Testament,
> she had no manuscripts of any kind until after I had been
> studying six months.[22]

While Hiram eventually gave up his belief in spiritualism, his wife could not. Mrs. Crafts came to resent her husband's teacher, and Mary saw the wisdom of moving on. But before finally leaving, Mary made a trip to Sanbornton Bridge, New Hampshire. While there she healed her niece, Ellen Pilsbury, who was dying of enteritis, and had been given up by the family's medical physician (see pages 285–286). Neither Mary's visit, nor this healing, however, did anything to quiet her family's opposition to her "science."

Sibyl Wilbur's account of this opposition, bred of familiarity, compared it to the opposition Jesus faced "when in Nazareth. 'Is not this the carpenter's son?' they asked, and, 'Are not his brothers and sisters here with us?'" Mrs. Eddy was touched by this reference in Wilbur's biography, telling Irving Tomlinson, "Yes, it was even so."[23] This visit effectively ended Mary's relations with her sisters. Her brother George, too,

An exhortation   PSALMS.   *to bless God.*

25 Of old hast thou laid the foundation of the earth: and the heavens *are* the work of thy hands.

26 They shall perish, but thou shalt endure: yea, all of them shall wax old like a garment; as a vesture shalt thou change them, and they shall be changed:

27 But thou *art* the same, and thy years shall have no end.

28 The children of thy servants shall continue, and their seed shall be established before thee.

PSALM CIII.

1 *An exhortation to bless God for his mercy,* 15 *and for the constancy thereof.*

A Psalm of David.

BLESS the LORD, O my soul: and all that is within me, *bless* his holy name.

2 Bless the LORD, O my soul, and forget not all his benefits:

3 Who forgiveth all thine iniquities; who healeth all thy diseases;

4 Who redeemeth thy life from destruction; who crowneth thee with lovingkindness and tender mercies;

5 Who satisfieth thy mouth with good *things;* so *that* thy youth is renewed like the eagle's.

6 The LORD executeth righteousness and judgment for all that are oppressed.

7 He made known his ways unto Moses, his acts unto the children of Israel.

8 The LORD *is* merciful and gracious, slow to anger, and plenteous in mercy.

K   145

Mrs. Eddy's book of Psalms

would refuse to accept her aid and soon pass on. She returned to Taunton for a short time, and then found a home with Mary Webster in Amesbury, Massachusetts, where she met her second student, nineteen-year-old Richard Kennedy.

While living at Mary Webster's, Mrs. Patterson continued working on a verse-by-verse explication of the book of Genesis. In her introductory remarks to this work, she wrote of the "science" she had discovered: "[W]e . . . find the blessed statement of this science contained in the Bible, and its full demonstration in casting out error, and healing the sick."[24] When she wrote this, she first placed "healing the sick" before "casting out error" and then switched their order. The third verse in Psalm 103 would have confirmed this choice. She had been healed of an illness during childhood when her brother Albert read the psalm aloud to her. The third verse refers to the Lord "who forgiveth all thine iniquities; who healeth all thy diseases."[25] Mary knew that the sick could be healed with her "science" only as the Truth of being first cast out error, or sin, in the thought of both the physician and the patient. And she knew that turning to God in prayer was the only way to do this.

Chapter 5

MORAL SCIENCE
(1868–1870)

$\mathcal{I}$N 1868 MRS. GLOVER, AS she was then calling herself, was seeking a thorough understanding of the Principle and rules of the divine Science that had healed her. The Bible had become her only textbook, and she was healing others in accord with the divine laws she was discovering in those Scriptures.

A telegram from Manchester, New Hampshire, addressed to "Mrs. Mary B. Glover" arrived at the Websters' home on May 30, a Saturday. It read, "Mrs. Gale is very sick, please come Monday morning if possible. Answer yes or no." Mrs. Glover packed her bag immediately and went to see Mary Gale. When she arrived, the doctors informed her there was no hope: Mrs. Gale could not live; she was dying of pneumonia. Yet Mrs. Glover healed her on the spot.[1] In later years when asked by a student what had prompted her to write *Science and Health with Key to the Scriptures*, Mrs. Eddy told her about this healing. The student, Clara Shannon, relates in her reminiscence:

> . . . when [Mrs. Glover] entered the room the patient

was propped up with many pillows, and could not speak. Our Leader saw that what she needed was an arousal, and quickly pulled all the pillows away from behind her. As she fell backwards the patient said "Oh! You have killed me." [Mrs. Glover] told her that she could get up and that she would help her to dress. [Mrs. Gale] was instantaneously healed and well. [Mrs. Glover] asked the doctors to leave the room while she helped her to put on her clothing, after which they rejoined the doctors and [Mrs. Gale's] husband in the sitting-room.

One of the doctors, an old, experienced physician, witnessed this, and he said, "How did you do it, what did you do?" [Mrs. Glover] said, "I can't tell you, it was God," and he said, "Why don't you write it in a book, publish it, and give it to the world?" When she returned home she opened her Bible, and her eyes fell on the words "Thus speaketh the Lord God of Israel, saying, Write thee all the words that I have spoken unto thee in a book" Jeremiah 30:2.[2]

After four more years of healing others and beginning her teaching, she started writing *Science and Health* in 1872.

On returning to Amesbury, Mary found that Mrs. Webster's son was bringing his family to stay in the house for summer vacation. As a result, all the boarders were forced to move. Mary's next home was with Sarah Bagley, who introduced her to the poet John Greenleaf Whittier, whom Mary healed of consumption when they met. Mrs. Eddy referred to this in the last class she taught thirty years later: "In one treatment the poet Whittier was raised from an advanced stage of consumption to perfect health and freedom, but not until the past few years did I know that his niece and former friends gave the credit to Christian Science."[3]

After two months Mary moved again. This time she found a home south of Boston with the Wentworth family in Stoughton. Mary had met the Wentworths when she was living with her first pupil, Hiram Crafts, and his wife. She had healed Mr. Wentworth of sciatica and his daughter, Celia, of consumption. These healings prompted Mrs. Wentworth to ask Mrs. Glover to teach her how to heal. Mrs. Eddy would later write about her experience with the Wentworths:

> When I was called to go teach Mrs. Sally Wentworth at Stoughton, I did so at a great sacrifice. They were *very* poor. Mr. Wentworth was a shoemaker by trade but had been sick for a long time & unable to work. I healed him of so-called incurable hip-disease in one treatment.
>
> They had scarcely enough money with which to provide food and lived in a house black for want of paint with a great boulder directly front of their door. I paid for having the house painted and for making a lawn front of their house. I healed Mr. & Mrs. Wentworth and their 2 girls free of charge, taught Mrs. W. & remained in their family & directed & assisted her in getting up a practice. She told me when I left their home that she was averaging $50 per week from her practice at healing....
>
> I had an agreement with Mrs. Wentworth that she should give me rent and board while with them and pay

me a percentage on her practice in return for teaching her, but ... I never received any money from her.[4]

Mary healed Mrs. Wentworth of chronic throat disease and her younger daughter, Lucy, of deafness. The clearest evidence of moral regeneration within the family took place when, after healing Alanson Wentworth of hip trouble, Mary healed him of smoking and chewing tobacco.

Another of Mrs. Glover's healings in Stoughton offers a particularly poignant example of the thorough regeneration her patients often experienced. Within an hour, she not only cured John Scott of enteritis and bowel stoppage but transformed his nature:

> I was once called to visit a sick man to whom the regular physicians had given three doses of Croton oil, and then had left him to die. Upon my arrival I found him barely alive, and in terrible agony. In one hour he was well, and the next day he attended to his business. I removed the stoppage, healed him of enteritis, and neutralized the bad effects of the poisonous oil. His physicians had failed even to move his bowels,—though the wonder was, with the means used in their effort to accomplish this result, that they had not quite killed him. According to their diagnosis, the exciting cause of the inflammation and stoppage was—eating smoked herring. The man is living yet; and I will send his address to any one who may wish to apply to him for information about his case.

Now comes the question: Had that sick man dominion over the fish in his stomach?

His want of control over "the fish of the sea" must have been an illusion, or else the Scriptures misstate man's power. That the Bible is true I believe, not only, but I *demonstrated* its truth when I exercised my power over the fish, cast out the sick man's illusion, and healed him. Thus it was shown that the healing action of Mind upon the body has its only explanation in divine metaphysics.

Especially interesting for what it adds to this account, is the write-up of it in the *Boston Traveller* in 1900:

> . . . Remarkable as was the man's physical healing, even more remarkable was the transformation in his thought and life. His wife told Mrs. [Glover] a few days later that she had never before seen him [hug] his children as other fathers did, but on the night of his recovery he called them to him, and taking them in his arms he told them that he loved them; and with tears rolling down his cheeks he said to his wife, "I am going to be a better man." It is not strange that the happy wife said to Mrs. [Glover], "Oh, how I thank you for restoring my husband to health, but more than all, I am grateful for what you have done for him morally and spiritually."[5]

This type of moral regeneration set Mrs. Glover's "science" apart from any other healing method. She saw it as the most important part, which very likely caused her originally to call her discovery Moral Science. This name first appeared in the title of her teaching manuscript mentioned earlier: "The Science of Man, by which the sick are healed. Embracing Questions and Answers in Moral Science." She completed this work while at the Wentworths'.

In this manuscript Mrs. Glover had written, "The sick have only to waken from this dream of life in matter—of pain, and disease in matter, yea, of sensation in matter that you call personal sense, to realize themselves well: but to break up this illusion requires much growth on your part, much progress from sense to Soul."[6] She followed this statement a little further on with:

Ques. What is the proper method and the one Jesus employed to heal the sick?

Ans. To cast out error with truth, and this heals the sick, and is Science, and no other process is.

Ques. How can I succeed in doing this so that my demonstration in healing shall be wonderful and immediate?

Ans. By being like Jesus, by asking yourself am I honest, am I just, am I merciful, am I pure?

Mary's work during this period was not confined solely to Stoughton. She lectured a few times in Southborough, Massachusetts, at St. Mark's, a private boarding school of the Episcopal church in South Framingham. Fifteen-year-old D. Lee Slataper was at that time a student at St. Mark's, and his roommate was

Oscar Whitcomb, a nephew of John B. Gough, a nationally known temperance lecturer. Both Lee and Oscar belonged to the I. O. of Good Templars. Many years later Lee wrote about this:

> Mrs. Mary Baker Eddy, then known under the name of Mrs. Patterson, came ... and gave us some good lectures, etc.
>
> On one of these trips my roommate was sick with a fever and after her lecture was over [she] came home with us and in a short time Oscar was free from all fever. This was my introduction to what is now known as Christian Science, and frequently afterwards she was called upon for relief. This was in 1868.[7]

In a sermon she gave in Boston several years later, Mrs. Eddy shared with the congregation another of her healing works that occurred around this time:

> I had an interview this last week with a gentleman who had escaped from a mad-house in 1868. He was a raving maniac, and they were in pursuit of him. He stopped at the place where I boarded, and the lady ran for me and said, "I am well nigh frightened to death; won't you come? Here is a maniac threatening our lives. My daughter has fled, and I am come for you."
>
> I went with her. He took a chair, and poised it, but I looked upward, and he dropped the chair, and asked if I had something to say to him. I said I had, all from the spiritual side, "The first thing is you have no disease of the brain; you need never have been in the insane

hospital." Then came the comfort and relief, and the poor maniac fell on his knees before me; he was cured. I saw him last week, married, the father of children, a well man. He never was insane after that.

Now I feel like asking your forgiveness for what I am saying, you must think it so perfectly incomprehensible. He said to me last week, "Do you remember, Mrs. Eddy, when I sat at your feet and you toyed with my curls. I said what are you doing and you said, I am anointing your hair with oil, and," he continued, "my hair was covered with oil; for months I could feel it like dew upon my head."

I remembered it; I remembered that when he fell before me, I reached out my hand in benediction. It touched his head, and he said, "What are you doing?" [I replied,] "Anointing your head with oil." I meant what David said, "He anointed my head with oil, so that my cup runneth over." I meant the anointing of Truth like the dew or the gentle rain, coming upon that poor, agonized brain, and he thought it was hair-oil and that I was toying with his hair![8]

After a year and a half at the Wentworths', Mary went back to Amesbury to teach Sarah Bagley. At one point they encountered a small boy who was feeling ill when they were visiting his grandparents. Many years later Stephen Babcock wrote about their visit:

. . . My Mother's parents were Quakers (Mr. & Mrs. Charles Wing), living in Amesbury, Mass. There was a so-called "Faith Healer" living there who used to give treatments to my grandparents—her name was Bagley and we used to call her "Auntie Bagley." She wore gray corkscrew curls on the side of her head—and to my child mind they looked like cast iron or steel turnings. One day [Miss] Bagley and "another lady" (who I afterwards learned was Mrs. Eddy) were at my grandfather's house. I was taken with a stomachache, and [Miss] Bagley tried to help me by holding me in her lap—but those "steel curls" frightened me. The other lady who I just remember as a kind gentle lady then took me in her lap—and I felt very peaceful. I cannot remember the actual healing—but I am quite sure the pain left me.[9]

During her stay with Sarah Bagley, Mary met with Richard Kennedy, her second student whom she had taught two years earlier, soon after she moved to Amesbury. Mr. Kennedy was twenty-one years old now and very eager to start in the full-time practice of healing. He convinced Mrs. Glover to form a teacher/practitioner partnership with him. He would treat patients, and she would guide his practice. Before agreeing to this, Mary cautioned him: "Richard, this is a very spiritual life that Mind Science exacts, and the world offers many alluring temptations. You know but little of them as yet. If you follow me you must cross swords with the world. Are you spiritually-minded enough to take up my work and stand by it?"[10] With more enthusiasm than wisdom, he assured her he was.

Because she saw the need to establish her student's practice in a larger town, Mrs. Glover and Mr. Kennedy moved to Lynn in May 1870. Her hope was that Richard's practice would prompt calls for teaching. As can be seen from her letter to Sarah Bagley in July, she was not disappointed:

> I have all calling on me for instruction, and why,
> if I am not better than others I am not fit to teach God
> beyond them and could not. Richard is literally overrun
> with patients; as soon as it was known that I had brought
> a student here, the people began to throng him.[11]

Mary's guidance of her student's practice was more active than passive. Richard Kennedy did not have the confidence to treat his patients without resorting to physical manipulation, rubbing the head or stomach. Though she never used this method herself, Mrs. Glover allowed it to continue with the hope that he would grow out of it. He never did. A girl who knew her during this period wrote, "Mrs. [Glover] used to do the treating and Dr. Kennedy the rubbing."[12] And Mrs. Eddy wrote in a letter in 1888:

> When my second student went into practice, I did
> the healing for him sitting in a cold gloomy ante-room
> while he was in the front office as the physician. This I
> did because my first student stopped his practice the first
> year, so great was the persecution, and to get one started I
> had to do the work at first, and not be seen in doing it.
>
> I was pleased with this out-of-sight labor, liked it
> much better than to be in front....[13]

In 1909, Mrs. Eddy told Irving Tomlinson more about what her life was like during that time:

...At one time in Lynn I had something like one hundred cases, but a student was perceptively the practitioner. I refused to take patients because I was carrying the Cause and my time was occupied with many other matters.

I remember one case brought to the rooms well nigh prostrated and one which had been given up as hopeless. I happened to be in the ante-room when the only seat was an upturned tub. Down I sat upon it, silently treated the patient, and she left fully healed.[14]

The "many other matters" Mrs. Glover was concerned with at that time involved teaching, writing, and counseling. In August 1870 she taught her first class of six students. Three months later, she taught another class of similar size. Samuel Putnam Bancroft was a member of that class and wrote extensively of his experiences with his teacher during this period. True warmth and appreciation flow through his words as he describes what it was like to be taught by Mrs. Glover and, in particular, her great concern for the welfare and progress of her students. At one point she saved the life of his young child, who was severely ill.[15] Mr. Bancroft writes:

Mrs. [Glover] did not claim to be a teacher of religion, however, but of a method of healing the sick without the use of medicine. That was what induced us to study with her. The object of some was to regain health; of others, to commercialize the knowledge acquired. They considered it a sound business proposition. Her religious views, while not concealed, were not capitalized. Later, we learned that our success or failure in healing depended on the purity of our lives, as well as on the instruction she gave us.[16]

Mrs. Glover's ongoing Bible study furnished a strong foundation for her healing and teaching. To facilitate the latter, Mary wrote papers for her classes. The titles included "The Soul's Inquiries of Man," "Spiritualism," and "Personal Sense." She used these in conjunction with her teaching manuscript, *The Science of Man*. Occasionally a question would be asked in class that she felt was important enough to answer in writing. One of these was from Mr. Bancroft, who asked how they should metaphysically view the process of teaching. As part of her answer, Mrs. Glover wrote:

> When I teach science it is not woman that addresses man, it is the principle and soul bringing out its idea. … My scholars may learn from me what they could not learn from the same words if uttered by another with less wisdom than even my "grain of mustard seed," hence, it is not the words, but the amount of soul that comes forth to destroy error.[17]

For Mary, the ability to heal came from far more than an intellectual understanding of metaphysical concepts. It was a matter of whether spiritual sense or material sense governed the practitioner. Without the spiritual aspect, the healing practice turned into a mesmeric exercise of one human mind controlling another. This is why she kept stressing to her students the need for greater goodness and purity in their thoughts and lives. As she stated in a revision of *The Science of Man,* "A student of Moral Science, and this is the Science of man, must be a pure and undefiled Christian, in order to make the most rapid progress in healing...."[18]

Mary Gatchell, who lived for a time in the same house as Mrs. Glover, described her in part as "the purest minded woman I ever knew."[19] This is how Mary could instantaneously heal a badly deformed man sitting on the sidewalk in Lynn by simply telling him that God loved him. Mrs. Eddy described this healing to a member of her household in 1907:

> ... I was walking along the street ... and saw this cripple,
> with one knee drawn up to his chin; ... The other limb
> was drawn the other way, up his back. I came up to him
> and read on a piece of paper pinned on his shoulder,
> "Help this poor cripple." I had no money to give him so
> I whispered in his ear, "God loves you." And he got up
> perfectly straight and well. He ran into [Lucy Allen's]
> house and asked who that woman is, pointing to [me.]
> The lady told him, "it is Mrs. Glover." [He replied,] "no it
> isn't, it's an angel."[20]

In *Science and Health,* Mrs. Eddy writes that one "must prove, through living as well as healing and teaching, that Christ's way is the only one by which mortals are radically saved from sin and sickness."[21] Before she wrote these words, she lived them.

Chapter 6

TEACHER, COUNSELOR, AUTHOR
(1871–1874)

As MARY BAKER EDDY WENT forward in her life as teacher, author, and founder, sharing Christian Science with mankind, she never stopped healing. In fact, she would not have been able to carry out the duties that each of these roles demanded, without her ability to heal, which she felt was God-given. It permeated everything she did.

In 1871, Mrs. Glover was conducting classes in Moral Science. She taught in the evenings in the same building where she lived, Susie Magoun's school for young girls. One day Miss Magoun told her about a girl in her school who was mute, but could hear perfectly well. Mrs. Eddy wrote about this in 1898:

> The next time the child passed my door on her way to school I met her and spoke a few words to her. When the question came around to her in class, she astonished the whole school by promptly answering in a clear strong voice.[1]

Mrs. Glover tried earnestly to teach those interested in learning how to heal quickly and completely just as she did. For the most part, her students came from the working-class people of Lynn. The price she put on her lessons was $300, more than one-half of a Lynn worker's annual salary. In today's economy the fee would be equivalent to about $6,400. Not only did this show the value she placed on what she was teaching, but it also helped to ensure that the student's interest was deep and abiding, and not just a matter of idle curiosity. However, she did take a number of students at a reduced fee, and some needy students were taught gratuitously if she felt they were sincere. For Mary, her discovery of divine Science, which had come as a revelation from God, was a "pearl of great price."[2] And scientific Christian healing was a lifework, not simply another way to earn a living. She knew that a total commitment was essential to success in this healing work.

Mrs. Glover taught only one class in 1871. It was held in April. The rest of her time was spent counseling and supporting her students in their healing practices. Caring for one's pupils after formal lessons have been completed remains to this day, at Mrs. Eddy's impetus, a moral imperative for teachers of Christian Science.[3] Mary watched over her students as if they were her own children, and she hoped that through their practices, the continual call on her personally to do healing work would decrease. This was not the case in the beginning, however. As she wrote in 1901: "I could not at first make a student see how to heal the sick with prayer alone, for each student that I taught thirty years ago was not enough of a Christian to pray with sufficient faith and understanding to heal the sick."[4]

Recognizing her students' need for growth, Mrs. Glover told them "to practice as best they could," working with what they understood. This meant that some resorted to rubbing the heads of their patients. She commented in that same 1901 document:

> This went on till I had gained a clearer sense of the divine Principle of Science through which I learned it was impossible to practice it by any material method of manipulation. Then I hastened to instruct my students not to lay hands on the sick but to accept only the spiritual interpretation of that Scripture, namely, to apply through prayer the power of God to heal the sick, & by that time some of them had grown to the point of spiritual understanding sufficiently to take in my meaning. . . .

As she waited for the spiritual growth of her pupils, Mrs. Glover naturally continued to respond to calls for healing. At one point, she was asked to help a man with a severe fever who had refused to eat anything for a week. His two physicians declared he would die. When she entered his room, the man was delirious. He was saying, "This tastes good and that tastes good," but there was no food in the room. Mrs. Glover said to the doctors, "With that consciousness he can live without eating anything." When they laughed at her, she replied, "Well, then he *can* eat," and immediately he was in his right mind. He recognized someone in the room and asked for something to eat. After finishing his meal, he dressed, went outside, and was completely well. Many years later, Mrs. Eddy told a member of her household that she had not given any thought to the man's physical condition, only to the fact that "'God is all,' and [she had] shut out what the physicians had said and everything else from the [material] sense side."[5]

In healing, Mrs. Eddy could speak with authority because of the depth of her spiritual under-standing and compassion, tempered by the need to reach her patient. She recounted to the same individual another healing that occurred during this period:

PHOTO: W.T. BOWERS, © CSPS

Mrs. Eddy in 1871

> A lady in Lynn was so angry at me she would not speak to me after healing her daughter because she said I spoke disrespectfully to her dying daughter. The physicians had said there was only a little piece of her lung left and she was dying. I was called and there were spiritualists around. I tried to reach her thought, but no, could not get at it. So I said, "Get out of that bed." Then I called to those in the other room, "Bring her clothes." The girl got up and was well; never even coughed again. . . . I speak sharply sometimes, but the thought must *move*.[6]

Mrs. Glover herself never practiced physical manipulation in her own healing work. But when she told her students, at the beginning of 1872, that they must drop it completely from their practice, this caused a stir with some of them. Her second student, Richard Kennedy, refused to comply. She tried for a time to make him see the importance of taking this step, but he would not change his ways. As a result they dissolved their formal partnership that had been agreed on when they first came to Lynn two years earlier. Richard Kennedy would spend much of the rest of his life working against Mrs. Eddy's interests. In particular, he tried to cause disaffection among her students and followers, working to turn them against her.

A number of years later Mrs. Eddy would write at length exposing Kennedy's malpractice in this direction. About one young student, George Barry, who had grown especially devoted to her, she wrote:

> Another victim of the aforesaid mesmerist [Kennedy] was a young man [Barry] who was consumptive, and went to him to be doctored. He was bleeding at the lungs, etc., when he joined our class. Being poor, we receipted to him in full for one half our usual tuition. After our instructions he regained perfect health, and professed great gratitude to us. . . . During a period of about five years the mesmerist evidently nourished his hatred and purpose to destroy that young man, and from no cause apparent but our interest in his welfare. . . . Had we understood then, as now, the demonology carried on by the aforesaid mesmerist, that young man would have been saved what will be to him the saddest recollection in his whole history.[7]

Also at the beginning of 1872, another former pupil, Wallace Wright, used a Lynn newspaper to attack Mrs. Glover's teaching and practice, calling it mesmerism. In her response, she made her first public statement about her "science" through the same newspaper. Wright's published reply prompted a second statement, which Mrs. Glover titled "Moral Science and Mesmerism." She ended this letter "To the Public" this way:

> I am preparing a work on Moral and Physical Science, that I shall submit to the public as soon as it is completed. This work is laborious, and I have not much opportunity to write, hence the delay in publishing. I withhold my MSS [manuscripts] from all eyes but my students', first, because they are mere outlines of my subject, that require me to fill up by explanation, and secondly, because I think the mass of minds are not yet prepared to digest this subject.[8]

The "work" she was preparing would become the textbook for her "science." In March of 1872, she held one more class and then stopped teaching in order to devote her entire effort over the next three years to writing *Science and Health*.

When Mary first considered the problem of what to do for her students, having taken away their crutch of physical manipulation, she did not immediately see the solution. She wrote about this years later on the flyleaf of one of her Bibles:

> Before writing *Science and Health with Key to the Scriptures*, I had asked God for weeks to tell me what

next I should do, and each day I opened the Bible for my answer, but did not receive it. But when I grew to receiving it, I opened again and the first verse I looked at was in Isaiah 30:8.[9]

This verse reads, "Now go, write it before them in a table, and note it in a book, that it may be for the time to come for ever and ever."

Regarding her role as author, Mrs. Eddy told Irving Tomlinson in 1900 that it was important to include in a biographical piece he was working on something she considered to be a significant "epoch" in her life. At age seven when her friends asked what she was going to do when she grew up, she replied, "Write a book."[10] As it turned out, she wrote not just *any* book but a hands-on textbook that would explain the "science of Life"[11]—a textbook that enables a student, entirely through prayer, to overcome life's problems, whether they be moral, mental, or physical. But the author made a demand on the student: "...those who would learn this science without a high moral standard will fail to understand it until they go up higher."[12] Mr. Wright, who had attacked her in the newspaper, was among those who felt too much was being asked in order to go up higher. In a letter to her he complained, "While I do not question the right of it, it teaches a deprivation of social enjoyment if we would attain the *highest* round in the ladder of Science."[13]

Mrs. Glover did not advocate asceticism, but she did counsel her students, in line with Christ Jesus' teaching, that while they may be "in" the world, they must not be "of" the world.[14] Her own life was certainly an example of this. Every waking hour of her day was devoted to her "science." Although she planned most of it to be spent in writing, calls for help came to her constantly, and she could not refuse those in need. One can see the blessing this brought to her writing, however, as she included some of these healings in the first edition of her textbook:

> The following is a case of heart disease described in a letter from a lady at New York. "... The day you received my husband's letter I became conscious, for the first time for forty-eight hours; my servant brought my wrapper and I rose from bed and sat up. The attack of the heart had lasted two days, and no one thinks I could have survived but for the mysterious help I received from you. The enlargement of my left side is all gone and the M.D.s pronounce me entirely rid of heart disease. I have been afflicted with it from infancy, until it became

Jan. 20, 1872

For the Transcript.

MR. EDITOR:—I casually noticed in the *Transcript* an attack by W. W. Wright on the Moral and Physical Science that I teach, in which he states it is mesmerism, and that the MSS. he holds prove this. Mr. Wright is under a three thousand dollar bond not to show those MSS. Can he annul this agreement and *practice* or *understand Moral* Science? But the same MSS. are in the hands of other of my students in this city, who will answer this question, and if the reader of his article, or any one desiring to learn this Science, will call on me, at 29 South Common street, they shall have the opportunity to judge for themselves, as I will satisfy them on this point; or, if I am out, one of my former students, Dr. Kennedy, with whom I am in business, will answer this question of Moral Science.

Mr. Wright says his principal reason for writing on this subject was to prevent others from being led into it. Here he is honest. 'Tis but a few weeks since he called on me and threatened that, if I did not refund his tuition fee and pay him two hundred dollars extra, he would prevent my ever having another class in this city. Said he, " My simple purpose now is revenge, and I will have it,"—and this, too, immediately after saying to individuals in this city that the last lesson the class received, of which he was a member, was alone worth all he had paid for tuition. The " whistle " was not so "dear" then. Very soon after this, however, I received a letter from him, requesting me to pay him over and above all I had received from him, or, in case I should not, he would ruin the Science. I smiled at the threat, and told a lady at my side, " If you see him tell him first to take a bucket and dip the Atlantic dry, and then try his powers on this next scheme." The student in Knoxville, to whom he referred, wrote me :—" Mr. Wright puts a false construction on the Science, but says ' he does not question its *morality* and *Christianity.*' " Also, in his letter to me he never referred to mesmerism, but said, (here I copy *verbatim*) :—" While I do not question the right of it, it teaches a deprivation of social enjoyment if we would attain the *highest* round in the ladder of Science." Was not this the " side " referred to in his newspaper article, in which he said, " Had I been shown both sides nothing could have induced me to take it up "?

Christianity as he calls it at one time, and mesmerism at another, cannot be the " two sides," for these are separated by barriers that neither a geometrical figure nor a malicious falsehood would ever unite.

My few remaining years will be devoted to the cause I have espoused, viz :—to teach and to demonstrate the Moral and Physical Science that can heal the sick. Well knowing as I do that God hath bidden me, I shall steadfastly adhere to my purpose to benefit my suffering fellow beings, even though it be amid the most malignant misrepresentation and persecution.

MARY M. B. GLOVER.

In response to Wallace Wright's article, Mrs. Eddy wrote this Letter to the Editor to the *Lynn Transcript*. It was published January 20, 1872.

organic enlargement of the heart and dropsy of the chest. I was only waiting, and almost longing, to die; but you have healed me; and yet how wonderful to think of it, when we have never seen each other! We return to Europe next week. I feel perfectly well."[15]

and

The following is from a lady in Lynn: "My little son, one year and a half old, was a great sufferer from disease of the bowels, until he was reduced to almost a skeleton, and growing worse constantly; could take nothing but gruel, or some very simple nutriment. At that time the physicians had given him up, saying they could do no more for him, but you came in one morning, took him up from the cradle in your arms, kissed him, laid him down again and went out. In less than an hour he called for his playthings, got up and appeared quite well. All his symptoms changed at once. For months previously nothing but blood and mucous had passed his bowels, but that very day the evacuation was natural, and he has not suffered since from his complaint, and it is more than two years since he was cured. Immediately after you saw him, he ate all he wanted, and one thing was a quantity of cabbage just before going to bed, from which he never suffered in the least."[16]

There's more to this last healing than appeared in the first edition of *Science and Health*. When Mrs. Glover came to the home, she also found not only the woman's husband confined to his bed with rheumatism but a little daughter who was deaf. By the time she left the house, less than half an hour after she had arrived, both of these cases had been healed, too.[17]

Many years later Mrs. Eddy told one of her students about this experience, which prompted the question, "When will we be able to do work like that?" Looking off in the distance, Mrs. Eddy replied, "It is Love that heals, only Love!" The student, Miss Nemi Robertson, repeated the question, "But when will *we* be able to do such work?" This time her teacher looked directly at her and said quietly, "When you believe what you say. I believe every statement of Truth that I make."[18] Mrs. Eddy recorded those statements of Truth in her textbook, *Science and Health with Key to the Scriptures*, so that all who study it may be purified and heal as she did.

Chapter 7

THE "CAUSE OF TRUTH"
(1875–1879)

ETWEEN 1872 AND 1875, MARY Glover was writing the textbook to explain the Science she had discovered through divine revelation in 1866.[1] Since that discovery, she had been intensively studying the Bible, healing the sick through prayer alone, and teaching others how to heal. She suspended teaching in 1872 in order to devote her full time to writing *The Science of Life*. This was the original title for her work, which she changed after learning of a book with that same title already in print. Mrs. Eddy later wrote about this experience:

> Six weeks I waited on God to suggest a name for the
> book I had been writing. Its title, Science and Health,
> came to me in the silence of night, when the steadfast
> stars watched over the world,—when slumber had
> fled,—and I rose and recorded the hallowed suggestion.
> The following day I showed it to my literary friends, who
> advised me to drop both the book and the title. To this,
> however, I gave no heed, feeling sure that God had led me

to write that book, and had whispered that name to my
waiting hope and prayer. It was to me the "still, small voice"
that came to Elijah after the earthquake and the fire.[2]

At the beginning of 1875, Mrs. Glover was boarding with
Amos Scribner and his wife at 7 Broad Street in Lynn, Massachusetts. One night, Mr. Scribner was called to stay with a friend
who had been very ill for some time with two kinds of fever. He
was reluctant to go because the friend was now said to be dying.
Years later, she wrote about that evening:

> When I heard of the circumstances I said to him,
> "go & I will heal him for you." I also told him the signs
> that he would see as my work on the case progressed. He
> said, "well supposing when I get there he is dead?" I said,
> "he won't be, & at 9 (this was 7) I will cure him if you will
> ask everyone but yourself to leave the room."

> "But," he said, "supposing he is dying before then?"

> "Then I will cure him at that time." He had seen
> me heal his wife of child bed fever & his son of choler
> infantum & had utter confidence in my ability & said,
> "I will go." When he arrived there the man was very low
> & he soon requested all to leave the room that he might
> have the man wholly in his care.

> Soon the man opened his eyes & said, "hello!
> Amos! Is that you, how glad I am to see you." Amos said,
> "would you not like to get up?" He said, "yes, it is rather
> early to go to bed," & he got up & dressed himself &

then wanted something to eat. The next day he was out of the house perfectly well.

> This case was so well known that people would gather on the corner of streets & talk about [it;] the whole city was shocked by it.[3]

Mrs. Glover may have had healings like these in mind when she wrote in the Preface of her soon-to-be-published book: ". . . we propose to settle the question of 'What is Truth?' on the ground of proof. Let that method of healing the sick and establishing Christianity, be adopted, that is found to give the most health, and make the best Christians. . . ."[4] Her "method of healing"—demonstrating the reality of the divine Science that had been revealed to her by God—did "give the most health, and make the best Christians"; it treated the whole man, transforming human character while it healed the body. This defines what a full Christian Science healing accomplishes.

On October 30, 1875, Mrs. Glover's book, *Science and Health,* was published in its first edition of one thousand copies. The months leading up to that luminous day had been exceedingly full. In the spring and summer, Mary had been occupied with not only correcting printer's proofs but also adding her observations on mental malpractice to the book's last chapter, "Healing the Sick." She described the writing of this addition as a "painful task,"[5] but as one she had become convinced was necessary in order to alert readers to the danger of straying from Christian healing into mesmerism. These sixteen pages were written at 8 Broad Street, her new home in Lynn. Mary had purchased the house in March and resumed teaching in

April, using the front parlor as her classroom. A month after this, on May 23, she delivered a lecture entitled "Christ Healing the Sick" at Concert Hall on Market Street in Lynn. This was her first public address on Christian Science in that city.

Whether teaching or lecturing, *healing* was at the center of all Mary's efforts. She wrote a prospective student in 1876 about her teaching, ". . . if I do not make [pupils] capable of healing, I will refund the money to them."[6] To her, teaching was not about pupils learning previously unknown facts; its purpose was to produce students who could heal through Christian prayer alone. Though it became necessary to move gradually from a public to a private practice of spiritual healing as the demands of establishing the Christian Science movement grew, Mrs. Glover's own healing work continued as calls for help kept coming. One of these was from the son of a widow in Lynn; he had a degenerative shinbone. The boy's doctor had prescribed an opiate, which he took every two hours, to dull the pain. When Mrs. Glover came to him, the day he was to have his leg amputated,[7] there was a question whether he would live. She wrote about the results:

> The next day after my visit he was out on the street, took
> no more morphine, and that winter attended the dancing
> school. About a month after I healed him, he called
> on me and I noticed that his foot turned unnaturally
> outward. I immediately changed that and he walked
> across the floor with the foot in its natural position.[8]

In 1901, Calvin Frye, Mrs. Eddy's private secretary, wrote in his diary that she had spoken of this healing to him and said,

No. 8 Broad Street, Lynn, Massachusetts. The skylight window is in the attic room where Mrs. Eddy wrote.

The title page of the first edition of *Science and Health*

PREFACE.

_____

LEANING on the sustaining Infinite with loving trust, the trials of to-day are brief, and to-morrow is big with blessings. The wakeful shepherd tending his flocks, beholds from the mountain's top the first faint morning beam ere cometh the risen day. So from Soul's loftier summits shines the pale star to the prophet shepherd, and it traverses night, over to where the young child lies in cradled obscurity that shall waken a world. Over the night of error dawn the morning beams and guiding star of Truth, and " the wise men are led by it to Science, to that which repeats the eternal harmony reproduced in proof of immortality and God. The time for thinkers has come; and the time for revolutions, ecclesiastic and social, must come. Truth, independent of doctrines or time-honored systems, stands at the threshold of history. Contentment with the past, or the cold conventionality of custom, may no longer shut the door on science; though empires fall, " He whose right it is shall reign." Ignorance of God should no longer be the stepping-stone to faith; understanding Him " whom to know aright is Life " is the only guaranty of obedience.

Since the hoary centuries but faintly shadow forth the tireless Intelligence at work for man, this volume

3

The opening page of the first edition of *Science and Health*

"I knew that if he died he would awake to find he had not that disease, and I wanted to wake him to it *before he died*." [9]

Waking thought to the truth about the allness and goodness of God, and of man as His perfect reflection, is central to Christian Science, and it produces healing. Under God's impulsion, Mrs. Eddy wrote *Science and Health* for the awakening of mankind. But she was not content simply to produce the book and then leave the outreach of its message to the whim of public interest. Mary Baker Glover understood that part of her divinely appointed mission was to see that the book's message reached all that "hunger and thirst after righteousness"—purity, health, and wholeness—so that "they shall be filled."[10] So a month and a half after her book appeared, Mary wrote to a student about "our glorious cause."[11] What had started out more than thirty years earlier as a search for true health, had, through God's gracious preparation, transformed an invalid into a healer, teacher, author, and now founder of the "cause" of Christian Science.

In 1876, one of Mrs. Glover's primary concerns was getting *Science and Health* in the hands of the public. She appointed Daniel Spofford, one of her students, as publisher, to be responsible for the sale of the book.[12] In May she wrote him: ". . . what you most need is Love, *meekness*, and charity, or patience, with everybody. These things would increase your success. . . ."[13] And a year later she wrote him of the need to "get students into the field as practitioners, and their healing will sell the book and introduce the science more than aught but *my* lecturing can do."[14]

Of course, the reason Mary's lectures introduced her "science" so effectively is that healings occurred as a result of them.

She makes reference to this in her autobiography, *Retrospection and Introspection*, where she writes, "Our last vestry meeting was made memorable by eloquent addresses from persons who feelingly testified to having been healed through my preaching. Among other diseases cured they specified cancers."[15] Mrs. Eddy was referring to a series of afternoon sermons she had given in the Tabernacle Baptist Church in Boston, beginning November 24, 1878. Clara Choate, one of Mrs. Eddy's students who was present at one of these afternoon meetings, described it:

> In an octagonal church in the vestry on Shawmut Ave. near & opposite Hammond St., a meeting of the Christian Scientists was held about the year 1879. The time was in the cold weather, since Mrs. Eddy wore a fur-trimmed velvet coat, & the Dr. [Asa Gilbert Eddy] an overcoat. . . . One person, it might have been Rev. Williams the pastor, asked if she could restore the *blind*—She replied *no*, but *God* could, if we would let Him do the work. . . . There was no specified time for closing and we lingered on till quite dark. But though nearly every Christian Scientist was present, the audience was not over 40 & some present were strangers. . . . The spirit of the meeting rather than any words was felt by all, and some wonderful healing was reported from this meeting. Mrs. Eddy claimed it as her thanksgiving to God, and we were loath to part or to close, but Mrs. Eddy told us if we were to be her followers we must be particular in the promptness & the proper hour for the meetings.
>
> From this time on a new impetus was given the

Cause of Christian Science and the healing gained
favor, the textbook sold rapidly, and a new interest was
created in the various denominations, for Dr. Williams
even could not help talking about Mrs. Eddy & her
wonderful claims. . . . Mrs. Eddy sat beside a table,
with the people gathered informally about her, so quiet
& inconspicuous that people about me asked which
was she. But when she spoke, her voice and manner
betrayed at once her unusual mind; one could not help
listening for the words were with power, & one present
wished to tell [that] she had come in a stranger with
dreadful headache, but it left her, though no one knew
but herself, and she wondered at God's impersonal
power, which to some degree Mrs. Eddy had awakened
her to realize.[16]

Several significant events had taken place in the three inter-
vening years since her book had been published. In March of
1876, she met Asa Gilbert Eddy, her future husband, who came
to her for healing of heart disease. After they married on January
1, 1877, she wrote a pupil:

I need not vindicate this step to a student who
knows the interest of the cause of Truth is all the earthly
interest I possess, and with a view to promote this cause
and to find in union there is strength, to bring another
into my department of labor, and last though not least
to unite my life to one whom I know will bless it. I have
changed its tenor after so many years of struggles *alone*.

Last Spring Dr. Eddy came to me a hopeless

invalid. I saw him then for the first time, and but twice.
When his health was so improved, he next came to
join my class.... In four weeks after he came to study,
he was in practice doing well, worked up an excellent
reputation for healing and at length won my affections
on the ground alone of his great goodness and strength
of character.[17]

Gilbert Eddy became the first of her students to announce
himself to the public as a "Christian Scientist." The publication
of *Science and Health* had established "Christian Science" as the
permanent name for the divine revelation Mrs. Eddy taught and
for "the cause of Truth" she led.

Also significant in the development of this "cause" was the
organization of students into the Christian Scientist Association
on July 4, 1876. Through her Association, Mrs. Eddy was able to
continue the spiritual education of her pupils at regularly held
meetings. She cared deeply about her students, who would turn
to her for help when unable to meet a challenge alone. In one
instance, a mother of six months had been driven by the ceaseless
crying of her baby to appeal to her teacher for relief. Mrs. Eddy
spoke of this in a class she taught in 1888. A member of that class
later wrote in her reminiscences:

Mrs. Eddy said she returned to the home with the
mother, took the baby on her lap, and asked the mother
to leave the room. The child cried and screamed terribly,
and Mrs. Eddy silently declared the truth, but did
nothing else. She said the struggle went on until it
seemed as if the baby might die, but she continued to

know that the real child could not die and that error had no life and that it could not continue to manifest itself. After a short time the child stopped its screaming and crying and went to sleep, and this was the end of that error. Mrs. Eddy went on to explain to the class that the mother, before the birth of her child, had been treating a patient who had a violent temper, and that the mother had not taken the precaution of protecting herself or her unborn child.[18]

Mrs. Eddy was keenly alert to the need to defend her own "child," the newborn "cause of Truth." The materialistic, or worldly, thought of others resisted this "cause" to the point of trying to destroy it. Such was the case when Gilbert Eddy was falsely charged on October 29, 1878, with being party to a conspiracy to murder Daniel Spofford. By this time, Spofford had turned against Christian Science and Mrs. Eddy (for more information, see Spofford's biographical note on pp. 512–514). Gilbert Eddy was incarcerated in Boston's Charles Street Jail for ten days before bail was posted.[19] Three months later the malicious lie was exposed, and the charge was dismissed as having absolutely no validity. In March 1879, Mrs. Eddy wrote a friend:

> The cause is prospering again, rising up slowly from
> the awful blow of malice and falsehoods dealt it last
> Autumn—in which two of my students (one, my darling
> husband) were so shockingly belied, and I dragged into
> the newspaper articles. It was got up by Spofford to stop
> the sale of my Book after I took from him the license
> to sell it because of some shocking immorality and his

broken agreement. . . . My husband became publisher of the Second edition of my work and it had been issued but a week when the blow fell.[20]

Mrs. Eddy had begun this letter by relating how she was then conducting regular Sunday services in Boston at the Parker Memorial Building. In less than a month, she and her students would organize the Church of Christ (Scientist), "designed to perpetuate the teachings of Jesus, to reinstate primitive Christianity, and to restore its lost element of healing."[21] Materialism's attempt to ruin "the cause of Truth" proved impotent. Mrs. Eddy swerved not, nor slowed, in leading this healing cause forward under divine direction.

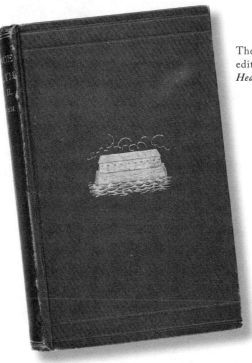

The second, or Ark, edition of *Science and Health*

Chapter 8

Pastor
(1879–1881)

$\mathcal{O}$N APRIL 12, 1879, AT Mary Baker Eddy's home in Lynn, Massachusetts, the Christian Scientist Association of her students met and cast an important vote:

> On motion of Mrs. M. B. Glover Eddy, it was seconded & unanimously voted, that we organize a church to be called Church of Christ.[1]

It was subsequently discovered that another congregation in the state had already incorporated under that name, so in August, Mrs. Eddy's students obtained a charter for the Church of Christ (Scientist).

During that same month, rules and regulations were drawn up to govern the new Church. One of these rules set high standards for the Church's pastor:

> The Pastor of this Church must be able to heal the sick

after the manner of Christian Science, must be strictly moral, and an earnest and devoted follower of Christ.[2]

Mrs. Eddy had been conducting Sunday services in Boston since the previous November, and the congregation naturally called her to preach for the new Church that August. She certainly met all the moral and spiritual qualifications of a Christian Science healer!

During this period a suffering child turned up one day on Mrs. Eddy's doorstep in Lynn. Many years later, Mrs. Helen M. Grenier wrote of this incident:

> I was a little girl at the time, with a child's natural antipathy for medicine, as well as an inherent dread of doctors, and being taken suddenly ill with an agonizing pain in my side, decided to keep my suffering to myself. The eyes of love are keen, however. My mother noticed my unusual pallor and listlessness and questioned me, with the result that a physician was to be called next day unless I was much improved. I grew worse instead of better and set my wits to work to find a way out of the difficulty.
>
> In visiting a relative on Broad Street, I had often noted a house on which was a sign decorated with a gold cross and crown. A woman doctor lived there, it was said, and in my desperation I reasoned thus: "If I must have a doctor I will go to the lady on Broad St. The sign shows she is a Christian, and a Christian woman—even if she is a doctor—wouldn't hurt a little girl." Accordingly I ran away and went to see Mrs. Eddy.

I have never forgotten Mrs. Eddy's gracious womanliness as she met me and led me to a seat, saying "dear child, did you wish to see me?" After a few generalities she closed her eyes for a brief period. She asked me no questions as to symptoms, ailment, etc., but taking my hand said, "if you are not better tomorrow, come and see me again." As I rose and asked the fee, she simply said—"nothing, dear."

I could not understand it. It was so unusual. No questions asked—nothing done to my body—no medicine and no money, and yet—the pain was gone! I knew nothing whatever about Christian Science, and nothing was said regarding it either by Mrs. Eddy or her husband, who met me at the door. I was filled with wonder at the loving kindness of the people who were so good to a little girl, but I no longer wondered at the beautiful cross and crown over the door and in my heart enshrined them as true Christians.

That treatment has never been paid for except in love and grateful appreciation. I was perfectly healed in that one treatment and walked—or rather—*ran* all the way home.[3]

Mrs. Eddy especially cherished the childlike thought. This was evident in the friendship she developed with fifteen-year-old Alice Sibley, whom she had met through one of her students. On September 14, 1879, Mrs. Eddy wrote her:

Darling Alice, keep yourself pure from contamination. Let not the grosser element of other people's thoughts touch the finer fabric of thine own to interweave a single thread not golden. Aim at all that is exalted, put aside as worthless all that degrades or can only dim the luster of the jewel of mind. Let the perfect thought be the parent of the perfect deed, keep the fountain of mind unsullied by a single wrong thought, carelessly cherished, and then the bright promise of your sweet girlhood will meet the expectancy of riper years and of those who so tenderly love thee.[4]

Two months later, Mrs. Eddy's own child, George Glover, came to visit her in Boston. They had not seen each other in twenty-three years. Mr. and Mrs. Eddy had moved to the city in November, primarily to be closer to the Church's services, which were held first in Charlestown and then in downtown Boston at Hawthorne Hall.[5] Though mother and son held a deep affection for each other, their opposite outlooks on life created a gulf between them that could not be spanned. He was a gold prospector in the Black Hills of the Dakota Territory, while she had already found her gold in the kingdom of God. Before returning home, George mentioned to his mother that his three-year-old daughter, Mary, had crossed eyes. She told him, "You must be mistaken, George, her eyes are all right." Later on, the granddaughter confirmed this healing: "When he returned to our home in Deadwood, and during a conversation with my mother at my bedside while I was asleep, they awakened me and discovered that my eyes had become straightened. Mother has a picture of me taken before this incident showing my eyes crossed."[6]

In April 1880, Mrs. Eddy delivered a sermon titled "Christian Healing." The following month it appeared as a pamphlet, becoming the first of her works to be published for the public after *Science and Health*. In it she cautioned her followers, "See to it, O Christian Scientists, ye who have named the name of Christ with a higher meaning, that you abide by your statements, and abound in Love and Truth, for unless you do this you are not demonstrating the Science of metaphysical healing."[7] This was a problem Mrs. Eddy had seen almost from the beginning of her teaching efforts. So many early students, though grasping somewhat her "Science," found it difficult to "abide by" and "abound in" the righteousness that Christian metaphysics demands. Wrong or failed actions undermined their healing practice, which in turn eroded their support of the Cause of Christian Science. Because of this lack of support, Mrs. Eddy considered resigning from the pastorate of the Church toward the end of May 1880. In hopes of persuading her not to do so, the members of both her Association and the Church passed several resolutions. The second of them read: "That while we feel that she has not met with the support which she had reason to expect, we venture to hope that she will reverse her decision, and remain with us."[8] She did so for one more month, but then in July she and her husband, Gilbert, left to spend the rest of the summer in Concord, New Hampshire.

Mrs. Eddy saw great danger in what she later described as "the mistake of believing in mental healing, claiming full faith in the divine Principle, and saying, 'I am a Christian Scientist,' while doing unto others what we would resist to the hilt if done unto ourselves."[9] This led her to investigate "the metaphysical mystery of error."[10] She knew evil to be an illusion, but she also knew that unless its true nature was specifically uncovered, thought could be influenced by it unconsciously.[11] Her next edition of *Science and Health* expanded the original sixteen pages on this subject into a forty-six page chapter entitled "Demonology." Her reasons for giving so much thought to this problem can be understood from what she later added to her textbook:

> Every Christian Scientist, every conscientious teacher
> of the Science of Mind-healing, knows that human will
> is not Christian Science, and he must recognize this in
> order to defend himself from the influence of human
> will. He feels morally obligated to open the eyes of his
> students that they may perceive the nature and methods
> of error of every sort, especially any subtle degree of evil,
> deceived and deceiving.[12]

In September, the Eddys moved back to their house in Lynn, and Mrs. Eddy resumed her previous activities of preaching and teaching. At one of their church services a young lady from Connecticut, Julia Bartlett, witnessed a healing: "The first Christian Science Sunday service I ever attended was at this time and was held in the little parlor at 8 Broad Street, Lynn. There were about twenty people present. Mrs. Eddy preached the sermon which healed a young woman sitting near me of an old chronic trouble which physicians were unable to heal." Many years later Miss Bartlett told another Christian Scientist that the woman had suddenly become "very pale, and was taken from the room by her husband. The next day the gentleman came to Mrs. Eddy and reported that his wife on that occasion was instantaneously healed of chronic troubles of many years' standing which had baffled the physicians." Miss Bartlett wrote in her reminiscences, "That was the greatest sermon I had ever heard, but few were there to hear it."[13]

While Mrs. Eddy's preaching and teaching took up most of her time, her primary concern was the revision of her textbook, *Science and Health*. She spent all her free time working on it. In August 1881 it was published in two volumes with a cross and crown emblem on its covers for the first time. This third edition of *Science and Health* is particularly notable for the addition of the chapter "Recapitulation." As Mrs. Eddy explained, "This chapter is from our class-book, First edition, 1870."[14] (The class-book had been privately published in 1876 as *The Science of Man.*) To this day, "Recapitulation" remains the basis, or class-book, for teaching Christian Science. And even though this third edition of *Science and Health* was a significant revision, its message and vision remained unchanged. She revised the textbook "only to give a clearer and fuller expression of its original meaning."[15]

As noted previously, Mrs. Eddy felt that the condition of her students' thought at that time called for a more thorough elaboration of the mesmeric workings of evil, or the carnal mind, which she put into the chapter "Imposition and Demonstration." She wrote, "Uncover a lie, and, snake-like, it turns to give the lie to you."[16] Later, in the final edition of *Science and Health*, she phrased it, "Uncover error, and it turns the lie upon you."[17]

Two months after the third edition of *Science and Health* was published, a letter from eight of Mrs. Eddy's students was delivered to both her Association and the Church.[18] They accused their teacher of "temper, love of money, and the appearance of hypocrisy" and declared her unfit to lead them.[19] Most likely, the accusations, though patently false, were not what hurt Mrs. Eddy most. Rather, it was that some of her most intimate students had broken their oath to her and the Church: "[I]f thy brother shall trespass against thee, go and tell him his fault between thee and him alone."[20] The signers had given no prior indication of any dissatisfaction.

Two weeks after this, on November 9, 1881, the students who remained loyal ordained their teacher as Pastor of the Church of Christ (Scientist). A week later they passed a set of resolutions, which Mrs. Eddy edited and approved, declaring her "to be the Chosen Messenger of God to bear His Truth to the Nations," and deploring the dissidents'"wickedness and abuse of her."[21] These resolutions were subsequently published in a Lynn newspaper.

Even during times of persecution, divine healing was never far from Mrs. Eddy's thought. She told one of her secretaries in 1908:

> When I was in Lynn, those opposing me said that I had been a very good woman but now I had become very bad. There was one gentleman . . . who was a member of the Congregational Church who always stood up for me. He would say, "I do not understand her, but I know she is good." One day he appeared at my house with a message. He came with a crutch for there was trouble with his hip. As he stood before me leaning on his crutch, I said to him, "Which do you lean on the

more, that crutch or on God?" He looked at me and said, "On God," threw away his crutch, which fell against the door, and stood erect and free. . . .

This gentleman left his crutch behind him and went from the house well.[22]

A similar healing took place during one of Mrs. Eddy's sermons. She recorded the incident in an article she wrote a few years later for the "mind-body" magazine *Mind in Nature*:

On March 15, during my sermon, a sick man was healed. This man had been assisted into the church by two men, a crutch and cane, but he walked out of it erect and strong, with cane and crutch under his arm. I was not acquainted with the gentleman, was not even aware of his presence.[23]

In fulfilling her role as Pastor—and in spite of opposition—Mary Baker Eddy demonstrated the nothingness of sickness and sin by revealing the omnipotence of divine good. The result was healing.

Chapter 9

LAUNCHING OUT DEEPER
(1882–1885)

THE THIRD WEEK IN JANUARY 1882 arrived cold, gray, and rainy. In the Eddy household in Lynn, Massachusetts, however, there was little time to notice the weather. Mary and Gilbert were preparing for an extended trip to the country's capital, Washington, D.C., and there was much to be done. The Church and Mrs. Eddy's students needed guidance and encouragement. Arrangements had to be made for their Sunday sermon in the absence of Mrs. Eddy, their recently ordained pastor. The students would need to work together. She counseled one of them:

> Let the church work together and not separate. Let each who can, take a part, and be not weary in well doing and God will help you. . . .
>
> I would recommend that your Sunday service be [held] alternatively in Boston at your rooms and in Charlestown, and you and Mrs. Whiting, Miss Bartlett,

and Mrs. Poor's name be registered alphabetically to take care of the services.[1]

And to another student, she wrote:

> This I beg that you "love one another even as I have loved you." That no root of bitterness springs up among you. That no pride comes up or vain inquiry "who shall be greatest," but remember I have made myself the servant that I might lead others to Christ.[2]

The Eddys spent ten weeks in Washington, charmed by its beauty and fully occupied in a vibrant, crowded schedule of activity. She taught and lectured; he devoted much of his time to studying copyright law. Toward the middle of March, enthusiasm sparkling through her words, Mrs. Eddy wrote a Boston student:

> I have had parlor lectures for two evenings. About fifty have listened to me and expressed themselves as pleased. Editors, Colonels, teachers, one clergyman, etc. ... This is the most beautiful city I was ever in.[3]

Two weeks earlier she had written:

> I have worked harder here than ever! Fourteen consecutive evenings I have lectured three hours every night besides what else I am about. Go to bed at 12, rise at 6, and *work*.[4]

The "what else" she was about included a notable healing of a prominent clergyman whom the Eddys met when they went one Sunday to the church the President normally attended. After being introduced to the Eddys, the minister asked if he might call on them and was warmly welcomed to do so. The minister spent the better part of an afternoon listening to Mrs. Eddy's explanation of Biblical truths. As the supper hour approached, he was invited to stay. He told them he was not able to eat solid food but would enjoy their company. Doctors had diagnosed stomach cancer and limited him to a liquid diet. Mary's heart went out in compassion to the man. In 1901, Mrs. Eddy recounted the minister's healing:

> I said to him briefly, that this was an excellent opportunity to put to test our talk of the afternoon. He replied by saying that he hardly could consent to test the doctrine for the sake of killing himself. However, I voiced the Truth and asserted his ability to eat in comfort. He went with us to the table, soon forgot himself and his false fears and partook heartily of the salads, meats and pastry. At the conclusion of the dinner he said, "What have I done? Will I survive?" We assured him there was no danger. He felt no harm and never after was again troubled.[5]

If the time in Washington seemed overflowing with activity, the return to New England on April 4 was no less so. The next Sunday Mrs. Eddy took her place in the pulpit in the Church's rooms at Hawthorne Hall. She later told a student:

> Preached yesterday to a large audience . . . from the text "What I do thou knowest not now but shall

PHOTO: W. S. WARREN

Mrs. Eddy in 1882. She made the purple velveteen dress she is wearing for speaking engagements.

know hereafter." Spoke mostly of Jesus' healing that was not understood now but shall be and his Christ-character will *then* be understood. I wish you could see the wild enthusiasm here over this blessed Truth.

The reception was indeed a splendid affair. There was a crown of flowers and on the word Truth a large cross with the word Love, another bed of flowers on green leaves with the motto Welcome. This was over the door. The company was so large it took an hour to shake hands. This was my entry into Jerusalem. Will it be followed with the cross?[6]

At the end of April, the Eddys leased a brownstone on Columbus Avenue in Boston, providing a new home not just for themselves but also for the Massachusetts Metaphysical College.[7] But the brightness of this spring was greatly darkened by Gilbert's death on the third of June.[8] This was especially hard for Mary, a very bitter blow. She went to Vermont to a student's family home to regain her peace; only that student and one other accompanied her. She felt an urgent need for healing—and the healing came. Toward the end of July, she delivered an address at the Methodist church in Barton, on the subject that was ever in her heart and on her tongue: Christian healing. The minister called the next day, and they spent the morning talking about her lecture. On returning home, Mrs. Eddy wrote in her Bible, "Aug. 6th 1882 ... opened to Isaiah 54."[9] Among the many comforting verses in that chapter is "thou ... shalt not remember the reproach of thy widowhood any more." By the end of October, she could tell a student, "The ship of science is again walking the wave, rising above the billows, bidding defiance to the flood-gates of error, for God is at the helm."[10]

The next few years were to see a focus on publication and outreach. "I have so much writing on hand now, something I have not spoken of to the students," Mrs. Eddy confided in a letter.[11] When the Christian Scientists' first magazine, the *Journal of Christian Science*, appeared in April 1883, she served as its Editor and provided much of its content. The work, though stimulating, was arduous. She had little leisure, working seven days a week and resting solely in her love of the work and of God. Much to her delight, the leading religious papers in Boston sent her courtesy copies of theirs in exchange for her *Journal*. For more than a year she had also been revising her textbook, *Science and Health*. She made a significant addition to it by including in this sixth edition, published in September 1883, a section titled "Key to the Scriptures." Originally Mrs. Eddy had intended to put this "Key" into her second edition, which appeared in 1878, but serious problems with the printer and other circumstances prevented this.

The "Key" consisted of metaphysical interpretations of many Bible names and terms, which today can be found in the textbook's Glossary. Twenty-three of these terms and interpretations first appeared in the more than 600 pages of notes Mrs. Eddy had made on the book of Genesis between 1867 and 1868.[12] Echoes from these notes appear throughout today's textbook, as seen in the following two examples:

Heaven was happiness and not a locality but was
the atmosphere of a principle where all was harmony.[13]

and

This truth stands at the threshold of your thoughts
a guest so new and strange that we know it must knock
loudly and long before you open unto it—and yet once
[past] the iron portals of beliefs which close against it,
where truth sups with understanding, and ever thereafter
will you say of it: We have entertained angels unawares.[14]

The cover of Mrs. Eddy's manuscript on the book of Genesis

Christian Science was indeed knocking loudly at the threshold of the public's thought. The newspapers and churches were more and more raising questions and making criticisms of this new denomination. It would eventually cause Mrs. Eddy, a year and a half after the publication of the textbook's sixth edition, to issue two pamphlets—*Historical Sketch of Metaphysical Healing* and *Defence of Christian Science*.[15]

In spite of the continual demands of writing, publishing, and preaching, Mrs. Eddy still found time to teach classes and counsel her students.[16] In 1884 she even made a trip to Chicago to support the work there. Writing to a student after her return, she explained:

> I went in May to Chicago at the imperative call of people there and my own sense of the need. This great work had been started, but my students needed me to give it a right foundation and impulse in that city of ceaseless enterprise. So I went, and in three weeks taught a class of 25 pupils, lectured in Music Hall to a *full* house, got 20 subscriptions for my *Journal*, sold about thirty copies of *Science and Health*, etc. . . .
>
> A lady educated in a convent, a Catholic, . . . was healed mind and body by a few minutes conversation with me in Chicago. She changed her whole course of life, and her letter to me since my return alludes to it.[17]

Because she was no longer in the public practice, the question had arisen "Has Mrs. Eddy lost her power to heal?" She answered this in the June *Journal*. Her reply began, "Has the sun forgotten to shine, and the planets to revolve around it?"[18] Her students had no doubt about her healing abilities. Clara Choate went to Mrs. Eddy one night, asking her to come and help her four-year-old, who was ill. She had tried to heal him herself, but with no results. Mrs. Eddy came and prayed at his bedside for a few minutes. Suddenly the little boy turned and began kicking the wall next to his bed as hard as he could. Mrs. Eddy sat quietly without saying a word. He continued until he was tired; then he turned in bed again and fell asleep healed. Later, Mrs. Choate asked her teacher at a meeting of students how she had treated her son. Mrs. Eddy replied:

> The only thought that I had was "Warren Choate, your mother governs here with the Truth."

> Mrs. Choate, you don't govern that child morally when he is well, so you can't heal him when he is ill. You have done all that could be done except that you had neglected to handle the moral question, and this must be handled in every case whether it be an adult or a small child. You never make him mind, and if you give him a command you don't insist upon his carrying it out.[19]

The student who related this account went on to comment, "This lesson was brought home forcibly to us in the Association because we would never have considered that the moral question should be handled in the case of a child."[20]

Mrs. Eddy saw beneath the surface of things, and expected the same of her students. She was instant and loving both in her rebuke of the wrong method and in her explanation of the right way to heal. In answer to one student who said he had been foiled by a case, Mrs. Eddy alluded to Jesus' words to Simon: "Launch out deeper, Anchor yourself to God."[21] In a note to another she wrote, "Are you ready to help? You say yes, but why don't you help me if you are willing and can handle this? All you say is inconsistent unless you *do* as *you say*. I healed a case of softening of the brain in a minute, three weeks ago, but I didn't say I would do it—and then desert the sufferer."[22] And to another, "Let our lives make the difference between a false and a true Mind healer."[23]

Because she *lived* what she taught, and because she "let this mind be in [her], which was also in Christ Jesus,"[24] Mrs. Eddy was able instantly to heal a minister in Washington, D.C., a woman in Chicago, and a little boy in Boston. She constantly launched out deeper, and anchored herself to God. There is no other way to be a Christian Scientist.

Chapter 10

DEFENDER OF THE CAUSE
(1885–1887)

THE MENTAL ATMOSPHERE IN BOSTON'S Tremont
Temple on March 16, 1885, would likely have been daunting
to most speakers trying to explain what must have seemed a
very different way of being a Christian. The thoughts of the
nearly three thousand attendants ranged from benignly curious
to highly skeptical to openly hostile. But Mary Baker Eddy
stood before them all in order to defend her "child," the Cause
of Christian Science. At a previous Monday Noon Lecture,
the then quite prominent Reverend Joseph Cook had read a
harsh criticism of this relatively new face on Boston's religious
scene. Not only did the new faith promise healings after the
manner of Jesus, but it spoke in a new language that contra-
dicted a number of traditionally and, consequently, firmly held
doctrines. Even worse, it was led by a woman!

Mrs. Eddy had been allowed ten minutes in which to
reply to the Reverend Cook's criticism. She began, "As the
time so kindly allotted me is insufficient for even a synopsis

of Christian Science, I shall confine myself to questions and answers."[1] Then she posed and answered the following questions:

> Am I a spiritualist?
>
> I am not, and never was. . . .
>
> Do I believe in a personal God?
>
> I believe in God as the Supreme Being. . . .
>
> Do I believe in the atonement of Christ?
>
> I do; . . . .
>
> How is the healing done in Christian Science?
>
> This answer includes too much to give you any conclusive idea in a brief explanation. I can name some means by which it is not done.
>
> It is not one mind acting upon another mind; it is not the transference of human images of thought to other minds; . . . . It is Christ come to destroy the power of the flesh; it is Truth over error; . . . .
>
> … Is there a personal man?
>
> The Scriptures inform us that man was made in the image and likeness of God. . . .[2]

That day, Mrs. Eddy's students gave away eight hundred copies of her pamphlet *Defence of Christian Science.*

The following month, Mrs. Eddy wrote to her students in Chicago requesting that they publicly refute lies in the press about her and Christian Science. In a meeting of her students in Boston on May 6, the minutes record that "Mrs. E. Hopkins made a very satisfactory report for the Com. on Publication. Several Papers had been replied to. She had been able to get an article into the Boston Herald as had also Mrs. Hale." The minutes of this meeting continue:

> The President [Mrs. Eddy] stated that she was proud of the literary capacity of her students. Articles for the press should be arranged judiciously. There is a great work to be done with the Clergy. They have got to be talked with lovingly. In this spirit call upon them to recall their assertions that are false.[3]

It's interesting to note that she concluded her remarks to her students: "Now if you want to be healers, be honest."

Healing always had a part in every effort Mrs. Eddy put forth. At a meeting of her students the previous February, she had told them:

> . . . the grand secret of all your success is in your Christianity. Just in proportion as mortal sense is hushed, just in that proportion will healing be done.

> Some say "we are doing all we can." Stop the utterance. *Do more.* God is making the extreme trial an occasion for your good. Such moments are the most glorious of all experience, because God's hand is stretched out over them.

We have God on our side to meet *all* questions, and I have never found an hour when He would not deliver me.[4]

Mrs. Eddy's ability to hush mortal sense was certainly evident on a shopping excursion she made with a student, Julia Bartlett, to look at carpets in a Boston rug emporium:

A gentlemanly and kindly man waited upon them. The women could not help noticing that his face was partially bandaged. After just a few moments, Mrs. Eddy seemed to lose all interest in the purpose of their errand. . . . "Come Julia, let us not look further to-day. We can come again." On the second or third day after, Miss Bartlett returned alone to the store. The same salesman advanced to serve her. The bandage was no longer on his face. Very earnestly the man asked her who might the lady be who had come with her on the previous occasion. Then, in a reverent and awe-struck voice, he said, looking intently at Miss Bartlett, "I can't explain it, but that lady had something to do with a very wonderful thing which has happened to me." Then he told her that not long after she and her companion had left the store on the earlier visit, his face, which had been scarred, began rapidly to heal; and, looking, she saw it was perfectly clear. The affliction had been cancer.[5]

This kind of experience was not at all uncommon for Mrs. Eddy; on another shopping trip, accompanied by a different student, Mrs. Eddy healed a furniture salesman of an abscess on his eye. (See page 330–331.)

At the end of 1884, a Boston University professor had made a rather sarcastic public offer of one thousand dollars if Mrs. Eddy or one of her students could reset a hip or ankle dislocation without physical manipulation, and two thousand dollars to restore the sight of one born blind. This challenge was brought up at the next monthly meeting of her students' association. Several spoke of their recent practice: healings of pneumonia, a sprained wrist, diphtheria, and opium addiction. Pleased with these reports, Mrs. Eddy told them, "the higher grew the affection of Jesus, the grander grew his demonstration. Affections teach us the way to liberty. We sail into the great, glorious sea of possibilities through the storm and not the calm."[6]

The next month, February 1885, Mrs. Eddy responded to the professor through the pages of her *Journal of Christian Science*. With characteristic kindness she replied: "Will the gentleman accept my thanks due to his generosity; for if I should accept his bid on Christianity he would lose his money. Why? Because I performed more difficult tasks fifteen years ago. At present I am in another department of Christian work, where 'there shall no sign be given them,' for they shall be instructed in the principle of Christian Science that furnishes its own proof."[7]

From 1885 through 1887, Mrs. Eddy taught a total of seventeen classes: eight Primary, seven Normal, and two in Obstetrics.[8] In addition to her teaching, throughout 1885 she was working on a major revision of *Science and Health with Key to the Scriptures*, striving to make ever clearer the science of Christian

The Massachusetts Metaphysical College on Columbus
Avenue in Boston, where Mrs. Eddy lived and taught.

healing. At the end of July she engaged a Unitarian, the Reverend James Henry Wiggin, as an editorial assistant to help her.[9] At that time students had no way of easily locating ideas or subjects in *Science and Health*, except to rely on their memory or personal notes. Their Bible concordances and reference books were worn out from constant use; but there was nothing similar to that to assist students with their teacher's book. Mrs. Eddy met the need with an index, which the Reverend Wiggin prepared for the new edition under her direction.

The first printing of the sixteenth edition, published in February 1886, sold out in ninety days, and the second printing was half spoken for even before it arrived from the printer, University Press. Mrs. Eddy marketed her book through bookstores and booksellers, as she had been doing for a number of years. Now, dozens of new inquiries came, and purchasing agents bought *Science and Health* in bulk. Students were selling the book, too. To one she wrote: "How important that this book that God dictated should be our only standard, especially now that so many are trying to raise false standards in the name of Christian Science. Let us as loyal adherents draw up nearer to the book that has the *divine* signet upon it and hold this one banner aloft. Then we shall put to flight the aliens."[10]

The "aliens" were, for the most part, a number of disaffected students who had left Christian Science and were attempting to build up their own "mind-cure" schools.[11] Mind-cure was a generic name for any number of mental healing theories that had sprung up suddenly and flourished for a time in the mid-1880s. They all had one very significant feature in common—none of them saw the need for pure Christianity as the sole basis of healing. Regardless of the unique aspects of each, and for all their differences, they were simply various forms of mentally directed willpower, or mesmerism. The problem was that they claimed to stand under the umbrella of Christian Science, hoping thereby to gain acceptance and respectability.[12] At the same time, however, that they sought to benefit themselves by

Mrs. Eddy in 1886

associating with Christian Science, they were highly antagonistic toward Mrs. Eddy, many falsely accusing her of stealing Science from Phineas Quimby.

Mrs. Eddy saw great danger in this. For her, mesmerism, which she referred to as animal magnetism, was the very antipode of her discovery. In order to counter mind-curists' misleading efforts to teach what decidedly was not *Christian* healing, she requested her loyal students who had been trained to teach Christian Science to establish formal "Institutes" for teaching and healing and sponsoring church services in their own cities around the country. (This was before Christian Science churches had begun regularly organizing in local communities.) And she told these loyal students, ". . . be careful and put Christians to the head of your College, *old tried* Christians that shall control its management."[13] Lecturing was another method Mrs. Eddy felt could do a great deal to offset the claims of the mind-curists. She asked a few students who had shown particular promise to prepare themselves for public speaking, even suggesting that professional tutoring would help.

For the questioning public, Mrs. Eddy chose to differentiate Christian Science more clearly through pamphlets. She revised and expanded *Defence of Christian Science*, giving it the new title *Christian Science: No and Yes*. She also wrote a new pamphlet, *Rudiments and Rules of Divine Science*. Her students' association provided the funds to publish the Reverend Wiggin's *Christian Science and the Bible*. And she herself paid for the publication of Hanover P. Smith's *Writings and Genius of the Founder of Christian Science*. A student of Mrs. Eddy's since 1880, Hanover first became interested in Christian Science at nineteen when Mrs. Eddy healed him of being both deaf and mute, conditions he had experienced since birth.[14]

William Gill was another student (and briefly a worker) whom Mrs. Eddy healed. Before coming into Christian Science, he had been a minister, and partly because of this background, she had made him Editor of the *Journal.* Unfortunately, he lasted only four months before going astray and joining the mind-curists. However, before he left at the end of 1886, she healed him of an injured foot. More than ten years later Mrs. Eddy referred to this in a letter to a student:

> Oh! I was glad to hear that you, at least, demonstrated *Christian* Healing. When I united the joint of Gill's toe—in a minute—and he said why could not your students have done this? I made an excuse as best I could... .

> My students are doing more for, and against, C.S. than any others can do. They are the greatest sinners on earth when they injure it; and doing more good than all others when they do the best they know how.

> Here I must leave it; but the fruits of my awful experience in preparing the hearts of men to receive Christian Science, is *patience* in tribulation, hope, and *faith,*—before these graces of the Spirit evil *must fall.* May you, my *faithful dear one* be strengthened and uplifted by the cross of others—by seeing sin and so avoiding it in your own dear self.[15]

Christian healing—this is what distinguished Christian Science and Mrs. Eddy from the mind-curists, who prescribed less demanding paths without the Christian cross to bear. Yet the heart of *Christian* healing for Mrs. Eddy—that God is All and entirely good—also separated her from most of the theologians of her day. For in order to heal as Jesus did, one needs to understand that God does not know evil, and therefore one must treat evil as an illusion of the carnal mind. This was a more radical premise than most denominations could accept. Yet Mrs. Eddy taught—and proved through her own healing work—that to the degree the purity of the divine Mind was reflected in the student's mind, to that degree would the student find success in healing.

Chapter 11

"THOSE WHO WATCH AND LOVE"
(1888–1889)

*W*HEN GEORGE GLOVER, MARY BAKER Eddy's son, wrote that he, his wife, and their three children were coming to Boston to spend the winter of 1887–88 with her, the news came at an especially busy time for Mrs. Eddy. Her days and weeks were filled with teaching classes on Christian Science, meeting with her students' association in the chapel of Tremont Temple, regularly writing for *The Christian Science Journal*,[1] maintaining a constant and growing correspondence with students, and serving as Pastor to her Church.[2] Nevertheless, she welcomed her son and his family. Mrs. Eddy loved her grandchildren, and she enjoyed introducing them to the members of her Church.

Children were one of her heart's delights. Mrs. Eddy loved their receptivity to good, and they loved her in return. There were two occasions in the overly crowded months that began 1888 when children and church would combine to lighten an otherwise heavy calendar. The first of these was reported in the March *Journal*:

Chickering Hall was crowded Feb. 26, for a service which has long been desired by many of the members of the church. . . . twenty-nine children, including a few babes, were led to the platform, and placed in semicircles. Rev. Mrs. Eddy then moved about slowly among them. From each she received a card on which was written the child's name. Raising her hands over each in turn, she then repeated the name, and very slowly and emphatically pronounced this blessing: "May the baptism of Christ with the Holy Spirit cleanse you from sin, sickness, and death." No water was used in the rite, but it was nevertheless impressive. . . .

The short address which followed, by Mrs. Eddy, was on "Names and Baptism." In the Bible we read that names were changed . . . but these indicated changes of character and career, not of name only. The baptism of the Christian should be a baptism into Spirit, and should represent "the answer of a good conscience toward God," as says Peter in his First Epistle. . . .[3]

Mrs. Eddy's grandchildren were among those christened that day in the only formal occasion of christening that ever took place in the Church.

The second happy occasion combining children and church early in 1888 occurred on Easter Sunday at a Chickering Hall decorated with lilies. The service that first of April was largely a concert by the Sunday School children. No fewer than eighteen hymns and anthems cheered both Pastor and congregation, the fresh young voices often in harmony, sometimes not quite on key.

Halfway through, twelve young ladies each answered a question, responding with a passage from *Science and Health with Key to the Scriptures*. The Pastor's grandchildren, Edward, Evelyn, and Mary Glover, were among the singers.[4] The following day Mrs. Eddy wrote to Captain Joseph Eastaman and his wife, who had directed the concert:

> I have no words to tell you how much I enjoyed the beautiful occasion that you got up for Easter Sunday.
>
> The whole was a perfect *success*, even the *little* mistakes of the "darlings" were *beautiful* —and my "April fool" finished the symbols of the day. You ask why did you not finish up the singing and your part of reading Hymns?
>
> I answer, Because I got so absorbed by the children's entertainment that I *forgot* it, and that was the *April's fool*, and the compliment to you, Mrs. Eastaman.[5]

Mrs. Eddy's joy in and love for children had a decidedly healing effect on them, too. The daughter of one of Mrs. Eddy's students was twice quickly healed by Mrs. Eddy. The first was an instantaneous healing of inherited lung trouble and chronic coughing (see p. 520–521).[6] This occurred a few months after the mother, Emma Thompson, had attended one of Mrs. Eddy's classes. The second healing occurred during a subsequent visit when the young girl, Abigail, and her mother were in Boston. Abigail later recounted:

> . . . I was stricken down suddenly and confined to my

bed with a most distressing hip trouble. . . . Finally
the pain became so intense that my dear courageous
mother found herself overwhelmed with discouragement and fear, . . . she hastened at five o'clock in the
morning to Mrs. Eddy's home. Mr. Frye met her at the
door. . . . Mrs. Eddy heard them talking and . . . listened
to the conversation in the hall below. . . .

[Later Mrs. Eddy told Mrs. Thompson] "when I
heard your conversation I said to myself, it is time for
Mother to step in on this case and save that child, and
hurrying back to my room I dropped into a chair and
immediately reached out to God for the healing."

So quick was the response that when my mother
returned to me a few minutes later, even before
reaching the bedside, she was greeted with the cheery
ring of my voice calling to her the welcome message,
"Mother I am better"—and soon we both realized
with overwhelming joy that I was not only better, but
completely healed.

Through the many years that have followed I
have never spent another day in bed, and from the
depths of a grateful heart I give the entire credit for my
abounding health to the completeness and permanency
of our Leader's realization of the healing power of
God.[7]

When Mrs. Eddy was preaching in Boston two years earlier,
another mother, Mrs. Mary Dunbar, had been reaching out for
healing:

... Mrs. Dunbar's only child, a daughter then about four or five years of age, never had walked. She could creep on her hands and knees but below her knees the bone had never hardened, but was like cartilage, so that her feet dangled and were useless. Mrs. Dunbar tried to interest members of her family and friends to go with her to hear Mrs. Eddy preach, but as no one seemed willing to go she decided to go alone. She did go one Sunday afternoon and sat in the audience. Mrs. Eddy did not know she was there by anything Mrs. Dunbar said or did.

On her return home her family were waiting for her with curiosity. They asked her if she had actually seen Mrs. Eddy and what she looked like. Mrs. Dunbar replied that she had seen her but did not know what she looked like. They then asked her what Mrs. Eddy wore, and Mrs. Dunbar replied, "I do not know." They inquired what Mrs. Eddy had said, and again Mrs. Dunbar replied, "I do not know." In jest they then asked her what she *did* know. To this Mrs. Dunbar replied, "I know I have found the Truth. I know I have found that for which I have always sought."

The sleeping room of little Ethel Dunbar adjoined her mother's bedroom on the second floor of their home. Ethel had never been able to get in and out of bed as other children of her age could do. The following morning, before Mrs. Dunbar was up, Ethel climbed out of bed and ran across the floor to her mother, perfectly normal. She was healed.[8]

It was not at all uncommon for healings to result from Mrs. Eddy's public speaking. A young woman from Germany, Bertha Reinke, who had come to America to study medicine and also hoped to find a cure for her own illnesses, came to hear Mrs. Eddy speak; she came out of curiosity, because it was unheard of in her country for a woman to preach. She had never heard of Christian Science and had not known of its focus on healing before she attended the service:

> Human energy and will power alone had enabled me to come to this lecture and while I was waiting for the "Lady Preacher" to appear, it seemed as if I could not endure my mental and physical condition much longer.

> Then something wonderful happened. Escorted by a gentleman, the "Lady Preacher" appeared on the stage. For a few moments she gazed silently over the audience. I felt an atmosphere such as I had not known before. She spoke with a gentle, low but very clear voice. As I was not accustomed to hear an address in English, and as I sat so far from the stage, the words themselves were not understood. But as I listened I experienced an inexpressible feeling of relief, and the pains and misery, with which I had gone to this lecture hall, had fallen away from me.

> Not knowing to whom I had been listening, I asked an usher for the name of the "Lady Preacher." In utter astonishment he looked at me and answered,

"Why, that was Mrs. Eddy!"—Mrs. Eddy?! I had never heard the name before—I left the hall free and well.[9]

One of the most outstanding examples of the healing effect of Mrs. Eddy's public speaking occurred when she traveled to Chicago and spoke at the Central Music Hall to an audience of about four thousand, a little less than a quarter of whom were students of Christian Science. She chose as her text the first verse of the ninety-first Psalm and the address that followed, "Science and the Senses," was given extemporaneously, as she had had no idea she was expected to speak until she arrived at the hall.[10] *The Boston Evening Traveller* described what happened at the end of the address:

When she had finished, the scenes that followed will long be remembered by those who saw them. The people were in the presence of the woman whose book had healed them, and they knew it. Up came the crowds to her side, begging for one hand-clasp, one look, one memorial of her, whose name was a power and a sacred thing in their homes. Those whom she had never seen before—invalids raised up by her book, *Science and Health*; each attempted to hurriedly tell the wonderful story. A mother who failed to get near held high her babe to look on her helper. Others touched the dress of their benefactor, not so much as asking for more. An aged woman, trembling with palsy, lifted her shaking hands at Mrs. Eddy's feet, crying, "Help, help!" and the cry was answered. Many such people were known to go away healed.[11]

Some of the other healings that occurred during Mrs. Eddy's talk in Central Music Hall involved rheumatism, paralysis, and diabetes. One in particular was noted by several people. A woman in the front row had come in with great difficulty on crutches. At the conclusion of the talk, she arose and spoke to Mrs. Eddy, who leaned over the platform to reply. Immediately the woman laid down her crutches and walked out healed and free.[12]

Mrs. Eddy expected her students to heal as she did. A year after her talk in Central Music Hall, she urged her pupils, during a class, to heal quickly and completely:

> Why do you give long treatments? Because you don't give them on the right side. . . . It's the power of the living God we want. If the voice of God were heard, all would be healed. You are so buried in the life of the senses! That's what makes long treatments. It's spiritual want that prevents healing. It is knowing that your life is hid in Christ that gives power. There is a belief of lethargy where mind is attached to personality,—When you realize Truth, Love, you heal. . . .

> When a student doesn't heal, it's his own fault. I am out of patience at hearing a student ask his patient to work when the patient is up to the ears in the waves. Don't ask anything of your patient. Show him your Science and when he is healed he will work.[13]

To one who had told her of a quick healing, she wrote, "Your consciousness of Truth healed instantaneously. Thus you see it is our fault not to be more filled with the realization of

God, good, and so reflect this true consciousness. Your cases of cure were so satisfactory I want to publish them in the June No. of our Journal."[14]

Mrs. Eddy's standards were very high. When students fell short, she was not shy about correcting them. Unfortunately, there were those who had neither the humility nor maturity to see that she was not rebuking them personally—she was rebuking the errors that prevented them from doing as they should. Before she had left for Chicago, Mrs. Eddy had requested that her students' association hold a meeting while she was away to resolve a disagreement that had arisen at their previous meeting. At this special meeting, a number of outspoken students who objected to their teacher's methods and actions withdrew from the association and influenced others to do likewise (for more information on this event, see Robert Peel's *Years of Trial*, pp. 237–244). In all, thirty-six left without allowing Mrs. Eddy the opportunity to meet with them face to face to respond to their accusations. Mrs. Eddy expressed her feelings about this rebellion in a letter to two of her Chicago students, John and Ellen Linscott:

> It is to "kill the 'heir' that the inheritance may be ours" for which they are at work. But my greatest regret is that as in the parable when the Lord took away the inheritance from the wicked stewards and gave it unto others—because of this motive and means, so will it, must it, be with them. Oh, if they only knew that the heir gained the inheritance by helping every one else up instead of pulling them down, to rise over other errors,

Mrs. Eddy at 67

then would they be wiser and understand how to gain
and retain this inheritance.[15]

Mrs. Eddy continued to love these students in spite of their
rebellion. Several weeks later she tenderly invited two of those
who had influenced others against her to come to church:

> I shall preach next Sunday, and I hope you will be
> there to learn more of the way to heaven, the joys that are
> imperishable.

I never felt my Father so near as now. May God
bless you and save you from sin is the prayer of your
Pastor and Teacher.[16]

Love was the only way Mrs. Eddy knew to respond to hate
or settle disagreements. A number of years after this, she would
write a poem entitled "Love." It is a beautiful lesson on healing
disputes. In it she points out, "The arrow that doth wound the
dove / Darts not from those who watch and love," and she ends
with

> ... Love alone is Life;
> And life most sweet, as heart to heart
> Speaks kindly when we meet and part.[17]

In the autumn of 1888, Mrs. Eddy expressed her great
love for humanity not only through her own healing works but
by teaching others how to heal by spiritual means alone. In the
middle of a class in September, after finishing a lesson one day,
she healed an insane woman who had been brought to her by
the woman's brother. Believing she was being crushed by a giant
serpent, the woman fell on the floor screaming. Clara Shannon, a
member of the class, witnessed this healing. She later recounted:

> Our Leader looked upwards, as if she had seen
> the face of an angel in her communion with God. In
> a moment, she said to the woman, "Has it gone?" but
> there was no reply. Mrs. Eddy repeated her question, but
> the woman still seemed not to hear it. Then she spoke
> with authority and asked, "Has it *gone*?" and the poor

woman looked up, and her whole body was shaken and quivering as she answered, "Yes!" I watched the changes of expression that came over [the woman's] face, from fear to peace and joy. And, oh! the love that was expressed in our Leader's face as she looked down on her, stretched both arms and lifted her up, saying, "Get up, darling!" Then our dear Teacher put that needy one's head on her shoulder and patted her face, as she lovingly talked the truth to her. Mrs. Eddy then went out of the room and talked to the brother, who took her home, and then she asked me to come and have supper with her, and to sing to her. During the evening she turned to me and said, "You saw what happened to that lady today? Well! She will never be insane in this world again." And she has not been.[18]

In November, Mrs. Eddy wrote a student: "We are gaining in the onward march slowly, but surely, through the clouds of selfishness out into the light of universal love. God speed the dawn. Our Cause has had a great propulsion from my late large classes. Over fifty members have gone into our C. S. Association since the stampede out of it."[19]

What also resulted from the experience with the rebellious members was a heightened awareness of the great need to alert students of Christian Science to the influence of animal magnetism. In her textbook, *Science and Health*, Mrs. Eddy defines animal magnetism as "the false belief that mind is in matter, and is both evil and good; that evil is as real as good and more powerful. This belief has not one quality of Truth."[20] The problem of animal magnetism is not one of overcoming a real power, but of not being influenced by the false suggestion that matter or brain or human methods have power.

The minutes of Mrs. Eddy's students' association for November 7, 1888, record:

> Our Teacher ... gave a synopsis of the history of animal magnetism from its first appearance to the present time. ...
>
> She also instructed her students how to detect its touch, and named its antidote which is love. "Love," said our Teacher, "will meet and destroy every claim of error," and [she] urged her hearers to rise into its atmosphere and thereby win victories over sin. Her words, always so encouraging and instructive, were especially so today.[21]

In a letter the following month, Mrs. Eddy wrote, "I consider the most important point in teaching today is the proper instruction on handling this basic error, Animal Magnetism. ... I have warned all my students of this need."[22]

Mrs. Eddy would teach only one more complete class in Boston. A few days after her March 1889 class ended, she wrote a friend that she did not want to teach anymore, but wanted the Bible and her textbook, *Science and Health with Key to the Scriptures*, to serve as teacher.[23] Just prior to this class, she had met with her students' association and impressed upon them "the great need of constant and careful study of the Scriptures in connection with *Science and Health* to enable us to follow our Master [Christ Jesus]."[24] These two books formed one foundation on which rested the demonstration of Christianly scientific healing.

During this period, Mrs. Eddy was also taking steps to forward her Cause, this Christian movement of spiritual healing, outside of Boston and the United States. She wrote students about promoting her textbook in Europe, especially in England. She also requested her followers to start organizing churches in towns where Christian Science healing was being publicly practiced. Boston, though, was to remain the center of operations. She wrote the Editor of the *Journal*, "As I have said before, Boston is to be the headquarters of Christian Science. God has made it so."[25]

In some respects, Mrs. Eddy was pleased with the progress her Cause was making. In May 1889, she wrote a friend, "My students are doing wonderful works at healing. Their letters surprise me with their records."[26] In other respects, however, she saw signs that concerned her. Word had reached her that some Christian Scientists were using written formulas in their healing work. She strongly warned against this, writing one student:

> Tell every one whom you know of doing this, that it is as far from scientific as it would be to give or order drugs. The written direction, beyond a general scientific rule for practice which is already given in *Science and Health*, confines the practice to mortal mind and is nothing more or less than human directions, mind cure, and will produce the effect only of animal magnetism.[27]

Mrs. Eddy was also concerned about the loss of Christian fellowship among her students. In August 1889 she wrote a friend: "I do not approve of all that is done by my students. When they take sides against each other, it almost prostrates me. O! when will this Spirit of Truth and Love prevail throughout the ranks of those who profess to be Christian Scientists? I reprove, rebuke, exhort with a depth of love that has no soundings, but the harvest has not come." She ends the letter, "Do remember the influence that is exerted mentally to prejudice my students against one another and by which they misjudge."[28]

Because they continued to "misjudge," Mrs. Eddy dissolved her students' association and suspended the formal organization of the Church in Boston. As she wrote to Laura Sargent at the end of 1889, "This was after ten years of internal feuds caused always not by the main body, but by two or three members that mesmerism used to do as the Bible says, one sinner destroyeth much good."[29]

Mrs. Eddy wrote the Church on November 28:

Dear Brethren: –

The Church of Christ (Scientist) in Boston was my patient seven years. When I would think she was well nigh healed, a relapse came and a large portion of her flock would forsake the better portion, and betake themselves to the world's various hospitals for the cure of moral maladies. These straying sheep would either set up claims of improvements on Christian Science and oppose The Mother Church, or sink out of sight in religious history. This state of the Church has lasted ten years. It even grew rapidly worse when, about three years ago, I, for lack of time to adjust her continual difficulties, and a conscientious purpose to labor in higher fields and broader ways for the advancement of the glorious hope of Christian Science, put students in my pulpit.

Six of these students became at different times candidates for pastor's assistant. One of them preached over a year; all the others had spoken in my pulpit. Some of them were true Christians and tolerable expositors of Christian Science, but all of them were ruled out.

Mrs. Eddy bought the house with the tower—385 Commonwealth Avenue, Boston—in 1887 and lived there until 1889.

This and much more of a *severe nature* caused me as the Mother of this Church to ask earnestly "What shall she do to be saved?" and I think God has answered me and bidden her to disorganize, saying, "I will try her and prove her on the pure basis of spiritual bonds, loving the brethren, keeping peace and pursuing it. I will test her love which seeketh not its own but another's good, is not puffed up, is not easily provoked, envieth not, doth not behave herself unseemly, beareth all things, hopeth all things, endureth all things, and if she is saved as a Church, it will be on this basis alone."[30]

As one who is treating patients without success remembers that they are depending on material hygiene, consulting their own organizations and thus leaning on matter instead of Spirit, saith to these relapsing patients, "Now quit your material props and leave all for Christ, spiritual power, and you will recover," so I admonish this Church after ten years of sad experience in material bonds to cast them off and cast her net on the spiritual side of Christianity. To drop all material rules whereby to regulate Christ, Christianity, and adopt alone the Golden Rule for unification, progress, and a better example as The Mother Church.

When this is done I have already caused to be deeded to those who shall build a Church edifice, the lot of land designed for the site of such an edifice, and which is now valued at $15,000.

This offer is made on condition that the question of disorganization shall be settled by affirmative vote at

the Annual Meeting of this Church held December 2nd,
1889.

Please read in *Science and Health* page 92
paragraph 5.[31]

Owing to the spirit of the letters received from
certain members of this Church, and their persistent
determination to keep me embroiled in their quarrels one
with another, notwithstanding my oft expressed desire
that they should do their own work and leave me to do
mine, God has confirmed the purpose of this letter.

The hearts of the main body of this beloved
Church are trying to be right in the sight of God, and
for this and their faithful devotion as Christians, I send
them at this time the assurance of my abiding love and
fellowship.

Mary B. G. Eddy[32]

Mrs. Eddy requested her students in Boston to continue to
conduct church services, but as a voluntary association that acted
under the commandment to love one another, rather than under
congregational rules.[33] Feeling she should refocus her own efforts,
Mrs. Eddy announced to the Field that she was retiring and
moved back to her home state of New Hampshire.[34] In addition
to wanting uninterrupted time to work on a major revision of
Science and Health, she was also praying and listening for God's
guidance about the final form the Church of Christ, Scientist,
should take so that divine Love and Christian healing would fill
it to the exclusion of all else.

At the close of the year, she sent a message to the Christian Science Field describing good healing as "instantaneous cure." The "way" to this accomplishment, she told them, was marked by three milestones: self-knowledge, humility, and love.[35]

Chapter 12

IMPELLED BY LOVE
(1890–1892)

*T*HE DAWN OF 1890 FOUND Mary Baker Eddy at one of the most significant crossroads in her life. She had left Boston, Massachusetts, settled in Concord, New Hampshire, and resigned as Pastor of her Church. By the end of 1889, she had given the responsibility for publishing *The Christian Science Journal* to a "Publication committee" of her students, and she had closed the Massachusetts Metaphysical College, of which she was President and teacher. Also by the end of 1889, and under her direction, a Board of Directors had been appointed and made responsible for maintaining church services in Boston, including the employment of another pastor who would preach in strict accord with the teachings of Christian Science. Having thus cleared the decks, Mrs. Eddy devoted herself to revising her book. Her purpose was not to add new ideas, but rather to elucidate and illuminate more thoroughly the divinely inspired concepts that had been there from the first writing.

The fiftieth edition of *Science and Health*, issued in

January 1891, included a number of highly significant changes: there was a new arrangement of chapters, including several new chapter titles; marginal headings had been incorporated for the first time; Scriptural quotations had replaced literary ones at the beginning of each chapter; the previous thirty-eight-page index had grown to seventy-one pages; throughout the book, portions of text had been shifted, and forty pages of new material had been added; and almost every page showed evidence of some rewriting. Of this new edition Mrs. Eddy wrote two of her students, "I made it a special point . . . to so systematize the statement of Science as to compel the *scholar* to see it is demonstrably true, and *can be* understood on the basis of proof."[1]

The Discoverer of Christian Science did not write *Science and Health* from a theoretical basis. While all of its concepts had first come to her as divine revelation, she hadn't begun the book until she had first proved its practicality by healing others through scientific, Christian prayer. Perhaps to emphasize this point, she added these lines to the new edition:

> . . . Working out the rules of Science in practice, the author has restored health in cases of both acute and chronic disease, and in their severest forms. Secretions have been changed, the structure has been renewed, shortened limbs have been elongated, cicatrized joints have been made supple, and carious bones have been restored to healthy conditions.[2]

In regard to the "shortened limbs," Mrs. Eddy may have been thinking of a healing that occurred a year or so before she left Boston. The man who was healed related his experience to a Christian Scientist in Los Angeles in 1903:

> About eighteen years ago, while living in Boston, I fell from the third story of a building on which I was working, to the pavement. My leg was broken in three places. I was taken to a hospital, where they tried to help me. They said that the leg was so bad that it would have to be amputated. I said, "No, I would rather die." They permitted it to heal as best it might, and as a result I had to wear an iron shoe eight or nine inches high. I was called to Mrs. Eddy's home on Commonwealth Avenue, in Boston, to do some light work. Mrs. Eddy came into the room where I was busy, and observing my condition, kindly remarked, "I suppose you expect to get out of this some time." I answered, "No; all that can be done for me has been done, and I can now manage to get around with a cane." Mrs. Eddy said, "Sit down and I will treat you." When she finished the treatment she said, "You go home and take off that iron shoe, and give your leg a chance to straighten out." I went home and did as I was told, and now I am so well that, so far as I know, one leg is as good as the other.[3]

Mrs. Eddy healed the same way she loved God: it was simply in her nature and had been from childhood. Nothing was more important to her than doing God's will, which she perceived through daily prayer. She was continually urging her students to lean more on God instead of turning to her for advice, sometimes referring them in her letters to Proverbs 3:5, 6: "Trust in the Lord with all thine heart; and lean not unto thine own understanding. In all thy ways acknowledge him, and he shall direct thy paths."

But this by no means meant she had stopped caring for them. Quite the contrary, Mrs. Eddy felt toward her pupils as a mother feels for her children. As she wrote to one of them: "God has given me new lessons, and I too must 'be about my Father's business.' Do not think it is for lack of love, but only a conviction of duty that makes me desire to be isolated from society."[4]

The need to love one another dominates Mrs. Eddy's correspondence during this period. A beautiful example of this can be seen in her words to one pupil:

> Oh may this Easter Sunday carry you my prayer…
> "Little children love one another"…you must love *all*.
> No matter if they persecute you even, you must love all.
> But you must love especially the brethren. You must
> meet with them, cheer them, in their labors, point the
> way of love to them and show them it by loving first, and
> waiting patiently for them to be in this great step by your
> side, loving each other and walking together. This is what
> the world must see before we can convince the world of
> the truths of Christian Science.[5]

When Christian Scientists in Chicago were at odds over the controversial pastor of their Church of Christ, Scientist, George Day,[6] Mrs. Eddy wrote to a Christian Science teacher[7] there of how she "had a great love for all of his good sayings and doings, and had forgiven and forgotten any things that he had uttered against [her]." She closed this letter:

> O do show me how great is your love for God
> by forgiving, yea more, by loving all mankind, and for
> once I ask it show yourself the best Christian of the two
> by taking the *first* step towards reconciliation. Will you
> do this dear? My heart bleeds with this name among
> men—that we are *not brethren*. I would humble myself in
> the dust to have this otherwise.[8]

The week before writing this letter, Mrs. Eddy had heard that Mr. Day was ill and had sent him "a letter calculated to heal him."[9] Two days after writing the Chicago teacher, Mrs. Eddy learned that her earlier letter to Mr. Day had accomplished its purpose.

In writing to another student about the relationship of divine Love to healing, Mrs. Eddy said:

> The healing will grow more easy and be more
> immediate as you realize that God, Good, *is all* and
> Good is *Love*. You must gain Love, and lose the false
> sense called love. You must feel the Love that *never*
> *faileth*,—that perfect sense of divine power that makes
> healing no longer power but grace. Then you will have the
> Love that casts out fear[,] and when fear is gone doubt is
> gone and your work is done. Why? Because it never was
> *undone*.[10]

In the spring of 1891, Captain Joseph S. Eastaman, one of the Board of Directors of the voluntary Boston church, witnessed a demonstration of this healing "grace" in action. Two days after the following incident, he recounted the experience to Arthur Maxfield, who included it in his reminiscences:

> Captain Eastaman had an appointment with Mrs. Eddy. . . . He arrived at her home at the appointed time, was met at the door by Mrs. Eddy's secretary Calvin Frye who ushered him into the reception room, then went up the stairs to inform Mrs. Eddy that the Captain had arrived. As he started to return down the stairs he suddenly pitched head first to the foot of the stairs, apparently with a broken neck caused by the fall.

> Mrs. Eddy, hearing the noise, came to the head of the stairs and said what is the matter? then she noticed Mr. Frye lying on the floor. She said, "Calvin get up on your feet." She said again, "Calvin get up at once." The third time she said calmly, "Calvin arise immediately you are all right." Mr. Frye arose at once, looked up at Mrs. Eddy who was coming down the stairs, and then walked into another room. Captain Eastaman had his interview with Mrs. Eddy and then left to take the train back to Boston. Captain Eastaman was positive that he had witnessed a demonstration over the claim of accidental death.[11]

Calvin Frye's diaries show that his daily work for Mrs. Eddy went on completely uninterrupted and unhampered by this incident.

About four months later, another student, David A. Easton,

visited Mrs. Eddy in her home. He told her he was dying of consumption. A week later, he wrote her:

> I am healed. I realized it the next day after I saw
> you. . . . When I called on you, I seemed to be in a swift
> current of mortal thought, that I could not resist and
> that was carrying me down, down. Your few but vigorous
> words seemed to lift me out of that current. I feel like a
> new man.[12]

In her reply Mrs. Eddy wrote, "I felt it when I held your hand and God touched you. I told you I could do nothing for you, but I knew that moment of God's power. Oh tell your wife to let you this time go preach the gospel of healing. Remember this duty yourself when the hour comes."[13] A year and a half later, Mrs. Eddy would ask the Board of Directors to call Mr. Easton to serve as pastor of The First Church of Christ, Scientist, in Boston.

When Mrs. Eddy reorganized the Boston church in the summer of 1892, she changed it from a local church to what would become an international one. More importantly, she would gradually replace the former congregational government and its member involvement with a church governed by divinely inspired laws.[14] She had purposely caused the previous organization to dissolve because of continual disputes within the congregation sparked by a few members. In stark contrast to this, her ideal of church government was one supported by the members' love for one another.

In the March 1892 issue of the *Journal*, Mrs. Eddy wrote

of church organization in the same terms she used to describe marriage: "If our Church is organized, it is to meet the demand, 'suffer it to be so now.' The real Christian compact is love for another. This bond is wholly spiritual and inviolate."[15] The prosperity and progress of the organization rests on the love felt and expressed by its members for each other.

In order to support this concept best, Mrs. Eddy was inspired to have her reorganized church governed by rules which she wrote—rules based on the law of God. If the members obeyed these rules, their human opinions would have no place and consequently could not inhibit their love for one another.

On September 1, 1892, Mrs. Eddy established The First Church of Christ, Scientist, through a Deed of Trust which created the Christian Science Board of Directors to administer the Church in accordance with the rules she had written. Each of these rules, or By-Laws, was divinely inspired to meet the need not only of the moment, but of the future as well.[16]

In October, Mrs. Eddy wrote to a student:

My task the past summer, to breast the storm of blind guides, and deliver the people and establish Christ's Church in Boston, has been beyond description. But I was enabled to accomplish it. This new form of Church government is a light set upon a hill.[17]

This "light" is produced by the flame of divine Love,

the power and grace that exist for the healing of mankind, individually and collectively—the same power and grace that underlay all of Mary Baker Eddy's healing works.

Chapter 13

THE DEMAND FOR MORE GRACE
(1893–1895)

$\mathcal{I}$T BECAME MARY BAKER EDDY'S practice, after she moved to Pleasant View, her home in Concord, New Hampshire, to take daily carriage rides through the town and surrounding region. These drives usually lasted no more than an hour and provided a break in a very demanding work schedule. Sometimes she would stop at the Western Union telegraph office to send a message to her church workers in Boston. On those occasions Henry Morrison, the office manager, usually came out to her carriage. One afternoon, while he was talking with Mrs. Eddy, she asked if he was "feeling as well as usual." He told her of a chronic stomach problem. After their conversation he never again had trouble with his stomach, nor with severe colds, which he had been subject to.[1]

At another time when Mrs. Eddy was watching the approach of a storm, she noticed a man on crutches enter her gate. She sent word to offer him shelter and food. After eating, he stayed in the carriage house until the rain had stopped. A few months later when some members of the Pleasant View household were going to Concord, a workman who was breaking stone on the road stopped their carriage. He asked if they remembered him. When none did, he told them that he was the one to whom they had given shelter. He went on to say that, while waiting for the storm to pass, he had fallen asleep, and upon waking, "I rose and walked without my crutches, and have never needed them since." He didn't know what had healed him, but when told about this on their return, Mrs. Eddy recalled the man and acknowledged that she had prayed about the situation.[2]

On another occasion, when telephone wires were being put up in Concord, a young lineman working in front of Pleasant View was hit in the eye by a wire. He was brought into the house, and Mrs. Eddy talked with him. The next day he was back at work, completely healed.[3]

Healing was central to Mrs. Eddy's nature. She was continually counseling her students in their practice of Christian Science. To one she wrote:

> The healing of my students changes its stages as they learn from experience. It starts a marvel of power and then becomes a marvel of *grace*. The latter is gained by the spiritualization of practice which acts on the moral more than the physical degree of healing, but is sure to produce the latter which never relapses. More of the spirit than letter is required to reach this Christ-stage of healing sickness and sin. This, dear one, is what I want you to attain.[4]

To encourage "more of the spirit than letter," Mrs. Eddy spent much of 1893 working with James Gilman, an artist from Vermont, who was illustrating a poem she had written early in the year. In this poem, titled *Christ and Christmas*, she wanted to convey her feelings about the impersonal expressions of the Christ and Christian Science. In an article in *The Christian Science Journal* she wrote:

> I never looked upon my ideal of the face of Jesus, but the one in my work approximates it.
>
> . . . Pictures are parts of one's ideal, but this ideal is not one's personality,—note this. When looking behind the veil of the temple he that perceives a semblance between the thinker and his expressed thought, cannot blame him for it, but must credit himself.[5]

It was important to Mrs. Eddy that not only Christian Scientists but everybody have a correct concept of who she was as the Discoverer and Founder of Christian Science. To this end she prepared an address to be given at the World's Parliament of Religions, which was being held in conjunction with the 1893 Chicago World's Fair. The Editor of the *Journal,* Judge Septimus J. Hanna, delivered Mrs. Eddy's address, but, unfortunately, afterward he allowed the press to have the manuscript against Mrs. Eddy's prior instructions. The next day the newspapers reported that it was the Editor's address and named him the leader of Christian Science. Mrs. Eddy was greatly disappointed: a rare opportunity had been lost through disobedience. As she wrote to one of her Chicago workers several weeks later:

For the world to understand me in my true light, and life, would do more for our Cause than aught else could. This I learn from the fact that the enemy tries harder to hide these two things from the world than to win any other points. Also Jesus' life and character in their first appearing were treated in like manner. And I regret to see that loyal students are not more awake to this great demand in their measures to meet the enemies tactics.[6]

(By "the enemy" Mrs. Eddy was referring to the "carnal mind" St. Paul speaks of in Romans 8:7.)

She also saw the demand for Christian Scientists to be awake to the need for readily practicing Science at all times: "Oh how I wish all of my students were awake and demonstrating as they ought the divine Love pouring out upon us such miracles of favor. Today a runaway horse with a sleigh dangling behind him was making gallops towards my sleigh—but when I turned and looked him in the face, he turned away from the sleigh and rushed by us—and turned just as if reined by a driver."[7]

In 1894 Mrs. Eddy's predominant concern was the completion of the construction of the Original Edifice of The Mother Church. She had been constantly encouraging the Church's Board of Directors to finish the building before the end of the year. But as the months passed, this appeared less and less likely. Mistakes and delays seemed to be the order of the day. A railway strike, recalcitrant contractors, and continual postponements had to be overcome. By the beginning of September, only one exterior wall had been completed. The Directors— Joseph Armstrong, Stephen Chase, William B. Johnson, and Ira O. Knapp—had little or no experience with such a large building project, but they kept going forward because Mrs. Eddy constantly turned them to divine Mind. Earlier in the year, she had written one of her students: "Am glad that the demand for more grace to meet the emergencies of this hour is being realized by many of my students. Our prayer in stone, our monumental church, that is to be built in Boston will tend greatly to unify our numbers. May God give us the true *substance* of this type of Love."[8]

By December, things looked hopeless: the bell tower was unfinished; the auditorium, filled with scaffolding, still had no balcony or pews; and the walls and ceiling had yet to be plastered. At this point "lack" was the overriding problem: lack of laborers, lack of supplies, lack of time. However, when an incident of lack appeared in Mrs. Eddy's own town of Concord at the same time, she showed clearly how it was to be overcome.

The Original Edifice of The Mother Church under construction in November 1894

There had been no rain in the Concord area throughout November. The farmer who delivered Pleasant View's milk told the cook that his well was empty and his cows were beginning to go dry. When Mrs. Eddy was told about this, she smiled and said, "Oh! if he only knew, Love fills that well."[9] The next day when the farmer came, he was overjoyed to tell the cook that that morning he had found his well full of water. And what was amazing to him was that there had been no rain to fill it. Mrs. Eddy wrote to the Board of Directors on December 10, telling them about this experience. The challenges faced in building the Church were met and overcome. Love had filled the void.

The first church service was held in the new edifice on Sunday, December 30, 1894.[10] It was also the first Christian Science service

2748

Pleasant View.
Concord. N.H. Dec. 19, 1894,

Christian Science Directors—
My beloved Students,
The day is will nigh won.
You will soon rest on your arms. Thank God you have been valiant soldiers—loyal to the heart's core.
"Who is so great a God as our God."
Present no contribution box on Dedication day.

2748 P. 2

When you know the amount
requisite and have re-
ceived it form finishing
the church building —
close all contributions
and give public notice
thereof.
Hold your services in
the Mother church, Dec. 30,
1894, and dedicate this church
Jan. 6th The Bible and
"Science and Health with Key
To the Scriptures" shall hence
forth be The Pastor of the
Mother church. This will tend
to spiritualize thought. Person
al preaching has more or less of
human views grafted into it.
Whereas this pure Word contains only
the living health giving Truth
With love mother.
Mary Baker Eddy.

in Boston where the pastor was not a preacher delivering a sermon, but two books from which a Reader read a Bible Lesson. On December 19 Mrs. Eddy had instructed the Board:

> The Bible and "Science and Health with Key to the Scriptures" shall henceforth be the Pastor of The Mother Church. This will tend to spiritualize thought. Personal preaching has more or less of human views grafted into it. Whereas the pure Word contains only the living health-giving Truth.[11]

The Mother Church was dedicated on January 6, 1895. One who attended that service wrote:

> When I went home after the dedication of The Mother Church, I manifested a belief of a severe bronchial trouble which seemed very tenacious. During this time I was called back to Mrs. Eddy's home for an interview. While there, no manifestation of the trouble appeared, and when taking my leave she accompanied me to the door, and putting her hand on my arm she said, "That is not in your body, but in consciousness, and you can put it out." I returned home, but the healing was not in evidence for a few days, when it suddenly disappeared. When I returned to stay in Mrs. Eddy's home, she suddenly asked me, "How long was it before you were free? I only ask the question because I wanted to see how long mesmerism could seem to hold my work. You were healed when you left here, but you did not know it."[12]

To keep the members of her Church awake and alert, Mrs. Eddy had been establishing church duties and rules as the need arose for them. Those that were first adopted also supported and confirmed the main points of the September 1, 1892, Deed of Trust, which had served to reorganize the Church. In March 1895, Mrs. Eddy requested that all these rules be put together in a *Church Manual*. She later wrote to the committee given this task: "Let the Manual be brief and gotten out *soon*. There is a great call for it so that the By-Laws shall be read by all its members."[13] Mrs. Eddy expected her Church members to be healers. A number of years after the *Manual* was first published, she wrote:

> This Church is impartial, its rules apply not to one member only, but to one and all equally. Of this I am sure, that each Rule and By-Law in this Manual will increase the spirituality of him who obeys it, invigorate his capacity to heal the sick, to comfort such as mourn, and to awaken the sinner.[14]

The Mother Church was designed so that healing would permeate all its activities. To emphasize this in the midweek church meeting, Mrs. Eddy requested changes in the conduct of this service, which up to that time had been a continuation of Bible Lessons from the Sunday service.[15] On January 15, 1895, she sent the following notice to be read at the next meeting:

> My dear Students: Make broader your bounds for blessing the people. Have Friday evening meetings to benefit the people. Learn to forget what you should not remember viz. self, and live for the good you do.

The Mother Church, circa 1899

Conduct your meetings by repeating and demonstrating practical Christian Science. Tell what this
Science does for yourself and will do for others. Speak
from experience of its Founder—noting her self sacrifice
as the way in Christian Science. Be *meek*, let your mottoes
for this meeting be, Who shall be least and servant and
"Little children love one another."

Affectionately yours,
Mary Baker Eddy.[16]

Meekness was a quality Mrs. Eddy especially valued.
She taught that it is essential in the healing practice. Consis-
tently evident in her own healing work, it is one of the defining
qualities of the Leader of Christian Science, together with her
purity, fearlessness, honesty, wisdom, unselfed love, and absolute
faith in God. With these as her foundation stones, she built a
Church that offers mankind the Science, or divine laws, of
Christian healing. In her understanding and demonstration, this
divine Science is the Comforter promised by Jesus.[17] Her own
estimation and recognition of what God had done for mankind
through her can be seen in a reply she made to a student who
had asked her, "Tell us what you are, that is, tell us what you are
to the world." Mrs. Eddy responded: "As Mary Baker Eddy, I
am the weakest of mortals, but as the Discoverer and Founder of
Christian Science, I am the bone and sinew of the world."[18]

Chapter 14

THE FOUNDER AT WORK
(1896–1898)

*M*ARY BAKER EDDY BEGAN 1896 by delivering a communion address in her Church in Boston, Massachusetts—The Mother Church, The First Church of Christ, Scientist. In her talk she turned thought away from the persecution of Jesus of Nazareth to his demonstration of divine, infinite Love in forgiving his enemies, which enabled him to overcome the cross and the grave.[1] As often occurred on such occasions, one of her listeners was both healed and transformed:

> This man had been a pronounced invalid for
> years and had grown so irritable that his family could
> scarcely live with him. He was unable to walk without
> support. . . . he was visiting in Boston not far from
> the Christian Science Church there. Sunday morning,
> hearing the chimes, he asked to what church they
> belonged. On being informed that it was the Christian
> Science Church, and that the worshipers in that church
> claimed to heal the sick, he went to the service. He

said he had not been there long when a woman came in who was announced as Mrs. Eddy, and she gave a talk. She had not talked long, until all of a sudden he felt that he was healed. He did not miss his canes until after he reached the house of his friend. The next day he bought *Science and Health,* a book written by the same Mrs. Eddy who spoke in the church. Since then he has been an ardent student of that book. [An old friend said of this man], "I don't believe even he realizes the transformation that has taken place in him. I assure you I never saw so great a change in any person."[2]

A week after the service, Mrs. Eddy wrote to one of her students: "Oh let us love our dear enemies and show them in our own lives even as we try to—the way to Heaven. . . . The communion was very sweet on Sunday and impressive. I felt sure I did some healing and have since heard of a few cases."[3]

One of the other healings she may have been referring to happened before the service as Mrs. Eddy was entering the Church. She passed a man on crutches in the street and nodded to him, smiling. Charles Howe later wrote of the experience:

When I returned into our home, both Mother and sister noticed a change in me—I had noticed it immediately for I was stronger and could walk so much better on my way to the house—the next day or two the neighbors and my friends noticed the change— Dr. Marr said he had never known of such a quick comeback [from typhoid fever] and was surprised.[4]

Mrs. Eddy was continually counseling her students on the need for more effective healing. At the end of January she wrote to one student, "To know there is but *one* God, one Cause, one effect, one Mind, heals instantly. Have but One God, and your reflection of Him does the healing."[5] The following day she wrote to another, "Love is the only and all of attainments in spiritual growth. Without it, healing is not done and cannot be either morally or physically. Every advanced step will show you this until the victory is won and you possess no other consciousness but *Love* divine."[6] In the February issue of *The Christian Science Journal*, in reply to a question about whether she would teach again, Mrs. Eddy said in part, "The hour has struck for Christian Scientists to do their own work; to appreciate the signs of the times; to demonstrate self-knowledge and self-government; and to demonstrate, as this period demands, over all sin, disease, and death."[7]

The needs of the world beyond the United States were also drawing Mrs. Eddy's attention during this period. She sent one of her students, Julia Field-King, who had previously established a Christian Science church in St. Louis, Missouri, to London, England, to build up a church there through healing and teaching. Mrs. Eddy also began to consider the need to translate *Science and Health with Key to the Scriptures* into French and German.

As the weather warmed in the late spring, Mrs. Eddy became acquainted with a sixteen-year-old girl who lived on a neighboring farm in Concord, New Hampshire. Her family had emigrated from England three years before. This girl, Minnie Ford, had spent most of the previous winter (1895–96) in the hospital with tuberculosis. Homesick, she returned to her family's farm against the judgment of doctors who did not expect her to recover. As a result of Mrs. Eddy's daily carriage drive, the two met and she invited the teenager to visit her. They soon became friends. Minnie later recounted one occasion when she accompanied Mrs. Eddy on a walk:

> [Mrs. Eddy] invited me to go with her to feed the gold fish in the fountain. She called them to her by saying "come to Mother," and to my surprise they came instantly and took the food out of her hand. She looked at me and smiled, she was so sweet. During this time my illness was entirely forgotten, and the first thing I knew I was well.[8]

Later in the summer, Mrs. Eddy asked Minnie's parents if their daughter could join her household staff to help with the cooking and cleaning. They said no, feeling she was too young. Of this decision Minnie wrote, "As I look back over the years, I feel my parents and I were most ungrateful; she had saved my life, and her dear face will be in my memory always."[9]

What drew most of Mrs. Eddy's thought during the latter half of 1896 was the preparation of her book *Miscellaneous Writings 1883–1896*. It was published the following February and comprised almost all of her contributions to the *Journal*, which she had started fourteen years earlier as publisher and editor. In the March 1897 *Journal*, Mrs. Eddy announced that all Christian Science teaching by her students would stop for one year. Her notice read, in part:

> "Miscellaneous Writings" is calculated to prepare the minds of all true thinkers to understand the

Christian Science Text-book more correctly than a student can.

The Bible, Science and Health with Key to the Scriptures, and my other published works, are the only proper instructors for this hour. It shall be the duty of all Christian Scientists to circulate and to sell as many of these books as they can.[10]

At the end of January, just before *Miscellaneous Writings* was published, Mrs. Eddy had written to one of her most promising students, James Neal, telling him she wanted to give him a copy of her new book. This letter also speaks eloquently of his recent decision to devote his life to the healing practice of Christian Science. She wrote:

> Your letter is my best New Year's gift. I had felt for some time the fitness you possessed for healing, I knew it when you were a member of my College class. It looked a waste to have you in a counting room. Now, thank God, I have at least one student in Boston that promises to be a Healer such as I have long waited and hoped to see. Oh may the Love that looks on you and all guide your every thought and act up to the impersonal, spiritual model that is the only ideal—and constitutes the only scientific Healer.
>
> To this glorious end I ask you to still press on, and have no other ambition or aim. A real scientific *Healer* is the highest position attainable in this sphere of being. Its altitude is far above a Teacher or preacher; it includes

Pleasant View, Mrs. Eddy's home in Concord, New Hampshire

all that is divinely high and holy. Darling James, leave behind all else and strive for this great achievement. Mother sighs to see how much her students need this attainment and longs to live to see one Christian Scientist attain it. Your aid to reach this goal is *spiritualization.* To achieve this you must have *one God,* one affection, one way, one Mind. Society, flattery, popularity are temptations in your pursuit of growth spiritual. Avoid them as much as in you lies. Pray daily, never miss praying, no matter how often: "Lead me not into temptation,"—scientifically rendered,—Leave me not to lose sight of strict purity, clean pure thoughts; let all my thoughts and aims be high, unselfish, charitable, meek,—

spiritually minded. With this altitude of thought your mind is losing materiality and gaining spirituality, and this is the state of mind that *heals* the *sick*. My new book will do you much good. Do not purchase one, Mother wants to give you one. I welcome you into the *sanctum* of my fold. God bless you.[11]

Seven months later, she alerted Mr. Neal to the trap of human praise, writing him again:

Now dear one, watch that worldliness and the natural mortal love of human applause or any possible pride or vanity creep not into your thought, for these are among the thieves that would steal into the good man's house and spoil his goods—take away the riches of purer and higher thoughts—which weigh in God's scale helping you to heal the sick and reform the sinner. To this end pray to divine Love daily; for if the good man watch, his house will not be broken open.[12]

The student who had been sent to London was also successful in her mission, and First Church of Christ, Scientist, London, was dedicated on November 7, 1897.[13] With the exception of the $1,000 Mrs. Eddy had sent to help with the purchase of a church edifice, the Christian Scientists there had triumphed on their own, under Julia Field-King's guidance.

1898 proved to be a landmark year for the Cause of Christian Science and its healing activities.[14] In January, Mrs. Eddy established the Church's Board of Lectureship and reorganized The Christian Science Publishing Society, which had been an independent corporation, and made it part of The Mother Church. In February, she established the Church's Board of Education. In April, she provided the twenty-six subjects for the weekly Bible Lessons. In May, she changed the testimony meeting from Friday evening to Wednesday evening. In September, she established the *Christian Science Weekly*, which she renamed *Christian Science Sentinel* four months later. In November, Mrs. Eddy taught her last class, to which she invited seventy students. And in December, she established the Church's Committee on Publication. At the end of 1898, she wrote to a lecturer whom she had appointed, "I have wrought day and night this year to make way for our Church and a systematic order of action in the departments of Christian Science."[15]

Earlier in the year, in February, Mrs. Eddy had addressed a meeting of Church members in Concord. Her talk focused on the ninety-first Psalm, which she considered one of the foundation stones of the Christian Science religion.[16] She said that this psalm "contains more practical theological and pathological truth than any other collection of the same number of words in human language except the Sermon on the Mount of the great Galilean and hillside Teacher."[17] She went on to say that the first verse of this psalm emphasizes an essential point of Christian attainment—dwelling "in the secret place of the most High":

> But what is the sacred secret of the Almighty?
> So far as experience reaches and Truth has unfolded
> its immortal idea through spiritual sense, this secret is
> spiritual *Love*, whereon David has based all Christianity,
> all healing, all salvation. This Holy of holies is indeed to

human sense a secret, for it involves God's own nature. The bodily senses are shut out from it. Eye hath not seen it, ear hath not heard it, neither do the human affections abide in the sanctum of Spirit, even though they are oft touched by its holy influence, rebuked, chastened, uplifted, purified by spiritual Love. The sole habitat of this secret place is infinite, and infinity is a secret to the finite senses. In fact Spirit, Divine Love, destroys all fear, pain, sorrow, and sin.

Because the senses of Spirit are spiritual and divine, they dwell in the understanding, abide in the secret of Infinity and demonstrate Life, Truth, and Love. How then can human sense or intellect attain the secret of Spirit or Divine Love? By turning away from the false evidence or material sense testimony and listening to the teachings of Spirit.

This solid secret, this substance enduring, this place wherein if a man dwell he can never lose the true sense of God, of Life, and Love is not even sought by the five material senses and is found only by "My Spirit saith the Lord."

1. The secret place of the Most High is spiritual Love.
2. The way thereunto is Christ Truth, but the way to find this Way is:
   1. The knowledge of God
   2. The understanding of God.[18]

This "spiritual Love" enabled Mrs. Eddy to heal quickly and to meet challenges of whatever nature with authority. One of her students recounted an example of this divine authority that she and another student had witnessed while at Mrs. Eddy's home in Concord:

> While she was giving us some instruction of work to be done, there came a very heavy thunder storm. Mrs. Eddy stepped to the window. It made me so still, for I felt the divine presence as she spoke with God, and immediately the storm ceased and a double rainbow was over the home at Pleasant View.[19]

The book of Genesis in the Bible says that God gives man dominion "over all the earth."[20] Mrs. Eddy shared the revelation she received from divine Mind in her book *Science and Health* so that her own age, and ages to come, could demonstrate that dominion through Christian healing. After that, God led her to found a Church based on that revelation and to structure The First Church of Christ, Scientist, in such a way that its activities could bring about "the healing of the nations."[21]

Chapter 15

THE "WEDDING GARMENT" OF DIVINE LOVE (1899–1901)

*A*T THE BEGINNING OF 1899, Mary Baker Eddy received a letter from a student she had taught eleven years earlier. He wrote that he had served as Reader in his branch Church of Christ, Scientist, and recounted how much time and effort since his class instruction in Christian Science from her had been devoted to healing—and how he was "still working for that great Prize to be able to have on the wedding garment."[1] He also hoped to be taught further by her. In reply Mrs. Eddy wrote about that "wedding garment":

> It is first the desire above all else to be Christ-like, to be tender, merciful, forgetting self and caring for others' salvation. To be temperate, humble, pure, whereby appetite and passions cease to claim your attention and you are not discouraged to wait on God. To wait for the *tests* of your sincere longing to be good, and seek through daily prayer for Divine teaching. If you continue to ask

you will receive,—provided you comply with what you must do for yourself in order to be thus blessed. Reading, or listening to my teaching the truths of Christian Science will not do for you what this earnest *seeking* and *knowing* and *following* can do for you. . . . Be of good cheer, you cannot *seek* without *finding*.[2]

The *wedding garment* is a term Jesus used in a parable about those invited by a king to his son's wedding to which "many are called, but few are chosen."[3] In her *Message to The Mother Church for 1900*, Mrs. Eddy wrote: "To-day you have come to Love's feast, and you kneel at its altar. May you have on a wedding garment new and old, and the touch of the hem of this garment heal the sick and the sinner!"[4] Mrs. Eddy was speaking out of her own experience. A number of years earlier she had told her students' association:

> . . . One of the best cures I ever performed was, apparently, under the most adverse circumstances. I had spent one year of incessant toil upon the [manuscript] of my book, *Science and Health*, and put it into the hands of a printer for publication, who, I found, had allowed it to be taken from his possession, and I was thus obliged to return, in the sackcloth of disappointment, without it. A student soon called desiring me to assist in a case that was dying. I put on the wedding garments at once and healed the case in twenty minutes.[5]

Mrs. Eddy's "desire above all else to be Christ-like" was constant. Her healing ability remained undiminished throughout her life. Clara Shannon, a cherished worker in Mrs. Eddy's Pleasant View home during the late 1890s, was living proof of this. At one point Clara became severely ill with diphtheria and went to stay with nearby friends so as not to burden Mrs. Eddy. Mr. and Mrs. Ezra M. Buswell helped her to bed and began to pray earnestly. Clara's condition, however, continued to worsen until it appeared that death was imminent. At this point Mrs. Eddy arrived at the Buswells in her carriage. Upon learning of the situation, she told Mr. Buswell to go tell Clara that she need not be afraid, divine Love was with her, and that she, Mrs. Eddy, was praying for her. The effect was immediate, and the suffering ceased. Clara then fell asleep and the next morning arose, dressed, had breakfast, and walked back to Pleasant View completely healed.[6] Less than two years later, Mrs. Eddy healed another household worker, her cook, Lydia B. Hall, of the same illness.[7] But Mrs. Eddy's thought was not confined just to her own home. She was deeply involved in the activities of her Concord, New Hampshire, community, of her son and his family, who lived in South Dakota, and especially of her Church in Boston, Massachusetts.

Mrs. Eddy had a new house built for her son as a Christmas present. She also oversaw and paid for the private schooling of her grandchildren. In Concord, New Hampshire, she gave shoes to all of the impoverished children of the city. She also initiated the paving of Concord streets and contributed financially to this endeavor. In connection with this latter benevolence, a remarkable transformation occurred. A student wrote Mrs. Eddy a number of years after the fact:

> There was a splendid testimony given last evening
> at First Church [Chicago]. A man who said he was

formerly an actor, was ill, despondent, discouraged, without a God, and most forlorn in the world; drifted into a [Christian Science] lecture one night; listened, was interested, afterwards wrote the Lecturer, and upon hearing that he might find the true God, secured the textbook [*Science and Health*], and notwithstanding he was just then offered a good position, he declined that and went to Concord instead, took a job on the road then building out Pleasant Street, where he could see you pass every day in your carriage, and although it was pretty rough work for an actor, unaccustomed to the uses of pick and shovel, he actually enjoyed his work, was healed, soundly converted, has known God ever since, and would not take anything in exchange for what he has learned through your teachings.[8]

At the top of this letter, Mrs. Eddy wrote in her own hand, "Case of healing by me on street, person unknown."

Such healings were not at all uncommon. On another occasion during this period, Marie Chalmers Ford, who was fairly new to Christian Science and had been visiting her brother in New Hampshire, came to Concord before returning to her home in Ohio. She wrote Mrs. Eddy about what had happened:

As the time for my departure [from my brother's] drew near, I became so ill that I could scarcely walk without great suffering, and it seemed as though I would not be able to go alone, if at all. All the time I was holding to this one sentence in Science and Health, page 494, "Divine Love always has met and always will meet every human need," and I found myself on the train for Concord. When I reached there I went directly to Christian Science Hall [a combination church and Reading Room] and was told that in a short time your carriage would pass. I sat down in one of the windows to read, but my suffering was still so intense that I could scarcely see the pages. Very soon someone came to me quietly and said that your carriage was coming. Of course I expected you only to drive past, but instead you drove up and stopped almost directly in front of where I sat in the open window. Someone from the Rooms went out to your carriage, and you talked with them several minutes. Many times during those few minutes you glanced up at the window where I sat and looked straight into my eyes. You drove away and I arose from my chair perfectly healed. There was not the slightest sense of pain or suffering left, and I had not been free from pain night or day for almost a week.[9]

On the front of this letter's envelope, Mrs. Eddy wrote, "case of my healing."

In June 1899, Mrs. Eddy traveled to Boston to address the Annual Meeting of The Mother Church.[10] That year it was being held in Tremont Temple because of the large number of members attending. Mrs. Eddy told her listeners that the special demand of the hour was "the fulfilment of divine Love in our lives." She went on to say:

... Divine Love has strengthened the hand and encouraged the heart of every member .... Divine Love hath opened the gate Beautiful to us, where we may see God and live . . . .

Divine Love will also rebuke and destroy disease, and destroy the belief of life in matter. . . . Divine Love is our only physician, and never loses a case. It binds up the broken-hearted; heals the poor body, whose whole head is sick and whose whole heart is faint . . . .

The practical effect of divine Love was evident in many ways during this meeting. Take, for example, the transformation of a woman who had no affection for Mrs. Eddy. Another woman in the audience later wrote of this experience: "A friend who had persistently clung to an unreasonable dislike for Mrs. Eddy, told me that as Mrs. Eddy was coming down the aisle she turned and looked into her face, and the resistance melted away completely, her eyes filled with tears, and after that she was absolutely loyal to our Leader."[11]

As was usual when Mrs. Eddy spoke publicly, healings occurred. One of these was published in the *Christian Science Sentinel*:

I awoke on the morning of that day with a sense of suffering so severe that it was a great effort to get up. I could eat no breakfast, and after working [praying] an hour, was relieved, but by no means free. Ordinarily I should have thought it the part of wisdom to remain quiet, but so great was the desire to be present at the meeting and hear our Leader, that I arose, dressed, and went to the Temple, feeling that I should hear the needed word of healing and strength from her lips. Nor was I disappointed. While Mrs. Eddy was speaking, the pain lessened, and then I forgot it completely until later, during the services, I realized that all sense of discord had vanished. Not only this, but for many months afterwards I was better and stronger, did better healing work for my patients, and experienced an unusual degree of spiritual and mental freedom.[12]

A year after this address, Mrs. Eddy wrote this to one of her students: "Our churches spring up spontaneously from the

MRS. EDDY ADDRESSING THE CHRISTIAN SCIENCE CONVENTION IN TREMONT TEMPLE.

An 1899 drawing published in the *Boston Herald*.

soil of healing—but I know that a healer needs all her time to do her best in caring for patients. It is an absorbing subject to lift the mind above pain, disease, and death, and when I practiced I could not attend to aught else."[13]

Beginning in August 1899, however, a great deal of Mrs. Eddy's attention was focused where she would not have chosen. Josephine Woodbury, a former pupil, brought a libel suit against her. Mrs. Eddy knew the accusations against her to be foundationless, and over the next two years she was deeply involved in her own legal defense. She continually counseled her attorneys on how to proceed, and issued specific instructions throughout this period to those she had asked to pray about the case. One of the more preposterous allegations Mrs. Woodbury made at the time was that the Discoverer of Christian Science had never healed anyone. As a result of the evidence presented, the suit was decided in Mrs. Eddy's favor. While this suit was going on, she was inspired to write the poem "Satisfied," which begins:

> It matters not,
> What be thy lot,
> So Love doth guide;
> For storm or shine—
> Pure peace is thine—
> Whate'er betide.[14]

Mrs. Eddy counseled others, including her own son, against instigating legal suits. To one student, in August 1900, she wrote:

> I have heard what pains me; I long to hear your

legal quibble is settled amicably. You know the scripture
saith brother must not go to law with brother and that
before unbelievers. Forgive, be unselfish, meek and
Christlike or you cannot be a Christian Scientist.[15]

Mrs. Eddy worked continually to foster brotherly love
within her Church as well. Toward that end, in January 1901, she
brought about a significant adjustment in the government of The
Mother Church when she made the Christian Science Board of
Directors solely responsible for the transaction of the Church's
business. Up until this time, a select group of "First Members"
also had limited responsibilities, though Mrs. Eddy had been
gradually diminishing their duties. A few years previously she
had written a letter, which was read at a Church business meeting,
admonishing, "When, if ever, will all the members of this church,
even while under the rod, behave themselves as Christian Scientists and not have to be put into straitjackets to keep them from
quarreling in the sackcloth of this solemn hour?"[16] In June 1901,
Mrs. Eddy wrote to a student, "Wisdom is one third of Christian
Science, the other two thirds is *Love*."[17]

Once, after reviewing a Christian Science lecture, Mrs.
Eddy wrote to its author: ". . . it lacked that appeal of Love that
touches the heart. Dear one, cultivate this tender emotion, have a
cell less in the brain and a fibre more in the heart in yourself, and
it will do much for your lectures and in healing the sick."[18]

At the end of April 1901, Mrs. Eddy granted a rare
interview to a newspaper reporter, Joseph I. C. Clarke.[19] When
asked "On what is Christian Science based?" she replied, "I
can tell you on what I based my conception of religion and

on which, so far as in me rests, I have laid its foundation in Christian Science: The Ten Commandments, The Ninety-First Psalm, The Sermon on the Mount, The Revelation of St. John the Divine."

Mrs. Eddy learned from the Bible not only how to wear divine Love's "wedding garment" but never to take it off. Her "desire above all else to be Christ-like" enabled her to heal as Jesus had. And she worked to see that this desire predominated in all the activities of her Church.

Chapter 16

"THE CAUSE NEEDS HEALERS"
(1902–1904)

$\mathcal{M}$ARY BAKER EDDY WROTE OF *Science and Health with Key to the Scriptures*: "The textbook of Christian Science maintains primitive Christianity, shows how to demonstrate it, and throughout is logical in premise and in conclusion. Can Scientists adhere to it, establish their practice of healing on its basis, become successful healers and models of good morals, and yet the book itself be absurd and unscientific? Is not the tree known by its fruit?"[1]

As evidenced by her correspondence, Mrs. Eddy was especially concerned about the need for more effective Christian healing. To this end, she was continually working to make clearer her textbook on the Science of Christ-healing. At the end of January 1902, the 226th edition of *Science and Health* was issued. Readers familiar with the book could immediately see it was a major revision. Mrs. Eddy, assisted by two of her students, Edward A. Kimball and William P. McKenzie, had spent months working on it. She significantly rearranged the chapters, putting them in the order they have today, and she added a new final chapter, "Fruitage," a compilation of healings from the pages of *The Christian Science Journal* and the *Christian Science Sentinel*. What ties these healings together is that they were all accomplished solely by reading *Science and Health*. Mrs. Eddy also reviewed the marginal headings in the book and rewrote some of them.[2] And she told Mr. Kimball and Mr. McKenzie to make sure that all Scriptural quotations in the book were according to the King James Version. Another new feature she added was line numbering, in anticipation of a concordance that was then being prepared. As a consequence, an index that had been a part of the book since 1886 was not included.

Mrs. Eddy devoted herself throughout 1902 to reading the new revision from beginning to end.[3] As a result, she corrected and standardized the capitalization of words relating to God, removed repetitive sentences and paragraphs, and added a little new material. In a letter to Albert F. Conant, who was compiling the Concordance, Mrs. Eddy wrote in the spring of 1903:

> My "last changes of *Science and Health*" may continue so long as I read the book! But I will stop now, and you may finish the Concordance immediately. Owing to the fact that the book should unfold in proportion as my thought grasps the spiritual idea more clearly so as to voice it more simply and thus settle many queries—I wished I had not commenced a Concordance, but had had an Index attached to S.&H.[4]

Her reason for not returning the index to her book at that time concerned copyright considerations, about which her attorney had advised her.

Revising *Science and Health* was just one of many continuing assignments Mrs. Eddy gave herself. As she wrote to a friend, "My whole time is employed in the work for humanity."[5] To two students who had given her a copy of Wycliffe's translation of the New Testament, she wrote:

The 226th edition of
Science and Health,
a major revision

> To-day it is a marvel to me that God chose me
> for this mission, and that my life-work was the theme
> of ancient prophecy and I the scribe of His infinite way
> of Salvation! O may He keep me at the feet of Christ,
> cleansing the human understanding and bathing it with
> my tears; wiping it with the hairs of my head, the shreds
> of my understanding that God "*numbered*" to make men
> wise unto salvation.[6]

Mrs. Eddy saw salvation as the scientific understanding and demonstration of God's supremacy, which heals sin and

A page of the 226th edition with Mrs. Eddy's corrections

sickness. Time and again during this period, she was writing to her followers of the great need for more quick, effective healing work. She wrote to Alfred Baker, a former doctor turned Christian Scientist:

> The sick need you and you can do great good by healing. The Cause needs healers a million times more than teachers. The best healer is the best Scientist and will take the place that God has for all to take.[7]

To the Editor of the *Journal* and the *Sentinel:*

> I started this great work and *woke the people* by demonstration, not words but works. Our periodicals must have more Testimonials in them. . . . Healing is the best sermon, healing is the best lecture, and the entire demonstration of Christian Science. The sinner and sick healed are our best witnesses.[8]

To a Boston student:

> . . . I retain my conviction that the greatest need that our Cause has is *better healers*. Those of experience, Christian character, and ability are more needed, much more, to fill this appointment in proof of Christian Science than to build up churches.[9]

To a Christian Science practitioner:

> Unless we have *better healers*, and more of this work

than any other, is done, our Cause will not "stand and having done all stand."

> *Demonstration* is the whole of Christian Science, nothing else proves it, nothing else will save it and continue it with us. God has said this—and Christ Jesus has proved it.[10]

And to a teacher of Christian Science:

> . . . healing the sick and reforming the sinner demonstrate Christian Science, and nothing else *can, does.*

> Beloved child, will you not address yourself to gaining this height of holiness? Nothing is so much needed for your own happiness and distinguishment, and for the success of our Cause, and for the glory of leading on and up the human race, as this one demonstration. By it I got the attention of the world; my words and writings, sermons and students, or adherents, could not, did not, do it. But my wonderful *healing* did it. I had hoped that you would have followed in these footsteps. Dear, dear Augusta, begin today. Leave all for this.[11]

Mrs. Eddy's healing work continued to be "wonderful," as a worker in her home recounted after a circus performer with an eye injury, whom Mrs. Eddy had seen at the 1901 New Hampshire State Fair, paid a visit to her:

> One day, a man whom she had seen jump from a

great height called to see her. He had on dark goggles.
She asked him if he were not afraid when he took that
leap. He explained to her that if he were to become
afraid the jump was too high, he would be killed.
After talking to him in a most heavenly way for some
time, one could see by the expression of his face how
enlightened he was mentally. Then she began again, and
talked to him about his lack of fear, he still asserting that
he had no fear when jumping—he knew he could do it.
She said to him, "Why not apply the same rule to your
eyes?" One, he told her had been destroyed through an
accident, the other was all right, but he wore the dark
goggles to hide the bad eye. They were sitting in the
library, and as she talked to him I could see and feel that
his fear was removed, and his thought was full of hope
and joy, although he did not then realise the blessing he
had received. A day or two afterwards the cabman who
drove him to the station reported there that he had two
perfect eyes when he reached the station.[12]

At the end of June 1903, Mrs. Eddy invited those who
had attended The Mother Church's Annual Meeting in Boston
to visit her home in New Hampshire. About ten thousand
came to Concord and heard her speak briefly from the balcony
of her Pleasant View home. A number of healings occurred at
this gathering: a man was healed of smoking, a woman cured of
exhaustion, and a crippled boy was healed of his lameness. Another
who was also healed wrote of her experience years later:

> I was in Concord the last time she spoke to the
> students who made the pilgrimage to her home. I was so

much impressed when Mrs. Eddy stepped on the balcony with her hands open and upturned with the simplicity to receive and to give, as the Father had made it possible for her. After leaving Mrs. Eddy's home I walked towards the city of Concord. And on my way I came in contact with Mrs. Eddy's carriage and was very close to her. And I had a wonderful realization of a blessing. And it surely was a blessing, for as I looked in those wonderful eyes almost transparent, I was instantly healed of a "spider cancer," and I realized God had made this blessing possible.[13]

Another wonderful healing happened during Mrs. Eddy's carriage ride after her talk, an account of which appears in the reminiscences of Lottie Clark, a Christian Science nurse:

. . . I was in a seven passenger car going to Hyde Park, Boston to a [Christian Science] lecture. Soon after we started the woman in the front seat turned around and said she wished to tell us of a woman who lived in Concord, New Hampshire. This Concord woman was paralyzed on one side, she had not a penny in the world, and her home was so unhappy she felt she could no longer live in it. So she decided to leave home and never return. As she left her yard she looked up the street and saw a large concourse of people. Out of curiosity she followed them, they were the ten thousand on their way to Pleasant View. When they arrived this woman was on the outskirts of the crowd, so far away that she did not even hear the sound of Mrs. Eddy's voice when she spoke. When Mrs. Eddy turned around and returned to the house[, to] this woman['s] helplessness, hopelessness, and despair was added this fresh disappointment at not hearing what she knew must have been a very important message to have attracted that size crowd. She turned around with tears flowing freely down her face to return to Concord. As she walked along she came to a vacant lot, she crossed this lot to the street on the other side, and there she stood weeping bitterly, her face drenched with tears, when she saw a team of horses coming. She stood idly watching them, and as they approached she recognized the woman in the carriage to be the same one who had spoken from the balcony, so she waited to see her at close range. As the carriage passed Mrs. Eddy leaned forward and looked at her. No word was spoken, but the woman was instantly healed. She returned to her home and found the home condition healed. This was the end of the story. We all sat spellbound and overwhelmed at the wonderful healings of Mrs. Eddy. All was quiet for a while, then the woman who sat beside me spoke up and said very quietly, "And I was that woman, and I have lived happily in my home ever since." Then she added, "Never before nor since have I seen the love and compassion in any human face that I saw in Mrs. Eddy's when she leaned forward and looked at me."[14]

Mrs. Eddy wrote to one of her students a year later, "Faith in and the spiritual understanding of the allness of divine Love heals. ... Work and wait, watch and pray till you know the allness of God, and in that understanding you will gain the desired result, the 'secret place,' when you can *abide* under the assurance spiritual, of His support."[15]

In 1903, Mrs. Eddy in her study at Pleasant View with Pamelia Leonard, Lida Fitzpatrick, and John Lathrop

At the time Mrs. Eddy spoke from her balcony, she had been at work three months on revising the *Manual of The Mother Church*. She finished this at the end of July, and it was issued on September 5, 1903. The twenty-ninth edition of the *Church Manual* contained seventeen new By-Laws, amendments to 122 existing ones, and the deletion of twenty old rules. Mrs. Eddy also revised the Church Tenets and "Historical Sketch." One of the new By-Laws she added to this edition was "Healing Better than Teaching":

> Healing the sick and the sinner with truth, demon-strates what we affirm of Christian Science, and nothing can substitute this demonstration. Neither the Teacher in the Board of Education nor a member of this Church shall teach the Normal course in Christian Science for three consecutive years, dating from August 1st, 1903. I recommend, that, during this interval, each member shall strive to demonstrate by his or her practice, that Christian Science heals the sick quickly, and wholly; thus proving this Science to be all that we claim for it.

A week after this new *Manual*'s publication, Mrs. Eddy provided the *Christian Science Sentinel* an article about it entitled "Mental Digestion."[16] In her eyes, the *Manual* was much more than a compilation of rules to operate her Church in an orderly manner. She also intended it to be a guidebook that, when understood and obeyed, would make its students better Christian healers. Like *Science and Health*, the *Manual* was to be applied to all aspects of one's daily life.

In 1904 Mrs. Eddy twice wrote to her Church's Board of Directors about the great importance of better healing work by Christian Scientists. In May she told them:

> I have just saved the life of one of my students and treated him only once. The demonstration of what I have taught them heals the sick. It absolutely disgusts me to hear them babble the letter and after that fail in proving what they say! It is high time that they stop talking Science or do prove their words true.[17]

And in August she wrote:

> As I understand it, God has His cause demonstrated in healing the sick. . . . Explain to those who write, that less teaching and more healing is *best for our Cause,* and for the students; fewer reports of new churches and more testimonials of our cures, argue more for the progress of Christian Science.[18]

Nothing was more important to Mrs. Eddy than doing God's will. To her, healing was the highest activity anyone could aspire to, and she devoted herself through her books and her Church to doing all that could be done to promote and extend this activity to all mankind.

Interlude

ADVICE FOR HEALERS

*F*OR MARY BAKER EDDY, GAINING and living a practical understanding of God was the purpose of life. And she demanded that this be done through spiritual understanding—a comprehension acquired through prayer, revelation, and working with the ideas gained from studying the Bible, *Science and Health with Key to the Scriptures*, and her other writings. To Mrs. Eddy, spiritual healing of human problems was the primary means for making practical one's understanding of God. She established her Church to awaken human consciousness to the understanding of man's inseparable relationship with God; the natural result of that understanding is healing.

From young adulthood until her discovery of Christian Science, Mrs. Eddy's attention was focused on finding relief from physical ailments that caused her almost continual suffering and invalidism. She investigated practically all the curative agents of her day: dietary practices, allopathy, homeopathy, spiritualism, hydropathy, and mesmerism. At one point she became a practicing homeopath, treating not only herself but others.

The emphasis on study and practice found in Mrs. Eddy's early search for cures plays a key role in her approach to spiritual healing as well. Christian Science is "no respecter of persons."[1] It is not a personal talent or ability; it can be studied, learned, and practiced. Mary Baker Eddy was—and still is—the master teacher of Christian Science, teaching today through her writings.

When Mrs. Eddy was teaching classes in Boston, applications for her instruction, especially in the latter half of the 1880s, would often exceed class size. As the October 1888 issue of *The Christian Science Journal* noted, "There were about one-hundred applicants waiting to enter Mrs. Eddy's Primary Class in September. . . . By the time this reaches our readers, a Primary Class of forty-five members, representing fourteen States and Canada, will have completed its course. In this class there are clergymen, physicians, a dentist, teachers, the wives of governors, besides other noteworthy members. . . . The other applicants had to wait for the next class."[2] Mrs. Eddy's last Primary class (March 1889) included sixty-five pupils. A brief account of that class appeared in the April 1889 *Journal* and is reprinted in *Miscellaneous Writings*.[3]

Mrs. Eddy did not allow pupils to take notes during her classes. C. Lulu Blackman, a student in her September 1885 Primary class, wrote:

> . . . She at no time made any explanation of this requirement, but all my days I have blessed her for this ruling, because it compelled us to let the form go so that limited finite statements of Truth might not circumscribe the pinions of her thought. Her impartations transcended

the medium of words. Words served only to convey her revelations. She gave both the letter and the spirit, but she took away the letter lest any should substitute it for the wine of the Spirit.[4]

Mrs. Eddy began her Primary instruction explaining who and what God is. Miss Blackman wrote:

> The first three days in the classroom gave overwhelming proof of Mrs. Eddy's understanding of God and her consistent acceptance of the fact that there was none beside Him. In my own experience, she seemed to have obliterated everything I had deemed substantial and actual. The word "God"—"God"—"God" was repeated over and over in my consciousness to the exclusion of all else.

> Mrs. Eddy awakened us to the realization that she taught no mere theory but the practical, living Truth when she closed the third lesson with these words: "Now go home and take your first patient."[5]

The demand for practicality was uppermost as far as Mrs. Eddy was concerned. She had no use for a theoretical understanding of Christian Science. Students understand her Science only to the degree they can practice it in healing. Yet she realized that learning to heal instantly and completely, on a consistent basis, cannot be accomplished in one class or even several classes. Mrs. Eddy knew that Christ-healing requires total devotion of thought and effort to its practice over years of experience and continuing spiritual growth.

In a By-Law of her Church, Mrs. Eddy states that teachers of Christian Science are

> morally obligated to promote their [pupils'] progress in
> the understanding of divine Principle, not only during the
> class term but after it, and to watch well that they prove
> sound in sentiment and practical in Christian Science.
> He shall persistently and patiently counsel his pupils
> in conformity with the unerring laws of God, and shall
> enjoin them habitually to study the Scriptures and *Science
> and Health with Key to the Scriptures* as a help thereto.[6]

Long before this By-Law was ever written, its author obeyed it.

Mrs. Eddy had taught her first pupil in 1867, the year after her discovery of Christian Science. In the years that followed, hundreds upon hundreds of students received her instruction. Over the next four decades, she continually counseled her students, personally when they came to see her and through thousands of letters. The following excerpts are from that correspondence and from notes students made after she spoke to them. It is essential to remember when reading these excerpts that what Mrs. Eddy tells a student is specific for that individual in a particular situation. Her instructions should never be used as formulas in treatment. The ideas used in each case of metaphysical treatment evolve from reason and revelation and are specific to that case. (Minor changes to spelling and punctuation have been made when necessary for clarity.)

The first ten excerpts focus on certain aspects to be considered in the general treatment of patients:

In about 1880 Mrs. Eddy wrote to George Choate:

> One thing is sure, if the case is unreal to you, you can make it unreal to her, and vice-versa. Look upon the right side and have more *fight* in you, more indignation at such an imposition as disease. You look at things *too materially*, you gather yourself in the thought of Life, Substance and Intelligence in matter, too insensibly, [and] your patient mesmerizes you ....[7]

A short while later she wrote to his wife, Clara:

> Do not go out of the house where your patient is, nor run before a lie, for that would be as if you believed it was the truth. When you hear her hawking, etc., remember you *do not hear* her, that hers is a dream, and yours a dream, also.
>
> Remember all is mind, there *is no matter*.
>
> Have you wakened some now? To see it is a dream and *not* a *reality*?
>
> When hearing your own dream that she is coughing, you must realize as much as in you lieth now, that you do not hear her and say it so to yourself and to her until you break both your dreams.[8]

Earlier, Mrs. Eddy had written Clara:

... Get her strongest fear, find it out by some means, and direct *all* your fire to *that* until you beat it down. You *can* master it. The only trouble ... is these so-called material conditions are too real to you.

Remember that sight is only an admission; it is only this—"I *see*"; remember that a loss of sight is only "I do not see"—it is only what mortal mind *says* about it. Now bend this mind to admit what you say is true—and you contend as stoutly and believe it as strongly that they *do see*, and you have got the case. You must first conquer your own doubt and then you can conquer their fear. Make it real to yourself that they are perfect in all the faculties and that the eye cannot help them or hinder them from seeing. If a patient fears anything, make them meet that fear—and do just what they feared to do.

Never allow *yourself* to think anything material can *hurt them* or help them; watch yourself here. Remember all is *Mind*, *there* is *no matter*. Do not allow yourself to get to thinking of a *lie*, of a material condition as a *reality*.

If you believe the lie, it will be difficult to make them disbelieve it. Say she can see and *believe it yourself*, cast the beam out of your own eye.[9]

In 1885 Mrs. Eddy wrote Mrs. Babcock:

... The book *Science and Health* is healing the most difficult cases of disease. My students use it as an aid to practice by having their patients read it, and if it rouses strong chemicalization, so much the more certain it is striking deeper at the root of disease than they have done. In which case, they treat the patient for the chemical and keep the patient reading this book until it cures them.[10]

That same year she wrote George Wickersham:

... Our Father is everywhere present, and it is His presence and power that heals. It is not the power of one mind over another, it is not the transference of mortal thoughts that heals, but the divine Truth that makes us free.[11]

Also in 1885 Mrs. Eddy wrote Sarah Heywood:

There is one general answer I can give for every case.

Do not concern yourself so much to get the argument, as to rise to a clear sense of the Science of Being, namely, that what you behold is an illusion of your own senses as well as the senses of your patient. And then work bravely, persistently, and Christ-like to dispel this illusion of sin, sickness, and death to yourself.[12]

In 1887 she wrote M. Anna Osgood:

... There is danger of your following the mistake of arguing too much and too long for patients. You know I instructed you not to do this....

Never take down the symptoms of your patients, but rise yourself *above* symptoms and arguments. If the patient is not getting well with them, drop them and *know* and realize you have nothing to talk about but God and His creation.[13]

In 1896 Mrs. Eddy wrote Annie Robertson:

To know there is but *one* God, one Cause, one effect, one Mind, heals instantly. Have but One God, and your reflection of Him does the healing.[14]

In 1901 Mrs. Eddy said to Irving Tomlinson:

When visiting a patient that is very low never say, "There is no death." Say rather, "All is Life and Life is eternal." To say, "there is no death" is to call up the image of the very thing they fear. And their fear may produce the effect they dread. Just as [we] see that which is reflected on the retina of the eye, so the thought given a patient is reflected by him.[15]

The following year she told him:

. . . Disease is but the image of a lie. It is not in matter or a part of matter. It is but the reflection of a falsehood. As Jesus said, it is but a liar and the father of lies. There is no truth in it. Disease, sickness, and sin you are to know as but the image of wrong thought, and seeing it thus, you destroy it.[16]

The next four excerpts are about what to do when having difficulty in healing:

In 1885 Mrs. Eddy wrote Janette Weller:

> Do you find any difficulty in healing? If so, strike for the higher sense of the *nothingness* of *matter*. Do not care to search into causation there, for there is no cause and no effect in matter; *all is Mind*, perfect and eternal. Whenever you treat a patient, include in your understanding of the case that no ignorant or malicious mind can affect the case. There *is no relapse*. Science tells us this—is all it manifests. *Progress* is the law of the Infinite, and finite views but supposition and belief. Now *realize* this. And be a law to every case when you commence treating it that there is but *one Mind*, and this one governs your patient, that there are no *minds* to interfere. Error is *not mind*, has *no power* over *you* or the patient. These are the rules for you to work out every hour of your life. . . .
>
> Realize constantly that no mortal mind (so-called) can affect *you* or make you believe you cannot *cure* your patients. There is no *malice*, no *envy*, no *will power*. All is Love and Truth. *Argue this* way.[17]

Mary Adams and Elizabeth Webster wrote Mrs. Eddy in 1887:

> Since we returned from Boston, our cases do not respond as they should. All seem to hold on, or do not acknowledge being helped, or seem to relapse.

We do not leave a stone unturned, that we know how to turn. We are working almost constantly. Never doubt the Science for a moment. Deny, as you have taught us, knowing "God is All," seeking earnestly for the Light, *trying* to realize His ever presence.

What is it?

Mrs. Eddy replied:

Nothing but malicious mesmerism and a *scare*.

Stop trying so hard, make less of *personality*, know yourself, that you have nothing to treat; quit arguing so much. Have faith, by understanding that if *you believe* what you argue, it is already done.[18]

In 1901 Mrs. Eddy told Irving Tomlinson:

Suppose you had two vessels into which you were pouring water. While one filled rapidly, you observed that the other made no gain. On investigation you found that there was a leak, and as fast as you poured it in, it ran away. Your remedy would be to pour in a larger stream until the vessel was filled. So, in healing the sick if the case does not respond, pour in the Truth in larger stream until the patient feels the presence of life and life alone.[19]

Later that year she told him:

Observe that our harvest is already here if we will but see it. It is but our blindness that delays the reaping.

Know this, "and look on the fields: for they are white already to harvest."

If you have a case that seems protracted, dwell no longer upon it, lift up your eyes and realize the eternal presence of peace and harmony. Know that the harvest time of health and life is even now with you.[20]

The next two excerpts are about treating for relapse:

In 1885 Mrs. Eddy wrote James Wiggin:

When, if ever, you have a return of your complaints, fix your mind steadfastly on this thought: No mortal mind, or malice, can affect my mind or body. Be strong in that consciousness of Truth, and if you gain the point of conviction of its truth, and the perception that it was a directed shaft of mortal mind, you will destroy the suffering.[21]

In 1902 she wrote Charlotte Allan:

No disease can *relapse*, no fear return. Truth, Life, Love is the same forever; a reversal of them is impossible. The old beliefs of fear, sin, or disease cannot return. They never were; and there are no *new beliefs* of these, or fear of them to come, for there are none in doing good. Our life consists of good; our health and happiness all come from thinking rightly, and acting rightly. The law is that we are healthier and happier for helping or healing others. It is only thus that we fulfill the law of Christ.[22]

The following four excerpts are about the need to keep the sense of person out of treatment:

In 1893 Mrs. Eddy wrote to Ann Otis:

> Never address the person who errs by treating them mentally, or treating yourself against it. Never recognize the person in your argument—you must not. But take it up, the error, only, and never doctor the error much but make yourself so conscious of the opposite Truth that the error disappears, e.g., Know that nothing can come to you, or go from you, but what God sends, and therefore, that no mortal mind can influence you; for only one Mind exists, and this is Immortal *Love*. Overcome the evil mind with good. Never talk to it, or of it, but hold steadfastly to Good, Love, and do not feel that any other power exists. This will deliver you. If you dwell in thought on any person, it will hinder you from overcoming personality in your healing and casting out sin. There *is no personality*, and this is more important to know than that there is no disease. Your lifelong mistake has been your strong sense of personality. Drop it and remember you can never rid yourself of the seeming effects from a personality while holding in mind this personality. The way is to put it wholly out of mind and keep before your thought the *right* model.[23]

In 1894 Mrs. Eddy wrote Clara Shannon:

> ... think of an error as having no *cause whatever*. If it is hate or envy, think of it as no part of individuality, but

only error, illusion, in fact *nothing*. Hence it has no person back of it, and thus you separate the tares from the wheat and never think of any person when treating for error, but only of error itself.[24]

In 1895 she wrote E. J. Foster Eddy:

. . . do not name or think of personality; only know there *is none*. I find that is best for you. Daily treat yourself against *personality*. It is the basis of all *sin, sorrow,* sickness, and death. Neither *love* nor *hate* it.[25]

In 1896 Mrs. Eddy wrote Lida Stone:

. . . What our Cause needs most is the *impersonalization* of thought. I see little if any growth in this direction. To destroy an effect we must remove its cause. The first error was limiting Mind, or personality, which was supposed to contain mind. Now to love or hate or fear or believe in this finity of mind called mortal personality is to preserve the cause of all error. . . . No persons can grow into Christian Science until they have grown out of attaching themselves to personality either through fear, love, or hate.[26]

The next two excerpts are about assisting in childbirth:

In 1885 Mrs. Eddy wrote Clara Choate:

In reply to your question, [I] will say take up the case in thought as you would think of a bud unclosing without pain. There is no pain attendant on it, matter has no pain. Now put all belief that pain attends childbirth out of mortal thought, and there would be no suffering whatever, and the labor would go on faster and the birth be less protracted.

The only thing that delays the birth is fear. Let your firm faith in God, Truth and Love, cast out all fear.

It was turning away from God as the only *Mind* that caused pain. There is no other mind to suffer, and matter cannot suffer.[27]

In 1898 she wrote Alfred Baker, formerly a medical physician:

During parturition your mind can assist your patient or the prospective mother. At the birth let your mind govern the action, prevent pain, and control the presentation of the babe. Mind is master of all the rules and conditions pertaining to obstetrics. Mind governs the results in every respect contingent on delivery, and the condition of the infant and mother, and the treatment thereof. ...

Teach your student all this and teach him apart from this the purely mechanical parts of obstetrics. Do not drill him in unnecessary detail therein but qualify him according to law how to proceed in all cases and under difficult circumstances. Qualify him first how to conduct safe and harmonious cases of childbirth, then how to treat the abnormal cases.

Advise your students in case of serious obstacles at childbirth that they do not overcome, to summon an M.D. for counsel in order to avoid our state laws coming down on them. And guard well mentally the mother's thought so as to prevent fear or inflammation.[28]

The next six excerpts are about treating oneself:

In 1885 Mrs. Eddy wrote Flavia and Ira Knapp:

... The case named of rupture is considered very difficult, but God says all things are possible to Him. You have only to rouse yourself from a stagnant sense of God's power and presence. ... Never yield for a moment to doubt or dismay. There are plenty of sick, and you can heal them, and will .... God is perhaps trying you as He has tried all his own, and if you stand the test, all at once you will come into the kingdom of our Lord, a clear and abiding sense of your power to heal. Only be faithful over a few things, and He will make you ruler over many, and then you will enter into the *joy* of your work. Rupture is only a thought of matter, but there is *no matter*, and man's entire substance is Spirit. *Rouse* yourself from the dream of matter, and pluck the beam out of your own eye; help others, and you are helping yourself; help yourself, and you will help others. You know what I taught you is true. Now do not let the *enemy sow tares* while you sleep—be awake, and watch. Deny with all boldness that you cannot heal, for to admit it is dishonoring God since He it is who heals, worketh through us, and we must see that we *reflect* Him,—reflect the divine power. I know, my dear students, the way is the way of our Master, full of crosses and crowns.[29]

In 1876 Mrs. Eddy wrote Eldridge Smith:

You can be well, yea, *you are well.*

That which is sick is not you; it is a belief instead of *you.*

There never was and never can be a pain or sensation in matter. The body you name you, is but a belief; it is not you. One of its beliefs, for which the ignorant doctor is responsible, is an utter absurdity, namely, that a lung that is governed by mind in all its action could cease to act because of matter and thus matter beat mind when it has no power outside of mind. God governs and clothes the lily. He, as the Truth of your being, would govern your body as harmoniously, if a separate thought besides His did not control it.

Your lung never stopped acting on account of matter, be it solid or fluid, water or what not.

If it ever acted, mind produced the action; if it ever stopped acting, mortal mind or belief stopped the action. Just what you believe about it will be carried out on your body. Look out for what you *believe* and your lung will be right. . . .[30]

In 1888 Mrs. Eddy wrote Fremont Snider:

> You are in the right way now. Be strong in the
> *sense* of Truth, the truth that nothing ails you. The truth
> that you are not in your body and have no material
> heart—that heart is affection—that all is Mind [and]
> there is no matter, no material body. You are not afraid
> of your own concept, are you? If you are, change it. You
> make it. Nobody can make what you see or feel; you
> alone are responsible for this. Now stick to this. Above all,
> know that God is *all*, that He *is all*. Then you must lose
> fear in the sense of Love. *He* cares for you and will hold
> you in eternal health.[31]

In 1896 she wrote Edward Kimball:

> . . . Your mind is all that determines the case whether
> you are better or worse. The body and its symptoms have
> nothing to say about it. Now be strong, calm, conscious
> that you are well and trouble has no power over you. Oh,
> I have learned to meet this awful ordeal by just casting
> all sense of it out of mind and finding *love* lighten the
> burden, and resting in Good. There is no evil.[32]

In 1897 Mrs. Eddy wrote Septimus Hanna:

> Take the First Commandment for your
> medicine—it cures all disease. There is but one Mind, and
> no person can or is harming you. It is a *dream*, a falsity,

an illusion. You have no material heart, head, back! There is no electromagnetism, no nerve centers for fools or demons to play on with glamour.

You, dear one, are God's appointed to stand if others do not. "A thousand shall fall at thy side, . . . but it shall *not come nigh thee.*" Not but you can go apart to pray—this we all need to do, and I want you to do it. But note this, do not go where, if you get frightened, you have no one *well skilled* in *truth* to encourage you and neutralize error with Truth.[33]

In 1902 she wrote Edward Kimball:

. . . Dear one, meet it thus, and stand on this platform. *There is no liver*, no pneumogastric nerve, and no nerves, no solar plexus. Then *stand*; having done all, *stand* on *this Rock.* There is no matter, no *substance* but *Spirit.* Stand there, know it, draw all other physical conclusions from this and *all Truth.*

. . . To run before a lie is to accept its terms. This works like running before the enemy in battle. You will be followed, pursued *till* you face about, *trust* in God, and stand on *Spirit*, denying and facing and fighting all claims of matter and mortal mind, both *one.*[34]

The next four excerpts illustrate Mrs. Eddy's treatment of Pamelia Leonard through her correspondence:

In 1900:

> There is no hernia except in *thought*; the body cannot cause it, *cannot have it*. Drop your false image, and have one Mind, and that Mind will be minus a breach, a bloat, an ache—and you will be *free*.

> Drop your chains; you are free. Thought is *above* captivity; it has all it *wants* from *Love*. Accept Love's *gift* and it is *yours at once*.[35]

In 1904:

> You have *no dropsy*, no swelled bowels nor limbs nor feet any more than you have horns and hoofs. You are His *image* and *likeness*. Now awake from your dream! It has no reality. There is not *within*, all is without. You do not see or feel a *dream*, and there is but one Mind. There is no other Mind affecting you, and you are not self-mesmerized to believe a lie. You, the grand, true, strong child of God, cannot be self-deceived. Your spiritual sense has destroyed the false evidence of material sense. The Surgeon only repeated a lie, and Truth destroys this lie; and I declare in the name of Almighty God that it *is destroyed* for I *cannot see it*.[36]

In 1905:

> Never let a "scalding tear" fall on your dear cheek, but joy and rejoice in the God of your salvation all ways, for Christ, Truth, is the *way*, and you are walking in it and are *well now*.

Do realize that the cross is over and you are risen. Matter has no part in your life work. *Mind is all,* and this Mind is *Good, Life,* Love. *These you have now.* Do not look into the past or future, "into the place where they have laid him"—even the belief of substance or sensation in matter, but look to Mind, the divine Mind, that acts upon the human and causes it to relinquish the belief in disease, and to have but one Mind, one God. Keep this *commandment.*[37]

And in 1906:

... "He that abideth in my word shall know the truth, and the Truth shall make him free." It *has made you free.* There is but *one* Mind and you have none other; evil is not Mind, not presence nor power. There is no evil mind, and matter is only a *dream,* and you have wakened from this dream, and no night is there. The Revelator, in the flesh, beheld this vision of *"no pain,* no night" (doubt or fear) ... and no more sorrow. Such is *your present vision. Mind alone* gives you health, and matter is out of the question now, and forevermore must be.[38]

The next five excerpts are on the need for self-purification:

In 1889 Mrs. Eddy wrote Joshua Bailey:

... God has given you the word and power; now do not obscure His presence by yielding to temptation. Look your heart over every day and see if it is right in the sight of divine Truth and Love, and if one single sin or seed of human self and dishonesty be there, wrestle all day, all night, and until the light comes and the victory is won. "The morning light is breaking."[39]

In 1897 she wrote James Neal:

... Pray daily, never miss praying, no matter how often: "Lead me not into temptation,"—scientifically rendered—Leave me not to lose sight of strict purity [and] clean, pure thoughts; let all my thoughts and aims be high, unselfish, charitable, meek—*spiritually minded.* With this altitude of thought, your mind is losing materiality and gaining spirituality, and this is the state of mind that *heals* the *sick.*[40]

A little later that year Mrs. Eddy wrote John Lathrop:

... Search out, dear one, your most obstinate belief and there pitch your battle. I would think you had no besetting error, so pure, innocent, and faithful you seem to me. But I have views beyond the external sense that tell me mortal mind needs watching and subduing, however much is fair and promising. Watch and guard well and early, and subdue finally all that is not good, of God, and the law of the hillside Sermon.[41]

In 1899 she wrote Sarah Conger:

Yes, dear one, begin at home as you said; labor for your own sanctification, spirituality, health, holiness. I find that in proportion as I do this for myself, the whole world feels it. That is why I greatly desire more time to give to this self-purification. God hears your sigh and sees your smile. Be sure of His ever presence—the ever present Father-Mother Love is ready to bless you and is pouring in His floodtide just as fast as you can receive the blessing. Be strong in faith, divine understanding, and love. Then are you fully equipped for your work and will feel the assurance that Good is guiding you and never will leave you comfortless, but will come to you at need and abide with you, and you will abide in Good. Then the heathen will be moved to seek and find and love God and [to] bless His servant and the Divine Love leading you.[42]

In 1901 Mrs. Eddy told Calvin Frye:

... the Apostle made the condition of the mind of him who prays, that is, the righteous man or the good man to be he who heals by prayer and none other can, for the prayer of the unrighteous availeth not. . . .

On this rock of Christ's prayer, Christian Science plants its standard of healing in contradistinction to all other forms of mortal mind cure, faith cure, or any other mental or material process of healing the sick.[43]

The next six excerpts are on the need to grow spiritually:

In 1886 Mrs. Eddy wrote Malinda Lancaster:

... That you are feeling "Who is sufficient for these things?"

is not strange. But you must remember that our heavenly Father does not require of us more than we can do. Each victory won over self and sickness strengthens you for the next contest, and so on, until you can say with the Apostle, "I have fought the good fight." We shall never know our strength until it be put to the test, and then *His* strength is made perfect in our weakness, and we learn from humility the might of divine Truth and Love.[44]

In 1890 she wrote Joseph Eastaman:

... How good it is to remember our mercies, and to remember nothing else.

The only thing is to be mindful of Good and un-mindful of evil. To see that we ourselves are emptied of the old wine so that the new (new to us) can be poured in plentifully by the divine energy without bursting the bottles. The lilies grow without toiling or spinning. God clothes them. We can, we do, grow from the same *Source*, and as unconsciously, and it should be as gently, from His dear hand who careth for us. But we toil, struggle, and what does it all avail? Better be still and know that *God is all* and there is none beside Him. Know that health, harmony, heaven is here and everywhere, and the whole world of sense *is powerless*. Oh! for a big rift in the clouds, the mists of earth, whereby to behold all this, and never lose sight of it.[45]

In 1891 Mrs. Eddy wrote Ira Knapp:

... The birth out of matter into Spirit is not gained by *argument*, nor by force. It is *growth, hourly*; it is forever getting nearer *Love* that *is Love*; universal divine *presence* and power, alias *might* and dominion. First over the body, then its reflection is dominion over all the earth.[46]

In 1892 she wrote M. Bettie Bell:

... I know you are growing, and then is the time to keep your garden of Good well weeded. It is strange how I note the tares in this garden of my own, that others cannot see, and every day I pull them up, and then they sprout again. How little these little things seem! But a breath human dims the dial of God. I long to be perfect even as the Father. Humility, temperance, love must clothe us as with a garment. We must render to Caesar the things that are his before we can give ourselves to God....

... The lurking snare prepared for the feet of students now, is developing a fall, unless they see it and thus escape. It is *vanity* and forgetfulness of the way that has led them, and the unconscious effort to avoid the Way-shower and appropriate the path as one of their own finding and foundations.[47]

In 1895 Mrs. Eddy wrote Elizabeth Moulton:

... God has enabled you to be faithful over a few things, thence His promise that you shall be ruler over many things and then enter into the joy of our Lord—the bliss of omnipotent Love, omnipotent Truth, Life everlasting. Do you want this 3rd degree in growth and its infinite joy? Then, dear one, ask the Divine Love for it, constantly plead for it, that you may know you are in earnest, and if you persevere, then you will find your prayer will be granted. This prayer is not made on bended knee, but with a bowed heart, a longing after righteousness, hungering and thirsting after it, that you may be filled. Your mental petition will be granted. Why? Because you will have gained a fitness for the blessing so you can receive it normally and never can lose it. You have clothed me, dear one. Oh, may my words clothe you in robes of white and crown you with the might of Christian Science.[48]

In 1896 she wrote Caroline Noyes:

Love is the only and all of attainments in spiritual growth. Without it, healing is not done and cannot be either morally or physically. Every advanced step will show you this until the victory is won and you possess no other consciousness but *Love* divine.[49]

The next two excerpts are about demonstrating health:

In 1903 Mrs. Eddy wrote John Lathrop:

A belief of health is grown out of in one of two ways—viz. suffering or Science. Do not *sentence yourself* to *suffer* out of a belief, but rise to the understanding that takes you out. This understanding is *spiritual*; it is not human will that takes you out, but the spiritual, and not material, sense of being. . . .

Now rouse yourself to know you are not living *in* the body but in God, in Spirit, in the good you do and are. Then you get out of the *belief* of *health* into the understanding of health, and *are* out—and out through Science, *not suffering.* Keep your mind happy in getting out; keep your thoughts away from me and grounded on divine Principle, not on a person.[50]

In 1908 Mrs. Eddy said to her household staff:

The healthiest person is the one who loathes sin the most.[51]

The next two excerpts are about the need to turn thought away from the body:

In 1902 Mrs. Eddy told Irving Tomlinson:

We are not to look to the body for life. Life is not of the body. Life is of God. Life does not grow old. Life *is* immortal.

It is written, "Let him that is on the housetop not go down." Do not go down to the body for the consciousness of Life, Truth, and Love. Live above and without the body, and eternal life is yours.[52]

In 1905 she wrote John Lathrop:

. . . The body and you are not one. You are not in the

body talking for it, and it cannot talk for itself. You are John, the beloved; you are spiritual not material. You are my good faithful follower of Christ—the image of God; indeed, you are this idea and have no strife with the flesh; you reflect God and are His image and like unto Spirit not matter. The flesh has no connection with you. Realize this and you are master of the situation.[53]

The next ten excerpts are about overcoming evil—animal magnetism, mesmerism, malpractice:

In 1884 Mrs. Eddy wrote Caroline Noyes:

...It is time for you now to handle the malicious mesmerism or belief just as you do sickness. Declare for God as *All* and that there is nothing beside Him. Don't take up a personality, but class it all in one lump of error.[54]

In 1886 she wrote Hattie Jones:

Animal magnetism in some form is all that is sin, sickness, or death, and it's our province to meet and to master this triad of mortal mind in the strength of God, who gave us this demonstration through His spiritual son Jesus.[55]

In 1887 Mrs. Eddy wrote Emma Thompson, who had been a patient of Phineas Quimby's in 1862:

You have nothing to fear from 10,000 mind curers. Why do you feel shocked at things *unreal?* There is no power in evil; a million ciphers make no number. Evil [being] a naught, why do you call it a unit and units? You must not forget my teachings. Rise from this *nightmare* of mesmerism. Quimby left this stain on your mortal belief; now wash it off *in Science*—Christian Science that rests in calm strength on the sure foundation that *God is all,* and whatever else seems to be, *contradict* and *know it is not.*[56]

That same year she wrote Alfred Farlow:

Be sure and mind what I say: *Never think* of *animal magnetism* or any power but good. If you do this, it will be *right* and keep you safe and others from any other power. Don't let your mind out into the realm of mind. I find there is too much magnetism in mortal minds to do this safely. You make hate too *real.* Argue all is *love.*[57]

Around 1889 Mrs. Eddy wrote Caroline Frame:

. . . never treat *personally* to ward off malicious animal magnetism. If you do, it is, as God has revealed through *Science and Health,* a fight of the beasts; it is error meeting error, and the best of the two persons will always get the worst in this warfare.

Let our finite judgment never settle on *who* is troubling us, and never defend ourselves against a person. Rather ask *what* is troubling, and then meet the *what.*[58]

In 1891 she wrote Laura Lathrop:

...Trust in *Good*, and you will always be delivered from evil in every line of its attack.

Thus it is really good to be afflicted; it teaches us what nothing else can teach of Truth.

Permit me again one word of caution. Never deal with evil as evil deals with you. Never return personal arguments to meet personal arguments, or you will be continually subject to their return. Evil *is not real*; there are no talkers on the side of evil. *Know* this, dear one, and demonstrate thus your knowledge of Christian Science.

Love will gird you with strength and hide you from the tempest. But any deviation from this sense and consciousness is dangerous.[59]

In 1893 Mrs. Eddy wrote her adopted son, E. J. Foster Eddy:

...He that has the proper idea of Good loses his sense of evil.

Think only on the *right side*; let not the *unreal* decoy you into combat. Remember this.

Practice mentally not against the discord—but for the chord. If you *tell* nothing [that] it is destroying itself, you are *making something* of it to yourself.[60]

In 1899 she wrote Harriet Betts:

...Malicious animal magnetism is but a dream! It has only *nothing* of its own; do not give it suppositional something. There is no Armageddon. God, Love, *is all there* is. Choose ye this day. But while you know the truth, defend yourself against the subtlety of error's *claims*.[61]

In 1900 Mrs. Eddy wrote George and Nellie Moore:

> You must not address [Josephine] Woodbury personally as you do a patient. I think you do not know how to treat against animal magnetism. You need not think of the individual but only know there is no evil mind. Also know there is but *one* Mind and that is *God*, for God is *all* and in all. Treat yourselves that you cannot be made to believe a lie, that you cannot be mesmerized nor made to think the *reverse* of what is correct about anything or anybody. Do not name Woodbury in your argument; keep her out of your minds.[62]

In 1909 Mrs. Eddy told Irving Tomlinson:

> You ask why Gilbert [Eddy] died. Because he would not waken to defend himself from animal magnetism. He declared [that] he could not be mesmerized and would not work against it. You must handle mesmerism or it will handle you.[63]

The next six excerpts are about defending oneself metaphysically:

In 1893 Mrs. Eddy wrote Pamelia Leonard:

> Study daily *Science and Health*, put the world, the flesh, and evil under your feet. Treat yourself against the

influence of mortal mind. Watch that you are not led away from the true statement and the spirit of Christian Science. We all must do this, hourly. What I say unto you, I say to all, *watch*.[64]

In 1897 she wrote William McKenzie:

Commence at once a prayer to Divine Love to deliver you from the temptation to believe that you feel other minds or can be *influenced* by them to love, to hate, or to suffer from them, for there is but *one* Mind.

This prayer and its tendency causes you to love your neighbor, to hate no one, and will give you a determined strength in morals and Christianity, and save you.

Call, yea demand, yourself to keep the first command: *no other God*. This means that you must not allow yourself to fear or to believe that there is a mind apart from God, a power or a person that can govern or affect you but God. Now go to work bravely, and when you conquer this weakness, you will bind the strong man and destroy his goods. That is, you can resist all else but God. You can know there is naught else and destroy all supposed effects of any supposed power over you but Good, Life, Truth, *divine* Love.[65]

Two months later Mrs. Eddy wrote him again:

. . . Every day pray that you have one Mind and love thy neighbor as thyself. This fulfills the law. Then watch that you *fear* no other mind (since there is *none*) and that you do not admit that you *feel* any other mind. Make your prayer and demand and watch one—even the trinity reflected of Life, Truth, Love.[66]

In 1899 Mrs. Eddy instructed Alfred Baker:

… Every day treat yourself that no evil suggestion nor argument can swerve you or frighten you—or deter you from healing and doing just what is needed here. Tell your dear wife to do the same. No evil mind can touch you if you realize there is but *one Mind*. Three times each day treat yourself for this temptation; then watch that your house be not broken open.[67]

In 1901 she warned Mrs. Alfred Wolcott:

Permit me to name to you that instances are constantly occurring of hypnotism whereby the person is made to feel a mistaken sense of duty. My students protect themselves by mental power against this insidious attack—by realizing the allness of God, and evil as powerless to harm them. Therefore they cannot be subject to hypnotism. It were well for those who are not sensible of its influence to thus shield themselves against it.

God, Divine Love, is our shield and buckler; let us be mentally armored with this defense and watch, as the Scriptures demand, that our minds be not invaded.[68]

In 1905 Mrs. Eddy wrote John Lathrop:

> ...Dear one, there is but *one Mind*—this one is yours, mine, and governs all. All our thoughts come to us from this Mind and return to their source. In this Mind, there is no material sense, and there is *no other Mind*—no mortal mind to tempt, to harm, to control us. Now know this, realize it, and you are the master of the occasion, the master of yourself and of others.[69]

On the utmost need for love, Mrs. Eddy wrote Malinda Lancaster in 1892:

> Your statement of the points of Christian Science was quite as much as a mortal can reach through the letter in so short a time. But darling, the letter kills our growth unless the genuine spirit of *Love* accompanies every word of it. And this I trust has been your greatest achievement, that of the Spirit.[70]

About unforeseen events Mrs. Eddy wrote Minnie Hall Perry [later DeSoto] in 1905:

> ...Take up your accidents as impossible in Truth—there is no falling in truth, and accidents do not occur. Nothing is accidental, but all is law and order in God, and you live and move in Mind, in Spirit, not matter. You have been a brave little body—and now you could be, are, a good, grand, courageous soul outside the body and never liable to be influenced adversely.[71]

About Peter healing the lame man (recorded in Acts 3:1–8), Mrs. Eddy told Irving Tomlinson in 1907:

> That is just what we have to do today, heal the physical ailments. We have to show the falsehood of physical sense. There is but one Sense, Truth and Love; that Sense governs. It controls all the human mechanism. It governs until the human yields to the mechanism of the divine Mind.[72]

About working hard, she told Tomlinson in 1908:

> When I began this work, I never took any thought of fatigue or weariness. If at evening after I had done a hard day's work, and I thought of something which needed attention in Boston, I put on my things and at once made the journey and attended to the business. So should the students give no heed to the claims of material sense, but they should know that one does not grow weary in doing good.[73]

About raising children, Mrs. Eddy told her secretaries in October 1909:

> . . . If you had a child who was too young to understand, how would [you] teach him not to sin?
>
> While he was too young to understand the words, I should talk to him mentally and say, "You cannot sin." This I should say to him each day. Then [when] he became older, I should tell him so audibly. This done

faithfully would put him leagues in advance of where he would be otherwise.[74]

When Mrs. Eddy moved to Pleasant View in Concord, New Hampshire, in 1892, she continued her practice of setting "watches" for her home and sometimes for the Cause. Their primary purpose was to defend the mental atmosphere of her home through metaphysical work. She would select different members of her household to conduct these watches at various times depending on the need of the moment. Sometimes, she would also select certain Church members for this work during times of challenge to the Cause. The following are examples of directions she gave to these workers:

In 1894 Mrs. Eddy told Laura Sargent to tell them:

> Mother said in the old way mortal belief had one devil [and] now it had many; but we should no longer call it *they*, but *evil*.

> She said when we take up our watch, we do not help her with *our* thought; we simply clear our own thought of the belief of evil, and this is getting rid of *our* thought and getting out of God's way so the Light can shine through, and this blessed Light helps *us* and *all* in its shining. *This* is the blessed, blessed way from *sense* to *soul*.[75]

On the second day of 1900, Mrs. Eddy instructed her watchers:

"Hear O Israel, for the Lord our God is *one* God."

You are not to come in your own name to pray; you are not to try to control any mind. You are only to come in the divine strength and know that God will rule and does, and that hypnotism and evil minds cannot and do not control men nor governments. *All power is God, good.*

This is my only formula to Christian Scientists for prayer; and God will give you faith that you can remove mountains.[76]

Later in 1900, concerning the Woodbury lawsuit, Mrs. Eddy wrote to Joseph Armstrong:

... See all the watchers and especially Mr. Farlow, and tell them that Mother says they must not pray over this subject of court with any hatred or resentment in their thought. They must not take up Woodbury personally or refer to her personally, but when they pray, they must know that evil and lies cannot sway the judgment of the Court, and that the Judge of the whole earth will govern the judges, and they will do right.[77]

In 1903 Mrs. Eddy wrote a prayer for the watchers to work with:

The effect of this prayer *is not reversed.*

God, good, reigns, there is no *other mind.* Love reigns, there is no hatred, no envy, no revenge. All things are working together for good to those that love good. We do love good, God, and He gives us all our thoughts, motives, and governs all our acts. The divine Life preserves our life and health, and they cannot be taken from Christian Scientists, and Christian Scientists cannot be made sinful. We love God, and God loves us and is guiding us every moment. This prayer cannot be reversed!

This prayer bears fruit after its own kind. It does good, it blesses us and all others.[78]

Mary Baker Eddy's advice to her students was prompted by her understanding of the essential need for healing to be quick and complete in order to turn humanity's thought to God as "supreme in the physical realm, so-called, as well as in the spiritual."[79] In addition to what is presented in this chapter, there are a number of letters best considered in their entirety rather than excerpted. These can be found in Appendix A.

Chapter 17

THE CROSS
(1905–1907)

*B*Y 1905 MARY BAKER EDDY had become a national figure. Her Church, The First Church of Christ, Scientist, in Boston, Massachusetts, was prospering far beyond the world's expectations. Consequently, the media of that day were focusing more and more of their attention on her as Founder and Leader of the Christian Science movement. A good deal of this interest was not friendly. But no matter what confronted her, Christian healing remained at the forefront of her thought.

On May 25, 1905, Mrs. Eddy wrote to one of her longtime students:

> What I need for help in my life-labor more than all else on earth is a—*healer* such as I [was] when practising … . Gain that *one point*, [be] an instantaneous healer of all manner of diseases. I [was] that, and you should be. Our great Master was that and called upon his followers to do likewise. You can be this and must be in order to be a

Christian Scientist. Now address yourself to this duty of yours, watch, pray, labor, and have *faith*!—*Know* that you can be what God demands you to be and now are—His image and likeness—reflecting God, the one and only Healer, reflecting God, Life, Truth, Love.[1]

Four months earlier, Mrs. Eddy had demonstrated exactly what she refers to in this letter. In a reminiscence, George Kinter, a worker in Mrs. Eddy's home during this period, recounts what happened "late one winter night of January or February in the year 1905." Mrs. Eddy had called several times for her longtime personal secretary, Calvin Frye, but without response. She then summoned Mr. Kinter to see why Calvin had not come. Upon entering Frye's bedroom, George found him slumped in a chair: "Mr. Frye had passed on—he had no pulse, he was stone cold—and rigid. His closed eyes were fixedly set, and there were none of the common evidences of life." When informed of this, Mrs. Eddy came immediately to the bedroom and "began at once to treat him, making such bold, audible declarations . . . . [She] continuously denied the error and declared the Truth with such vehemence and eloquence for a full hour, as I never had heard on any other occasion . . . . I remember quite well many of her utterances and actions. She said, for example:

> Calvin, wake up and be the man God made!
> You are not dead and you know it! How often have
> you proved there is no death! Calvin, all is Life! Life!!
> Undying Life. Say, God is my Life. Say it after me!
> Say it, so that I shall know you realize it! Say it in a
> whisper, if need be, but make the declaration for yourself.

Declare—I can help myself. I know there is no animal magnetism. I am not the victim of malicious animal magnetism. I have proved a thousand times that my knowledge of good in Christian Science is paramount to every attempt of error to put me out through malicious mental practice. I am victorious over evil thought and action for I know that God is All-in-all, all-powerful, all-loving and always present. Callie dear, are you, yourself, repeating what I am saying to you—and for you? Are you? Do you hear me? Do you understand me? Mother loves you for all your years of faithful service, but our dear God loves you infinitely better, and you cannot, you need not, die tonight! You are not dead, Calvin Frye. Rouse yourself. Shake off this nightmare of false, human belief and of fear. Don't let error mesmerize you into a state of believing Satan's lies about man made in God's image and likeness! Your life-work is not done. I need you. Our great blessed Cause needs you.

Life is as deathless as God Himself, for Life is God and you are His spiritual offspring. Calvin, there is no death, for the Christian Christ Jesus has abolished death and this treatment is not reversed by error.

After an hour, Calvin moved a little and then spoke in very low tones: "Don't call me back. Let me go, I am so tired." To which Mrs. Eddy replied, "Oh, Yes,—We shall persist in calling you back, for you have not been away. You have only been dreaming, and now that you have awakened out of that dreamy sleep, you are not tired. . . . Thank the dear God, who is Mind, is omnipresent good, you do not concede any claim of the material senses. . . . Now then, give God thanks for He hath redeemed you. You are strong and well." By the time another half-hour had gone by, Calvin had completely recovered. The rest of the night was peaceful, and Mr. Frye was at his post the next morning, doing his usual work for Mrs. Eddy.[2]

A month after this experience, Mrs. Eddy received a letter from a Mary Crane Gray, who had just been introduced to

Calvin Frye at his desk in Chestnut Hill, Massachusetts

Christian Science. Her husband had become insane after losing a considerable fortune through bad financial investments, and the doctors had said he was incurable, recommending he be put in an asylum. Instead, Mrs. Gray wrote to Mrs. Eddy, begging her to heal her husband: "I poured out my heart's anguish in a ten-paged letter to Mrs. Eddy. I did not know that she was not taking cases of healing at that time. The third day after the mailing of that letter, my husband arose healed." He had no memory of being ill. His wife told him what she had done in writing to Mrs. Eddy. He told her, "I will seek employment at once."[3]

Mrs. Eddy no longer had a public healing practice because she was devoting all her time to helping humanity through her work as Leader of the Cause of Christian Science. And she knew that in order to succeed in this role, she must continue to grow spiritually. She told a newspaper journalist in June 1905, "All that I ask of the world now is that it grant me time, time to assimilate myself to God."[4]

As Leader, Mrs. Eddy was continually urging her followers to leave all for Christ. In her message "'Choose Ye'" to The First Church of Christ, Scientist, in Boston (written for the dedication of its grand Extension to the Original Edifice built more than a decade earlier), Mrs. Eddy reminded Christian Scientists of the Scripture, "He that taketh not his cross, and followeth after me, is not worthy of me."[5] And then she wrote, "On this basis, how many are following the Way-shower? We follow Truth only as we follow truly, meekly, patiently, spiritually, blessing saint and sinner with the leaven of divine Love which woman has put into Christendom and medicine."[6] For Mrs. Eddy, this "leaven of divine Love" was Christian healing. She had written as much to the First Reader of The Mother Church: "Is not healing the sick the highest and best thing done in the field? Yes, it is: our great Master made it thus."[7] And to a Christian Science lecturer she wrote:

> Now I name a need that is above all others to ensure the perpetuity of the present success of Christian Science and its continued advancement, namely a higher and more practical *healing*. A definite immediate cure is the demonstration of what you promulgate in theory, and theory as to religion or philosophy without practice is worse than nothing, for it disappoints the seeker of it and destroys the evidence of its truth, making the situation more hopeless, than even ignorance.[8]

Mrs. Eddy did not limit healing to praying for sick men and women alone. In May 1906, a Christian Scientist in the Philippines wrote to her about treating animals and received the following reply:

> ... heal the animals as well as mankind. When I [was] in practice I healed them and found them responsive to Truth in every instance. God gave man "dominion over the beasts," and we have no authority for supposing that He ever recalled that gift or took away from man his rightful spiritual heritage.[9]

Three days after sending that letter, Mrs. Eddy wrote to the Board of Directors of The Mother Church regarding the need to pray about destructive weather conditions:

PHOTO: D W BUTTERFIELD

The Mother Church and Extension in 1910

... consider this my proposition—that you require some of the best C[hristian] Scientists in Boston and vicinity to pray once each day that no thought of earthquake, tornado, or destructive lightning enter thought to harm it, but that He who reigns in the heavens and watches over the earth saves from all harm.[10]

A year and a half later, on September 24, 1907, Mrs. Eddy wrote in her notebook that one time when she prayed, "Terrific clouds all over the sky changed instantaneously by me, and a gentle rain and *rainbow* appeared."[11]

Mrs. Eddy's primary tool for teaching others to heal was

her textbook, *Science and Health*. Since the early 1870s when she began writing *Science and Health*, Mrs. Eddy had been continually at work on making it clearer for readers to understand. Six major revisions had been the result of her efforts, the last one occurring in 1902. In October 1906, she wrote to a helper: "It becomes necessary to publish a new edition of S&H because of the *over worne* [printing] plates. I have given much thought day and night to revise this book so as to make its meaning clearer to the reader who knows not Christian Science."[12] For the next eight months she devoted herself to this task, and when she was finished, she added this statement to the book's Preface: "Until June 10, 1907, [the author] had never read this book throughout consecutively in order to elucidate her idealism."[13] Certainly, Mrs. Eddy had read through her book before, but this was the first time she had done so solely for this purpose.

Perhaps the most prolific healer over the years has been *Science and Health*, Mrs. Eddy's textbook of Christian healing. She felt this last minor revision was necessary to support its healing purpose. *Science and Health* had been the outcome of God's revelation of His nature and laws to Mrs. Eddy. Over the years, the book has proved its divine origin in its ability to heal those "honest seekers for Truth"[14] who read it. In November 1907, Mrs. Eddy had read a newspaper interview with the founder of the Salvation Army, General William Booth. The article reported that his health had failed. This caused Mrs. Eddy to write to a Christian Scientist in England, instructing him "to find a way" to present her book to the General, adding that "now is the time to heal this man of faith."[15]

In the middle of her work of revising *Science and Health*

came one of the most severe challenges Mrs. Eddy ever faced. What began as sensational, competitive journalism between *McClure's Magazine* and the *New York World*, a major newspaper, culminated in a legal suit brought in her name by her "Next Friends" against certain members of her household and officers of her Church. These "friends" were her son George, one of his daughters, a nephew and a cousin of Mrs. Eddy's, along with her estranged adopted son, Dr. Foster-Eddy. As "Next Friends"

PHOTO: CALVIN FRYE, © TMBEC

Mrs. Eddy in her study at Pleasant View

they claimed she was mentally incompetent and being taken advantage of by those around her.

Mrs. Eddy's metaphysical approach to this suit can be seen in the directions given to someone she had asked to pray about this case: "She wanted the belief of 'lawsuit' handled with absolute metaphysics. I was not to outline what the verdict would be but to know that Truth would prevail and that divine Mind would direct the verdict—which it certainly did."[16] After Mrs. Eddy was interviewed by a court-appointed group of "Masters,"[17] the suit was dismissed.

An especially interesting sidelight of this experience was Mrs. Eddy's healing of a newspaper reporter who had throat cancer and could no longer talk. This reporter, who had come seeking scandal, left completely healed. In his later years, he turned to Christian Science and felt "he owed a debt of gratitude to Mrs. Eddy for his healing . . . ."[18]

During the same month in which the "Next Friends" suit ended, Mrs. Eddy invited the Countess of Dunmore, a Christian Scientist from England who was in America with her two daughters at the time, to visit her. One of the daughters, Lady Victoria Murray, later recounted:

> My last visit to Pleasant View was in [October]
> 1907 with my mother and sister after the passing on
> of my father. . . . Nothing could exceed the kindness
> and sympathy shown to us at that time, especially to
> my mother who was suffering severely from the sense
> of loss. Mrs. Eddy, "moved with compassion," tenderly

assuaged my mother's grief, lifting her to a higher recognition of Life[. T]hen turning to me, she asked if I had any questions. "Yes," I replied, "I would like to know how *you* heal the sick." Leaning back in her chair she smilingly said, "I will tell you. I heal the same way today as I did when I commenced. My original way was instantaneous. The students did not understand any more than an English scholar could understand a foreign language without learning it. They therefore put it into their language. The argument used in healing is simply tuning-up. If your violin is in tune, it is unnecessary to tune it up. Keep your violin in tune." This last sentence was repeated quite imperatively and much emphasized.[19]

No matter what the world threw at her feet—disease, storms, insanity, death, or a legal attack that threatened everything she had worked to establish—Mary Baker Eddy treated them all as occasions for healing. To her they were opportunities to show the world that God is an ever-present Father-Mother, an unfailing Physician, and a perfect Judge.

Chapter 18

CROWNED BY LOVE
(1908–1910)

*O*N THE AFTERNOON OF JANUARY 26, 1908, Mary Baker Eddy left her home of fifteen and a half years in Concord, New Hampshire, and moved to Chestnut Hill, a suburb of Boston, Massachusetts. That morning Mrs. Eddy had turned to her Bible, as was her daily custom, and it opened to I Corinthians, chapter 9. After reading verses 10 through 14 to her household, she gave what John Lathrop described as a "grand talk" on "healing the sick [being] the only test of a Christian Scientist."[1] When Mr. Lathrop left Mrs. Eddy's service a month later, she told him, "Give all your time to the healing. *Perfect* yourself in this."[2]

Nothing was more important to Mrs. Eddy than Christian Scientists' devotion to the practice of Christian healing. To encourage and support this devotion of thought and action was the underlying purpose of her efforts to establish the Cause of Christian Science, which is to save the world from sin and sickness. Earlier in January, a letter to Mrs. Eddy from another former household worker had appeared in the *Christian Science*

Sentinel. It began, "*My Beloved Teacher*:—Just a word to express my love and deep sense of gratitude to you for all you have done and are doing for mankind."[3] Over the previous forty-two years, Mrs. Eddy had devoted her life to sharing with her fellowman the revelation she had received from God. Recalling the initial revelation in *Science and Health*, she said:

> In the year 1866, I discovered the Christ Science
> or divine laws of Life, Truth, and Love, and named my
> discovery Christian Science. God had been graciously
> preparing me during many years for the reception of this
> final revelation of the absolute divine Principle of scien-
> tific mental healing.[4]

And further on in her textbook, Mrs. Eddy wrote,

> God selects for the highest service one who has
> grown into such a fitness for it as renders any abuse
> of the mission an impossibility. The All-wise does not
> bestow His highest trusts upon the unworthy. When He
> commissions a messenger, it is one who is spiritually near
> Himself.[5]

Mrs. Eddy wrote *Science and Health* on the basis of the "final revelation" and on her own life experience in the healing practice. Using this book and the Bible as her only textbooks, she personally taught Christian Science to several thousand students. She went on to serve as Pastor of the first Church of Christ (Scientist), which she established with the help of her students; founded the Massachusetts Metaphysical College, serving as its

President and Teacher; was the first Publisher and Editor of *The Christian Science Journal*; and reorganized her original church into The Mother Church, The First Church of Christ, Scientist, in Boston, Massachusetts, creating for it a government founded on divinely inspired rules and By-Laws. All this was done in order to give to mankind an understanding of God that enables one to heal the ills of the world through prayer based on the laws of God.

It was natural for Mrs. Eddy to expect that any situation which suggested a denial of God's ever-present goodness could be healed through Christianly scientific prayer, so she applied it constantly, even to the minor annoyances of the day. After Mrs. Eddy moved to her new home in Massachusetts, she found an occasion for healing there on her property. One of her secretaries later recounted the incident:

> [Mrs. Eddy] noticed that one of the trees on her place did not appear to thrive, but was drooping and showing every evidence of dying. She learned that the superintendent of her grounds proposed to cut the tree down and remove it. Immediately she sent word to him to do nothing of the kind, but to do what he could for the tree in his way, while she took the question up according to Christian Science. In a remarkably short time the tree began to grow and thrive, and today [in 1926] it occupies a place on her grounds.[6]

For Mrs. Eddy, no problem was too small or too big for Christian Science healing. When she took up residence in

Chestnut Hill, her thought turned more than ever to reaching the world with this practical, healing truth. In the April 11, 1908, *Sentinel* she issued a statement titled "War," which began, "For many years I have prayed daily that there be no more war. . . ." Her message concludes by pointing out the need for arbitrating disagreements between nations and the necessity for arming navies to prevent war and preserve peace.[7] A copy of this *Sentinel* was sent to the President of the United States, Theodore Roosevelt, by a Christian Scientist. He responded with a personal note which said, "That is interesting and important. I wish that all other religious leaders showed as much good sense."[8]

A few weeks after this, the editor of the *Minneapolis Daily News* requested a statement on what Christian Science could do for universal fellowship. Mrs. Eddy replied:

> Christian Science can and does produce universal fellowship as a sequence of divine Love. It explains Love, it lives Love, it demonstrates Love. The human material so-called senses do not perceive this fact until they are controlled by divine Love, hence the Scripture: "Be still and know that I am God."[9]

Impelled by divine Love, Mrs. Eddy was led at this time to establish a daily newspaper. As early as 1878, she had publicly declared an interest in having a newspaper at her disposal "to right the wrongs and answer the untruths."[10] This desire was part of her motive for starting the *Journal* in 1883, the weekly *Sentinel* in 1898, and the German *Der Herold der Christian Science* in 1903. Then, in the summer of 1908, she called on the Board of

THE WHITE HOUSE
WASHINGTON

From Chestnut Hill Files.

9772

Personal.

April 20, 1908.

My dear Mr. Davis:

I have your letter of the 18th instant, with en-
closure.   That is interesting and important.   I wish
that all other religious leaders showed as much
good sense.

With regard, believe me,

Sincerely yours,

Theodore Roosevelt

Mr. Hayne Davis,
    381 Central Park West,
    New York, N.Y.

Hayne Davis sent President Roosevelt
the Sentinel for April 11, 1908, which
contained Mrs. Eddy's stand on
Armament and Arbitration. This is
President Roosevelt's reply.
2195

The letter from Theodore Roosevelt commenting on Mrs. Eddy's statement about war that had been published in the *Christian Science Sentinel*.

Directors of The Mother Church and the Board of Trustees of The Christian Science Publishing Society to start *The Christian Science Monitor.*

Mrs. Eddy wanted a newspaper for the home, but she expected it to have a healing effect on the world. She said it is "to spread undivided the Science that operates unspent."[11] In this she was paraphrasing a line from Alexander Pope's 1733 poem "An Essay on Man," which speaks of the "MIND of ALL" that "spreads undivided, operates unspent."[12] For Mrs. Eddy, this "MIND" was nothing less than the one omnipotent God, who is divine Love meeting all mankind's needs. And "a newspaper edited and published by the Christian Scientists"[13] could be a healing manifestation of that divine Mind. On the morning of November 25, 1908, the day the *Monitor's* first issue was published, Mrs. Eddy opened her Bible to Song of Solomon 8:6, 7. These verses speak of the strength and power of love to withstand the forces of the material world.

It was extremely important to Mrs. Eddy that Christian Scientists express divine Love in *practical* ways. For the Communion service of The Mother Church on June 14, 1908, she instructed that the sermon be on the subject of "Works," especially as illustrated in John 15:2: "Every branch in me that beareth not fruit he taketh away: and every branch that beareth fruit, he purgeth it, that it may bring forth more fruit."[14] Two days before this service was held, Mrs. Eddy wrote:

> Faith without works is the most subtle lie apparent.
> It satisfies the student with a lie—it gives them peace
> in error, and they never can be Christian Scientists

without that faith which is known and proved by works.
Words are often impositions, and faith without works
is dead and plucked up by the roots; it is not faith but
is a deceiving lie, lulling the conscience and preventing
demonstration.[15]

Though Mrs. Eddy expected Christian Scientists to heal quickly and permanently, she recognized that if, on occasion, healing was not immediate, a patient might require practical care while the metaphysical treatment continued until the healing was accomplished. Therefore, on November 16, 1908, Mrs. Eddy requested the Christian Science Board of Directors to adopt this new Church By-Law, which established the requirements of a Christian Science nurse: "A member of The Mother Church who represents himself or herself as a Christian Science nurse shall be one who has a demonstrable knowledge of Christian Science practice, who thoroughly understands the practical wisdom necessary in a sick room, and who can take proper care of the sick."[16]

While such nurses may be needed in cases where healing is not immediate, this does not mean that Mrs. Eddy expected her students to be less than radical in their reliance on God for healing. In July 1909, she wrote to Alfred Farlow, who was serving as the Church's Manager of Committees on Publication and had had a minor accident: "If you use a crutch you are not depending on Christian Science. Choose ye this day whom you will serve.... Now take God's side. You *can walk* without a crutch, do *it*."[17] The next day, Mr. Farlow replied, "I have not used the crutch during the time since I received your first letter. This morning I am wonderfully improved and will spend the day at home. I can now see how the crutch has hindered me. I have neglected working for myself because I could get around on the crutch and have the time for other work."[18] Mrs. Eddy had her secretary respond, "Mrs. Eddy says that what she tells a student to do absolutely, she expects them to do it, but not before they can do it *scientifically* and then it can't hurt them, and they cannot suffer from it."[19]

Mrs. Eddy expected Christian Scientists, when confronted with physical ailments, to pray—relying solely on God to "resolve things into thoughts, and exchange the objects of sense for the ideas of Soul."[20] This was certainly how she worked for herself. Less than a week after her correspondence with Mr. Farlow, Mrs. Eddy told one of her secretaries: "Our thought must be scientific in all things, even the littlest of any. One time my hair was coming out in handfuls, and I could not stop it until I thought God will protect,—'the very hairs of your head are numbered,'—then it stopped."[21]

From time to time Mrs. Eddy found it necessary to call on different members of her household to work for her metaphysically. On Christmas Eve 1909, she gave George Kinter, one of her secretaries, instructions for such work:

> A lie is powerless, it has no effect whatever. A lie does not harm Mrs. Eddy, she does not feel it. It has no power; it has no effect; it is nothing whatever.
>
> The Truth is power, is Life; it has in itself all power, all good, all happiness, all blessing. The truth is that Mrs. Eddy is not sick; she is not old, nor weak, nor feeble. She

is strong, she is in perfect health, and it does her good to walk and to go over rough roads. She is stronger for it; she is healthier for it; she is better for it; better for overcoming a lie, and knowing the truth, and the truth does make her free. It makes her healthy and happy. It takes away all fear and gives her peace, health, and life everlasting.[22]

One of the things that most concerned Mrs. Eddy was the danger to Christian Scientists of becoming complacent. In August 1909 she wrote Alfred Farlow to "stir the dry bones all over the field, to more words, actions, and demonstrations in Christian Science. I am weary waiting for the impulse of Christian Science to become more active all over our field. Get somebody—and more than one—to ring out the first arousal. 'Awake thou that sleepest, and arise from the dead, and Christ shall give thee light.'"[23] Two days after sending this letter, she completed her work on the manuscript of *The First Church of Christ, Scientist, and Miscellany*. It was a collection of articles, notices, and letters that had appeared in print since the 1897 publication of her first compilation of similar pieces in *Miscellaneous Writings 1883–1896*.

Six months before Mrs. Eddy moved from Concord, New Hampshire, Arthur Brisbane, a New York journalist, interviewed her. He later recounted to friends:

> . . . it was my privilege to discover one of the keenest intellects I had ever encountered and the most gentle and sweet woman I had ever met. Her very presence was restful to me.

During our conversation I mentioned this, telling her how very tired I was. She then asked me if I would like to have a Christian Science treatment and I told her I would. All I can say is that it was a most unbelievably beautiful experience ... that treatment proved to me the great need in the world today for Christian Science.[24]

Without the proof of healing, there is no Christian Science. Such healing does not come from mere belief or blind faith in God, but is based on a scientific understanding of God as divine Principle, Love. Healing results from leaning on God alone through intelligent prayer, from denying that which is ungodlike and affirming the perfection, omnipotence, and omnipresence of the one divine Principle, Love, and man as this One's perfect spiritual manifestation: this is healing as the outcome of divine law scientifically understood and prayerfully realized. Mrs. Eddy's emphasis on "scientific" healing, as opposed to "faith" healing, is clear in a short article she wrote in September 1910:

PRINCIPLE AND PRACTICE

The nature and position of mortal mind are the opposite of immortal Mind. The so-called mortal mind is belief and not understanding. Christian Science requires understanding instead of belief; it is based on a fixed eternal and divine Principle wholly apart from mortal conjecture, and it must be understood, otherwise it cannot be correctly accepted and demonstrated.

The inclination of mortal mind is to receive Christian Science through a belief instead of the understanding, and this inclination prevails like an epidemic on the body; it inflames mortal mind and weakens the intellect, but this so-called mortal mind is wholly ignorant of this fact, and so cherishes its mere faith in Christian Science.

The sick, like drowning men, catch at whatever drifts toward them. The sick are told by a faith-Scientist, "I can heal you, for God is all, and you are well, since God creates neither sin, sickness, nor death." Such statements result either in the sick being healed by their faith in what you tell them—which heals only as a drug would heal, through belief—or in no effect whatever. If the faith healer succeeds in *securing* (kindling) the belief of the patient in his own recovery, the practitioner will have performed a faith cure which he mistakenly pronounces Christian Science.

In this very manner some students of Christian Science have accepted, through faith, a divine Principle, God, as their Savior, but they have not understood this Principle sufficiently well to fulfill the Scriptural command, "Go ye into all the world, and preach the gospel." "Heal the sick." It is the healer's understanding of the operation of the divine Principle, and his application thereof, which heals the sick, just as it is one's understanding of the principle of mathematics which enables him to demonstrate its rules.

Christian Science is not a faith cure, and unless human faith be distinguished from scientific healing, Christian Science will again be lost from the practice

of religion as it was soon after the period of our great
Master's scientific teaching and practice.

Preaching without practice of the divine Principle
of man's being has not, in nineteen hundred years,
resulted in demonstrating this Principle. Preaching
without the truthful and consistent practice of your statements will destroy the success of Christian Science.[25]

That "truthful and consistent practice" must extend far
beyond oneself. The crown of divine Love comes in unselfed
living for others. Mrs. Eddy wrote to a student a number of
years earlier: ". . . you never can be a practical Christian Scientist
without healing the sick and sinner besides yourself. It is too
selfish for us to be working for ourselves and not others as well.
God does not bless it."[26]

Feeling God's blessing was a vital element for those healed
by Mrs. Eddy. Miss Elsie Bergquist, a Christian Scientist, left the
following account of an incident related by her father, who was
not a student of Christian Science at the time:

During the year 1909 he was working on a
building in Chestnut Hill, not far from Mrs. Eddy's
home. One day, feeling very tired, he left work early
and decided to go to see the architecture of Mrs. Eddy's
home. As he approached, Mrs. Eddy's carriage came out
of the drive way. She smiled upon him, and he felt so
uplifted that he could have run along side of the carriage
for miles. Of course he did not do this, but he forgot to
look at the architecture of the house and started to walk.

He walked all the way to Boston [more than 5 miles]
without fatigue and did not feel tired again for a week.
My father told the members of his church about the
spiritual uplift that he received from Mrs. Eddy, how he
had felt that the Spirit of the Lord had descended upon
him. . . .[27]

This account and the following more dramatic incident
prove that Mrs. Eddy's ability to heal never diminished. In the
summer of 1910, the household staff told visitors to Chestnut
Hill about a healing that had occurred two days before: "A servant
fell on a meat-hook and tore her cheek open from chin to eye.
It seemed so serious they thought it best to tell our Leader. They
[did] so, and instantly, every trace of it disappeared—just as if it
had never happened. . . ."[28]

Untiring in her work for mankind in the name of Christian
Science, Mrs. Eddy, through her prayer and private correspondence, remained active in guiding the Cause up to the time of her
passing on December 3, 1910. Calvin Frye, Laura Sargent, Adam
Dickey, Irving Tomlinson, and William and Ella Rathvon were
with Mrs. Eddy on that Saturday evening.[29] The last thing she
said to them was "I have all in divine Love, that is all I need."[30]

Earlier in the year, Mrs. Eddy had written these words of
truth and comfort to one of her students who had just lost her
husband:

Your dear husband has not passed away from you
in spirit; he never died, only to your sense; he lives and
loves and is immortal. Let this comfort you dear one,

and you will find rest in banishing the sense of death, in cherishing the sense of life and not death. Your dear husband is as truly living to-day as he ever lived, and you can find rest and peace in this true sense of Life.

Mind not matter is our Life, and we can rejoice in knowing that Mind never dies. Sin and a false sense of life is all that dies. Immortality and blessedness never die, hence we should banish this false sense, it is not real.[31]

There was never a more loving or practical Christian Scientist than Mary Baker Eddy. Her lifetime of healing testifies to this. The Discoverer and Founder of Christian Science continues to lead mankind to the comfort of divine Science through the healing activities of her Church, and, most of all, through her writings, chief of which is *Science and Health with Key to the Scriptures*. To understand Mrs. Eddy in her true light, however, depends on gaining a practical understanding of the divine revelation in the Bible and her writings to such a degree that one can heal as she did.

Part Two

MORE HEALING WORKS
OF
MARY BAKER EDDY

More Healing Works
of
Mary Baker Eddy

URNING TO GOD IN HEALING prayer with compassion for all was as natural to Mary Baker Eddy as a flower's turning to the light. There are numerous accounts of Mrs. Eddy's healing works, in addition to those already related, in the collections of The Mary Baker Eddy Library. Some are in her letters to others, some are in her words as recorded by those who heard her speak, others come from relatives of those healed or from those healed themselves.

Although it has not been possible to verify some of the healings, all of them are consistent with her character and work, and the accounts are from reliable sources. Mrs. Eddy wrote in the twentieth edition of *Science and Health*: "I never believed in taking certificates or presenting testimonials of cures; and usually, when healing, have said to the individual, 'Go, tell no man.' I have never made a specialty of healing, but labored, in every way that God directed, to introduce metaphysical treatment. I offer a few testimonials, simply to support my statements about Christian Science" (p. 199).

The accounts of healing in this section—quite a few not published before—are quoted directly from the original documents. Sometimes, for fuller details, there are accounts of the same healing from more than one writer. Minor corrections to spelling and grammar have been made for clarity. When known, dates of healings have been included.

Growth on girl's neck healed (1865)

When about thirteen years old a growth developed in my neck. When I first noticed it, it was about the size of a pea, but it grew very rapidly until it was about the size of a walnut, and very hard. At that time our physician was called and he thought it best to lance it—which was done. Shortly after that it began to gather pus and it continued to do so until healed. During that time or condition, the cords on one side of my neck became drawn so that I could not turn my head. At that [time] Mrs. Eddy was in Portland, Maine, staying at a Mrs. Baker's. A niece of Mrs. Baker's lived in the same town I did. She learned of some of the healings by Mrs. Eddy, and she asked my mother if she might tell Mrs. Eddy of my case and ask her to treat me. She told Mrs. Eddy we were not able to pay for treatments, but that made no difference; the treatments were given. The only request Mrs. Eddy made was that I did not take medicine, which was agreed to. In less than three weeks I was healed. The only evidence is a small scar. I was about fifteen when the healing took place. (Mrs. Grace M. Chaffin letter, February 9, 1931)

Niece healed of enteritis (1867)
(Elizabeth P. Baker, Mrs. Eddy's stepmother)

Miss Ellen C. Pilsbury, of Sanbornton Bridge, now Tilton, N.H., after typhoid fever, was suffering from what her physicians called enteritis of the severest form. Her case was given up by her medical physician, and she was lying at the point of death, when Mrs. Glover (afterwards Mrs. Eddy) visited her. In a few moments after she entered the room and stood by her bedside, [Ellen] recognized her aunt, and said, "I am glad to see you, aunty." In about ten minutes more, Mrs. Glover told her to "rise from her bed and walk." She rose and walked seven times across her room, then sat down in a chair. For two weeks before this, we had not entered her room without stepping lightly. Her bowels were so tender, she felt the jar, and it increased her sufferings. She could only be moved on a sheet from bed to bed. When she walked across the room at Mrs. Glover's bidding, she told her to stamp her foot strongly upon the floor, and she did so without suffering from it. The next day she was dressed, and went down to the table; and the fourth day went a journey of about a hundred miles in the [train] cars. (*Science and Health*, third edition, pp. 152–153)

(Martha Rand Baker, Mrs. Eddy's sister-in-law, to Addie Towns Arnold)

I have never had an opportunity to tell this story, for no one was interested in Christian Science here, and as a son's wife, I have not wanted to take sides either way. When we found Ellen did not have a chance to live, we wrote Mary about it, and she came to us at once. We went to Ellen's room, and Mary sat beside her bed. Ellen had not known any of us for several days, but in a short time she looked up and said, "I am glad to see you, Auntie." Mary soon told her to rise and walk. We were horrified at this, and stood spell-bound. She rose, however, and walked seven times across her room, and then sat down. The next day she was dressed, and went down to the table. On the fourth day Mary took her home to [Taunton] with her. (Arnold reminiscences)

Internal tumor healed (1867–1874)
(Mrs. Eddy)

A lady having an internal tumor, and greatly fearing a surgical operation, called on us. We conducted her case according to the [S]cience here stated, never touched her person, or used a drug, or an instrument; and the tumor was wholly removed within one or two days. We refer to this case to prove the [divine] Principle. (*Science and Health*, first edition, p. 117)

Man yellow with disease healed (1867–1874)
(Mrs. Eddy to Lida Fitzpatrick)

I used to heal with a word. I have seen a man yellow because of disease, and the next moment I looked at him and his color was right; [he] was healed.

I knew no more how it was done than a baby; only it was done every time. I never failed, almost always in one treatment, never more than three. Now God is showing me how, and I am showing you. (Fitzpatrick reminiscences)

Friend healed of invalidism caused by hip trouble (1868)
(Mrs. Eddy in a letter to Sarah Bagley)

I had at Lynn a sweet visit, stopped at Mr. Winslow's. When I went there, Mrs. Winslow was very lame and sick, had not walked up stairs naturally for years and given up trying to go out at all. I stopped two days, and when I came away she walked to the Depot with me almost a mile. They were one and all urgent for me to stay there this winter, but I am not of their opinion. I don't want society, and what's more I won't have it; I detest the hollow heartedness of aristocracy, I loathe the hypocrisy of available friendship or in common parlance "such as pays." Mr. W. is a father to me; he attended to all my business, went through from one Depot to the other with me and set me right for here. (L08306)

. . . Mrs. Winslow had been for sixteen years in an invalid chair, and Mrs. Patterson [as Mrs. Eddy was then known], who occasionally spent an afternoon with her, desired to heal her.

"If you make Abbie walk," said Charles Winslow, "I will not only believe your theory, but I will reward you liberally. I think I would give a thousand dollars to see her able to walk."

"The demonstration of the principle is enough reward," said Mrs. Patterson. "I know she can walk. You go to business and leave us alone together."

"But I want to see you perform your cure, Mary," said Charles Winslow, half mirthfully. "Indeed, I won't interfere."

"You want to see me perform a cure," cried Mary Baker, with a flash of her clear eyes. "But I am not going to do anything. Why don't you understand that God will do the work if Mrs. Winslow will let Him? Leave off making light of what is a serious matter. Your wife will walk."

And Mrs. Winslow did walk, walked along the ocean beach with Mary Baker and around her own garden in the beautiful autumn of that year. She who had not taken a step for sixteen years arose and walked, not once but many times. (Sibyl Wilbur, *The Life of Mary Baker Eddy*, pp. 143–144)

A lesson in healing (1868–1870)
(Mrs. Eddy to her 1898 Normal class)

We are all learning together, and I must tell you of some of the funny things I used to do when I first saw that I had this wonderful power. . . .

My family and the friends around me saw what was done and knew that if they sent for me they would be well, but I could not make them acknowledge it. I could not make them admit what had done the healing work. One day I said, "Oh, I *must* make them acknowledge it—I must make them see that God does this." Sometimes, as soon as they sent for me they would be healed, before I could get there, and then they would not *know* that it was God who had done it. So one day, when I was called to see a [child], I was so anxious to have [people] see the power of Truth and acknowledge it, that I said to myself, "He *must* not get well until I get there." Of course that was not right, for I knew I must leave it all to God, and so, because pride had come in and

I had lost my humility, I did not heal the patient. Then I saw my rebuke, and when I reached home, I threw myself on the floor, put my head in my hands, and prayed that I might not be for one moment touched with the thought that I was anything or did anything, . . . this was God's work and I reflected Him. Then the child was healed. (Sue Harper Mims reminiscences; the final sentence is from the Mims account published in *We Knew Mary Baker Eddy*, p. 133)

She told of being called to treat a child in the early days of her work, and how happy she was to be definitely asked to take this case, so she could try her power. She gave the treatment and was confident that she had done good work, but later a member of the child's family came to say it was no better. At this Mrs. Eddy wept and prayed to be shown what had hindered the healing. It came to her with great clearness that the work was God's and she had been trying to do it in her strength and as her work. She bowed her face to the floor and gave all to God. Shortly after, she heard the child was entirely well. (Emma Shipman reminiscences)

Cataract healed (1868–1870)
(Mrs. Eddy to Irving Tomlinson)

I had a patient once who had been blind from her birth. In one eye she was so blind that you might hold a lighted candle before it, and she would not know it was there. Under my treatment I saw the cataract pass off as a cloud passes off from the face of the sun. The difficulty was with the left eye, and I recall that the cataract seemed to move from left to right until it had entirely disappeared.

Then, strange as it may appear, no sooner had this patient regained her sight than she exclaimed, "I hate you. I hate you. I could sit up nights to hate you."

I have always observed that there is a certain class of people so constituted in their moral nature that the help I give to them and the sacrifices I make for them [are] requited by their bitter hatred of me. I have often resolved not to do for this class of people, but my love to bless others has caused me to break my resolution. But I pray God to be henceforth and forever delivered from such as these. (A11440)

A child was brought to her with a cataract on each eye, blind. Mrs. Eddy began to talk to her of God, Truth and Love, when the child, animated by error, stamped her foot and said, "I hate you. I hate you. I could sit up all night to hate you!" Mrs. Eddy replied, "My darling, I love you. I love you, why I could sit up all night to love you!" and at once the cataracts fell out and the child saw. (Edward E. Norwood reminiscences)

[This healing, told here by two different writers, has similarities to the healing of cataracts for twelve-year-old Miss Eaton in Anna B. White Baker's entry in the Biographical Glossary.]

Little lame boy healed (1868–1888)

While [I was] living with Mrs. Eddy at Pleasant View, she

told many wonderful things, proving more and more the power of her healing work through Christian Science.

… She told us of the case of a child who was born helpless. While out walking one day, Mrs. Eddy observed a small boy drawing another and younger child in a little cart. She inquired of the older boy what was the matter with the little fellow. He replied: "He is my brother and he has never walked." Mrs. Eddy looked into the sweet face and beautiful blue eyes of the little boy lying flat on his back in the cart, his legs dangling over the edge, limp and helpless. In relating the incident, she said the sense of the perfect child of God was so clear to her that the boy slid out of the cart and went running down the street, saying: "See me yun [run]!" He reached his home, which was nearby, crying out: "Mamma, see me yun! See me yun!" (Julia E. Prescott reminiscences)

Horticultural demonstrations (1869–1879)

(Demonstrations such as the one involving a dying tree in Chestnut Hill [page 268] were not uncommon in Mrs. Eddy's experience. In the early years after her discovery, she would prove her Science on plants and trees.)

While staying with the Wentworths in Stoughton, Massachusetts, (September 1868 to March 1870), Mrs. Eddy (then Glover) brought out a blossom on an apple tree in winter:

At a social gathering of Boston Christian Scientists, Mrs. Eddy "narrated some incidents about the unusual and seemingly supernatural (but really natural) growth of apple blossoms in icy winter, and of fresh shoots from dry stems in summer, – through the power Mind." (*The Christian Science Journal*, July 1886, p. 94)

"I remember that while Mrs. Glover was with us a blossom appeared on a fruit tree on my father's premises out of season." (Charles O. Wentworth reminiscence file, February 18, 1907)

During the early 1870s when Mrs. Eddy constantly had to move, she asked a woman if she might have a room in her house. The woman, who had evidently heard ill rumors of her, agreed with one condition.

... [She] pointed to some dried stems in flower pots on her steps and said, "If you can make those plants live you can come in."

Mrs. [Glover] thanked her and came into the house. There was a closet off the room that Mrs. [Glover] took where there was neither light nor outside air. Mrs. [Glover] told the woman to put the crocks in the closet and to shut the door. A few days later Mrs. [Glover] called the woman to come and take out her crocks and the plants were all green and living. (Julia Michael Johnston reminiscences)

One of Mrs. Eddy's neighbors was raising house plants, but they were not hardy and would not bloom. She remarked to Mrs. Eddy one day that she did not know what was the matter with her plants; she gave them plenty of sun and water and the best of care, but they looked so sickly and would not bloom. Mrs. Eddy told her to send them all over to her house, which was done, and Mrs. Eddy ordered them put in the basement in a dark corner. They had neither sun nor water and no care but in a short time were returned to their owner sturdy and blooming beautifully. (Lottie Clark's notes in Julia Bartlett's reminiscence file)

Also during the 1870s, Mrs. Eddy "was called to help a family where several members were very ill and she had to remain for some days. Before going to them, she left a pot containing a plant [an oxalis] with a beautiful flower on the window-sill of her sitting room. On returning home, when she went into the room, there was the plant all withered, and the earth cracked; the sun had been pouring in through the glass of the closed window and had dried up the earth. A friend who was with her saw it. She [Mrs. Eddy] then went to the next room to open windows, and in a short time she heard the friend exclaim; when she went to see the reason for this exclamation, she found the plant had revived without being watered, and the leaves and flower were just as beautiful as when she left them." (EF136)

Severely crippled man healed (1870)
(Mrs. Eddy to Lida Fitzpatrick)

I was at a house [Mrs. Charles Slade's] and the woman came running into the room as white as ashes, and said a cripple was at the door and he looked so dreadful she slammed the door in his face. I went to the window, and there was—well it was too dreadful to describe; his feet did not touch the earth at all; he walked with crutches. I gave him through the window all I had in my pocket—a dollar bill—and he took it in his teeth. He went to the next house and frightened the woman there, but she did not slam the door in his face. He asked her to let him lie down a few minutes; she let him go into a bedroom and lie down. He fell sound asleep, and when he wakened up was perfectly well. Sometime afterward, the woman who was kind to him was in a store, and this man came rushing up to her and said, "Yes, you are the one, but where is the other woman?" Then he told her he was the one who was healed by me. The papers are writing up my history; the history of my ancestry; writing lies. My history is a holy one. (Fitzpatrick reminiscences)

Later, on being asked by her students as to how she healed him, Mrs. Eddy simply said, "When I looked on that man, my heart gushed with unspeakable pity and prayer." (Judge Septimus J. Hanna, *The Granite Monthly*, October 1896)

Girl's inability to speak healed (1870–1872)
(William Preble's account to Irving Tomlinson of his mother's healing)

At the time of her cure by Mrs. Eddy, she had been afflicted with a trouble which for long periods made her dumb. She had been treated by many physicians but to no avail, when a friend proposed that she see Mrs. Eddy. Mr. Preble said that at that time Mrs. Eddy was considered a strange woman, but so desperate was his mother's condition that she decided to seek her help. In those days Mrs. Eddy was working in connection with one of her students [Richard Kennedy]. The case was slow in yielding, and each day when Fannie returned from seeing Mrs. Eddy, the first words of her mother were: "Fannie, can you speak?" Fannie would sadly shake her head in the negative. The mother and daughter were in despair, but decided to continue visits to the first Christian Science practitioner. On the daughter's return, the mother again greeted her with the old question, "Fannie, can you speak?" Instantly the answer came back, "Yes, I can." Then she told the story which is as clear to [her] now, Mr. Preble said, as on the glad day when her speech was first restored. Mrs. Preble's words, as her son related them to the writer, were in substance:

"When Mrs. Eddy saw that I still could not speak, she asked me to come with her. She took me into another room, then into a hall, up a flight of stairs, and down a long hall. Mrs. Eddy then turned suddenly and said with authority, 'In the name of God, speak!' Instantly, I spoke my first word, saying, 'Oh.'"

Mrs. Preble found herself fully healed and for more than sixty-five years has been free from her former affliction. (Tomlinson reminiscences)

Dead child restored (1870–1872)
(Mrs. Eddy to Henry Robinson)

One little child was put into my hands. I did not come soon enough. Utterly helpless, utterly prostrated, and the doctors said he was gone. The little arms hung down, and it looked limp as a corpse, no appearance of life. I could not feel the pulse. The mother was crying and said, "He is dead; you have come too late."

I said, "Go out a little while." She did and that little creature rose right up, yawned and rubbed his eyes. I set him down. He walked to the door and his mother took him. (Historical File: Henry Robinson, Longyear Museum)

Mrs. Eddy told me she was called to treat a child. When she went in, the mother was holding it and thought it had passed on. Mrs. Eddy said, "Let me take the babe." She did and the mother went into the next room. In about ten minutes she put the child down and it walked toward the door. Mrs. Eddy opened the door, and when the mother saw the child walking (it had never walked before), she screamed and the babe sat down, and Mrs. Eddy said, "I saw I had another patient on my hands." (Victoria H. Sargent reminiscences)

Woman in agony, given up by the doctors, healed (1870–1872)
(Mrs. Eddy to Irving C. Tomlinson)

A student in Lynn had a patient who to every appearance was [a] very serious case. Before coming to Christian Science, a counsel [sic] of physicians had pronounced the case hopeless; then my student was appealed to. He [had] treated the patient for some days when I was called in. I found the sick one in great agony. The face was purple and the head was rolling from side to side. In fifteen minutes after my arrival, the pain had departed. The face had assumed a normal color, and the patient was at ease. When a member of the household who had gone out on an errand for the invalid returned, he found her up and about her work. (A11423)

Chronic invalid healed (1870–1874)
(Jenny Coffin to Mrs. Eddy)

Your wonderful [S]cience is proved to me. I was a helpless sufferer six long years, confined to my bed, unable to sit up one hour in the long, long twenty-four. All I know of my cure is this: the day you received my letter I felt a change pass over me. I sat up the whole afternoon, went to the table with my family at supper, and have been growing better every day since; I call myself well. (*Science and Health*, first edition, p. 352)

Chronic liver complaint and convulsions healed (1870–1874)
(Mrs. Eddy)

A case of convulsions produced by indigestion came under our observation; they said she had chronic liver complaint, and was then suffering from obstruction and bilious colic. We cured her in a few minutes. She had said, "I must vomit my food or die," and immediately afterwards said, "My food is all gone, and I should like something to eat." Contending persistently against error and disease, you destroy them with Truth. (*Science and Health*, third edition, p. 203)

Solidified knee joints healed (1870–1874)
(Mrs. Eddy to Irving Tomlinson)

I was called by a brokenhearted mother to attend her young son who was afflicted with ankylosed joints. The bones of the knees appeared to be solidified and the verdict of the doctors was, "a hopeless case—the boy will never be able to walk again."

I treated the little fellow and told his mother that she need have no further fear, for her son would be able to walk and run with other children. Three days after, the boy was playing in the yard with his companions. [The physician who had condemned him to hopeless invalidism] saw him romping with his friends [and sternly] asked him what business he had to be out there and [ordered] him to go into the house, and stay there. The response from the little fellow was: "You are not my doctor. Mrs. Eddy is my doctor, and I [shan't go into the house]." Sometime later his mother brought him to me to thank me for his wonderful healing. As he walked across the floor, I noticed that he toed in with one foot, and spoke to him of it. He said: "My mamma said I should tell you about that. I have always walked that way." I told him to walk in the right way, just like the other boys. He did so at once, being healed instantaneously, and ever after walked naturally. (Irving Tomlinson, *Twelve Years with Mary Baker Eddy*, pp. 62–63; A11771)

Broken foot healed (1870–1874)
(Mrs. Eddy)

Mr. R. O. Badgely, of Cincinnati, Ohio, wrote: "My painful and swelled foot was restored at once on your receipt of my letter, and that very day I put on my boot and walked several miles." He had previously written me: "A stick of timber fell from a building on my foot, crushing the bones. Cannot you help me? I am sitting in great pain, with my foot in a bath." (*Science and Health*, twentieth edition, p. 199)

Fatal disease healed (1870–1874)
(Letter from Grace M. Clarke)

I married John H. Clarke in 1889 and went to live in the home of his parents, Mr. and Mrs. John C. Clarke, 82 Hollingsworth St., Lynn, Massachusetts.

The story of Mr. Clarke's healing was told to me by his wife (my mother-in-law). . . .

Mrs. Eddy called at the house where they were living and asked if she might see Mr. Clarke.

I asked her [my mother-in-law] if she was sure that it was Mrs. Eddy, and she replied that the woman said she was. At the time Mr. John C. Clarke had been in bed for eight months, the sickness being caused by a fall on a spike when he was a boy; this brought on a running sore, and when Mrs. Eddy called, the doctor was present. His verdict was that there was no help for Mr. Clarke as the sore had affected the bone.

Mrs. Eddy remained in the room with the patient some time. When she came out she said that he was cured and could get up at any time that he liked. He did get up the next morning with the sore healed and feeling fine, eating breakfast with his family.

As his daughter-in-law, I never knew him to be in bed with any sickness afterward, and he lived to be over eighty years of age. (Grace Clarke letter, July 29, 1955)

∽∾

(Mrs. Eddy)

We were called to visit Mr. Clarke, in Lynn, confined to his bed six months with hip disease, caused by a fall, when quite a boy, on a wooden spike. [Saw him in the afternoon for the first time.] On entering the house, we met his physician, who told us he was dying. He had just probed the ulcer on the hip, and said the bone was carious for several inches,—even showed us the probe that had the evidence of that on it. The doctor [went] out. [(Mr. Clarke's) wife stood over him weeping.] He lay with his eyes fixed and sightless, the dew of death upon his brow. We went to his beside, and in a few moments his face changed; its death pallor gave place to a natural hue, the eyelids closed gently, the breathing became natural, and he was asleep. In about ten minutes he opened his eyes and said, "I feel like a new man, my suffering is all gone." It was between three and four o'clock, P.M., this took place. We told him to rise, dress himself, and take supper with his family. [In a few hours he] did that, and the next day we saw him out in his yard. We have not seen him since, but are informed he went to work in two weeks, and that pieces of wood were discharged from the sore as it healed, that had probably remained there ever after the injury in boyhood that was done to the bone, as the surgeons termed it. Since his recovery we have been informed that his attending physician claims to have cured him, and his mother has been threatened with an insane asylum for having said, "It was none other than God and that woman that healed him." (*Science and Health*, third edition, Vol. I, pp. 154–155; the bracketed sections are primarily from the account given on p. 353 of the first edition of *Science and Health*. See pp. 192–193 in current edition.)

Assassin thwarted (1872–1879)

[Mrs. Eddy] also told of being in her room and having the impression that someone was coming to shoot her, and her first thought was to close and lock the door, but she left it open, and a man entered her room and pointed a revolver at her, and she said to him, "You cannot shoot," and his arm became as if paralyzed; his revolver dropped to the floor, and he said using an oath, "I came to kill you." At that he left the room. (James Brierly reminiscences)

My mother [Annie Rogers Michael] told me that once as Mrs. Eddy sat at her desk she felt a sense of something wrong and turned and looked behind her. A man had entered the room and closed the door behind him. In his hand was a weapon pointed at Mrs. Eddy. She said, "You cannot do this wicked thing." The man's arm fell helpless at his side and the weapon on the floor. He said, "Well, I came to do it but I can't," and he left the room. (Julia Michael Johnston reminiscences)

Little girl restored (1872–1879)

A lady residing in Reading, who had lived in Lynn, Massachusetts, for a number of years, told me that one morning while shopping on Market St., Lynn, she saw an Italian woman run out from a side street, and crying, "My little girl is dead, help me!" Almost immediately another woman came around a corner and spoke to this Italian woman, stepped into her house and healed the little child. This lady was Mary Baker Eddy. In broken

English the Italian woman began to express, in her emotional nature, her gratitude, saying, "O that lady must be a saint, she has healed my child."

Afterward I asked the lady who witnessed this healing of the child, "Did you become a Christian Scientist?" She answered, "No," and added, "My husband and I were members of a Congregational Church. Many of our friends attended that church also. Moreover, Christian Science was not popular. It was even ridiculed."

Later, however, she and her husband became Scientists. (Lewis Prescott reminiscences)

Child with fever healed (1873)
(Charles Green to Alfred Farlow)

Thirty-four years ago. Spring or early fall; drizzling rainy day. Mrs. Eddy came to my house, and wanted to know if she could rent a room. We told her that we had no rooms to rent. She said she knew that, but desired to get in that locality [Lynn], but my wife told her we had no room to rent, and then said, "You will have to excuse me, I have a sick child." Mrs. Eddy asked if she might see the child. We had quite a little chat with Mrs. Eddy, I think, before she saw the child. She went in and saw the little girl, Josephine, three and one-half or four years old. She had been very sick with brain fever. I had gone away for a few days, but was called back suddenly because she was so much worse. She rallied, and we thought was some better. Mrs. Eddy went into the room and stood at the bedside. She took the little girl's hand and spoke with her in a low voice. In about twenty minutes or half an hour she said let me dress the child. We could not understand, but let her do so. Then she said, let me take the child out. We protested on account of it being such a rainy day, but we could not resist her. We had confidence in that woman. She took the child across the street and back. Although we were afraid, the child was all right the next day. The doctor came the next morning, but could not understand it. The child came along all right. (Subject File: Alfred Farlow, Charles Green statement.)

(Mrs. Eddy, writing years later)

When at Lynn one morning I was impressed to call at the house of Mr. Green residing on Sagamore St. . . . I found the child in what is called brain fever; her physician of the regular school had given her up. I sat by her side a few moments [and] then called for her child's clothes. She was dressed & went out with me into the street. It rained; we walked a few blocks and returned to the house. She called for something to eat, ate heartily, and that night slept alone in her room. In the morning her parents were assured of her perfect recovery. (A10193)

Rheumatism healed (1873–1879)

I have heard both my grandmother and my father, John Cluff, speak of Mrs. Eddy healing my father in his youth of what seemed to be a case of rheumatism.

Mrs. Eddy (who was fond of my father), not seeing him about as usual one morning when she called at my grandmother's, inquired concerning him, wanting to know what was the matter, whereupon my grandmother told her that John was upstairs with what she thought was rheumatism, and that he was unable to get out of bed. Mrs. Eddy then went upstairs and found John with one leg doubled back on his body. Despite his protest that he could not move it and get up, Mrs. Eddy firmly insisted that he could get up and walk. My father related that he did get right up and hobbled downstairs, mostly on one foot and with the aid of the banister, but after walking about a little, the leg straightened out to its normal position, and he found himself free. (Alice Cluff French reminiscences)

Painless childbirth demonstrated (1874)
(Miranda R. Rice of Lynn, Massachusetts)

I take pleasure in giving to the public one instance out of many of Mrs. Glover-Eddy's skill in metaphysical healing. At the birth of my youngest child, [now] eight years old, I thought my approaching confinement was several weeks premature, and sent her a message to that effect. Without seeing me, she returned answer the proper time had come, and she would be with me immediately. Slight labor pains had commenced before she arrived; she stopped them immediately, and requested me to call a midwife, but to keep him below stairs until after the birth. When the doctor arrived, and while he remained in a lower room, she came to my bedside. I asked her how I should lie. She answered, "It makes no difference how you lie," and simply said, "Now let the child be born," and immediately the birth took place without a single pain. The doctor was then called into the room to receive the child, and saw I had no pain whatever. My sister, Dorcas

B. Rawson, of Lynn, was present when my babe was born, and will testify to the facts as I have stated them. I confess my own astonishment. I did not expect so much, even from Mrs. Eddy, especially as I had suffered before very severely in childbirth. The M.D. covered me with extra bed-clothes, charged me to be very careful about taking cold, and to keep quiet, then left. I think he was alarmed at my having no labor pains, but before he went out I had an ague coming on. When the door closed behind him, Mrs. Eddy threw off the extra bedding, and said, "It is nothing but the fear the doctor has produced that causes these chills," and they left me at once. She told me to sit up when I chose, and as long as I chose, and to eat whatever I wanted. My babe was born about two o'clock in the morning, and the following evening I sat up several hours. I ate whatever the family did; had a boiled dinner of meat and vegetables the second day, made no difference in my diet, except to drink gruel between meals, and never experienced the least inconvenience from it. I dressed myself the second day, and the third day felt unwilling to lie down, and in one week was about the house, well, running up and down stairs and attending to domestic duties. For several years I had been troubled by prolapsus uteri, which disappeared entirely after Mrs. Eddy's wonderful demonstration of metaphysical science at the birth of my babe. (*Science and Health*, third edition, pp. 134–135)

Little girl healed of internal injury from a long fall
(1875–1876)

In reference to a healing which I as a little child received from Mrs. Eddy. At the time, I was living in the brick house on Franklin St. in Lynn, Massachusetts. I was very young and curious, & wandered across the street up to the old [Cobbet] schoolhouse and grounds, where my sister was in school. I decided to investigate the stairway, which was built in a square form, & when I got to the top, decided I would look down the center space to see how high I had climbed. They picked me up at the lower floor, and everybody supposed I was broken and internally injured. They carried me home. At that time Mr. Daniel Spofford was boarding with my grandmother. He came in the room when my little mother was holding me, and took me out of her arms. In a short time I was apparently very much improved, and by noon seemed quite well. Childlike, I thought it would be nice to show myself at the school just to show how *smart* I could be, and when I did so, the fear expressed overpowered me & I was taken home in a similar condition. Mr. Spofford's efforts this time were not successful & he left the house and went over to see Mrs. Eddy about me. The healing came before he returned. I was well & had no more trouble from the accident. I remembered this very forcibly because I was given a very large sack of candy for "being a good girl and not crying." (Ethel West letter, May 17, 1917, reminiscence file)

Infected finger and blood poisoning healed (1875)

While sewing, my mother had stuck the needle into the quick of her finger and made a sore. It grew worse and blood-poisoning set in. The physicians, of whom we had many and of the best, all said that it would be necessary to have it amputated. Mother was unwilling to have this done, though they told her that she would die if it was not amputated. The finger was about three times its normal size, and she suffered intense pain from it.

We went to Lynn, and the first day Mrs. Eddy spoke to mother about her finger. In eight days it was perfectly well except that the nail which had come out had ridges on it and was shaped like a parrot's beak, growing down over the top of the finger. Mother spoke to Mrs. Eddy about this, who said it would be all right. It *was* in about a week.[1] (Subject File: Alfred Farlow, Mary Godfrey Parker statement)

Fractured skull healed (1875–1880)

My personal acquaintance with Mrs. Eddy was very slight. I studied with her in the last Primary class of March 1889. While on a visit to Boston in the autumn of 1888, I was taken by a student of Mrs. Eddy's to call upon her and we spent the evening at her house. I remember her speaking of a wonderful demonstration in the case of a workman, who, while repairing the roof of her house, fell to the pavement below and fractured his skull— within a short time the man returned to his work, healed.

On taking leave of me that evening, she took my hand in hers and said, "Put your hand in God's hand, let Him lead you," words never to be forgotten, a priceless admonition. (Marguerite Sym reminiscences)

Man run over by a heavy wagon restored (1875–1880)

[Mrs. Eddy] spoke more than once of a man who was run over at Lynn. She said she saw the accident from her window, and it seemed to sicken her. He was carried into the house, and she was called down to see if she could do anything for him. She turned her back on him and lifted her thought to God, and the first thing she knew he was standing behind her, speaking as if he were awakening from a dream. He was healed instantly. (Adelaide Still reminiscences)

Story of a man run over by a heavy wagon; [Mrs. Glover] saw the accident. He was run over the bowels, was bleeding from mouth and nose. They carried him in a house for dead. Attempted an autopsy, but someone demanded Mrs. Glover. She healed him instantly; he put his hands to his head and found he was all right. (Harriet L. Betts reminiscences)

Cancer healed (1875–1880)
(Ellen Brown Linscott to Mr. Carol Norton)

For several months, during the year 1883, I was one of four students besides her private secretary that resided in the Massachusetts Metaphysical College, Boston, with our teacher, the Rev. Mary Baker G. Eddy. . . .

One day I was in Mrs. Eddy's private room assisting her in some small way, when the housemaid appeared and said a lady wished to see Mrs. Eddy. She was occupied at the time on some work for the Cause of too much importance to leave, even for a short time, so she asked me to see the visitor for her, etc. Going down to the reception room, I met a very quiet, dignified woman, who at once impressed me as being a person of great sincerity and earnestness. I shall never forget the look of disappointment that came into her eyes and face when I said Mrs. Eddy was so occupied that she could not possibly see her. I felt very sorry indeed for her. In answer to my question, Have you ever met Mrs. Eddy? she replied, "Oh yes, she healed me of a dreadful disease several years ago, and as I am passing through Boston, I thought I would like to see her, for she certainly saved my life. But for her I would not be here today." I was all attention, and immediately asked, "What did Mrs. Eddy heal you of?" She replied, "A dreadful cancer. It had developed to the point where it was liable to terminate fatally any time." Again I asked, "How many treatments did you have?" She replied, "Only one." In answer to the next question put by me, "Did the cancer disappear all at once while Mrs. Eddy was treating you?" she replied, "No, not at once, but it began to dry up and to heal at once and never gave me any pain again. In a very short time all trace of it had entirely disappeared." When she said this her voice had dropped to a very low tone and her eyes were filled with tears—of gratitude no doubt. She left the college keenly disappointed at not seeing Mrs. Eddy. To quote her own words as nearly as I can recollect them, she said, "I wanted to see the woman that performed such a miracle once more and thank her. I never saw her but once, you know. Give her my love. I am pleased to have met you and hope we may meet again sometime. I leave Boston today and only stopped over to see Mrs. Eddy." (Ellen Brown Linscott, January 21, 1899, letter to Carol Norton, quoted in Linscott reminiscences)

She [the woman] gave me to understand the claim of cancer was in the chest—a little above the breasts. (Incoming Correspondence: Ellen Brown Linscott to Mary Baker Eddy, September 19, 1904)

Effects of fright healed (1875–1880)
(Mrs. Eddy's dinner story at Pleasant View)

Miss Proctor's music teacher had been cruel in his treatment. After she had had a third lesson, sitting up all night to practice, he kicked the piano stool with her on it into an adjacent room. She was so frightened, she could sing and play no more. . . . [Having been asked to help, Mrs. Eddy] sent for [Miss Proctor] and asked her to sing. The poor girl grew white and said she couldn't do it. At last she was persuaded to go to the piano. Back came the music. She sang up and up and then "turned somersaults away up in the sky;" then she put her arms around [Mrs. Eddy] and kissed her over and over again. (Harriet Betts reminiscences)

Severe abdominal pain healed (1876–1877)

In about the year of 1876 or 1877, when Mrs. Eddy was living on Broad St., Lynn, I was living in Beverly, Massachusetts, and was very ill with pain in the abdomen, and the doctor had not been able to relieve me. Some one proposed that I go to Lynn to see the "medium" who healed without medicine. I said I did not care who it was if they could help me. So I went to Lynn to see her.

Mrs. Eddy opened the door herself and invited me in. I told her what seemed to be the matter, and she talked with me a few minutes and then said, "Now we won't talk anymore." She closed her eyes & sat with her hands in her lap for about ten minutes, and then she said, "You will not have that trouble anymore," and I said, "Aren't you going to rub me—or do anything?"—and she said, "You are healed," and I was.

As I went back to the carriage, I said to the friends that it was the queerest kind of healing I had ever heard of, for she did not even look at my tongue or feel my pulse.

When I asked Mrs. Eddy how much I owed her, she said fifty cents, but I was healed and never had this pain again. (Alice Swasey Wool reminiscences)

Little girl healed of membranous croup (1876–1877)

A few months after we went home I was healed of membranous croup. I remember it well. On the way to the station, my aunt thought I would die. Mrs. Eddy came to the door and said that if I would go upstairs to play I would be all right. I never had another attack. It used to come on five or six times in a winter. The doctors said there was nothing they could do for me.[2] (Subject File: Alfred Farlow, Mary Godfrey Parker statement)

Sick baby healed (1876–1878)

My mother often related the following experience in the Lynn household: I was sick, and my mother called a medical doctor. The physician gave my father a prescription to fill at a drug store. While he was gone, Mrs. Glover came in. She stopped at the door and listened to my mother's fears about me. Mrs. Glover said, "Put away the medicine. Flora is all right." When my father returned with the medicine, I was playing on the floor, perfectly well. (Flora Glover Nash Duff reminiscences)

Withered and paralyzed arm healed (1876–1879)

A carpenter came to our house, for some reason, who had his arm in a sling. Father asked him what the trouble was, and he said that he had strained the ligaments and paralysis had set in. The arm was partly withered, and all the physicians said that it would continue to wither. He said that he had been to the best physicians and hospitals there were. Father told him about Mrs. Eddy and asked him if he went to her to come and tell him the result. About a week later the carpenter came to the house to tell father that he was completely healed. (Mary Godfrey Parker reminiscences, September 1932)

The Mother Church already has my record, in Mr. Farlow's account, of the carpenter with a paralyzed arm who father sent to Mrs. Glover and whom she healed. I might add that when this man came to see Mrs. Glover, she was too busy to come down to talk with him and just opened a window in her parlor room on the second floor and called down to him. Father never told me any details of this experience other than those I have related, but as far as I know this was the only conversation Mrs. Glover had with the man, and he came away healed. (Mary Godfrey Parker reminiscences, December 1932)

Eye restored (1876–1882)

An engineer came to her whose eye had been put out by a hot cinder. Mrs. Eddy gave him a treatment, and an eye was manifested, but it was smaller than the other and deficient. She looked at it and said, "Is it possible that my understanding of

God is as little as that?" Again she treated him and the eye was *perfect.* (Edward E. Norwood reminiscences)

Dying pregnant woman healed (1877)
(Mrs. Eddy)

At one time I was called to speak before the Lyceum Club, at Westerly, Rhode Island. On my arrival my hostess told me that her next-door neighbor was dying. I asked permission to see her. It was granted, and with my hostess I went to the invalid's house.

The physicians had given up the case and retired. I had stood by her side about fifteen minutes when the sick woman rose from her bed, dressed herself, and was well. Afterwards they showed me the clothes already prepared for her burial; and told me that her physicians had said the diseased condition was caused by an injury received from a surgical operation at the birth of her last babe, and that it was impossible for her to be delivered of another child. It is sufficient to add her babe was safely born, and weighed twelve pounds. The mother afterwards wrote to me, "I never before suffered so little in childbirth."

This scientific demonstration so stirred the doctors and clergy that they had my notices for a second lecture pulled down, and refused me a hearing in their halls and churches. This circumstance is cited simply to show the opposition which Christian Science encountered a quarter-century ago, as contrasted with its present welcome into the sick-room.

Many were the desperate cases I instantly healed, "without money and without price,"[3] and in most instances without even an acknowledgment of the benefit. (*Retrospection and Introspection*, pp. 40–41)

(Laura Sargent to Mrs. Eddy)

In the town of Westerly, Rhode Island, where you went to lecture long years ago, and could not stay because you healed a woman, there are *three ministers* who are studying "Science and Health," and one of them, a Baptist, is preaching it from his pulpit. His wife and step-daughter have both been healed by Christian Science treatment. (Incoming Correspondence: Laura Sargent to Mary Baker Eddy, September 29, 1902)

Woman with consumption healed (1878–1879)
(Mrs. Eddy)

One memorable Sunday afternoon, a soprano,—clear, strong, sympathetic,—floating up from the pews, caught my ear. When the meeting was over, two ladies pushing their way through the crowd reached the platform. With tears of joy flooding her eyes—for she was a mother—one of them said, "Did you hear my daughter sing? Why, she has not sung before since she left the choir and was in consumption! When she entered this church one hour ago she could not speak a loud word, and now, oh, thank God, she is healed!"

It was not an uncommon occurrence in my own church for

the sick to be healed by my sermon. Many pale cripples went into the church leaning on crutches who went out carrying them on their shoulders. "And these signs shall follow them that believe."[4] (*Retrospection and Introspection*, p. 16)

Diphtheria healed (1878–1881)

(Clara Elizabeth Choate, Boston, Massachusetts, originally published with a comment from Mrs. Eddy)

One of the most delightful and sacred memories I hold of my experiences in Christian Science, and its Discoverer and Founder, Rev. Mary Baker G. Eddy, is of her healing me of acute and severe diphtheria about 1881. I had once before been very ill with this malady, and was treated by a famous physician, some years previous to my knowing anything of Christian Science. This last attack was worse than the former. My neck was swollen badly, I could not swallow, had not eaten for twenty-four hours, had chills and fever, no sleep, and was unable to rise from my bed. On this particular Sabbath afternoon, our Pastor Emeritus, Mrs. Eddy, called, and at once came into my room. How shall I describe it all! She seemed to float lightly and fearlessly to my bedside, calmly uplifted in demeanor, spiritually confident, unaffected, no professional airs,—just sweet, quiet, and soothingly graceful. To my joy she sat upon my bedside and kissed me. In a few minutes she told me I was healed. But what had come over me? The fever was gone, I felt perfectly natural,—no soreness of throat, all swelling had disappeared; I was hungry, and was chatting and laughing. I was free, and what a glorious, exalted freedom. Nature was again beautiful; divine Love had triumphed through His truth, as revealed and applied in Christian Science by our beloved Leader and Teacher, Mrs. Eddy, whose noble and unselfish example is a divine inspiration to all who are seeking and following after God's way,—in Spirit and in Truth. I also wish to say that she did this without money and without price. At that time she was preaching Sundays without a salary; I state this because the money thought has been brought to the fore so often. I would also add that I have never had any recurrence of throat trouble since then; for all of which blessings I am most deeply grateful to God, and to our beloved Leader, Rev. Mary Baker G. Eddy.

The above testimony comes from one of my early students, who has had much practice, who has learned by experience, who has done much good.—Mary Baker Eddy. (*Christian Science Sentinel*, May 12, 1906, p. 586)

Neck cancer healed (1878–1883)
(Mrs. Eddy to Irving Tomlinson)

Once a man came to me with a cancer that had eaten into the neck, and the jugular vein stood out. I turned from sense testimony, closed my eyes, and lifted my thought to God in prayer. When I opened my eyes, the man was perfectly restored, neck normal and natural. This is Christian Science healing. (A11935)

(Mrs. Eddy)

... When I have most clearly seen and most sensibly felt that the infinite recognizes no disease, this has not separated me from God, but has so bound me to Him as to enable me instantaneously to heal a cancer which had eaten its way to the jugular vein. (Mary Baker Eddy, *Unity of Good*, p. 7)

Diseased bodily organs healed (1882)

In 1853, when a small child, Susie [M. Lang] moved with her parents from Boston to Lawrence, [Massachusetts,] where she attended public schools and graduated with honors from the Lawrence High School. She studied piano and organ after graduating, and became a talented musician. She served as organist in the Haverhill Street Methodist Church in Lawrence, which church her family attended at that time.

About the year 1878 she was afflicted with an illness which her family physician in Lawrence was unable to cure. Her parents took her to a private hospital and sanatorium in Boston, near Massachusetts Avenue, in the vicinity of Columbus Avenue—where Mrs. Eddy established her Massachusetts Metaphysical College. When Miss Lang entered this hospital she was suffering from one physical disability, but after lingering there for more than a year, she was informed by her attending physician that every organ in her frail body was diseased; and she was given up to die. During the many months of her prolonged illness in the hospital, she daily read and studied her Bible, confident of God's love and goodness. It was then that God came to her rescue, for "Man's extremity is God's opportunity." Miss Lang and her father, Alfred Lang, then became aware of Mrs. Eddy's system of Christian healing and of the Massachusetts Metaphysical College, close by at 569 Columbus Avenue. Her father went to call upon Mrs. Eddy to ask for Christian Science treatment for his daughter. Mrs. Eddy took the case and the result was marvelously successful. Miss Lang was perfectly and permanently healed. She thereafter devoted her life to this wonderful Truth, to the teaching and healing ministry of Christian Science which had so uplifted and saved her from the "last enemy" and made her well and strong again. (Subject File: Susie M. Lang, Albert Lang reminiscences)

Injuries from an accident healed (1882–1884)

[Mrs. Isaac Foss] was driving with a span of horses, runaway; she was thrown out. When she was taken up, they found she was internally injured, and her ankle was sprained. For years her only relief was under opiates, suffering dreadfully all the time. Mr. Choate was her healer. He was located somewhere in New Hampshire. Took his patients to his house. This lady was there. He did not seem to reach the case. One day he told her he was going to Boston to see Mrs. Eddy and he would ask her to treat this lady. It was about six o'clock when she felt a very strange sensation; she was so stirred they put her to bed. When she got up, she got up well. She is now keeping boarders and does her own work and is a well woman. (Subject File: Alfred Farlow, Elizabeth Moulton statement)

Rheumatism healed (1882–1885)

A student came to Mrs. Eddy with a case of rheumatism which he had been unable to heal. The patient was bedridden and deformed from the disease and seemed to give no response to the treatment. Mrs. Eddy told the student how to work on it, but still there was no improvement. Upon his telling her there was still no lifting of the error, Mrs. Eddy said, "Oh, Lord, let the door be opened," whereupon the door of the room in which they sat swung slowly open. She then told the student to go, the patient was healed, and so it proved. (Grace Greene Felch reminiscences)

Weak back and limbs healed (1883)
(Ellen Brown Linscott to Mrs. Eddy)

That same season [summer 1883] I was suffering from a belief of a very weak back—could only *crawl up* stairs & more than one flight of stairs alarmed me. You healed me of that instantaneously. I had been healed of various claims by reading *Science & Health* before I studied with you in March 1883. (Incoming Correspondence: Ellen Brown Linscott to Mary Baker Eddy, September 15, 1904)

Mrs. Linscott also said, "From early girlhood I had an infirmity in the limbs that prevented me walking up stairs easily. One day at the College, I was going up to my room on the third floor, groaning and complaining, and as I reached the landing on the second floor said aloud, 'I know I'll never get up to the next floor.' Just as I said it, the door opened, and Mrs. [Eddy] came out and heard me. She gave a sweep of her hand, and commanded, 'Run up those stairs! Run up those stairs!' I started running, and have been running up stairs ever since." (Edward E. Norwood reminiscences)

Fifteen-year invalid healed (1883)

Previous to the year 1883, I, Jennie E. Sawyer [from Milwaukee], had been an invalid for fifteen years; pronounced incurable as I had chronic and organic diseases that would not yield to medicine or treatment of any material nature; and on three separate occasions my life had been despaired of and I had faced death, but had rallied and continued suffering until a relapse into another hopeless and dangerous condition.

Thus, life had become an endless torture; physicians gave me no hope of recovery as medicine seemed to poison the system, so there came a time when they recommended only fresh air, pure water, and sunshine together with absolute quiet, as the only hope of relieving the body of constant suffering and pain, as there was no waking moment that I was not enduring pain, and life had become a grievous burden until my constant prayer was that I might die,—thinking thereby I should enter into eternal rest. Finally I was sent to a resort or Rest Cure where no medicine was given, and patients were required to do nothing but lie out in the sunshine or shade, ride in row boats on artificial ponds, read, or remain idle as they chose; but at first I was too utterly weary to even avail myself of these privileges. It seemed an amazing thing that one could be so tired and utterly weary that even breathing exhausted them, and still I lived!

But gradually, after gaining a degree of strength, I was able to sit up a portion of the day and wear my clothes a few hours at a time, and avail myself of a few moments of boat-riding or of lying out on the porch; but before I was able to rely on myself at all,—after about seven weeks,—a letter came from my husband informing me that several friends had been urging him to try a mental method of healing which included no medicine and no physical exertion on the part of the patient,—and even mentally they did not require the patient to accept it until relief came and they could better understand it.

He had not at first been favorably impressed as such a method was unknown, and he, having studied medicine to a degree,—being a druggist and having practiced dentistry; his thought was that medicine having failed, there was nothing one could resort to; it was like having done everything [and] then expecting nothing to heal one. We had tried diet and travel, baths and electricity, and many different doctors and their remedies and methods, and were trying at that time to gain strength sufficient to have an operation, hoping to gain help in certain directions but not promised any sure relief.

Some people from Boston were visiting friends of ours and had brought these vague statements as regard a method of healing they had heard about, but could give no definite idea of what it really was except that a lady in Boston, through what was supposed to be a silent prayer, was healing people. He finally purchased *Science and Health* by Mary Baker G. Eddy, relating to her own experience of years of invalidism, and of her method of healing, which he could not understand but which seemed more Christian and spiritual than the ordinary faith of the church; and he, knowing that I firmly believed that the only ease I obtained was from God, he suggested that we go to Boston and consult Mrs. Eddy.

The very thought of such a proposition caused a relapse, for in my condition a trip of that distance was a momentous undertaking;—as I had lived for several years under the impression that any unusual exertion would end my life, I preferred dying at home and was opposed to the idea of attempting such a journey, feeling I could not endure it nor hope to reach the journey's end alive.

But my husband through reading *Science and Health* had gained a thought that had deeply impressed him as wholly different from any other Christian faith; it seemed a practical, workable, demonstrable faith, and he desired to meet the author personally. I had not seen, nor was I able to read the book; I was too weak physically or mentally to read or remember anything very long; and so a month or two passed before arrangements could be made to move me or I could gain courage or strength to attempt such a journey. It required closing his dental office and discontinuing business during our absence;—but finally the trip was accomplished, and we arrived in Boston one evening about the middle of December of 1883.

Dr. Sawyer, leaving me at the Hotel, called at once on Mrs. Eddy at 571 Columbus Avenue where her home and College were situated; he gained an appointment for me the following morning. On his return to the Hotel from this first call on Mrs. Eddy, I remember he said, "I don't know how you will be impressed; I don't know what you will think! She seemed very much of a lady, and very sincere in her faith and work in Christian Science; she talked of God and of man's relation to God in a manner we are not familiar with; her talk seemed sensible and convincing and very interesting, but very strange and unusual. She did not even inquire specially about your physical symptoms or condition, but in some way I feel there is help for you in it."

The following morning on seeing Mrs. Eddy, I felt favorably impressed with her sincerity and womanly, motherly kindness; there seemed no opposition in my thought of trying this method of healing. She did not apparently diagnose my case, nor did she act as though I were an invalid; there was no talk of sickness; it was a strange experience, for my appearance plainly showed that I was a constant sufferer, and after having exhausted all material means to expect by doing nothing I should be healed;—even at that very moment I was too weary to listen or to grasp hold on what she was saying, feeling I would [have] liked to have stopped breathing to catch up on strength sufficient to go on living; and so during this call I was unable to consider or follow the line of thought she was bringing out; still, there was something attractive and alluring in the idea of gaining rest and health through abiding in God's omnipotence, in the sure confidence and trust that she presented as possible. . . .

The only hesitation I felt of being healed was the dread of an invalid's convalescent state:—of gradually, slowly, gaining a degree of strength, and then through some cause suffering a relapse; then again, gaining a hope of health and then dying—that was more appalling to me than to die at once. I said to Mrs. Eddy, "If I gain my health, it will be such a slow process, and then I must sooner or later die, and I would rather go now, as I feel willing and ready to die." In those days a Christian who was reconciled to die had reached a state of mind most commendable; I realize the absurdity of it now, for my readiness to go was not so much because of my love and service to God as to free myself of suffering and pain; not wholly unselfish, although I was young and the world held many attractions. Mrs. Eddy assured me there would be no convalescent state if I were healed in Christian Science; and she also startled me by saying, "If you die you will awaken to the realization that you are not dead, and still have your problem to solve, for Life is from everlasting to everlasting."

Another fear that greatly troubled me was that this thought might be contrary to my Christian faith of the Congregational Church, or that it might separate me from my mother who had died a few years previously; also fearing it might be an anti-Christ of which we were warned in the Scriptures. I felt I must voice my convictions and fears before taking up this new faith. It was fortunate for me that Mrs. Eddy had been an invalid, also a member of an orthodox church, for she understood my nervousness and fears, and she showed the utmost consideration for all my doubts and misunderstanding.

The most astounding thing was that she did not physically diagnose my case, nor ask what the different physicians had thought my trouble was. She did not give me any treatment, but rather questioned my thought about God and mankind and Life; and finally she said, "I would advise you to sit in my class and let me teach you." That was the most astonishing thing; for I had not been able to remember three lines of anything I read for months! I was too tired to think; and the presence and conversation of people wearied me almost beyond endurance; and physicians had repeatedly told me there was nothing to build on, and had warned me that I was liable to die at any moment. But she paid not the slightest attention to the doctors' verdicts but answered, "Your husband is in good health, and together you might gain a thought that would heal you." At that time to imagine that a "thought gained" would heal incurable, hopeless organic disease, seemed almost an insane idea. Up to that time I had been unable to bear the weight of my clothes but a few hours each day; still she assured me, "You will be able to sit in this class; for as you learn your true relationship to God, you will forget these things that now trouble you."

...Thus, I entered Mrs. Eddy's class with trepidation and involuntary fear; a confusion of thought possessed me, for it was like entering a new unknown realm of thought wherein I might lose my old sense of faith and die before arriving at this new realization of how to trust God fully and entirely. I feared letting go of my personal sense measurement of life which had held me so long in bondage.

Mrs. Eddy at this time was a woman past sixty years of age, a well preserved beautiful woman;—not so much because of her physical charm as because there was discernible an inward light or reflection of thought that shone through her countenance that was an entirely new expression of being; this had its own influence,—one felt drawn to a better Life just from being in her presence. This realization of Life that she possessed gave impulse to her every action, word, and speech. She was prepossessing, attractive, and kind in her manner, and most considerate in guiding the thought of the members of this class away from the discussions in relation to matter as the only tangible evidence of life.

She guided the argumentative beliefs wisely into an acceptance of infinite Mind's power and presence; and this became a time marked by an absolute change of consciousness as regards Life and its demand together with its motive, purpose, desire, and aim; thereby changing the whole current of thought from a material mortal mind basis to a spiritual perception of man and the universe as reflecting God and His handiwork in the world; thereby enabling one to recognize God's everpresence, protection, and care in every way, at all times and under all circumstances ... .

Our first class was taught by Mrs. Eddy in her home and College at 571 Columbus Avenue in Boston, Massachusetts, beginning in December 1883. She gave us about three weeks of time; she told Dr. Sawyer and myself that we were the first students to have come from the West for instruction with her, and she formed this class especially to accommodate us as we had come so great a distance. There were but twelve students in this class and only three besides ourselves were paying students, as she had gathered these people together who had been asking for instruction. Thus she made up this class during the holiday season; and she had an intermission of a few days on my personal account, as the new thought stirred me to a feverish condition, trying to change the consciousness from a material personal sense of life and body to a recognition of the spiritual mentality of being.

Our faith and trust was so vague and uncertain compared with her grasping hold on God's promises, that it was literally like being born again; this learning to abide in the kingdom of Truth and Love seemed a mighty effort, and created a fever of fear and unrest and disquietude that she claimed it were better to discontinue her explanations for a few days until the balance was adjusted on the side of trust and assurance. I felt I could not discontinue or cease learning more, as I was not well enough established in the new way to treat or pray in Christian Science, and my former way of praying I could not go back to. She noticed my unrest and asked before the class disbanded, "Mrs. Sawyer, do you ever stir yeast when it is rising?" I answered, "No, but what has that to do with this?" She answered, "God's hand is leading you, and I would not do more just now." I did not understand it, and could not repress my tears. She sent one of her older students to meet me as I went from the classroom alone, and he said, "Mrs. Eddy wants you to know that you are in the most favorable condition of mind of anyone in the class." I said, "This is too serious a matter to say anything like that; I don't know what I am here for; I cannot grasp it, and I cannot go back to my old faith." He said comforting words that were wholly lost on me, and although I do not cry easily, I went out sobbing.

I remember taking *Science and Health* and thinking I will read until I know where and what God is; and suddenly as I was reading in the chapter on "Footsteps of Truth," it dawned on me that I was reaching far out for God as though He were a long way off—unapproachable and difficult to find. And out of that darkness and bewilderment, an illumination of thought encircled me, and I felt and knew and realized God's everpresence. It was like a conversion—a remarkable experience of "God with us" at all times, under all circumstances. My eyes were open to the truth of Being, and from that day to the present time it has been a daily, hourly, realization that my eyes need not be holden but may at all times recognize the bountiful mercy, love, and care of our heavenly Father that the Christ-thought brings to our consciousness, if we but turn our faces God-ward and realize His everpresence. Mrs. Eddy made a private appointment for that evening and gave us many new ideas and comforting thoughts.

We scarcely realized what a privilege we had in these private talks with her, but later on we learned to treasure the words given.

. . . at the end of the class, when Mrs. Eddy asked Dr. Sawyer if he would go to different cities and establish the work under her directions, and teach the Science wherever he found receptive minds, he accepted the call although he knew it would array public thought against him. He closed a lucrative business and followed along the line of Christian Science endeavor the remainder of his earth-life. Mrs. Eddy then asked me what I thought of it, and what I was going to do with the thought she had imparted to me. I answered, "I am filled with a wonderful Truth. I don't know what I am to do with it!" She said in a most convincing manner, "You are going to heal with it!" She seemed to foresee the future and felt that I would apply the knowledge gained to heal others whether present or absent. She assured me that I was practically healed of my infirmities and apparent disease—that had not quite dawned on me, and it seemed almost incredible to think there would be no return of those ailments.

I realized that to practice Christian Science would place me where I would be a target for severe criticism among my home friends and Church people, but I also realized that I had left my home and friends in a hopeless, dying condition that none could help; and my life had been prolonged and saved and my health restored and my faith renewed through and by this revelation of the Christ-healing taught by my Teacher, Mrs. Mary Baker G. Eddy,—and I could not do less than make a solemn compact with God to give my remaining days to His service; so I promised to do all in my power to help others to understand this blessed Truth of Christian Science.

We arrived home early in January 1884, and at once began the healing for whoever desired help. My first case was a young girl of about twenty years, born of a consumptive mother; she had never been strong, and at this time was suffering from inflammatory rheumatism, which rendered her right arm and hand useless. I began the treatment on Friday evening and did absent work until Monday morning, when she called and said, "See what I can do!" and she lifted a large heavy Atlas with her right hand! This girl had been afflicted with a double curvature of the spine from her birth; and through the treatment her back was straightened and healed in twenty-three days. . . .

I personally got the blessing, and took this healing so to heart that nothing could shake my faith in Christian Science healing. In all these years of having professed Christianity, I had never before realized that an actual possession of a living faith in our God could or would bring such a blessing into one's experience! At first only the chronic and apparently incurable cases came for treatment; and for several months we worked without compensation, and as suffering was relieved for one, they would tell another of benefit received. Thus in time a practice was established and, in a lesser way, we were pioneers of our Teacher's method of treating; hundreds of miles away from her, we were endeavoring to practice Christian Science.

Planting a new thought, especially if it be of a religious nature, is not wholly a thing of joy or happiness, except in one's own consciousness of right action. We had at once called on our own minister and physician, feeling sure they would appreciate this spiritual Truth and rejoice in the recovery of health; but our minister and church friends immediately turned a cold shoulder on us and many would not even allow an explanation in any direction, fearing it was of a mesmeric nature and in some way they could be made to believe in it without desiring to do so. They felt we had been innocently led astray by Mrs. Eddy's thought, and even the friends who had urged Dr. Sawyer to take me to Boston for this healing, dropped us socially. They simply judged it must be wrong because no minister had ever in all his study of the Scriptures discovered any such rendering of thought. . . .

Our physician was more lenient and kind and had to admit I seemed well, but he warned me that the moment "that woman's thought"—meaning Mrs. Eddy's thought,—"was off from me" I would pass [on], as it was but mesmeric effect. He emphatically said he knew my physical condition and I could not be healed! Both minister and physician watched my case for several years, but there was no relapse, and I have outlived most of these friends. . . .

It is now forty-seven years of continuous practice and teaching of Christian Science; and it has been one glorious experience,—of endeavor to undo self and sense and thereby serve God, the Giver of every good and perfect gift. (Jennie E. Sawyer reminiscences)

Abscess on eye healed (1883–1884)
(Pupil in Mrs. Eddy's December 1884 Primary class)

One member of the class asked Mrs. Eddy if she might tell what happened when she went with her to buy some chairs.

Mrs. Eddy said she might and she told the following story. She went with Mrs. Eddy to a furniture store to help her select some dining room chairs. The clerk who waited on them had a bandage over one eye. Mrs. Eddy seemed absorbed in thought while they were being shown the chairs, and when asked which she liked best, said, "Anything we can sit on, dear." The student told the clerk they would decide and let him know the next day. They were on the second floor, and the student opened a door and stepped out, thinking she was going down the stairs, but it proved to be a chute for sliding boxes down. Mrs. Eddy walked down the stairs and found the student picking herself up unhurt. When questioned about the chairs, Mrs. Eddy said, "Could I buy chairs from a man with his eye tied up?" When the student went back the next morning, the clerk said, "Who was the lady with you yesterday? When you came in, I had an abscess on my eye, and when you went out, I removed the bandage and there was nothing left of it." (Victoria Sargent reminiscences)

Girl healed of consumption (1883–1885)
(In an 1885 Primary class)

When the Christian Science services were held in Hawthorne Hall, the janitor brought his thirteen-year-old daughter to hear Mrs. Eddy speak. This girl was very ill, to mortal belief, with consumption, and had to be *carried* into the room. She was placed in the front seat before Mrs. Eddy. After the service Mrs. Eddy came down from the platform and spoke to her, whereupon the child was immediately made well. When she returned home and her mother asked if she felt badly, she replied, "Why should I feel badly, I am well." And they could never bring to her consciousness that she had ever been ill. (Grace Greene Felch reminiscences)

[Mrs. Eddy] told me that when she was first at [Hawthorne] Hall, holding services and preaching, the caretaker one Sunday brought his daughter, who was ill with consumption, and who had a distressing cough. After the congregation left the building, she was sitting in one of the end seats, waiting for her father. As Mrs. Eddy went down the aisle to go out at the front door, she saw the little girl and noticed how ill she looked. She stopped and spoke to the child, and said to her, "Don't you know, dear, that you haven't any lungs to cough with, or to be consumed—you are God's child!"; and she talked the truth to her and told her what she was as God's idea, and to know that she was well, and the child stopped coughing and was instantly healed. When her father came to take her home, he was amazed to find that she was well. (Clara Shannon reminiscences)

Lightning storm dispersed (1883–1888)
(Mrs. Eddy to Irving Tomlinson)

We should have the same control over the weather that we have over our bodies. I remember when I was preaching that on one occasion the sky became black and a flash of lightning was so severe that the soloist fell in [a] faint. I declared "Let there be peace," and almost instantly the sun came forth. (A11927)

Adulterer healed (1883–1888)

Mrs. Eddy had in one of her classes a woman whose face evidently showed great resentment. Mrs. Eddy asked her what the trouble was and found that she had an unfaithful husband. Mrs. Eddy explained how Jesus healed Mary Magdalene and said we must have the same mind Jesus had. Mrs. Eddy told her, "You will have to have it or you will never heal a case." The woman said she didn't have that mind and what was more, she didn't want it. But she was healed before she got through class and upon arriving home, found the husband changed—healed. (Irving Tomlinson reminiscences)

Malarial fever healed (1883–1888)

. . . A friend had spoken to [my mother] about Christian Science and expressed a desire to find out something more about it. Mother recommended that she take up the questions she had in mind directly with Mrs. Eddy and then wrote to Mrs. Eddy making an appointment for this friend. While on her way to Boston to keep the appointment [with Mrs. Eddy], the friend stopped in to see Mother to thank her, and to her surprise found Mother seriously ill with malarial fever. Mother had hesitated to ask for Mrs. Eddy's help, knowing that she was so busy, and Father had called in a doctor. He pronounced the case so serious that I remember Father came home early that day, and I stayed away from school. The lady, whose name I do not recall, kept her appointment with Mrs. Eddy and told her how ill Mother was. Upon returning to Chelsea, she stopped in to inquire about Mother, and to her astonishment found her up walking around. Mother always attributed this healing to

Mrs. Eddy, feeling sure that when she had been informed of her illness that Mrs. Eddy had immediately taken up the work and so restored her to health. (Mary Godfrey Parker reminiscences)

Pet bird's broken leg healed (1883–1888)

Mrs. Eddy was very fond of pets, especially birds. . . . On one occasion she had a little canary named Benny, and every morning he waited until Mrs. Eddy came down into the room, and would then burst into a flood of song. When she went to the Association meeting in Chicago, during her week's absence Benny never sang, but the day that the telegram was received, notifying the household of her return, he suddenly again burst into song.

On one occasion another little bird named May was given her, and in her spare moments, Mrs. Eddy would allow the birds to hop freely about the room. One morning someone in moving a heavy arm-chair rolled it on one of May's tiny feet. Mrs. Eddy picked up the bird, whose broken foot was hanging by a shred of skin, and laid her gently back in the cage. A few moments later a lady visitor called and while conversing with Mrs. Eddy suddenly stopped and said: "What *is* the matter with that bird?" indicating Benny, who was singing and chirping, flying to May's cage and back to them, and making a great noise. Mrs. Eddy replied by asking the visitor to look in May's cage, when the lady said: "Why, this bird has a broken foot!" Mrs. Eddy said: "Benny is sympathizing with her, and wants to tell us about it. But never mind, come back in three days." The lady did return at that time, and was amazed and delighted to see little May perfectly well, hopping about her cage and singing joyously. (Eugenia M. Fosbery reminiscences)

Dead goldfish restored (1883–1888)

A teacher whom I knew many years ago went through a class with Mrs. Eddy. She told me an incident that took place during this class from which she learned a great lesson. One morning at the beginning of the class Mrs. Eddy sat silently with her head bowed down. The members of the class all began to wonder if they had done anything which merited rebuke. At last Mrs. Eddy looked up and said: "I have been very wicked. Last night I saw one of my gold fish floating on top of the water, and I said, my gold fish is dead! But this morning I am happy to say, it is all right." Then she smiled at them. (Caroline Foss Gyger reminiscences)

Deformed man with withered limbs healed (1883–1888)
(Letter to Mrs. Eddy)

I had an uncle by marriage who was a helpless cripple and who was deformed. All his limbs were withered, and on very pleasant mornings a special policeman would wheel him out on Boston Common in his wheelchair. One morning a number of years ago, he sat there in his wheelchair as you were passing through the Common, and you stopped and spoke to him, telling him that man is God's perfect child, and a few other words. Later, after you had left him, he declared you had helped him. The next morning he looked and looked for you in the same place, and morning after morning continued to do so, until one day you came. Again you repeated to him what you had said before, and this time he was healed and made perfect—every whit whole; and after that he was able to go into business for himself and provide his own living. No doubt you will remember the whole circumstance. His bones had hardened so that when sitting or lying down, his knees were drawn up and rigid, his brother having to carry him up and down stairs, and feed him and care for him all the time; but after he was healed through your spoken word, he was able to be as active as other men and earned his own living; and whereas before he could not even brush a fly from his face, he regained the use of his hands, and became more than an ordinary penman. (Charlotte F. Lyon letter, July 2, 1908; *Christian Science Sentinel*, July 18, 1908, p. 912)

(A description of Mrs. Eddy's second encounter with the man, told to William Turner by Julia Bartlett, who was walking with Mrs. Eddy when this incident occurred)

. . . Mrs. Eddy suddenly paused, Miss Bartlett said, and abruptly leaving Miss Bartlett's side walked rapidly back to the afflicted man. Bending over him with her face close to his, she whispered something in his ear—Miss Bartlett never knew what—and then sped back, hurrying her companion from the spot, eager, as always, to avoid the conspicuous. But almost immediately the crippled man leaped up, endeavoring to run after the two women, crying out, "Stop that lady, stop that lady! She has healed me! She has healed me!" (William B. Turner reminiscences)

Spiritualist with gall-stones healed (1884)
(Mrs. Eddy to Lida Fitzpatrick)

I lectured one time where the spiritualists tried to break up the meeting; they would jump up and contradict without being asked. A lady in the audience—and the audience was large—was taken with one of her attacks of gall stones [and] fell on the floor in excruciating pain; I said to the spiritualists present—now is your time to prove what your God will do for you; heal this woman. They jumped about and did what they could, but she grew worse and worse; I stepped down from the platform, stood beside her a moment and the pain left; she arose and sat in her chair and was healed. (Fitzpatrick reminiscences)

(Mrs. Eddy to Irving Tomlinson)

When my students in Chicago sent for me to visit them and lecture, I wrote them that I was so tied down with work that it seemed well nigh impossible. They urged so insistently that at last I yielded, though it did not seem to be the leading of God, but I knew that the wrath of man would be made to praise God.

At that time the Spiritualists were almost in control of Chicago and, unknown to my students, they plotted to make of the lecture a failure. These Spiritualists planned to attend the lecture in a body and to attempt to break up the meeting by leaving while I was lecturing. The hall was crowded, people standing in the aisles and even on the windowsills to hear the lecture. In the midst of the lecture, there was a crash, and I saw that the leader of the Spiritualists had fallen on the floor. Several of the Spiritualists rushed to her and attempted their manipulations without avail. Stopping in my lecture I went to the fallen woman, spoke to her, and she arose healed. (A11837)

Blindness healed (1884)
(From a sermon Mrs. Eddy gave on November 16, 1884)

. . . A lady came to me, last week, and said, "I am blind; I have come hither only to say it, for I am told you take no patients. You have so much else to do, you cannot do good to the sick."

Well, I said, I am doing good to all through my address to the well; and I understand health is more contagious than disease, goodness more natural than badness, and the good and the health shall be the contagion in my church. We all shall catch it, as soon as we get in, and if you chemicalize under the attack of truth and error, you must not cry out, "Why art thou come hither to torment me before the time?" For the time now is to choose whom we shall serve, and to praise God, when we see His rule coming upon the earth, if we will leave the evidences material for the evidences spiritual, for man's happiness and eternity.

While I talked to her, she said, "I can see a little better." She went away without any further remark, and I have heard from her since then, saying her sight is perfectly restored. Now how is this done? Not by a material method, no hygiene, no oculist in the case, no humbug back to back séances, but the

Divine utterance of this stated fact which you all reject, which is universally rejected upon the face of the earth, namely, that you are not material, and never had a material pain nor a mind under the skull, nor an optic nerve that connected itself with the brain, and thus constituted something in the image of God's likeness, called man . . . . (A10088)

Invalidism and disappointment healed (1884)
(Sarah J. Clark)

December has a special charm for me, because of the glorious truths that were unfolded to me on the first Sunday of this month, in the year 1884, in Hawthorne Hall, Boston. I had received a few treatments from a Christian Scientist, and was physically more comfortable, as I had often been in using a new medicine, or from a change of climate; but no sense of permanent health had touched me, nor had I any idea that Christian Science was anything but a method of curing people without medicine.

I accepted an invitation to go and hear the Rev. Mary Baker Eddy preach, and went to the hall very indifferent as to the subject or the speaker. Every seat was taken, and I thought it would be my death to stand through the service; I was sure it would cause a relapse. There was a table in the vestibule, against which I leaned, thinking to stay but a few moments. I soon forgot myself, and when Mrs. Eddy ceased speaking, I was standing inside the hall.

As I passed into the street, the lady who had treated me asked me how I was. I looked at her in astonishment, for her words sounded strangely. I replied, "I am as well as you are"; for the sense of invalidism had left me. I was no longer disappointed with life. Verily, "old things had passed away, and all things had become new."[5] (From "Harvest Gleanings," *The Christian Science Journal*, December 1896, p. 418)

(Sarah Clark to Mrs. Eddy, when Clark was serving as Journal *Editor)*

. . . It is so good to hear you speak. Did you know I was healed by hearing you preach? (Incoming Correspondence: Sarah Clark to Mary Baker Eddy, January 27, 1891)

Inflammatory rheumatism healed (1884–1885)

I am a printer by trade, having learned the trade in Skowhegan [Maine] and serving first on the *Portland Express*. I afterwards came to Boston and worked on the *Boston Journal* for over thirty-four years, afterwards working on the *Boston Globe* and other papers. My last employment was as night watchman in the Christian Science Church, leaving there in 1912.

I was attacked by inflammatory rheumatism in my early thirties in such form that even the bedclothing proved to be burdensome and painful. I had heard about Mrs. Eddy's meetings in Hawthorne Hall on Park Street, near Brimstone Corner, and at the worst stage of the belief I was taken there on a stretcher, accompanied by the then Mrs. Littlefield. After the service ended Mrs. Eddy came down from the platform and greeted the members of the meeting personally—it was a small group of about a dozen people—and when she came to me and shook my hand and spoke to me, I felt the healing and responded by telling her that I was healed. I walked out of the Hall rejoicing, and that belief never made itself real to me again. (Henry A. Littlefield reminiscences)

Man on crutches healed (1885)
(*Emma Hopkins, Editor of the* Journal of Christian Science)

There is no professional practitioner in the field of mental healing doing so many, so marvellous, and instantaneous cures, as Mrs. M. B. G. Eddy. And that without being publicly known at present as a healer. This declaration we make upon evidence sufficient to forever establish the reputation of any preacher, or teacher, or practising mental physician on earth… . Not a Sabbath's preaching of the Word of Life, but looses the bonds of some poor sick or crippled prisoners. One which came under our observation after the sermon of Jan. 18 [1885], was that of a man who went into Hawthorne Hall on crutches, but the power of the Truth as [Mrs. Eddy] gave it utterance, set him free from his infirmities, and he went home without his crutches! (*Journal of Christian Science*, February 7, 1885, p. 5)

Journalist's fatigue healed (1885)

It was in my youthful days of journalism in Boston—in the eighties—that I became deeply interested in hearing of this remarkable woman [Mrs. Eddy] and ventured to write to her asking if I might have the privilege of a personal interview? A gracious reply came to me, naming an evening hour, on a given date. I recall that I was rather unusually fatigued that night, and upborne chiefly by the anticipation of meeting the eloquent speaker to whom I had listened more than once, and that I went up the steps to her door with feet that lagged, though my thought did not. Her most kind reception largely banished the fatigue, and I see before me now the slender figure, the luminous eyes, the faintly rose-flushed countenance; the simple, dainty grace of her gown, and the beauty of the hand that clasped mine … . From her conversation that evening I wrote a letter to "The Inter-Ocean," of Chicago,—very crudely and imperfectly interpreting the substance of what she said, I am sure; yet perhaps conveying something of the great truths she unfolded; and almost any matter referring to Mrs. Eddy and her work was read by the curious public and widely discussed. . . .

I have mentioned my state of fatigue, that evening, simply to record the striking sequence of that experience. It was a Saturday evening; I was then living in the Vendome, and after walking back to the hotel from Mrs. Eddy's home (then in Columbus Avenue), I was conscious of the most intense exhilaration and joyous energy. I felt as if I could walk any distance, indeed, almost as if I could fly through the air. The next morning, after listening to Phillips Brooks, in Trinity, I turned to some writing and was all the time conscious of that intense exhilaration of energy, that sense of joyous exaltation, of mind and body. My work seemed to fairly write itself, independently of my exertion. The sensation was so vivid that in the evening I mentioned to a friend that I had gone on, all day, in a sort of rapturous happiness, and she replied: "Why, that was the effect of Mrs. Eddy on you." That had not consciously occurred to me before. But it is true, as I look back and see this period in perspective, that this meeting with

Mrs. Eddy made itself a very definite date in my life,—one of those milestones in the onward march which one only adequately recognizes in after years. As I read it now, I can but regard this as the unconscious influence of a highly exalted spirit on another, who was so fortunate, perhaps, as to be sensitive to the spiritual vibration. (Lilian Whiting reminiscences)

(Alfred Farlow to Mrs. Eddy)

I am sending you a book which Miss Lilian Whiting has requested me to hand you. You will probably remember her. She still relates the story of the wonderful benefits she received from you twenty years ago, or more, when she called upon you on Columbus Avenue. She was much fatigued—worn out with her work. She said that after her interview with you, she went away entirely refreshed and invigorated. (Incoming Correspondence: Alfred Farlow to Mary Baker Eddy, July 7, 1909)

Woman dying in childbirth healed (1885–1886)
(Mrs. Eddy)

The late husband of Mrs. Janet T. Colman of Falmouth Street, Boston, Mass., hastened to me with a telegram received from Omaha, Neb., announcing that his wife was dying in childbirth and the Drs. could not save her. I immediately healed her. This was a case of absent treatment. (A10328) Mrs. Colman wrote Mrs. Eddy to express gratitude for the healing, saying the doctors were amazed at her recovery.

(Incoming Correspondence: Janet Colman to Mary Baker Eddy, November 28, 1885.)

A sequel to this healing occurred three months later when Erwin L. Colman returned to Boston to take class instruction from Mrs. Eddy:

(Mrs. Eddy to Irving Tomlinson)

When Mr. [Erwin L.] Colman was attending class at the Massachusetts Metaphysical College, I observed that he was one day handed a telegram and on reading it asked to be excused. On his leaving the classroom, I felt that all was not right and excused myself to speak to him. He handed me the telegram from their home in Omaha, Neb., which read in substance—your wife is dying; she will be gone before you can reach home. I instantly said, "She will not die. She will recover. You can return to the classroom." He took his seat in the class and later in the day received a telegram saying his wife was much better. Within a week she was completely healed. (A11768)

Girl healed of incurable disease (1885–1887)
(Anne Dodge)

When I was about sixteen years of age, I had been ill for two years of a disease my doctors said was incurable and which was most alarming to my parents. I had been given electrical treatments, and my mother had taken me to famous baths in Germany and in other parts of Europe. After a premature adolescence, a normal physical function had ceased, and I was anemic.

After returning from Europe, my mother and I went to Council Bluffs, Iowa, to spend the summer in our home there. . . .

At Council Bluffs we found that a Mrs. Jennie Edmonson, who had not walked for eighteen years and whose family was well known by my mother, had been healed through Christian Science by Mrs. Fenn of the neighboring city of Omaha, Nebraska. That was the first Mother had heard of Christian Science and Mrs. Eddy.

My mother took me to Boston to Mrs. Eddy for treatment.

After being in Boston a week or more, Mother and I had an appointment with Mrs. Eddy. We went to her home at 571 Columbus Avenue. I had not cared much about going as I felt so ill. We met Mr. Frye, Mrs. Eddy's secretary, on the first floor. Later Mrs. Eddy called for me to come to her library, or office, on the second floor.

My first thought on seeing her was what a spiritual woman she was and what wonderful eyes she had. Her curly hair at that time was still dark. She sat down in one chair, an easy, armed chair, and invited me to sit opposite her. I think the whole interview and the treatment took about an hour to an hour and a half. She put her hand over her eyes, and I thought she was praying. At first I felt rather restless, then I felt that it was all right to be there. I looked around the room at the pictures, etc. Very soon I had a wonderful feeling of peace and I felt uplifted. The flesh didn't seem real to me any longer. It was a really wonderful experience.

As we were leaving the house, my mother asked Mr. Frye what the charge would be and if she should pay in cash. He said he knew at which hotel we were stopping and he would let us know whether Mrs. Eddy wanted to see us again about the payment.

That same evening the illness vanished for all time. It never came back. *Mrs. Eddy had healed me in one treatment.* (Anne Dodge reminiscences)

Moral vices healed (1885–1888)
(Mrs. Eddy to Irving Tomlinson)

A gentleman who went to Boston and became a leading merchant, brought a parrot to me of which he was proud for his ability to talk. His first word was an oath. Said I to the gentleman, "Did you teach him that." He saw his mistake and said no. Then I said, "Could he ever have heard you use that word." Then I spoke to him of his influence for good or evil, and the silent influence of this conduct.

He afterward said that from that interview he was a changed man. He ceased his profanity, and forsook other vices, and lived a different life thereafter. (A12057)

Young woman with fatal stomach disorder healed (1886)
(Account from First Church of Christ, Scientist, Portland, Oregon)

In the winter of 1886, Mrs. Mary H. Mahon, then Mary H. Crosby, and at the time a student at the New England Conservatory of Music, was told by her physicians that the lining of her stomach was entirely destroyed and that she should return to her home in Oregon, prepared to live only a short time.

While she was weeping about this in her room at the Conservatory, the wife of the director of the Conservatory heard of her distress and came in to see her. She told her of Mrs. Eddy, then living on Columbus Avenue in Boston, saying that she heard that this woman healed as Jesus had healed. She advised Miss Crosby to see her before returning west.

Miss Crosby called on Mrs. Eddy and was received by her. Miss Crosby poured out the history of her illness and her symptoms. Mrs. Eddy quietly listened and at the end of the recital dismissed her, saying that she was not at that time taking cases, but that she could find help through some of the students of Christian Science.

Miss Crosby returned to the Conservatory and that evening found herself entirely healed of everything that she had voiced to Mrs. Eddy. (First Church of Christ, Scientist, Portland, Oregon, letter, acknowledged January 3, 1934, in Mary H. Mahon reminiscences)

Hacking cough healed (1886)

In the first class I was in, a woman from Georgia seemed to have a hacking cough. Mrs. Eddy called her by name and said, "Why do you blaspheme God that way?" She never coughed again.

[More than] a year later when Mrs. Eddy delivered her address in Central Music Hall [Chicago], I met this woman at the door and we knew each other. Almost the first thing she said was "Do you know I have never coughed since." (Ruth Ewing reminiscences)

Mrs. Eddy's estranged cousin healed (1886)

In one of our Leader's early classes (and as I recall my mother's Primary class), one morning soon after the session opened, Mrs. Eddy was called out of the room and did not return for over an hour. When she entered again she expressed regret for the delay, but said she felt they would realize its importance when she explained what had kept her. She then proceeded to tell them that at one time, early in her discovery of Christian Science, she passed through quite a period of misunderstanding with her family, and in her extremity turned as a last resort for sympathy and financial help to a favorite cousin, who, like the rest, disappointed her by rejecting her faith and refusing to give her assistance of any kind.

Our Leader said, "From that time on I relied absolutely upon God, and now, after all these years, this same cousin has become alarmed over a physical condition, and today came to me in tears to ask for healing. Under the circumstances I felt sure you would be willing to wait while I stopped long enough to heal her." (Abigail Dyer Thompson reminiscences)

Speech impediment healed (1886)
(A letter to Mrs. Eddy from Mrs. E. C. Heywood after her daughter, Flossie Heywood, was healed)

Will you please accept my sincere thanks for the good you

have done my daughter. ... the eve she called to see you at the College, she . . . had a slight impediment in her speech which was entirely overcome that night. (Mrs. E. C. Heywood letter, December 13, 1886)

Heart disease healed (1886–1887)

I came to New York [City] at the request of my dear Teacher, Mrs. Eddy. This was early in October of 1885. I had been in this city over a year when Mrs. Eddy sent for me to come to Boston to spend Sunday with her. I went Saturday night, reaching the College at 571 Columbus Avenue, where Mrs. Eddy then lived, at nine o'clock Sunday morning. She asked me no questions about my heart, although she told me nine years after that she had sent for me because of what one of her other students had said about me. One of them had called upon me in New York, and later had told Mrs. Eddy that I was in a very bad condition physically, that my heart constantly made a creaking noise, such as a gate would make when swinging on a rusty hinge. When it was time for dinner, I accompanied Mrs. Eddy to the dining-room, which was in the basement of the house. On returning to the parlor, she ran up the stairs like a young girl. I was ashamed not to make at least an effort to do the same, but for twenty-four years I had never run upstairs. Perhaps once or twice a year, if it were absolutely necessary, I would make the effort, going up two or three steps at a time, then sitting down to rest. This time I did go as fast as she did, but when I reached the top step I was in a sorry plight. How I looked I cannot tell. I only knew that I was seized with one of my old attacks, when it seemed as though an iron hand gripped my heart and was squeezing the very life out of it. She gave me one glance, and then, without asking me a question, she spoke aloud to the error. We are told that when Jesus healed the sick, he spake as one having authority. On this occasion Mrs. Eddy also spoke as one having authority.

As I look back on that wonderful event, I do not remember that the thought came to me at the time that she was healing me, neither do I remember that I had any special faith. The only sense I had was of her wonderful power. A few months after, I was seized with another attack, but it lasted only a moment and went, never again to return. That was eighteen years ago, and during all these years of unceasing work in Christian Science, I have constantly and fearlessly run up and down long flights of stairs when it was necessary to do so, and with no ill results. The belief of hereditary heart disease is not only dead, but buried. (Laura Lathrop, "Healed by Mrs. Eddy," *Christian Science Sentinel*, December 24, 1904, p. 259)

Effects of cold weather healed (1887)
(Annie M. Knott)

One morning stands out in memory: it was the first meeting with our Leader in the College at Boston, Mass., on a cold February day. I was removing my wraps in the corridor, preparatory to going to the class room, when a gentle voice bade me good morning. What a thrill passed through me; and as I looked up into the depths of those loving eyes, my own filled with tears of joy that God had been so gracious to me and enabled me to become a student of Mary Baker Eddy. I cannot disassociate from this meeting a little demonstration which must do good to many. My numerous ailments had been disappearing one by one since I had first accepted the Truth, but on this morning my hands were very cold—a condition or belief which had troubled me from childhood. As Mrs. Eddy took them in her own, she said as a mother would to her child, "Are your hands cold?" I think I said, "Oh no!" for my whole heart so warmed with her loving welcome that the hands were forgotten, but as I went into the class room I became very conscious of an indescribable glow and warmth going over [my] whole body, and I have never suffered from cold hands since. It was the healing touch of her great sense [of] Love.[6] (*The Christian Science Journal*, February 1901, p. 682)

Eyeglasses no longer needed (1887)

Dr. Henry Ives Bradley, my father, and my mother were in [Primary] class with us [Caroline Bates and her husband, Edward]. After my healing,[7] Father gave up his practice of medicine and accepted the teachings in *Science and Health*. For years he had been convinced that medicine never healed a disease, and did not use it for himself. Both my father and mother were healed of using glasses while in the class and never used them again. Father returned to New Haven and brought Scientific healing to his old patients, who became the nucleus of a Christian Science church. (Caroline S. Bates reminiscences)

Overwhelming fear healed (1888)

In August 1888 or about that time in one of the [*Journals*] appeared a notice that Mrs. Eddy would teach a class in September of that year. I made application and received a letter from Calvin Frye, Mrs. Eddy's Secretary, stating that my letter had been received and if I would fill out the Blanks that he enclosed, that if I was accepted I would be notified when to appear. I was accepted and the class was taught by Mrs. Eddy at [the College] on Columbus Avenue, Boston.

This was a wonderful demonstration to be made in a year, for prior to April 1887 I had been an invalid for ten (10) years, so in the year and a half, I had to acquire an entire new wardrobe, [make] several trips to Chicago in order to learn more of Christian Science, and also demonstrate over the needful supply for class instruction; just the day before I was to leave for Boston the demonstration was fully made. Thus proving that God does supply all our needs when we are wholly trusting Him.

In teaching the class Mrs. Eddy sat on a platform and my seat was just at her feet. When I entered the class I was so impressed by Mrs. Eddy's understanding of people and everything, that I was filled with such awe that tears flowed freely. When Mrs. Eddy entered the room where the class was assembled, it seemed as if she always surveyed the class, and it seemed as if she was looking into each face and seemed as if she was mentally greeting each one and seeing only the real man of God's creating.

One day at the close of the class, I told Mrs. Eddy that I was so afraid, just full of fear. Instantly came the question, "My dear, what are you afraid of?" And I told her I did not know just what the fear was; for an instant she stood still and then said, "You know, God is Love." I was healed and that sense of fear has never returned. (Cordelia Willey reminiscences)

Mental breakdown healed (1893–1897)

… One of [Mrs. Eddy's] followers in New York City, a woman of wealth and social position harassed by cares and weary with the weight of life's burdens, felt her mind giving way under the pressure, and so she fled one day from her home leaving no word where she had gone. She came straightway to Concord, New Hampshire, arriving late at night, and drove out unannounced to Pleasant View and there aroused the household and threw herself upon Mrs. Eddy's mercy, begging her to save her from the mad house. Mrs. Eddy took the poor weary and frightened woman into her charge. [She] soothed and treated her and sent her home [the] next day a healed and happy woman, too grateful for words to describe. Mrs. Eddy said that when the woman came to her she was insane but that [when] she went home she was restored. Mrs. Eddy made no claim about her personal power in the working of this cure but cited the incident to show me the power of Christian Science to heal and to minister to minds diseased.[8] (The Rev. Frank L. Phalen reminiscences)

Man on crutches leaves sermon healed (1895)
(An account by Edward Bates of a man's healing during Mrs. Eddy's address to the congregation on her second visit to The Mother Church, May 25–26)

… A man came in with two crutches, listened to her, and went out without them. When he reached the house he was visiting on Tremont Street, his friends asked him where his crutches were. He said he did not know; he had never seen them since he went into that church and heard that woman talk. The janitor looked for the crutches but never found them. (Edward P. Bates reminiscences)

Cyclone dispersed at Pleasant View (1895–1897)

At Pleasant View, dominion over weather, storms, etc., was just the same as over other seeming material conditions. After a prolonged drought, the inharmonious condition was met by our Leader's watching and praying, the effect being rain when there was not a cloud visible in the sky. At other times heavy, dark clouds appeared when there was no rain. Also Truth was demonstrated to quell storms.

During part of the year, cyclones were sometimes experienced at Concord, and one day Miss Morgan came to me and said that the clouds were gathering and there was going to be a dreadful storm, and she called me to look through the windows of her room, which was at the end of the house, looking towards the stables. Above, I saw dark clouds which seemed to be coming towards us very rapidly, and as Mother [Mrs. Eddy] had told me whenever I saw a cyclone or storm coming up I must let her know, I went to her room immediately and told her. She rose, and went to the verandah at the back of the house. By that time, the clouds had reached overhead. She then went into the front vestibule and looked on that side of the house. . . . I ran downstairs to the front door, opened it and went outside, looked up and saw the clouds hanging over the house—very heavy, black clouds, and in the middle, right over the house there was a rift—they were dividing—part were going one way and the other part in the opposite direction. This seemed to be such a strange phenomenon. I went in, closed the door, and went upstairs to Mother, on the verandah, and told her what I saw. I said, "The clouds are divided just overhead!" She said to me, "Clouds! What do you mean? *Are* there any clouds?" I said, "No, Mother!" She was looking up, and I could see by the expression on her face that she was not seeing clouds but was realizing the Truth. I saw the black clouds turn to indigo, the indigo to light grey, the light grey turn to white fleecy clouds which dissolved, and there were no more, and she said to me, "There are no clouds to hide God's face, and there is nothing that can come between the light and us—it is divine Love's weather."

That was early in the evening; the wind had been blowing terrifically, and Mr. Frye and another gentleman were in the attic, trying to pull down a large American flag. It was "Fete" day and a gentleman had sent this flag as a gift to Mrs. Eddy; it was very large, so she had it hoisted, and Mr. Frye and this friend were trying to pull it down, and the strength of the two men was not sufficient to pull down that flag, but suddenly the wind subsided and the flag yielded.

The next morning, early, when the mail was delivered, the postman was amazed to see that nothing had been disturbed in the garden, as, from a short distance down the road, and in the town there had been a great deal of damage. The lesson I learned then, through that experience, has since helped me through many storms by sea and on land. (Clara Shannon reminiscences)

Man in state asylum healed (1895–1902)

I did meet our beloved Leader, Mary Baker Eddy, in Concord one day at her home there. She asked me what work I did, and I said, "I am a school teacher." She said, "that is a good work helping the children." "Yes," I said, "I enjoy it; as I like children!" I used to see her riding with her driver around

Concord. I remember one day [when] she was riding past the State Asylum, a young man stepped out on a narrow porch, and he called to Mrs. Eddy, "Mrs. Eddy help me!" She answered, "Yes, I will!" and I heard later that he was perfectly healed! O, she surely was called of God to do such healing work! (Addie P. Forbes reminiscences)

Before going to Concord, Mrs. Eddy had set aside a certain time in her day for driving. She strictly adhered to this arrangement, planned as a refreshing interlude. As she drove along the valley she occasionally passed an insane asylum where an inmate watched her closely through the gate. Mrs. Eddy did not permit this sad picture to disturb her, but let her thought rest upon him with such understanding of his divine birthright that he was fully restored. (Julia Michael Johnston, *Mary Baker Eddy: Her Mission and Triumph*, pp. 130–131)

Young girl with boil on her head healed (1897)

It was the year 1897, on the 4th of July,[9] that Mrs. Eddy invited her church to her home in Concord, New Hampshire. She sent a telegram to a student here [in Kansas City, Missouri], telling him to come and bring his friends, and I was invited to go. I went with my sister and my two children.

When we were getting ready to start, we discovered that my little daughter, seven years old, had a boil on the crown of her head. Her hair was heavy and curly, and the boil was very much inflamed.

After we got on the train, she would not allow me to comb her hair. The confusion, the heat, and the crowded car made it difficult to work mentally, and her hair really went uncombed until we got to Concord. I did not try to comb it that night, because she cried so bitterly, but Sister and I put her to bed, and we sat down to do our mental work on the matter. The next morning we were to go out to Mrs. Eddy's home. The boil by this time looked like the small end of an egg. It stood up pointedly from her head and was more inflamed than before.

I took the scissors and cut the hair from around the boil. Then I washed her hair and combed it, my sister working for her mentally all the while, and I holding to the truth as best I could while I worked. The whole thing was a most trying ordeal, and it was only through showers of tears that we finally got her ready to go. She had a little light straw hat with a wreath of daisies on it. She did not want to put it on, because she said it hurt her head.

Mrs. Eddy and a number of others spoke to us. When the speaking was over, Mrs. Eddy sat upon the porch as the people passed through the carriage-way, greeting her as they passed. When my two children, a boy of nine and this little girl of seven, got in front of her, they stopped the whole procession, and stood looking up into her face with a most joyous smile. She looked at them and then looked at me; then she looked back at them again and threw a kiss to each one of them, and somebody told them to pass along. I followed them.

I wish I could make the world know what I saw when Mrs. Eddy looked at those children. It was a revelation to me. I saw for the first time the real mother Love, and I knew that I did not have it. I had a strange, agonized sense of being absolutely cut off from the children. It is impossible to put into words what the uncovering of my own lack of real mother Love meant to me.

As I turned in the procession and walked toward the line of trees in the front of the yard, there was a bird sitting on the limb of a tree, and I saw the same love poured out on that bird that I had seen flow from Mrs. Eddy to my children. I looked down at the grass and the flowers, and there was the same love resting on them. It is difficult for me to put into words what I saw. This Love was everywhere, like the light, but it was divine, not mere human affection.

I looked at the people milling around on the lawn, and I saw it poured out on them. I thought of the various discords in this field, and I saw, for the first time, the absolute unreality of everything but this infinite Love. It was not only everywhere present, like the light, but it was an intelligent presence that spoke to me, and I found myself weeping as I walked back and forth under the trees, . . . saying out loud, "Why did I never know you before? Why have I not known you always?"

I don't know how long it was until my boy came to me and said, "Come, Mother, they are going home." I got into the carriage and drove back to the hotel, but that same conscious intelligence and Love was everywhere. It rested upon everything my thought rested on.

When we got back to the hotel, there was no boil on my child's head. It was just as flat as the back of her hand. Afterwards the hair [came out] for about two inches around where the boil had been .... She was totally bald on the crown of her head, but the hair grew back as naturally as [if] it had never been out.

I know that this revelation of divine Love came to me by reflection from dear Mrs. Eddy, and for weeks it had a strange effect on me. I could not bear to hear anyone speak in a cross, ill-tempered tone, or do anything that would cause pain. (Jessie B. Cooper reminiscences)

Before leaving home my sister, Helen, had developed a boil on the top of her head which was very painful and caused us a good deal of trouble because travel afforded my mother limited facilities for caring for it, and Helen screamed every time they tried to dress it or arrange her hair. I was uncooperative and accused her of malingering and just spoiling the whole trip for us. Being settled in the hotel room gave my mother her first opportunity to properly cleanse the wound, cut away the matted hair around it and dress it and get her presentable for the visit to Pleasant View. Even then the swelling around the boil and the fiery red color made her an unpleasant-looking object. She rebelled against wearing a hat to cover it, but one was placed on her head anyway.

An omnibus, as we would call it, or a carry-all or barge as it was termed in New England in those days, was provided to take us to Pleasant View....

... There were chairs on the front porch of Mrs. Eddy's

house. The porch functioned as a carriage entrance. . . . . A prominent article of furniture on the porch was an upholstered chair, overstuffed it would be called today—a white piece of paper pinned on it had "MOTHER" written on it. I got close enough to read that before Mrs. Eddy came out of the door and seated herself. It was very warm and she wore no hat or wrap. She was dressed in a blue dress of some figured material. Her eyes were so searchingly bright that they held my attention. The blue of the pupils seemed to melt into the whites. . . .

When the word was passed that Mrs. Eddy would appear, we had gathered in the drive in front of the porch. I had managed to get myself in the front row directly in front of Mrs. Eddy's chair. . . . My mother reached over and took my hat off and handed it to me. This got me a smile and a personal wave of the hand from Mrs. Eddy, and from then on it seemed her eyes smiled every time she looked at me. . . . After Mrs. Eddy put in her appearance, I was too intent in watching her to pay any attention to anyone else or anything else that might have been going on. . . .

The house at Pleasant View was built, as I remember it, on a slope, the back part being lower than the front, making what we would call today a "split-level" house. At the side, where we were, a terrace led down to the lower level where a branch of the drive came for deliveries to the rear entrance. We walked to the terrace and my mother said, "Let us sit down here for a while." . . .

. . . While we sat there Mrs. Eddy's carriage came over from the stable, and she and Mr. Frye got in and went out, I suppose on her daily drive. Thereafter the party began to break up. . . . I saw our barge come in and told my mother, "Our people are getting ready to leave." She said, "Find your Aunt and Helen (my sister) and let us be going." ...

Upon return from Pleasant View and while my mother and I were calling on Mrs. [Mary M. W.] Adams [C.S.D.], my aunt was cleaning up my sister's head where her hair was matted from the dried discharge from the boil she had been suffering from ever since she had left home. When we returned to our room, my aunt called my mother to look at my sister's head. Her hair had been washed and the boil was completely healed. There was hardly even a red spot to show where it had been. (Will Cooper reminiscences)

Inherited illness healed (1897)
(Mrs. Eddy letter to Septimus and Camilla Hanna, Editors)

My dear editors,

You are by this acquainted with the small item that on October last I proposed to one of Concord's best builders the plan for the Christian Science Hall in this city. He drew it, showed it to me, and I accepted it. From that time, October 29, until it was finished, I saw the house every day, and suggested the details from the foundations to the top, outside and inside, and saw them carried out.

One day the carpenters' foreman said to me, "I want to be let off for a few days; I feel not able to keep about, am feeling an old ailment that my mother had." I healed him on the spot; he remained at work, and the next morning said to Mr. George H. Moore, of Concord, "I am as well as I ever was." (*The Christian Science Journal*, March 1898, p. 731)

... When they were building the Concord [Hall], Mrs. Eddy drove around from time to time. One day the contractor was not there. She sent for him to come to see her. Word came back that he could not come, for he was sick. She sent for him again. He came, and said that he was suffering from a trouble that his mother had had for a long time. The man was not a Christian Scientist, so Mrs. Eddy met him on the plane of his own thought.

She said, "No doubt your mother was a very estimable lady, but if she had been a drunkard, would you feel that you had to be a drunkard because she had been?"

The man was healed—so the work could go on at the church. (Emilie B. Hulin reminiscences)

Calvin Frye revived multiple times (1898–1908)
(Each of the following three healings is distinctly different from the accounts on pages 168 and 256–258. Eloise M. Knapp mentions all of them in her reminiscences, citing firsthand sources, as well as an additional healing of Mr. Frye related by Lottie Clark.[10])

I have heard of several restorations from the dead made by Mrs. Eddy, but as they were not given at even second hand, I refrain from quoting, except that Calvin Frye told me that Mrs. Eddy had restored him (in answer to my question). (Edward E. Norwood reminiscences)

1898–1901 *(Clara Shannon)*

One day, while I was writing to Mrs. Eddy's dictation, she sent me with a message to Mr. Frye, who was in his room. When I reached the door, which was open, I saw him lying on his back on the carpet, apparently lifeless. I returned to our Leader and told her about it, saying, "It seems as though he has fainted." She immediately rose and we both went to his room. She kneeled beside him and lifted his arm, which fell inert. Then she began to talk to him. I had been praying for him, but what she said to him was a revelation, to which I listened in wonder. Such heavenly words and tenderness, such expressions of love I have never heard, telling him the truth of man's relationship to God. After a while he opened his eyes, and, as soon as Mother saw that he was becoming conscious, her voice changed, and most severely she rebuked the error that seemed to be attacking him. Her voice and manner were so different, according to the need, that I was deeply impressed.

Presently, she told him to rise on his feet, and gave him her hand to help him to get up. Then she turned round and went out of the room down the passage where she had been sitting. Then she called out, "Calvin, come here!" And he followed her. She spoke to him for several minutes, striving to wake him up—at times, thundering against the error. Then she said, "Now you can go back to your room." He went from the passage towards his room, but before he entered she called him again and talked to him, and this was repeated several times.

I said, "Oh, Mother! Couldn't you let him sit down a few minutes?" She said, "No, if he sits down he may not waken again—he must be aroused—we mustn't let him die—he is not quite awake yet!" She began to talk to him again and reminded him of the time when she rented a farm for one day, not very far from Concord, when she, Martha, and Mr. Frye together drove out and spent the day there, and she began to remind him of the experiences of that day. That reached him, and she said, "You haven't forgotten it, Calvin?" and he said, "No, Mother." And he laughed heartily. Then she talked more of the Truth to him and told him he could go back to his room and his "watch."

She explained to me that when you speak the truth to anyone, if the truth you speak causes him to laugh, cry, or get angry, you have reached the thought that needed correction. (Clara Shannon reminiscences)

Miss Shannon made it clear to the writer that, to her sense of things, Mr. Calvin Frye had definitely passed on when they found him; and he lay on the floor for an appreciable period of time, during which our Leader was praying for him and talking to him, before he showed any signs of life, and sat up. Miss Shannon said that afterwards she was very keen to know what Mr. Frye was doing, to his then sense of things, during this time; and so [the] next day she went to him and said very earnestly, "Calvin, what were you doing yesterday when we thought you were dead? I want to know." Miss Shannon told the writer that he replied at once, "I was in the pantry, eating custard pie." (Richard St. J. Prentice letter, October 17, 1968)

1903 *(John Salchow)*

It was my privilege to witness a healing at Pleasant View in 1903 which was the result of Mrs. Eddy's own understanding of the truth. I always felt that at the time Mrs. Eddy actually restored Calvin Frye to life. My sister was then serving in Mrs. Eddy's household as maid. I remember coming down the second floor hall on my way to Mr. Frye's room and seeing Maggie running out of his room very much agitated. She told me that Calvin Frye was dead, said she had taken hold of him and his flesh was cold and stiff. As I stepped forward I could see him through the open door crumpled up at his desk, his face hanging white and limp against his chest and his arms and hands inert. Just then Mrs. Eddy's voice came from her room. She was out of my line of vision, but from the sound of her voice I could tell just about where she was. Apparently she had not received any response to her ring for Mr. Frye and was leaving her room to find out why he did not answer. I heard her voice coming nearer. It was evident that she had entered Mr. Frye's room and was approaching him, though from the sound of her voice I am sure she did not come directly up to him but stood still in the center of the room. I heard her ask over and over again, "Calvin, do you hear me?" It seemed to me that this went on for five minutes with no response on his part or sign of life. Then I heard him say very faintly, "Yes, Mother, I hear you." I turned and left the hall at that, feeling sure that all was well and that I would not be needed. As my sister had left the hall, as far as I know I was the only one who witnessed this healing. (John Salchow reminiscences)

1908 *(Irving Tomlinson)*

Mary Baker Eddy's motto as a Christian Science practitioner was *semper paratus* [always prepared]. She did not have to prepare herself to heal. She was already prepared. A striking instance was seen in her healing of Mr. Calvin A. Frye soon after she moved to Chestnut Hill. He was found by a member of the household on the night of November 9, 1908, unconscious and apparently in a death stupor. Three of us strove to restore him, but he seemed to have passed on.

When Mrs. Eddy was notified, she arose and was about to dress, but decided there was not time to do so. She asked that he be brought to her, whereupon Calvin was lifted into a small rocker and drawn into the chamber to which Mrs. Eddy had retired for the night. Mrs. Eddy, then in her eighty-eighth year, commanded Mr. Frye, with the voice of authority, to rouse himself, to awaken from his false dream. At first she met with no response, but this did not discourage her. She redoubled her efforts and fairly shouted to him her command that he awake. In a few moments he gave evidence of life, partly opened his eyes, and slightly moved his head. Seeking to rouse him, Mrs. Eddy said, "Calvin, don't commit self-murder." He replied, "I don't want to live."

"Disappoint your enemies and live," she commanded. "Say that you do want to stay and help me."

Then he took his first stand and answered, "Yes, I will stay." It was now about a half-hour since Mr. Frye had first been found. Mrs. Eddy told him to work for himself, and Calvin uttered the words, "Yes, I will come back." Soon he walked back to his room unaided. He retired, slept through the night, and arose the next morning in time to be down for breakfast at seven o'clock. After breakfast he was busy going over his accounts, and when I asked him to cash a check, he readily did so, thus showing his complete return to normality.

It is most inspiring to recall that throughout the entire experience Mrs. Eddy manifested tremendous spiritual strength and poise. Those of us who were present on that occasion can testify that this remarkable woman had lost none of her healing power in her eighty-eighth year. She spoke in strong, clear tones. There was no fear, no doubt, no discouragement; only absolute confidence, only perfect assurance of the victory of Truth. The following morning Mrs. Eddy was up at the usual hour, and at nine o'clock, when I entered her study, I found her busily occupied in reading her Bible. She called my attention to verses 7 and 8 of Psalm 138, which she marked in pencil:

> Though I walk in the midst of trouble, thou wilt revive me: thou shalt stretch forth thine hand against the wrath of mine enemies, and thy right hand shall save me.

> The Lord will perfect that which concerneth me: thy mercy, O Lord, endureth for ever: forsake not the works of thine own hands.

(Irving Tomlinson, *Twelve Years with Mary Baker Eddy: Amplified Edition*, pp. 64–66; corroborated in Adam Dickey, *Memoirs*, pp. 107–112)

Miss Still heard one of the workers say to Mrs. Eddy a few days after this incident, "Can I say that you brought Calvin back from death?" and Mrs. Eddy said, "No; he was not dead." (Robert Peel letter, M. A. Still reminiscence file)

A 1904 entry in Frye's diary possibly sheds light on his condition in this 1908 instance: "Mrs E saved my life from comatose suic'd." (Eddy/Frye diary, May 13, 1904)

Poverty overcome (1899)

I [saw Mrs. Eddy] once at a Jeweler's on Main St. [Concord] . . . and met her several times, and she always bowed, smiled, and shook her hand in such a beautiful manner I simply cannot describe it. I also sat on the seventh row of seats from the front when she spoke in Tremont Temple, June 6, 1899. Just before this I had no home and not one cent of money but received such inspiration that it seems simply unbelievable how I was provided for. I went to Boston from Toronto, Ontario, fully believing this time I would both see and hear her. I did not know she was going to be in Boston and have always given her the credit for this wonderful financial help and my instantaneous healing. (Walter Scott Day reminiscences)

Judge Ewing's cold and coughing healed (1899)

I had as I believed a very severe cold and during our conversation was constantly troubled with this little hacking struggle to get rid of what seemed to be a peanut shell which was lodged in my throat. I thought every time I made any effort I would get out of it. We sat on the sofa, and I turned in my conversation two or three times making assaults upon this peanut obstruction, and after the last one as I again faced [Mrs. Eddy] to resume the conversation, her whole expression had changed, and I thought she was entirely out of humor with me, and she said very sharply, "Why do you do that?" I hesitated for an instant and then said, "I am in doubt as to my ability to answer your conundrum, so I give it up." And then her face just smoothed out and came back to its natural expression, and she said, "Well, that's what you should have done long ago." (William G. Ewing reminiscences)

The following anecdote was told me by Judge Ewing. One time while calling at Pleasant View, he was manifesting a slight cold and coughed several times. Suddenly Mrs. Eddy turned towards him and said, "What are you doing that for?" He replied, "I don't know that I have a very good reason, Mother." With a quick smile, she responded, "I thought you hadn't, so you might as well stop it." He did instantly, and added, "I have never coughed since." (Abigail Dyer Thompson reminiscences)

Obsessive hatred healed (1900)

On page 16 of Mrs. Eddy's 1901 "Message to The Mother Church," she asks this question: "Shall it be said of this century that its greatest discoverer is a woman to whom men go to mock, and go away to pray?"

In the fall of the year before Mrs. Eddy penned this message to her Church, a shoe salesman of Hartford, Connecticut, who had for a long time hated Mrs. Eddy with an unreasoning and unprovoked hatred that amounted to insanity, went to Concord, New Hampshire, and stood outside her gate to see her as she came out to take her drive. He had a vacation about that time, and he was in the neighborhood, so took advantage of this opportunity to satiate his hatred by looking upon the object of his cruel obsession.

This man was in Asheville, North Carolina, a year later, and told of this experience. He said when Mrs. Eddy's carriage passed him at the gate, our dear Leader bowed and smiled sweetly upon him. There was something different in this greeting from what he had expected, for, said he, he felt a flood of divine love such as he never dreamt existed on this earth. It quite unnerved him, and before he realized what he was doing, he crumpled up and wept like a child. On his way home he bought a copy of *Science and Health* by Mrs. Eddy, and began the study of it. He was healed of some ailment (I do not remember what it was), and he became a devoted Christian Scientist. (Elizabeth Earl Jones reminiscences)

Menstrual pain healed (1902)
(Mary Eaton letter)

When I was in Mrs. Eddy's home in January 1902, she asked me where I suffered physically when error attacked me, and I replied that I suffered once a month during the period of menstruation. She then said to me: "You should not have it at all. I overcame it before I came into Christian Science. (I was then thirty years of age.) This is malpractice. It was Josephine Woodbury's belief and she would put her belief on you. Know there is no evil mind to intercept God and you."

As I did not know Josephine Woodbury, I was surprised to hear Mrs. Eddy say this. My practitioner, Mrs. Ella Williams of Chelsea, told me I was the first patient there she ever had who did not go to Josephine Woodbury, but she told me [Woodbury] was a hypnotist, and when some of her pupils urged me to visit her, saying she would teach me for nothing, I refused.

Two years after Mrs. Eddy had healed me of the pain from which I had suffered once a month for eighteen years, she asked me if I had overcome that belief, and I told her I had no more pain, and she replied: "I knew it was nothing but mesmerism." (Mary E. Eaton letter, December 26, 1934)

Sprained ankle healed (1902)

Mrs. [Elizabeth] Norton said that she and her husband [Carol] were in Los Angeles, California, and upon leaving a trolley car she slipped and sprained her ankle very badly. She was helped into the hotel and up to her room.

The following morning the ankle was discolored and so badly swollen that she could not walk. Mr. Norton went downstairs to breakfast, stopping at the office for mail, and among the letters was one from our beloved Leader, Mary Baker Eddy. This letter was addressed to them both and was dated Christmas Eve. Mr. Norton came upstairs and said, "What do you think we have received as a Christmas gift?" Whereupon he handed the letter to Mrs. Norton. As she read it, her eyes filled with tears and her heart overflowed with gratitude and love for our beloved one who had so greatly blessed the whole world with her unselfish love, and as she finished the letter and handed it back to her husband, she discovered that the ankle had been entirely healed, and she was able to walk. (Irving Tomlinson reminiscences)

Mrs. Eddy's letter was dated Dec. 24th, 1902. The above is an accurate account of the healing. [signed] Elizabeth Norton. (Irving Tomlinson reminiscences)

(Mrs. Eddy's letter)

Pleasant View, Concord, N.H.
Dec. 24, 1902

Beloved Student:

For your faithful labors, and your memory, through the pretty apples, of me—I thank you. My prayer is that our one Father-Mother Love hallow your life with His everpresence; and your way be the path of pleasantness—pure, holy, a beacon light to save the wrecks upon earth's siren shoals; to lure the wanderer, help the weak, and comfort the weary.

Mother sends her love to Mrs. Norton together with thanks for those sweet-eyed flowers that came from your "cottage by the sea." May this Xmas be a sweet benediction after your work is done or ready for renewal.

Tenderly thine mother
M. B. Eddy
(L04254)

Severe cold healed (1903)

(Miss Emilie Hergenroder and her sister, both of Baltimore, Maryland, visited Mrs. Eddy at Pleasant View. Emilie, a portrait painter, was working on a painting of Mrs. Eddy from photographs, and thought it would help to see her in person. This is the end of a letter she wrote fourteen years later describing that visit.)

My sister, who was really quite ill with a very severe cold, was instantly healed in Mrs. Eddy's presence. The world had pronounced Mrs. Eddy sick & feeble many times, but she expressed anything but that; indeed she looked very healthy.

Some of her last words were how much work was still for her to do for this great Cause and that her love was in it. (Emilie Hergenroder letter, January 28, 1917)

My first impression of [Mrs. Eddy] is indescribable. I expected to see a tall, handsome woman, almost masculine. It was a small figure which arose from beside the desk where she had been working. She was dressed in black silk, with the famous diamond cross on her breast. She greeted us with outstretched hands. Her great eyes were smiling so kindly as she said how sorry she was she could not see us the day before, but that she did double work to be able to see us that day. She carried her head, with her beautiful white hair, very erect, and had a calm, aristocratic bearing, and the charm of expressing much tender, motherly affection. We were deeply impressed. My sister, who was quite ill with a very severe cold, was instantly healed in Mrs. Eddy's presence. (Clifford P. Smith, *Historical Sketches*, p. 122)

Smoker healed (1903)

There was also a man named Strubble, I think the name was, from New York who was healed of smoking on this same occasion [when Mrs. Eddy spoke to a gathering of Christian Scientists from the balcony of her home]. He was a good Scientist but could not seem to overcome this particular belief. He was standing right opposite the gate at Pleasant View with a cigar in his mouth when Mrs. Eddy drove out in her carriage. He told me that as the carriage passed, she looked straight at him, and he took the cigar out of his mouth. That afternoon he lit another cigar and tried to smoke but found it made him sick. That was the last time he ever attempted to smoke, for his taste for tobacco had been completely destroyed. (John Salchow reminiscences)

[Wentworth Winslow's sister] spoke of the testimony of a noted actor which had appeared some time before in the periodicals and said that this same actor was still a slave to the tobacco habit when he was in Concord some time later, and that, while there, he was walking along the street one day with a big cigar in his mouth when our Leader passed in her carriage. She looked at him—he threw away the cigar and never had the least desire to smoke after that. He explained it by saying: "She saw the real man." (Caroline Getty reminiscences)

Elderly woman leaning on a crutch healed (1903)
(Elizabeth Earl Jones)

The Tuesday and Wednesday after Mrs. Eddy spoke from

the balcony at Pleasant View, in 1903, Mrs. Hazzard and I remained in Concord, New Hampshire, because we wanted to attend the testimonial meeting Wednesday night in Christian Science Hall, the gift of Mrs. Eddy to the Scientists in her home city. Wednesday noon I was in the Reading Room, when someone came in and said, "Mother is coming." We all went out and stood on the stoop at the front door to wave at Mrs. Eddy as she drove by. There must have been about ten or twelve of us there. Mr. Irving C. Tomlinson [C.S.B.], had a practitioner's office in this building, and an elderly lady of Concord was just arriving for her first treatment. With great difficulty she got out of her carriage, leaning on a crutch or stick. With the help of Mr. Tomlinson and her coachman, she joined the little group of Scientists on the stoop. This elderly lady was in the very front of us, leaning on Mr. Tomlinson's arm, and on her crutch or stick.

As Mrs. Eddy drove by, we all waved to her, but she seemed to see no one but this dear little old lady. Mrs. Eddy looked at her with that same lingering, loving, searching look that she had given me the year before, only this time our Leader was not serious, but was exceedingly happy looking. Mrs. Eddy was dressed in white, with a white tulle bonnet with violets on it, and with [a] white tulle nose veil, and bonnet strings. She wore no wrap, although the day was no warmer than the day before when she spoke from the balcony at Pleasant View. Her eyes looked as serene and blue as the summer sky, and she had the most heavenly expression on her lovely face. Indeed, I was so intently looking at this beautiful expression on Mrs. Eddy's face that I did not notice the elderly lady so much, until someone called my attention to her. She was standing erect without a crutch or stick, and was no longer leaning upon Mr. Tomlinson's arm. I heard her say joyously to

Mr. Tomlinson: "I do not need a treatment, I am healed." It all happened in much [less] time than it takes to tell it. (Elizabeth Earl Jones reminiscences)

Poor eyesight healed (1903–1904)

I thought you might be interested in hearing of a healing my husband received.... He was studying for the ministry, and in those days they sent students out on Sundays to conduct services in the country. My husband at that time was wearing glasses, could not see a thing without them, he said.... He was assigned [to conduct services in] Bow, New Hampshire....

He decided he would repair the church [Methodist Episcopal]. He found Mrs. Eddy's name on the church record, so he wrote and asked if she would like to give.[11] She wrote and said she would give fifty dollars towards a bell.... It was not long before he had the money raised for the bell, so he wrote her. She sent him a check for one hundred dollars. He thought there was some mistake, so he went to see her. She said fifty for the bell and fifty for repairs. She said, "What are you wearing glasses for, for style?" He went back to school and he could not see to study. He told the professor he would go out for the day. He never knew where he laid his glasses, but he never wore glasses again until the very last of his life to sharpen a very fine saw. He could read the finest print. (Alice M. Larmour to Will B. Davis, 1954, reminiscence file)

Injuries from an accident healed (1904)

While Mrs. [Ella] Sweet was at Pleasant View, the Concord church was in the process of building. Mrs. Eddy had said several times she wished my mother to see it. Some time, however, passed, when on a certain day she made arrangements to have Mr. Frye and Mr. Kinter accompany Mrs. Sweet to the church and show her through. She especially requested the two gentleman to look carefully after her.

During her walk through the unfinished building, as I understood, she stepped on a loose board or piece of wood, which flew up and struck her in the face leaving quite a wound; also her ankle was strained. Earnest work was done by all three. They returned home and each went to his room to continue work.

In a brief time my mother's bell rang summoning her to Mrs. Eddy's study. She responded, taking a chair a little behind or to the side of Mrs. Eddy, hoping the difficulty might not be noticed. Mrs. Eddy remarked, "Mrs. Sweet, why do you sit there, come where I can see you." She then asked to know what had happened and if help was being given. She wanted to know how mother was working for herself. Mother said she was handling the false claim of accidents. Mrs. Eddy replied, "That will not meet the case. Animal magnetism is trying to separate you from me and I need you." She talked a little and complete healing followed. (Clara Sweet Brady reminiscences)

Illness healed (1905)

One day when Mrs. Eddy was taking her daily drive, she passed an old acquaintance on the street. He could scarcely walk with a cane, but her sense of God and perfect man was so strong that he was healed. This was his statement in a letter following the incident, and which I heard our Leader read: "I have been very ill lately and have suffered a great deal, but was entirely healed the day you passed me on the street. I am grateful to God." (Julia Prescott reminiscences)

Arm disabled by neuritis, healed (1906)

... It was my privilege to attend the dedication of the Extension of The Mother Church and to visit Concord on Wednesday after the dedication. I was suffering with an almost helpless arm through a false belief of neuritis. When our beloved Leader passed Concord church on her daily drive, I looked in her beloved face and saw those marvelous eyes [looking] on her beloved children around the green. The chimes played "Saw ye my Saviour," [and] my tears of gratitude fell oh so lovingly toward her. I was healed and attended the evening service ..., not realizing I was healed until I stood in that meeting. I have never been able, since I saw her beloved countenance, to hold hatred or malice toward a human being, ... [though] before that I rather prided myself in forgiving but not forgetting. (Eleanor B. Whittemore reminiscences)

Severe throat condition healed (1907)
(Adela Rogers St. Johns to Irving Tomlinson)

When I had the pleasure of calling on you with Miss Allen last August, you asked me to write you details of a healing which I told you about at that time, and that is the occasion for this letter.

The story was told to me originally by Louis Weadock, who in 1906 was the star reporter of the *New York Herald*.

In that capacity, he was sent to Concord, with many other newspapermen, to "cover" the story about Mary Baker Eddy which was then occupying some space in the newspapers, and which is mentioned at length in the last part of Chapter XXI of Miss Wilbur's *The Life of Mary Baker Eddy*.

He told me that they were sent to Pleasant View at that time to dig up the truth about Mrs. Eddy. Their orders from the city desk were positive. They were to use what methods were necessary, but they were to find out the facts. If Mrs. Eddy was dead and someone was impersonating her, if she was mentally incompetent and physically in ill health, they were to bring back the story, sparing no one.

He also told me that naturally, being reporters, they hoped this would be the case—that something of a sensational nature would be uncovered. If Mrs. Eddy was merely living in saintly retirement, working and praying for mankind, it was not news. But if any of the other rumors about her were true, it would be a great story. All upon the old reportorial adage that if a dog bites a man it isn't news, but if a man bites a dog it is.

He said that they were a hard-boiled, belligerent bunch of old-timers who went down there. That they hoped and expected to "dig up" a lot of scandal. That they were news hounds baying on the trail.

As he told it to me, they were in Concord for some rather long period of time, investigating the story and, as I remember it, covering the happenings surrounding the suit brought by George Glover, Dr. Foster Eddy, and George W. Baker.

They took rooms at some hotel in Concord.

He said that while they were there a member of the Christian Science Church and someone close to Mrs. Eddy was appointed as a sort of news representative for Mrs. Eddy. This man was to give them the information from Mrs. Eddy's side of the case and to handle their requests and deal with them in all matters pertaining to the press.

The man appointed, so he said, was Mr. Irving Tomlinson.

He said that they were all greatly amazed at the kind and loving treatment accorded them. I remember his exact words: "If ever anyone had a right to hate anyone else, surely those Christian Scientists had a right to hate us. We were there to vilify their Leader if we could. We had no reverence and no decency, as I knew. We didn't believe anything but the worst about anybody. And we wanted if possible to hold Mrs. Eddy up to scorn and ridicule, to expose and denounce her if we could."

They were therefore much surprised to receive kindly treatment.

One member of their group—Mr. Weadock did not give me his name, and I am not just now able to get in touch with him, but I will later and will send it to you—was a reporter from a big New York newspaper, a hard drinker, and altogether the type of [an] old newspaper man.

He had been afflicted for some years with a very severe throat condition. Mr. Weadock did not know whether this was a cancer or not, but the boys thought maybe it was. Anyway, it was extremely painful, and at times overwhelmed this man completely.

One evening they were all sitting in his room at the hotel, drinking and smoking, bored with their stay in this small New England town. The reporter I have mentioned was at this time suffering tortures with his throat. He had lost his voice entirely and was not able to speak a word.

The telephone rang and it was yourself, calling and asking for this reporter. He had asked for some information and you were calling to give it to him.

Mr. Weadock answered the phone and said he would take the message as the reporter in question was too ill to come to the phone and couldn't speak anyway. But Mr. Tomlinson insisted upon speaking with him, saying that whether he could speak or not he could hear the message.

So the reporter went to the phone, showing decided anger. He listened a few moments, and those in the room of course could not hear what was being said. But when the reporter turned away from the phone, he could not only speak perfectly, but he was completely healed.

Mr. Weadock said the healing scared them all. They sat around, looking at each other, not able to comprehend this thing, and more startled by it than anything else.

They were closely enough in touch with Christian Science at that time to understand the claim of Christian Scientists to heal the sick, and they knew that their comrade had been healed.

They could not understand the method, but he said they did understand one thing, and all voiced it. If Christian Scientists were loving enough to want to heal those reporters who had come for the purpose they had, they were certainly loving their enemies and were showing a Christ-spirit far beyond anything they had ever before encountered.

They were just enough to give full credit for the great Love shown in the gentleness and the healing, even though they could not understand what had happened.

Mr. Weadock said that this circumstance completely changed their outlook on Christian Science, and swung them very decidedly over to a fair viewpoint in the proceedings, and animated them with a real desire to be fair in dealing with Mrs. Eddy and in fact made them hope that she would be thoroughly vindicated—which of course she was.

The reporters scattered after this, and Mr. Weadock does not know what became of this man, but he said he saw him several times afterwards and the healing was perfect and was still puzzling him greatly—so we know that we can leave him in God's hands, confident that his very wonder will one day lead him to the Truth.

Mr. Weadock himself has in the past two years turned to Christian Science for help. The claim of drunkenness had him pretty well down and out at that time, and the demonstration is not yet complete, but he asks for treatment, goes to church, and does his lessons, and believes entirely that Christian Science is the finest and most wonderful religion on earth today.

He has often stated to me that his contact with Christian Scientists in those early days, and his one interview with Mrs. Eddy, did so much to convince him of this, so that in his hour of greatest woe he turned back to it. And it has made me see more and more clearly that much of our "duty to our Leader"[12] is to live Christian Science in just this way, so that we will bring others to the Truth just by our daily living.

This experience as told to me has been a great help to me many times, and I have also given it as a testimony—without any names, of course—in several Wednesday evening meetings, and it has brought much help to others.

It is a great happiness to me to relate it to you.

(Adela Rogers St. Johns letter, October 25, 1926, in Irving Tomlinson reminiscences)

A healing which I recall with much interest occurred in the year 1907, at the time of the "Next Friends" suit, when many newspapers were sending their reporters to Concord in the hope of securing interviews with Mrs. Eddy. Since it would have taken nearly all her time if she had seen all these representatives of the press, she appointed me as a receiver and giver of messages. At this time there were three or four reporters particularly determined to see Mrs. Eddy. . . .

The chief man among this group, representing a big New York newspaper, was known as a particularly hard-boiled reporter and a steady drinker. He had been afflicted for some years with an extremely painful growth on his throat, which may have been cancerous and which at times completely overwhelmed him. . . .

Mrs. Eddy had asked me to call these men by telephone and inform them that it was impossible for her to see them. But she cautioned me at the same time, "Be sure to ask for the leading man and speak directly to him."

The telephone rang and one of the younger reporters answered the call. According to instructions, I asked to speak to the head man, . . . but was told that this man was too ill . . . . I said, "Tell him to come to the telephone; he can hear what I say even if he can't talk."

Accordingly, the suffering newspaper man came to the telephone . . . . He listened for a few moments. . . . [and] when this man turned away from the telephone, he not only could speak perfectly, but was healed. . . .

Some years later a relative of this man called at my office in Boston, and gave me the following message: "My uncle requested me to see you and to tell you in his last days he turned to Christian Science, and he knew that he owed a debt of gratitude to Mrs. Eddy for his healing in Concord." (Irving Tomlinson, *Twelve Years with Mary Baker Eddy*, pp. 69–71)

Storm dispelled (1907)

On several occasions I saw Mrs. Eddy dispel a storm; the first time was on August 3, 1907, in the late afternoon. The sky was overcast and it was very dark. Mrs. Eddy sat in her chair in the tower corner of her study, watching the clouds with a smile and a rapt expression on her face. She seemed to be seeing beyond the storm, and her present surroundings, and I do not think that she was conscious of my presence. In a few moments the clouds broke and flecked, and the storm was dissolved into its native nothingness. About half an hour later I took her supper tray to her, and she said to me, "Ada, did you see the sky?" I replied, "Yes, Mrs. Eddy." Then she said, "It (meaning the cloud) never was; God's face was never clouded." This agrees with what another student has recorded as having been said by Mrs. Eddy, namely, "When I wanted to dispel a storm, I did not say, 'There is no thunder, and no lightning,' but I said, 'God's face is there, and I do see it.'" (Adelaide Still reminiscences)

Lame arm healed (1908–1910)

Sunday afternoon, April 12, 1931, the writer [Irving Tomlinson] with Mrs. Tomlinson took for a drive Mrs. Martha McGaw. . . . While passing the Reservoir on Beacon Street, at the entrance to the Reservoir, Mrs. McGaw said: "Here a friend of mine had a wonderful case of healing. He had been troubled for a long time with a disabled arm. It was in such a bad condition that he could not lift his hand to his head. He hoped that he might see Mrs. Eddy, and while he was standing at the entrance to the Reservoir park, Mrs. Eddy came toward him in her carriage. He lifted his hand to his head to tip his hat to her, forgetting all about himself, forgetting that he had a lame arm, but he did it naturally and without inconvenience to himself. From that moment, he found himself completely healed and has been free from any inconvenience in that arm ever since." (Irving Tomlinson reminiscences)

Laura Sargent healed of exhaustion (1910)

One night in April 1910, error seemed to strike at Mrs. Sargent quite severely. Miss Eveleth and I stayed with her until midnight when she seemed somewhat better, but when morning came she said she was not equal to her work, and it seemed best for her to take a little time off to recuperate. Mrs. Eddy missed her very much and kept asking when she was coming back. She asked me what was the trouble with Laura, and I told her that she was just tired out and needed a rest. Mrs. Eddy immediately took a pad and wrote the article, "A Pæan of Praise,"[13] and gave instructions for it to be printed in the next issue of the *Sentinel*. She also wrote a note to Laura, and when she received an answer stating she would return in a few days, she was very happy. Laura came back a day earlier than she had promised, and surprised Mrs. Eddy. (Adelaide Still reminiscences)

COURTESY TMBEC

Residence staff of Mrs. Eddy's home in Chestnut Hill, Massachusetts

∽∾

(Mrs. Eddy's note)

April 17, 1910

Give my love to Laura and tell her I have taken her up and it helped her and she can come back to me. Tell me when she will come. Tell Laura I healed her. (L10875)

A PÆAN OF PRAISE

"Behind a frowning providence
He hides a shining face."

The Christian Scientists at Mrs. Eddy's home are the happiest group on earth. Their faces shine with the reflection of light and love; their footsteps are not weary; their thoughts are upward; their way is onward, and their light shines. The world is better for this happy group of Christian Scientists; Mrs. Eddy is happier because of them; God is glorified in His reflection of peace, love, joy.

When will mankind awake to know their present ownership of all good, and praise and love the spot where God dwells most conspicuously in His reflection of love and leadership? When will the world waken to the privilege of knowing God, the liberty and glory of His presence,— where

"He plants His footsteps in the sea
And rides upon the storm."

MARY BAKER EDDY

Chestnut Hill, Mass.
April 20, 1910

Appendix A

More Advice for Healers

Appendix A

MORE ADVICE FOR HEALERS

$\mathcal{U}$NLIKE MRS. EDDY'S LETTERS AND dictations excerpted in "Interlude," these are presented in their entirety since they contain extensive counsel on healing. All the material that follows ranges from 1888 to 1910; these documents are part of The Mary Baker Eddy Collection and may be found in The Mary Baker Eddy Library. Two items are not letters. One is dictation Mrs. Eddy gave to Calvin Frye on December 2, 1891, at 3:30 a.m. The second is a set of notes taken by Irving Tomlinson, describing the prayer he heard Mrs. Eddy speak at 10 p.m. on September 5, 1910. Once again, minor corrections to spelling and grammar have been made for clarity.

Throughout her letters, one can see Mrs. Eddy's insightfulness, wisdom, leadership, and tenderness, but most of all her love for her students. She cares for them as a mother cherishes her children. She wants only good for them. She calls on them to awake and to work. She rebukes the error they entertain, but not the students themselves. She puts demands on them with the full expectation that they will be able to meet those demands. One sees in these letters the wise counselor, the commanding Leader, and the gentle caregiver.

To Edward Kimball in 1888

Mr. Kimball
My dear Student,

I was delighted to hear from you, and I know from what you write that you are meeting all, now, and that this *all* is *nothing*! Now, dear Student, the lady that healed you is a good, loyal, noble woman, but she was not quite equal to the task of handling your mind. Hence you were never rid of *yourself*.

This task is left to be accomplished, and it will be, and it can be, and it must be done. You need to know that you are not the man you think you are. I never knew a dyspeptic that was either a man or a woman. They are nothing but *stomachs* all absorbed in digestion, of what? What you are is yet to be seen. I want to think of you as a *man*, a great, grand, noble, frank man such as stood up bravely and fought me in the class and when he was beaten knew it. Now, do you know as well on this occasion that you are not beaten and nowhere near it? You are a man! This I repeat, and you are not a stomach! And a stomach is not talking, arguing, feeling, and suffering. As a man you are occupied with a great demand on your time and talents. Now go to work full of business to *do good*, and have full confidence in God that all the good [He] wishes you to do you *can do*. He is too wise to say, "Go work in my vineyard" and then render you unfit for work! He says this to you and knows that you are able to do all the good that you are required to do. God says heal the sick. Malicious error says you can't heal and are sick; your stomach says I am the umpire and know this is true.

Now let God be found *true* and the last two aforenamed be proven *liars*.

I join issue with God. *I know* you are *well*, I know you are not frightened. You are *fearless*, strong, and well—this is the man I am addressing. There is *no malicious mind*, no mesmerism. There is but one Mind, and this Mind is Love. Nobody is *hurting you*, and you can't hurt yourself. This you will find out if only you stick to the statement of *Truth*, and declare on the right side, eat everything you please, and love everybody but especially your wife as she is one of the few who are worthy to be loved.

Just wake up! And see your real self ten minutes, or one minute, and all this ado about nothing will be found out. *God will* keep you from *falling*. You can't go down. He has given His angels charge over you; they (*true* thoughts) will hold you up, and you cannot dash your foot against a stone. Only let these thoughts hold sway.

Love to Mrs. Kimball.
Ever truly,
M B G Eddy[1]

To Mrs. Eddy's Christian Scientist Association in 1889

"He anointeth my head with oil; my cup runneth over" means the action of Mind on our consciousness.

Water corresponds to unconscious mind. All unconscious thought is in solution, when it comes to the surface it is dry land. The Red Sea spoken of in Scripture is figurative of fear in unconscious mind. Error—sin, sickness, and death—is sown and commences in the unconscious mind of your patients, and yourself. Your patients, through ignorant fear. Your own, through neglect, or willful sin.

"Baptism...by fire."

It corresponds to fear in mortal mind. All our suffering is from fear. We have got to pass through the furnace heated seven times hotter than it was wont to be. Man's extremity is God's opportunity. There is only one way to meet this rule of sin. Would we entertain a guest that was spoiling our house? Now instead of entertaining the guest that says "you cannot heal," old beliefs are re-established, you feel your patient's beliefs, etc.; it is your duty to eject this guest at once. No man can enter into a strong man's house and spoil his goods except he first bind the strong man; and then he will spoil his house.[2] You can make your house—the body—just what the mind is. The discouragement brought to you, you are to expel as an unwelcome guest. This is the ground on which all must work. Watch just what your thoughts are, and labor there until success greets your efforts. If you think you haven't time to attend to it, say I have; or if you think you need help, prove it otherwise. There is no one that can help you like yourself. There are no *conditions* hindering. They are only what you admit. Whenever you take this position, you go up higher. The opposite position is that of "I don't care."

Let me tell you something for your encouragement. The

one that has met the most and conquered it is the nearest heaven—harmony. Students are morally responsible to meet in themselves any error, and then it will disappear from the patient. It is not the patient. It is some moral wrong in the student. Never allow error (the use of medicines) indirectly to be used, not merely from a fear that they injure your patient for they have no virtue, but for the reason that God would not get all the glory of the healing.

The remedy for the trials of the hour, hatred with fear, is Love. How shall I meet this heated hatred, this envy, this malice, this poison of thought, is the question with the Christian Scientist. The answer is by the exercise of Love, which chastens the evildoer. Evil hath its own reward. The law in Israel today is—What you say or do to cause another to suffer, shall cause *you*, not them, to suffer. Because we do not observe this law is the reason we do not succeed. That the spirit of revenge in mortal mind may not prevail, students should see the necessity of, and strive to attain a clearer understanding of, the Law of Love.[3]

To Frank Gale in 1891:

385 Commonwealth Ave.

My very dear Student,

Your excellent letter and kind remittance just rec'd. Accept my *thanks*. You are *growing*. The Father has sealed you, and the opening of these seals must not surprise you. The character of Christ is wrought out in our lives by just such processes. The tares and wheat appear to grow together until the harvest; then the tares are *first* gathered, that is, you have seasons of seeing your errors—and afterwards, by reason of this very seeing, the tares are burned, the error is destroyed. Then you see Truth plainly, and the wheat is "gathered into barns"—it becomes permanent in the understanding.

The suggestions that enter your mind, such as you specified in [your] letter, are sown by the "wicked one"—and by night—when you are doubting or departing unconsciously from the light. Work on; the field is everywhere, and God will direct you where to be if you abide in this Scriptural rule, "Trust in the Lord with *all* thy heart, and lean not unto thine own understanding; in all thy ways acknowledge Him, and He will direct thy path." The healing will grow more easy and be more immediate as you realize that God, Good, *is all* and Good is *Love*. You must gain Love, and lose the false sense called love. You must feel the Love that *never* faileth—that perfect sense of divine power that makes healing no longer power but *grace*. Then you will have the Love that casts out fear, and when fear is gone, doubt is gone and your work is done. Why? Because it never was *undone*.

My tender love to your dear mother. My earnest desire for you both goes with this letter saying in the words of Jesus, "In the world ye shall have tribulation: but be of good cheer; I (Truth) have overcome the world," overcome the flesh and temptation. I did not expect the money, $100, and am most grateful to you.

Your loving Teacher,
Mary B G Eddy[4]

Dictation of Mrs. Eddy to Calvin Frye

Dec. 2 – 3:30 A.M. 1891
From Dictation of Mrs. E.
C.A.F.

1. The Principle of C.S. is Love.
2. The effect of Love is to destroy all sense of corporeality.
3. Whatever tends to diminish the sense of love & increase the sense of corporeality diminishes the understanding of C.S. and the demonstration of the Principle Life and Love.

The war
1. The fight between the world, the flesh, and the devil.
2. Their weapons: hatred and false personality.
3. Whatever diminishes the sense of love & increases the sense of personality casts your influence on the side of the world, the flesh, & the devil, and helps evil to destroy the idea of good. In other words, to kill the person who represents in the highest degree this idea & so to shut out the sense of love.

Moral
Watch & be sure that your love is increasing & your false sense of personality is diminishing & make everything that you say & do tend to produce this effect.

A strong sense of the false personality retards the growth of yourself & of those around you, the same as a strong sense of disease would prevent your healing & prevent your patient's recovery.[5]

To Ira Packard

July 7, 1896

My dear Mr. Packard, and Student,

You are held by a *mesmeric belief* to the thought that you cannot demonstrate Christian Science. Demand of yourself to awake from this glamour and know it is false and a "liar from the beginning." Do you think that divine Love has said "seek, and ye shall find" and "seek ye first the kingdom of God, and [His] righteousness; and all these things shall be added unto you," and then fail to fulfill His Word? Your faith is less than was his of old who said, "Because Thou canst, thou wilt make me whole." Rouse yourself from this spell of mesmerism and by no means return to your material pursuits. They cannot remedy your spiritual need but will add to it. Take God, *Good*, at His word and follow the teachings of my books, and I promise you that you can demonstrate what they teach. No bank note is half as sure as these promises, no business transactions can equal God's integrity and sure reward for doing rightly. Is matter the reality and Spirit unreal? And which is leading you, the real or the unreal when you contemplate turning from spiritual things to the material for consolation? Put down this temptation that you cannot heal the sick, preach the gospel, and raise your dead faith to the life-giving realities and possibilities that enable you to meet the command of Christ to his students today, the same as in the first century. Rise above this temptation by which Satan, evil, would bind you, and know the truth and "the Truth will make you free," and angels, right thoughts, will come to you.

Why should you go to students to explain what the Bible

and my books teach? Ask God in prayer to open your own eyes that having eyes you can see. And that your eyes be single, that you ... give up material pursuits and say I will not go back, having "put my hand to the plough," but will hold on to Truth, and error shall not deceive nor mislead me.

You have grown out of a sense that matter can help you in business or in grace, and you know that God can and will. Read the 91st Psalm and treat yourself daily against being governed by Theosophy or Hypnotism or m.a.m. [malicious animal magnetism]—and pray that His kingdom, the reign of peace and Love, be come in your understanding, and that your faith fail not, but increase daily. No matter what the senses testify for they are not your guide, but misguide.

Let me hear from you again after you obey my orders and heal the sick and cast out the evils in your own mind.

With love to your family and yourself,
Mother
Mary Baker Eddy[6]

To Judge Septimus J. Hanna

Aug. 5, [18]97

My beloved Student,

You are now taking the right steps. Go into your secret "upper chamber" (observatory), shut out observation and the world since the kingdom of good cometh not thereby—and pray. No better possible place hath earth for prayer than that. But to reap the reward, take up your cross, overcome the fear of man that bringeth a snare. Tell your wife and her servants never to disturb you at those hours of prayer; fix them at four hours each day for reading, prayer, and meditation *alone* with God. Let your rule for this have no more exception than if you were on an island in the sea. Be strong and *firm* on this basis till you are ready to feel, "I have had my vacation, I am ready for harder work." Life is not rest, it is action; doing good is Life, rest, and action. But turmoil and the world's *nothing* forced on one goads and thus tires *good folks*. You are an example of action that cannot weary; it bears the burdens that Christ, Truth, makes light. Love gives you rest in this toil and sweetens it. Oh if you knew my confused life *in the house* and outside of it, you would say it is a miracle every moment that she can live! But healing is to those who do it not, a miracle, but to those who do it—only natural and rests one on an immutable Principle that *all* must learn.

Lovingly,
Mother

P.S. — Treat yourself 3 times every day on the basis I name. And let a student treat you once, and make the basis point this: that you can help yourself and need not the help of man. God, good, Truth, Love is all the help you can have, for these are all power. Know this. Also *know* that if you *trust* in this help, you cannot fall. "Because he has put his trust in me, therefore will I deliver him" is the promise.

Now drop any of your offices but *Readership*, never that, and your salary shall increase in proportion to the loss.

Aside from 4 hours employed as designated, study the Word, meditate, pray, watch, work, but not weary. I mean by this, mental work. Remember this fixed fact. You *have no material heart.* Your heart God gave you, and He governs all its functions. It cannot cease to act so long as God acts, for it is His reflection of Love. Let alone all sense of anatomy, and hold this true consciousness of yourself. Pain is *not pain* and *you know it.*[7]

To Septimus J. Hanna

Aug. 14, 1897

My beloved Student,

Every time you have been, to my knowledge, tested by divine Love, in your faithful discharge of high offices, you have shown a loving charity and a most Christian spirit. And I do pray that I may not give you a single additional care or sigh.

Oh may God spare me this occasion. I never feel that you do wrong; you cannot indulge a wrong thought with your *own* volition turned as it is to Truth and Love. But the temptations that beset all true Christians are either to feel too sharply the burdens borne or to try to lay them down.

Now beloved in Christ, [neither] you nor I can *suffer* for *doing good.* It is our *life,* our growth, our spiritual element, that is mightier than all the means of mortals to thwart this result—yes, infinitely beyond them. Now just turn all your powers to find peace and rest in the *good you reflect,* and that *upholds* you.

Know this, that there the necromancers fail; they cannot

come nigh that secret place. There, you *are safe*, and because you put your trust in Good, God *will* deliver you, and you cannot fear but will *walk where you look* and be strong.

No person has ever since I left the [*Christian Science*] *Journal* filled its need but you, and God will give you power to continue [as] its editor. I beg of you to have rules like the Medes and Persians that change not. Make them imperative and unalterable viz.: That certain hours you cannot be seen nor communicated with. Do not let the caller in at those hours, nor a letter or message be sent to you. Had not I established this system for myself, I never could have accomplished what little I have done. I beg you not to feel the least regret or condemnation over your letter. It will do us all good. Be calm, full of *trust* and *joy*, for the blessings you have brought on us all by your fidelity to God and man must, will, return to you after due time.

With love to dear Camilla and Septimus,
Mother Mary Baker Eddy[8]

To Pamelia J. Leonard

Aug. 31, [1902]

My precious Student,

Excuse pencil. I want to say that you must know that your present changed thought on the nothingness of disease is *scientific*. True, there is in reality no disease. But Jesus said he that endures to the end is saved.

Suppose you fail to heal the belief of disease in one treatment, and because you have not healed it, you can do no more for the patient, for the disease seems so unreal to you! You cannot continue to argue it down! Now when the disease is unreal to you—you have *healed it*, and this is the only way to know it is healed.

I am sure it is fear that prevents you arguing and denying a disease so long as the disease lasts in belief. Now you must master this fear of yours or you cannot heal the patient. "Endure to the end" when the case lingers—fight the error till it is beaten [or] else conquer it in the beginning. Answer me on this point. You cannot bring back your belief by contending against the reality of error, for that cannot make error real to you.

And the error is real to you that you do not *destroy*. So you should not forget its name if to name it puts it out, and S. & H. [*Science and Health*] says that it does do this. You must not forget to watch against a robber, and if you forget how to handle the robber, he may break open your house. Examine yourself and treat disease either by arguing it down or by destroying it in the first instance.

Lovingly yours,
M B Eddy[9]

Written by Irving C. Tomlinson

Eddy
Prayer
Sept. 5, 1910

(While on watch) with Mrs. Eddy last night at 10 P.M., I heard her speaking. An investigation found she was in prayer. I stood beside her for at least 5 minutes, then sat down and for 5 minutes more prayer continued. The entire petition was scientific, orderly in its procedure, choice in language. It contained no request for a special blessing for health, comfort, or prosperity for herself or her Cause, but was a beautiful declaration of Truth for a full realization of truth of being for herself and for her followers and for all mankind.

The entire prayer was in accord with her characteristic phrasing and breathed the profound faith shown in her most spiritual writings.

She would voice her inmost desire for a realization of God's presence and power and follow it with a declaration that that presence and power was an eternal manifestation and fully realized by His children. She would petition that no temptation could assail; and follow it by the declaration that the real man was free from temptation. She affirmed that there was no lack in God's provisions for His offspring and asserted that this truth *was* realized by all.

The prayer had introduction, progress, and conclusion. The language was chaste and well chosen. She spoke of God's presence hourly and *momently* and asked that we might know that there was "no rift in the rhythm of the eternal harmony."

The prayer was a hint of the source of power in Christian Science and suggested the reason for its founding, growth, and fruits.[10] The prayer which I heard brought to my consciousness the truth that real prayer is the very heart and soul of Christian Science—its founding, its growth, and its fruits.

At its conclusion I spoke. Her response indicated that she was awake but in a realm apart from her surroundings. She asked, "Who is it dear?" and when I told her that the prayer was heard, she answered, "Yes, dear, it is."

Within 15 minutes she was again sound asleep.

Undoubtedly it was my privilege to hear the audible expression of the silent but ever present desires which for forty years have been wafted heavenward by this faithful servant of the Most High.[11]

Appendix B

BIOGRAPHICAL GLOSSARY

Appendix B

BIOGRAPHICAL GLOSSARY

THE FOLLOWING ARE SKETCHES OF individuals either mentioned in this book or whose reminiscences have provided source material for the accounts of Mary Baker Eddy's healing works. (When known, historical references are provided, including birth and death dates.) For many of these individuals, their association with Mrs. Eddy came about from the need for healing. Some were healed by her directly, others by reading her book *Science and Health with Key to the Scriptures*, and others were healed by her students. A number of the people discussed in this glossary are noted as having had Christian Science class instruction—Primary or Normal. A Christian Science teacher, one who has earned a certificate from the Board of Education of The First Church of Christ, Scientist, is qualified to teach Primary classes. Each teacher may hold one Primary class a year of not more than 30 pupils. A student who takes a Primary class is preparing to be a Christian Science practitioner, or healer. Attending a Normal class—taught every third year—prepares an experienced practitioner to be a Christian

Science teacher. Normal classes are taught by Christian Science teachers who are practitioners with well-established records both of Christian healing and of dedication to the Cause of Christian Science.

Joseph Armstrong (1848–1907) A lumberman and banker in Kansas, Joseph Armstrong took up the study of Christian Science after his wife's healing of invalidism in 1886. He took three classes taught by Mrs. Eddy. Early in 1893 she asked him to serve as Publisher of *The Christian Science Journal* and soon after placed him on the Christian Science Board of Directors, the governing board of The Mother Church under the guidance of the *Church Manual*; she also asked him to serve as Manager of The Christian Science Publishing Society. In 1896, Mrs. Eddy asked Mr. Armstrong to be the Publisher of her own writings after she dismissed her adopted son from that position in the same year. Armstrong's duties as Publisher of the *Journal* were assumed by the Board of Trustees of the newly reorganized Publishing Society in 1898. He served in all three capacities—Director, Manager, and Publisher of Mrs. Eddy's writings—until his passing.

In August 1901, Mr. Armstrong asked Mrs. Eddy what he should do to better sell her writings. In her reply she wrote:

> To your question, How to increase the sales of my books? I answer: By stopping the lies published about the author with the truth that destroys the lie. . . .
>
> . . . If you are willing to give your time to publishing my works and work for the Cause by attending more

to mental prayer which pours in truth to the boiling cauldron of lies, I would be glad to have you give up the other publishing and get the right one to take your place. I always said and say that the one work is enough for one man's pursuit. If you do this it will increase the sales and give you as much profit in the business as you would make by diminishing the sales [of] my books and publishing the rest of the literary stuff on hand.[1]

Addie Towns Arnold (1858–1937) Born in Tilton, New Hampshire, Addie Towns was acquainted with members of Mrs. Eddy's family there. Mrs. Eddy's niece, Ellen Pilsbury, was her schoolteacher. Addie was a child when she first saw Mrs. Eddy (then Mrs. Patterson) in 1862. Mrs. Patterson's husband Daniel was a prisoner of war in the South and she was staying with her sister Abigail Tilton. Mrs. Arnold became interested in Christian Science in 1885 when she was healed of invalidism caused by rheumatic fever. Not until after her healing, when she read of Ellen Pilsbury's healing in the twentieth edition of *Science and Health*, did she realize that Mrs. Eddy and the Mrs. Patterson she had known as a child were the same person.

During the winter of 1886–87, Addie was taught Christian Science by Susie M. Lang, a student of Mrs. Eddy's. She joined the Boston Church of Christ (Scientist) in December 1888. Mrs. Eddy personally greeted her and her husband after the Sunday Communion service when new members were admitted. She said to them, "Beware of the leaven of the scribes and Pharisees—the doctrines of men." After speaking with each new member, Mrs. Eddy addressed them all, saying,

"I need you, the Church needs you, and the world is waiting. Be faithful to Christian Science."[2] Mrs. Arnold devoted the rest of her life to the public practice of Christian Science healing.

Sarah Bagley *(1824–1905)* After being displaced from Captain Nathaniel Webster's house in Amesbury, Massachusetts, Mrs. Eddy (then Mrs. Glover) went to live in Miss Bagley's home for two months during the summer of 1868. Toward the end of that year, while staying with the Wentworths in East Stoughton, Massachusetts, she wrote Sarah of her plans to go west:

> I want a student at work. I am torn asunder almost by requests to heal the sick and somehow they keep me at it continually; this is all the way I can escape. I can go there and teach, have my travelling expenses all paid, and a pleasant board at a fashionable and excellent hotel, and it will be much easier for me than to build my own fires and toil through a hard winter here."[3]

Mrs. Glover spent another six weeks with Sarah in the spring of 1870.

Originally a spiritualist, Miss Bagley gave it up when she became Mrs. Eddy's fourth student. Although remaining a friend, Sarah never gave up head-rubbing as part of her practice after Mrs. Eddy told her students in 1872 that they must discontinue this method as part of their healing treatment. Miss Bagley never joined her teacher's students' association or the Church and never claimed to be a Christian Scientist. The two lost contact with each other after the mid-1870s.

Joshua F. Bailey (1831–1907) A Boston schoolteacher in the late 1850s, Joshua Bailey became a Special Agent of the United States Treasury Department in 1861. Working for Thomas Edison's Telephone and Light Company, he lived in South America from 1870 to 1874 and then in Europe until 1887. He took three classes from Mrs. Eddy: two Primary classes in 1888 and 1889, and a Normal class in 1889. She appointed him Editor of *The Christian Science Journal* in February 1889. Under her instructions he wrote the *Journal* article, "Christian Science and its Revelator," which is quoted on p. 29–30.

It was Mr. Bailey's idea to start the semi-monthly periodical *Christian Science Series* in May 1889. Mrs. Eddy stopped its publication in April 1891, after already having replaced him as Editor in December 1890 because of his headstrong impulsiveness. Nevertheless, she cared for him as her student. In July 1891, Mrs. Eddy wrote Mr. Bailey:

> Work on in His vineyard but do not help deluge
> our land with diluted or subverted statements of
> Christian Science.

> Your own sharp discrimination and sound
> judgement ought to shield you from being misled in this
> as others have been. But the grace of God *is sufficient* to
> save you, and to Him I commit you. Trust Love to lead
> you out of temptation and deliver you from evil. Be strong
> in the strength of Truth and Love. He girdeth thee.[4]

Mr. Bailey began teaching Christian Science in 1891 and continued in this work in New York City, along with his healing practice, until his passing.

Abigail Ambrose Baker (1784–1849) Mrs. Eddy's mother was a Puritan and very loving by nature. Her family was second in her affections only to God, and she felt closest of all to Mary, her youngest. Likewise no one was dearer to Mrs. Eddy than her mother. Mrs. Eddy told her household in 1908 that she thought her mother should be spoken of in terms of Song of Solomon 8:5: "Who is this that cometh up from the wilderness, leaning upon her beloved? I raised thee up under the apple tree: there thy mother brought thee forth: there she brought thee forth that bare thee."[5]

After her mother's passing, Mrs. Eddy (then Glover) came across a box of clippings Abigail had kept. They reveal more of her religious nature: "The Sabbath Bells" by Charles Lamb, "When is the time to Die?" "What Is life?" "The Dying Girl's Lament," and the longest—"Small Things Important." This last was an acrostic based on I Thessalonians 5:22: "Abstain from all appearance of evil."[6]

Abigail Barnard Baker (Tilton) (1816–1886) Mrs. Eddy's elder sister. In her later years, Abigail declared, "I loved Mary best of all my brothers and sisters," but this love could not endure Mary's devotion to Christian Science (see p. 62 and p. 74).[7] In 1837, Abigail married Alexander Tilton who owned a number of large textile mills. The town of Sanbornton Bridge was eventually renamed Tilton for his family. At the time of her passing, the newspapers reported, "Mrs. Tilton was the wealthiest lady in town and undoubtedly the most charitable, giving money liberally and in such a quiet manner that it was not generally known. She subscribed liberally toward the improvement of the village."[8]

Albert Baker (1810–1841) Mrs. Eddy's second eldest brother, whom she was closest to after her mother. One time when young Mary was sick in bed, Albert read Psalm 103 to her, and she was healed (see pp. 75–76). He served as her tutor between his terms at Dartmouth College. Mrs. Eddy recalled this experience vividly: "My favorite studies were natural philosophy, logic, and moral science. From my brother Albert I received lessons in the ancient tongues, Hebrew, Greek, and Latin."[9] Albert graduated with honors in 1834 and then accepted an offer from the former governor of New Hampshire, General Benjamin Pierce, to live with him and study law with his son, Franklin, a future President of the United States. In 1837 Albert was admitted to the bar of Suffolk County, where he established his practice in Hillsborough as successor to Franklin Pierce, who was then in Washington, D.C. Albert Baker served in the state legislature from 1839 to 1841. At the time of his passing, he had been nominated for the United States Congress in a district where such nomination by the political party practically guaranteed election.

Anna B. White Baker (c1860–c1928) Raised as a Quaker, she was married to Dr. Alfred E. Baker, a homeopathic physician from Philadelphia, Pennsylvania. They had Primary class instruction in 1896 with Flavia Knapp, whose husband Ira was a Director of The Mother Church. She went through Normal class with Mrs. Eddy in her last class in 1898. The following year Mrs. Eddy called Alfred Baker to serve as a Christian Science practitioner in Concord, New Hampshire. During his time there, she healed him of influenza.[10] Anna Baker was called to serve in Mrs. Eddy's household from time to time until they left Concord in 1902. In Mrs. Baker's reminiscences she recounts: "Mrs. Eddy had told us of Miss E[aton], a young child of 12 yrs. whom she had healed of cataracts in her early work in Science—She was visiting the parents, and seeing the child in a very ugly attack of temper, sternly rebuked her saying, '[W]hen you can see to do right you will see with your eyes'—then naming the expression, 'you have no eyes.' The child instantly became still and her sight was restored."[11] Mrs. Eddy wrote the Bakers afterwards, "I write to say I forgot my close to that sentence to the blind Miss Eaton. It was this, 'You have no eyes'—meaning 'having eyes ye see not' then the cataract moved off."[12]

Elizabeth P. Baker Mrs. Eddy's stepmother, who married Mark Baker on December 5, 1850. Elizabeth Baker was Daniel Patterson's aunt, and it was through her that Mary met her second husband. Stepmother and stepdaughter were on affectionate terms throughout their lives. Mrs. Baker's letter testifying to Ellen Pilsbury's healing of enteritis appeared in *Science and Health* from the third edition through the 225th edition (see p. 285). A glimpse into their relationship can be seen in a card Elizabeth wrote to Mary on April 6, 1875: "My own Dear Daughter. It is a long time since I have heard one word from you, hope you are well and enjoying the light of God's countenance and surrounded with kind friends, a good Minister, and good society...."[13]

George Sullivan Baker *(1812–1867)* Mrs. Eddy's youngest brother, whom the family often called Sullivan. When a boy, he was healed of a severe ax wound to his leg when his father put little Mary's hand on the gash. When George left home in 1835, he found employment teaching weaving at the Connecticut State Prison. Three years later he returned to Sanbornton

Bridge, joining his sister Abigail's husband, Alexander Tilton, as a partner in the mills, which would become famous for the tweeds produced there. In 1849 he married Martha Rand and moved to Baltimore, Maryland, to establish himself in millwork. Toward the end of his life he became blind and returned to New Hampshire to spend his remaining years close to his family. He turned down his sister Mary's offer to pray for him.

Mark Baker (1785–1865) Mrs. Eddy's father was a Calvinist and an orthodox Congregationalist who, according to his youngest daughter, "kept the family in the tightest harness I have ever known."[14] One example of this can be seen in a letter from Mrs. Eddy where she wrote, "My father was very particular about the books his children read. He even objected to my reading the books that my brother brought from College such as Locke & Bacon, & forbade my reading under his roof Voltaire or Hume."[15] Mark Baker was well respected in Bow, sometimes acting as a lawyer for neighbors and even for the town itself. Although a farmer by occupation, he was civically active. He served as clerk for his church, chaplain for the town's militia, county coroner, and for ten years as a trustee of Sanbornton Academy. Mark, along with his eldest daughter Abigail, was responsible for removing Mary's son, George, from her care when he was a young child.

Martha Rand Baker Married to George Sullivan Baker in 1849, she was Mrs. Eddy's sister-in-law. Martha and Mary had become good friends while George was courting her, but their lives went separate ways after Martha and George moved to Baltimore, Maryland. Martha was present when Mary healed their niece, Ellen Pilsbury, in July 1867. In the 1880s when Mrs.

Eddy invited Martha to attend one of her classes on Christian Science, she declined. Mrs. Eddy learned later that Martha had influenced Mrs. Eddy's father and her sister Abigail against her.

Martha Smith Baker (Pilsbury) *(1819–1884)* Mrs. Eddy's second elder sister was a schoolteacher before she married Luther C. Pilsbury at the end of 1842. Martha was Mary's nurse for a period in 1851 and 1852 to the extent that relatives had to care for Martha's two young daughters while she was caring for Mary. She also loaned Mary and husband Daniel Patterson money for their home in North Groton. After Mrs. Eddy discovered Christian Science, Martha called on her sister when her twenty-two-year-old daughter, Ellen, was dying of enteritis (see pp. 285–286). A number of years later, after Ellen had married, Martha again called on Mary for help after receiving news that Ellen was not expected to live through childbirth. Mrs. Eddy told her sister, "Go and when you reach there you will find her well." And so it was when Martha arrived at her daughter's home.[16]

Maryann Baker *(1746–1835)* Mrs. Eddy's grandmother, who shared the homestead with Mark and Abigail Baker and their family at the time Mary was born. With the Bible as a lesson book, she taught Mary to read.

Nancy Baker *(1802–1881)* Mrs. Eddy's cousin, daughter of Mark Baker's brother, James. Before Mark moved his family to Sanbornton Bridge, New Hampshire, Mary healed Nancy of a severe headache. Mrs. Eddy (then Mrs. Glover) and her student Miranda Rice visited Miss Baker in Bow, New Hampshire, in the late 1870s.

Samuel Dow Baker (1808–1868) Mrs. Eddy's eldest brother was responsible for introducing her to her future husband George Washington Glover. Samuel married Glover's sister Eliza in 1832. After Eliza passed away, he married Mary Ann Cook in 1858. In 1862 Samuel and his wife escorted Mrs. Eddy (then Mrs. Patterson) to Portland, Maine, to be treated by Phineas Quimby. From 1895 to 1902, Mrs. Eddy oversaw and paid for her sister-in-law's care, providing her with a home and a nurse in her final years.

Samuel Putnam Bancroft (1846–c1925) One of Mrs. Eddy's earliest students, Samuel Bancroft went through her second class, which she taught in November and December of 1870. He was a charter member of the Christian Scientist Association, organized in 1876, and he helped Mrs. Eddy establish the Massachusetts Metaphysical College in 1881. He privately published his reminiscences in 1923 under the title *Mrs. Eddy As I Knew Her in 1870.* In this work he writes:

> . . . When she told us that the Truth she taught was the "little leaven that would leaven the whole lump," we considered it as the work of ages, not dreaming that in less than fifty years, thousands, probably millions, would accept it wholly or in part, for there is hardly a person of learning who does not quote her and endorse her, to some extent, in teaching and preaching.
>
> Brave and untiring, in spite of discouragement, calumny, the desertion of friends and the ingratitude of pupils, this woman for forty years continued to repeat the story told by Jesus of Nazareth, and to explain his words.

She had the gift of the true orator, the ability to make her listeners forget the speaker in what she was saying. I have had the privilege of being present and listening to her discourse with the deep thinkers of the past generation, Emerson, Bronson Alcott, and others. I have heard her at the public forum, where questions were propounded, and have never known her to fail to interest or at [a] loss for an answer.[17]

Julia S. Bartlett (1842–1924) At age sixteen, Julia Bartlett was left parentless and had to care for and raise five brothers and sisters, the youngest being three years old. She came to Christian Science in 1880 for the cure of physical ailments that had made her bedridden for periods at a time. Mrs. Eddy's third husband, Asa Gilbert Eddy, treated and healed her.

Julia was taught by Mrs. Eddy four times and taught her own first class in Christian Science in 1884. She served in a number of prominent positions in the Church of Christ (Scientist) in Boston during the 1880s and was one of twelve chosen Charter Members of The First Church of Christ, Scientist, when Mrs. Eddy reorganized her Church in 1892. She lived for a time at the Massachusetts Metaphysical College in Boston in the early to mid-1880s when Mrs. Eddy was working and teaching there.

In her reminiscences, Miss Bartlett tells of a particularly trying time for her while at the College:

> . . . As Treasurer of the Church, I often found the subscriptions insufficient to meet the bills. This lack I

supplied from time to time from my own purse, in order
that the payments might be made promptly and that
there be no debts. There were many uses for what we had
and not a great abundance to draw from. The great part
of my time was given to work that brought no material
remuneration. . . . I took a few patients and had good
success in healing, and this supplied me with necessary
funds, until all at once not one came to be healed. I
understood the cause of this and worked assiduously to
overcome the error, in realizing God's government and
that He is the source of supply, and in actively doing
my part to start my practice again, yet with no apparent
result. To be sure I had all I could do with work for the
Cause, but my little practice which had met my daily
expenses was taken from me. To reduce expenses I then
began to take my meals out and to reduce the supply as
well, and for the first time I knew what it was to suffer
from hunger day after day. I did not trouble Mrs. Eddy
or anyone with the extreme conditions, so far as I could
hide them. It was my problem to solve. I finally thought
relief must come soon if I was to remain in the College,
and taking my Bible for my guidance, I opened to these
words: "Thou shalt remain in this house." It was no longer
a question with me. I must and could work it out. Then
one day patients began to come. The attempt to take me
away and deprive Mrs. Eddy of the help she needed had
failed, and I had no more trouble that way, and she said I
never would.

This experience which was new to me, and my
dependence for relief wholly on God, was a most valuable

lesson for which I have always been grateful. I remarked to Mrs. Eddy, "We are commanded to take up our cross daily, but I am not doing so, for I do not see any to take up." Her answer was, "It is because it has ceased to be a cross."[18]

William Bradford Turner came to know Miss Bartlett when they were both members of the Church's Bible Lesson Committee, and from time to time she would tell him of different experiences she had had with her teacher. A visit to the circus was one of the incidents she shared with him:

> . . . "A great circus is to exhibit in the city," [Mrs. Eddy] remarked one day quite abruptly to Miss Julia. "Will you go with me?" she asked. "It is the menagerie which interests me; it is said to be exceptionally fine."
>
> The two ladies went. "Mrs. Eddy always had a reason for everything she did," observed Miss Bartlett in the telling. "In front of the lions' cage we stopped; Mrs. Eddy's attention seemed riveted." The guard, inside the guard rope, for the greater safety of the onlookers, was, at regular intervals, pacing up and down before the barred cages reserved for the different great cats. "Mrs. Eddy's eyes followed him," said Miss Bartlett. "All at once he stopped, at the farther end of his beat. More quickly than I can tell it, Mrs. Eddy was under the line; and the next moment her hand was resting on the lion's paw near the edge of the cage directly facing her. She rested it there, looking into the face of the great majestic beast, for a moment; then, as quickly, she was under and outside the line again. 'Come Julia, that is all.'"[19]

After being taught by Mrs. Eddy, Miss Bartlett devoted the remainder of her life to Christian healing and to teaching Christian Science.

Elsie Bergquist A Christian Scientist, she gave a reminiscence to The Mother Church in 1951 in which she related her father's encounter with Mrs. Eddy in 1909 and the healing that occurred as a result (see pp. 277–278). She also wrote that her father "spoke so much about it [to the members of his church] that the minister of the church asked him not to relate the experience anymore there."

Harriet L. Betts *(1846–1937)* A Christian Science practitioner and teacher, Harriet Betts had Primary class with Mrs. Eddy in 1888 and Normal class in 1898. She worked in Mrs. Eddy's household for six weeks during December 1902 and January 1903. Mrs. Betts wrote of the time after she first arrived at Pleasant View:

> Those first days were very happy ones. Whenever I was called to [Mrs. Eddy's] room she had many things to tell me. . . .
>
> When she wished to impress on my mind some instruction she would turn to her Bible, open it at random apparently, then read aloud a passage and say to me, "There don't you see?"

Once, on such an occasion [Mrs. Eddy] said: "I could hear God's voice as distinctly as I could hear my son's voice."

At another time Mrs. Eddy spoke about her own healing work, mentioning one incident in detail. Mrs. Betts recalled the conversation:

> [Mrs. Eddy] wished she had taken certificates of her healing but people now would deny it. [She] healed every form of disease known. A dead body was nothing to her. A little corpse was handed to her, and he was alive. A mother sent for her saying, "You are too late, he is dead, but I wanted you to see him." She told the mother to go away for an hour. The mother went and never dreamed the child would be restored. Three times she told the child to arise, then he sat up and rubbed his eyes. Then she told him to get down from the bed; then she called him to her and took him in her lap. Mentally she commanded "Come out of him." The boy said "I *is* tick, I *is* tick," and doubled his fists to fight her. She had all she could do to keep him from pommeling her face. Then she made a plaything of two spools and he threw it on the floor. He was a wicked little boy of an awful temper. His face was purple for awhile from brain fever. In an hour's time he went to the door and met his mother.[20]

Mary B. G. Billings See Mary Baker Glover.

Clara Sweet Brady The daughter of Ella Peck Sweet, who was a member of Mrs. Eddy's household from June to November 1904. Mrs. Brady was a Christian Science practitioner from 1927 to 1935. In her reminiscences she recounted two of Mrs. Eddy's demonstrations of Christian Science that her mother witnessed:

dissolving a gathering storm and healing Mrs. Sweet of injuries received from an accident (see pp. 376–377). Regarding the storm Mrs. Brady wrote:

> During the period of [my mother's] stay at Pleasant View, frequent severe storms of weather occurred. Mrs. Eddy perceived in them certain threatening phases of evil to be overcome. She would often call all the workers together and instruct them to handle these weather conditions.

> On one particular occasion the evidences of gathering storm being unusually ominous, Mrs. Eddy directed them all to work. They assembled in a room, as I understood, downstairs where were long French windows or doors. They had stood for a time in a group near one of these windows working without much effect, when very quietly Mrs. Eddy was heard descending the stair and approaching. She presently stood in their midst, pushing them gently aside, and said, "It is very evident you are not making the demonstration, you are all mesmerized by the appearances." As she stood and worked a few moments, the clouds broke and the black ominous appearing faded away.[21]

James Brierly (1852–1926) Brought up in the Congregational church, James Brierly began attending the Methodist Episcopal church after he married. He recalls, "It was in the year 1884 that I first heard of Christian Science and became interested in it. It came about through the healing of my wife, who from a child 'had suffered many things of many physicians' who had failed to heal her of neuralgia, womb, stomach, and kidney troubles."[22] Mrs. Eddy taught Mr. Brierly in a Primary class in 1885 and a Normal class in 1887. In his reminiscences, he writes of her teaching: "In our class she told how at one time she stopped the wind, and caused to bloom an apple blossom on a tree in the yard in the winter, and that she saw in a room of one of her neighbors a plant that was gaunt . . . and without branches and said she would take it and bring out branches upon it, and make a beautiful plant of it, which she did."[23]

Arthur Brisbane (1864–1936) A nationally known journalist, he began at the age of nineteen working for the *New York Sun*. Later he was managing editor of the *New York World* for seven years, and after that, in 1897, became editor of the *New York Evening Journal*. At one point he was the publisher of the *New York Daily Mirror*. He finished his career as an editorial writer for the Hearst Syndicate and as America's highest paid newspaper writer. Mr. Brisbane was one of three newspapermen to whom Mrs. Eddy granted an interview in her home at Pleasant View just prior to the "Next Friends" suit in 1907. At this meeting, Mrs. Eddy healed him of fatigue. He told Helena Hoftyzer and her husband about his healing of fatigue at the time of the interview, and she recounted it in a letter to The Mother Church in 1942.

Ezra M. Buswell (1844–1906) A veteran of the Civil War, Mr. Buswell became interested in Christian Science in 1884. He was healed by reading *Science and Health* of a disease his doctors had told him was incurable. He had four classes with Mrs. Eddy, including her last class in 1898. In 1893 Mr. Buswell had been arrested for practicing medicine without a license in Nebraska; he was tried and acquitted. Mrs. Eddy called him to Concord, New Hampshire, in 1895 to practice Christian healing in her city. He also served, at Mrs. Eddy's request, as First Reader of the Concord church from 1897 to 1899. He returned to Nebraska in 1899 and devoted his remaining years to Christian healing and to teaching Christian Science.

Stephen Chase *(1839–1912)* Originally a Quaker, Stephen Chase became interested in Christian Science after being healed of blood poisoning. He was taught by Mrs. Eddy in a Primary class in 1887. She appointed him as one of the original Directors of The Mother Church, a position he held from 1892 to 1912. He also served as Treasurer of the Church during those years.

Clara E. Choate *(1850–1916)* Mrs. Choate went through a Primary class taught jointly by Mr. and Mrs. Eddy in 1878 and took another Primary class with Mrs. Eddy in 1882. Mrs. Eddy healed her young son, Warren, in the early 1880s (see p. 131) and healed Clara of severe diphtheria in 1881 (see pp. 315–316). Mrs. Choate served as one of the Directors of the Church of Christ (Scientist) in Boston for a period of time. She was dismissed from the Church and from Mrs. Eddy's students' association in 1884 for working against the interests of the Cause. In 1904, after expressing regret for past actions, Mrs. Choate, at Mrs. Eddy's suggestion, joined The Mother Church.

In her reminiscences Mrs. Choate writes of one of her first visits with Mrs. Eddy:

> One of my most precious memories of Mrs. Eddy

is an interview I had with her in 1877. She had invited me to call to confer about class instruction with her. I had been wonderfully healed and this fact kept our attention fixed upon the healing. She emphasized this work of Christian healing as laying the foundation for her future work in Science & Health, as we then termed the Cause, more often than its present term of Christian Science. As near as I can quote her from memory she said this, "Healing is what the world needs—Christ taught this healing—our religious advancement or righteous living, one and the same, can be better gained by *good healing* than in any other way."

"To be a good healer, or a true follower of Christ, you must demonstrate the law of God, for His law does overcome disease. In overcoming this you overcome sin." I replied, why this will be glorious, and she remarked in her sweet winsome and persuasive manner, "Your enthusiasm is just what I need to carry forward this work of healing to the hearts of the people, for healing is what *they* desire and what you and I and dear Gilbert and other of my students must give them. I must turn my attention from now on, to other departments of the work of Science and Health which I am trying to systematize. We must have system. This great Cause cannot progress in a desultory fashion. Everything must be done decently and in order." She then explained how the students might be led, or swayed into thinking of *less* important ways of the work, but healing is *the* work needed first and last. She wished us all to follow her plans of healing the sick for in so doing she could bring the Cause and *Science and Health* into the acceptance of the *whole* world and this could *not* be done in any other way. She praised my voice, so earnest and honest and said my work of healing the sick would be a great help to her in many ways, and of useful service to the world. The healing was the need of the hour, she strongly urged—just the faithful, patient healing work, by a life devoted and willing. This was what *she* prayed for, so *she* might write, and form, and plan, for the *wider* spread of the Cause and the *real* uplifting of man. I could not resist this appeal, who could? My healing had inspired *me*, and I longed to heal others, and by this wonderful truth as taught in Mrs. Eddy's book *Science and Health.*

As she sat so unconsciously stately, in her modest rocking chair of black hair cloth, with the curls of brown ringlets tossing unnoticed upon her shoulders, her plain gown unornamented except by a long gold chain with which she toyed, and with eloquent upturned face, beaming with the glorious hopes of a soul inspired, I felt she was pleading for the sick world; the *whole sick world*, and is still pleading for the students to do this work, though now from an impersonal standpoint she still speaks. I was then a very young mother, and oh this did touch my heart most deeply. She continued, "All the emoluments in the world, all the admiration that can ever be excited is not, nor can be *surpassed* by the gratitude of a sick person healed, or, by the dejected painful, suffering one relieved and restored." Mrs. Eddy never belittled this part of the work. She always impressed upon me that soul healing would inevitably come with the demonstration of *bodily healing*. "I join the work of Christ when *I* heal the sick." As she said this she rose and, laying her hand gently upon my shoulder, with tears in her deep glorious eyes, [said,] "Then are we the true soldiers of the Christ and His followers. What a help such work will be and how hopefully I am inspired to go on with my part and my writings." She pointed to the groups of manuscript that lay in little piles about the floor around her chair, the black rocker in which she had been seated. Here let me say, "Key to the Scriptures" and the chapter on "Recapitulation" [were] not then in *Science and Health*, and she was considering including them, so she told me.

In concluding this all too short interview with Mrs. Eddy, I resolved to join the class as she proposed, and remember the joy of my decision and the "God bless you, my dear girl" which she so tenderly and impressively uttered as she accompanied me to the door of her home, 8 Broad St., Lynn, Mass. All the way home I marvelled at her *faith* in God, at her divine healing, and still feel to this day Mrs. Eddy really walked and talked with God. The effect upon me was to read *Science and Health*, and that very night a clearer consciousness came to me of what her mission was, and of the purpose of her book *Science and Health*."[24]

Lottie Clark Miss Clark was Julia Bartlett's nurse at the Christian Science Benevolent Association in 1924. Eight years later she gave to The Mother Church her reminiscences of what Miss Bartlett had told her about Mrs. Eddy. In 1939 Miss Clark wrote to The Mother Church about Mrs. Eddy's healing of a partially paralyzed woman in 1903 when she had welcomed Christian Scientists to Pleasant View (see pp. 212–213). From 1948 to 1955 Miss Clark advertised in the *Journal* as a Christian Science practitioner in Boston.

***Joseph I. C. Clarke** (1846–1924)* A journalist, dramatist, and poet. Between 1870 and 1906, Mr. Clarke worked for the *New York Herald*, the *New York Journal*, and *The Criterion*. His interview with Mrs. Eddy (see pp. 203–204) was published in the *New York Herald* on May 1, 1901, and served as the basis for a chapter in his 1925 memoir, *My Life and Memories*. Excerpts from this interview appear in *The First Church of Christ, Scientist, and Miscellany*, pp. 341–346.

***The Rev. Joseph Cook** (1838–1901)* A well-known lecturer who spoke throughout the United States, as well as in Great Britain and the Far East. He was also the founder and editor-in-chief of the periodical *Our Day*. His "Boston Monday Lectures" in Tremont Temple were famous in their time. It was in response to a letter read at one of these lectures that Mrs. Eddy delivered a defense of Christian Science at the Temple in 1885 (see *Miscellaneous Writings 1883–1896*, pp. 95–98).

***Hiram Crafts** (1834–c1907)* A shoemaker by trade, Hiram Crafts was Mrs. Eddy's first student. She taught him in 1867 using her exegesis of Matthew 14 to 17. She lived in Mr. and Mrs. Crafts' home in East Stoughton (now Avon), Massachusetts, for five or six months during the winter of 1866–67. In April 1867 Hiram and his wife moved to Taunton, and Mrs. Glover moved with them, staying three to four months more. Hiram set up his healing practice under his teacher's guidance, but after she left, he returned to shoemaking. In 1901 when various charges were being made in the press about the early days after Mrs. Eddy's discovery of divine Science, Mr. Crafts came to his teacher's defense.

Sarah Crosby She and Mrs. Eddy (then Mrs. Patterson) met while both were patients of Phineas Quimby's. In the latter half of the summer of 1864, Mrs. Patterson stayed with Sarah Crosby in Albion, Maine. While there she healed Mrs. Crosby of injuries from vitriolic acid spilled on her face (see pp. 54–55). Mrs. Patterson taught her Christian Science in 1870; however, her spiritualistic leanings eventually caused her to put aside Mrs. Eddy's teachings.

George B. Day An ordained minister, George Day was taught twice by Mrs. Eddy in 1886, first in a spring Primary class and then in an autumn Normal class. He became pastor of the Chicago Christian Science church that same year. As chairman of the National Christian Scientist Association's convention in June 1888, he introduced Mrs. Eddy at the public meeting in Chicago's Central Music Hall. Even though she had previously stipulated that she would not be speaking, George Day told her, right as they were about to go on the platform, that the printed programs stated she would be delivering an address. "Science and the Senses" (*Miscellaneous Writings*, pp. 98–106) was the title she subsequently gave her talk, which she based on the ninety-first Psalm (see pp. 150–151). The Reverend Day left the church in 1890 when the clash between his former Protestant beliefs and Christian Science began troubling him.

Walter Scott Day In 1935 Mr. Day sent to The Mother Church his reminiscences of his encounters with Mrs. Eddy (see p. 368). He was taught by Pamelia J. Leonard, a student of Mrs. Eddy's, who also served in her household several times between 1900 and 1907. Mr. Day was listed in *The Christian Science Journal* as a Christian Science practitioner in Chatham, Ontario, Canada, from 1903 to 1948.

Adam Dickey *(1864–1925)* Formerly a Methodist, Adam Dickey became interested in Christian Science as a result of his wife's healing in 1893. He received Primary class instruction in Christian Science from Henrietta Graybill in 1896 and entered the full-time healing practice in 1899. He received his teaching certificate in 1901 after attending the Normal class taught by Edward Kimball, a student of Mrs. Eddy's. Mr. Dickey joined Mrs. Eddy's household as a secretary in 1908. While still a member of Mrs. Eddy's staff, he was elected to the Christian Science Board of Directors at her suggestion in 1910, and he served until his passing in 1925. He also served as Treasurer of the Church from 1912 to 1917.

In his memoirs Mr. Dickey writes of his three years as a member of Mrs. Eddy's household when she lived in Chestnut Hill, Massachusetts. At one point, in reference to *Science and Health*, she told him, "When I turn to this book, I am like a mechanic who turns to his tools and picks up the one he wants." At another time she called all of her household together and asked them, "Can a Christian Scientist control the weather?" After each one had responded affirmatively, she told them, "They can't and they don't." Then she said, "They can't, but God can and does." She continued:

> Now, I want you to see the point I am making. A
> Christian Scientist has no business attempting to control
> or govern the weather any more than he has a right to
> attempt to control or govern sickness, but he does know,
> and must know, that God governs the weather and no
> other influence can be brought to bear upon it. When we
> destroy mortal mind's belief that it is a creator, and that it
> produces all sorts of weather, good as well as bad, we shall
> then realize God's perfect weather and be the recipients
> of His bounty in that respect. God's weather is always
> right. A certain amount of rain and sunshine is natural
> and normal, and we have no right to interfere with
> the stately operations of divine Wisdom in regulating
> meteorological conditions. Now I called you back because
> I felt you did not get my former instructions correctly,
> and I want you to remember that the weather belongs to
> God, and when we destroy the operations of mortal mind
> and leave the question of regulating the weather to God,
> we shall have weather conditions as they should be.[25]

Mary E. Dunbar Mrs. Dunbar's mother was a Baptist; her
father was a Universalist who served as a justice of the peace and
a Vermont state senator. Mary Dunbar was chronically ill as a
child, and her health grew worse as an adult: "I never had health
until the healing power of Truth and Love in Christian Science
gave me my divine inheritance of health. All that human parents,
doctors, money and care could do was done for me."[26] She went
to a Christian Science practitioner for treatment in May 1886

and was healed in three days. The following Sunday Mrs. Dunbar heard Mrs. Eddy preach a sermon in Boston, and that night her little daughter Ethel was healed of lameness (see p. 148). Mrs. Eddy taught Mary Dunbar in an 1887 Primary class and an 1889 Normal class. She was called on occasion to serve in Mrs. Eddy's home for a day or two at a time. Mrs. Dunbar advertised in the *Journal* as a Christian Science practitioner in Boston from 1887 to 1929.

John Randall Dunn Mr. Dunn was taught Christian Science in 1906 by Sue Ella Bradshaw, one of Mrs. Eddy's students. He received Normal class instruction from another of her students, Ella W. Hoag, who served in Mrs. Eddy's home several times from 1908 to 1910. Mr. Dunn entered the public healing practice in 1907. He served on the Board of Lectureship from 1916 to 1920 and 1923 to 1943. He was First Reader of The Mother Church from 1920 to 1923 and was appointed Editor of the Christian Science periodicals in 1943, a position he held until his passing in 1948. Two of his poems appear in the *Christian Science Hymnal.* Nemi Robertson told John Randall Dunn about her conversation with Mrs. Eddy related on p. 101.

Joseph S. Eastaman *(1836–1910)* Joseph Eastaman was a sea captain for twenty-one years, having begun his career at sea as a cabin boy when he was just ten. When he returned from his last voyage, Captain Eastaman found his wife very ill. He turned to Mrs. Eddy to heal her, but she told him that he could learn how to heal her himself, so he went through Mrs. Eddy's Primary class in 1884. During this instruction he did heal his wife, and she accompanied him to the last lesson. For about a year Captain

Eastaman was a member of the first Christian Science Board of Directors. Mrs. Eddy created this Board through her 1892 Deed of Trust, which conveyed the land on which The Mother Church edifice was to be built.

Considered by Mrs. Eddy to be quite a good healer, Captain Eastaman devoted himself to its public practice. Six months before his passing, in 1910, he wrote Mrs. Eddy a letter of gratitude in which he said:

> ... You told me more than twenty-five years ago to take
> an office and to go to work on Christian Science healing.
> I did as you told me, and took *this room* on lease. It is
> just twenty-five years to-day since I began the most holy
> work (to my sense), and Oh, beloved Teacher, how many
> are the people that I have been the instrument to heal
> and help in that time, and how many are the people that
> are living in comparative health to-day who were given
> up by the medical profession and through my efforts
> in Christian Science to save them are to-day well and
> praising God for Christian Science.[27]

David Augustus Easton *(1843–1894)* A Congregational minister, the Reverend Easton became interested in Christian Science when his wife was healed of an incurable illness. He had previously attended Antioch College and Andover Seminary and was a member of the Alpha Delta Phi Society along with James Russell Lowell and Phillips Brooks. Mrs. Eddy healed Mr. Easton of consumption in 1891. With her recommendation, he was appointed as associate pastor of The Mother Church from

1893 to 1894. The Reverend Easton had previously been a guest preacher at the Church of Christ (Scientist) in Boston. On Easter Sunday, 1889, Mrs. Eddy introduced him:

> Friends, the homesick traveller in foreign lands greets with joy a familiar face. I am homesick for God. I have met one in my long journeyings who comes from the place of my own sojourning for many years, the Congregational Church. . . . He has left his old church as I did, from a yearning of the heart, because he was not satisfied with a man-like God, but wanted a God-like man. He found the new wine could not be put in old bottles without spilling—hence he came to us.

After the Reverend Easton's sermon, Mrs. Eddy spoke further about Easter, concluding her comments:

> In 1866, when God revealed to me this risen Christ, this Life that knows no death, that says, "because he lives, I live, I shall live,"—in this consciousness I was brought out from the dark shadow and portal of death, and my friends were frightened when they saw me restored to health. An old lady said to me, "How is it that you are restored to this world healed? Has Christ come?" I replied, "Christ never left: He is always here—the Impersonal Saviour."
>
> Then another person more material met me, and I said, "Touch me not,"—the words of my Master. I shuddered at this material approach; then my heart went out to God and I found the open door from this

sepulchre of matter. I love the Easter service when it
comes, for it speaks of Life and not of death. Let us first
do our work, then we shall have part in this resurrection
from material sense.[28]

Asa Gilbert Eddy (c1832–1882) Mrs. Eddy's third husband. They
were married on January 1, 1877. A native Vermonter, Gilbert
Eddy was a sewing machine salesman at the time he and Mrs.
Glover were introduced by a mutual friend, who knew he was
suffering from a heart condition. He benefited so much from his
future wife's treatment that he asked her to teach him Christian
Science. In the spring of 1876, four weeks after completing
his instruction, he established himself in the Christian healing
practice and became the first of her students to announce himself
publicly as a Christian Scientist. He also organized the first
Christian Science Sunday School in 1881.

Throughout their marriage, Gilbert devoted all his effort to
supporting his wife in her mission to establish Christian Science.
This can be clearly seen in a letter he wrote her from jail, after
being falsely charged with the murder of Daniel Spofford, who
was alive but in hiding. While his letter was primarily about
obtaining bail, he ended it:

> ... Do not fear for me or Mr. Arens. God doeth all things
> well; not a sparrow falls without Him and He will not
> forsake us whom He chasteneth. We are comfortable
> here and I have enjoyed myself during this experience
> so far, having as I have the assurance of being accounted
> worthy to suffer persecution for the Master's sake. Now

Mary Dear be of good cheer for though this is not the experience we should have chosen, yet the Master who knoweth better than we hath said it worketh out a more exceeding and eternal weight of glory.

Yours in Love,
Gilbert.[29]

Gilbert's tender love for his wife, his strong faith in God, and his loyal support of the Cause are evident here.

Ruth Ewing *(1846–1923)* Mrs. Ewing became interested in Christian Science through her husband's healing of incurable respiratory problems. She describes that time fondly:

> I love to recall my earliest experiences as an investigator of its merits. By its means my husband was raised from what physicians pronounced immediately impending death. When, after having been restored to health and activity, he manifested a tendency to relapse, I went to see the practitioner in Chicago—a young student from under Mrs. Eddy's personal tuition—to whom my husband had been referred by the one in the East who had so wonderfully helped him. Betraying my anxiety, as I told my story of hope uplifted and then again depressed, she said to me with great earnestness, "Why don't you study Christian Science and learn how to take care of your own family?" I was astonished and said to her, "Can anybody take it up?" Her answer was, "It is for every man, woman and child; it is simple Christianity."[30]

Mrs. Ewing took the advice and attended three of Mrs. Eddy's classes in the Massachusetts Metaphysical College. She lived in Chicago and devoted the rest of her life to the practice of Christian healing and to teaching Christian Science. Her husband, Judge William G. Ewing, was a well-known Christian Science lecturer from 1899 to 1910.

Alfred Farlow (1857–1919) Raised as a Methodist in Illinois, Alfred Farlow became interested in Christian Science when he first encountered *Science and Health* in 1885. A neighbor who had been healed of invalidism had loaned the book to Alfred's mother. After he was taught Christian Science by Janet Colman, one of Mrs. Eddy's students, he applied to Mrs. Eddy herself for instruction. He attended her class in May 1887. Mrs. Eddy taught him two more times: in the Normal class in the autumn of 1887 and another Primary class in 1889.

After his first class with Mrs. Eddy, Mr. Farlow left his manufacturing business to enter the full-time public healing practice. Later, he worked for the Cause in other capacities and enjoyed regular interaction with Mrs. Eddy. He wrote this comment about Mrs. Eddy's own healing in February 1866 and what she learned from it:

> At that time it was not clear to Mrs. Eddy by what process she had been instantaneously healed, but she knew that her thought had turned away from all else in contemplation of God, His omnipotence and everpresence, His infinite love and power. It eventually dawned upon her that this overwhelming consciousness of the divine presence had destroyed her fear and

consciousness of disease exactly as the light dispels the darkness. She afterwards "noticed that when she had entertained similar thoughts in connection with the ills of her neighbors, they too were benefited, and it was in this manner that she discovered how to give a mental treatment."[31]

Mrs. Eddy called Mr. Farlow to Boston at the beginning of 1899 to serve on the Church's three-member Committee on Publication, which was the organization's contact point with the news and publishing media. A year later she reduced the size of the Committee to one person, Mr. Farlow, and gave him the title of Manager. He served in this position until 1914, when he retired to California to resume his work as healer and teacher.

In 1909 Mr. Farlow wrote Mrs. Eddy a letter of gratitude:

Dear Teacher,

I have just been reading some of your answers to critics made nearly twenty-five years ago and published in *Miscellaneous Writings*.

The Committees on Publication will do well to study the Christian and skillful methods which you employed in the early days. Your replies are like a refreshing shower that washes away the dust so gently and completely that one forgets that it was ever in existence.

Your arguments are not only indisputable but they are utterly inoffensive. They are sensible, clear, and

dignified. They are full, and yet made with due respect
for the printer's space. They are so impersonal that, while
they sweep the critic off the earth, he does not even know
that he has been hit, but simply is glad that he is on our
side and is not as the critics are.[32]

Julia Field-King A student of Mrs. Eddy's, Mrs. Field-King
was originally a homeopathic physician, having graduated from
Oberlin College in Ohio and from Hahnemann Medical College
in Philadelphia, Pennsylvania. Mrs. Eddy taught her in an 1888
Primary class and again in an 1889 Normal class. She appointed
her as Editor of *The Christian Science Journal* in November
1891. Mrs. Field-King served in that position until September
1892, when she resigned. Four years later, Mrs. Eddy sent her
to establish Christian Science in England. Her efforts proved
successful and resulted in the formation of First Church of Christ,
Scientist, London, and the dedication of the church's edifice in
1897. In June 1902 Mrs. Field-King was placed on probation as
a member of The Mother Church due to her working against the
interests of the Church because of theological misconceptions of
Christian Science. Three months later she was dismissed at her
own request. She reunited with the Church as a probationary
member in 1917, remaining as such until her passing in 1919.

Lida W. Fitzpatrick A Methodist investigating Christian
Science in 1887 for her diabetic husband, Mrs. Fitzpatrick took
Primary classes from two of Mrs. Eddy's students: George Day
and Hannah Larminie. With this newfound understanding, she
healed her spouse. In 1888 Mrs. Eddy taught her in a Normal
class, and afterward Mrs. Fitzpatrick established a public healing

practice and taught Christian Science in Cleveland, Ohio. She was instrumental in organizing both First and Second Churches of Christ, Scientist, in that city.

Mrs. Fitzpatrick served in Mrs. Eddy's household three times: from May 1903 to February 1904, and from February to June and August to September in 1907. Mrs. Eddy would often share metaphysical ideas with her and the other members of the household. Mrs. Fitzpatrick records that on one occasion Mrs. Eddy said:

> Humility is the door, honesty is the way, and spirituality is the summit.
>
> Oh! If we could only see ourselves in God, "In Him we live and move and have our Being," we would have no other consciousness.

At another time she recorded her saying, "If you have a patient who does not respond, would you say, I have done the best I could, and give up? No; it is the opportunity to rise higher and meet the demand."

A few months before the end of her first period of service at Pleasant View, Mrs. Fitzpatrick wrote in her notebook this comment by Mrs. Eddy: "When a student is wrong, if it is not deep sin, I (Mrs. Eddy) walk with them away to help them out; even when they are working right against me sometimes; walk with them away and open their eyes to the error, then when they see, the error is gone. Not go at them denouncing them, pouncing upon them."[33] After Mrs. Fitzpatrick returned to

Cleveland, she devoted herself to healing and teaching until her passing in 1933.

Addie P. Forbes Miss Forbes became interested in Christian Science after her father, an American Civil War veteran, was healed by reading *Science and Health*. She went on to enter the full-time healing practice as a Christian Science practitioner. She wrote to The Mother Church in 1959 about her meeting with Mrs. Eddy while living in Concord, New Hampshire (see pp. 355–356).

Marie Chalmers Ford She wrote to Mrs. Eddy in 1906 about the healing she had experienced at the time they briefly encountered each other in Concord, New Hampshire, several years earlier (see pp. 198–199). In describing this incident, Mrs. Ford wrote, "My eyes were flooded with tears of joy and my heart was overflowing with gratitude to you for this wonderful healing which had come to me through the Christ-love radiating from your consciousness."[34] Five months after sending this letter, Mrs. Ford advertised in *The Christian Science Journal* as a full-time Christian Science healer in Toledo, Ohio.

Minnie Ford See Minnie Ford Mortlock.

Ebenezer J. Foster-Eddy *(1847–1930)* A homeopathic physician from Vermont, Dr. Foster graduated from the Hahnemann Medical College in Philadelphia, Pennsylvania, in 1869. After seeing a friend healed by reading *Science and Health*, he entered one of Mrs. Eddy's Primary classes in 1887 and was taught again by her in a Normal class in 1888. In November of that year, she adopted him as a son because of his apparent devotion to her and his support of her life's work.

Dr. Foster-Eddy served as Mrs. Eddy's publisher from 1893 to 1896. However, his high opinion of himself and continual disobedience of her instructions caused Mrs. Eddy to remove him from the Church's work in Boston. She sent him instead to Philadelphia to establish himself as a Christian healer in that city and to shepherd the church there. Unable to work in harmony with his fellow Scientists, he was expelled from the church in Philadelphia and went to visit his brother in Wisconsin for an extended stay. In 1899 The Mother Church dropped him from its membership. He resurfaced in 1907, at the time of the "Next Friends" suit, when he joined with Mrs. Eddy's birth son, George, as a plaintiff against Calvin Frye and Church officers. After the suit was dismissed, Mrs. Eddy wrote "Benny," as she called him, inviting him to come for a visit: "If you would like to call on me now, I have a little leisure, and would be pleased to see your dear face once more for a chat with you after the old way."[35] He did not accept the invitation, and the two never saw each other again. Her final way of wishing him well was a gift of $45,000 from her estate.

Alice Cluff French Born and raised in Lynn, Massachusetts, Mrs. French heard about Mrs. Eddy's ability to heal from both her father and grandmother. Her grandmother, Deborah J. Cluff, a Methodist, was a friend of Mrs. Eddy (then Mrs. Glover) at the time the latter was living in Lynn. In fact, Mrs. Glover

> asked Deborah if she might use the large front "spare" bedroom on the second floor to write in,— that she

was writing *Science & Health* and did not have much
opportunity to get entirely away from others in her own
home. Deborah graciously granted the request at once.
Then when Mrs. [Glover] had finished writing the book,
she asked Deborah how much she owed her for the use
of this spare room, but Deborah would not think of
accepting money for it. Then Mrs. [Glover] said she knew
what she would do—she would give Deborah a first
edition of the book—*Science & Health*—which she did
do, writing an inscription in it to Deborah from her.[36]

Mrs. French sent her reminiscences of her father's healing
by Mrs. Glover (see pp. 303–304) to The Mother Church in
1937.

Calvin A. Frye (1845–1917) His father attended Harvard College
and was in the same graduating class as Ralph Waldo Emerson.
Originally a member of the Congregational church, Calvin
became interested in Christian Science after his mother was
restored to sanity by one of Mrs. Eddy's students, Clara Choate.
Mrs. Eddy first taught him in 1881 in Lynn, Massachusetts.
He subsequently went through two other classes with her. As
noted on pp. 168, 256–258, and 362–368, Mr. Frye experienced
multiple significant healings as a result of Mrs. Eddy's prayerful
treatments.

Mr. Frye served as Mrs. Eddy's private secretary from 1882
until her passing at the end of 1910, never taking a vacation.
His duties as Mrs. Eddy's assistant changed and overlapped in
accord with her activities. Apart from his secretarial responsibil-

ities, he was, at times, her bookkeeper, coachman, aide, steward, spokesman, confidant, and metaphysical physician. Mrs. Eddy highly valued his unwavering devotion to her and her lifework.

In 1903 Mrs. Eddy asked the Christian Science Board of Directors to acknowledge Mr. Frye's service to her and the Church by giving him an appropriate gift:

> It is twenty-one years this month since he left his paternal home and at my husband's suggestion, Dr. Asa G. Eddy, first went to our home in Boston. After [Asa's] death Mr. Frye became resident physician at our College on Columbus Avenue, Boston, and has stood by my side to help *our Cause 21 years.* He has done more practical work in my behalf to aid our Cause than any other student.
>
> He should be acknowledged in this line of action for the entire field. I have given him a token of gratitude and suggest that the Executive Members of our Church notice this anniversary of one of its oldest actors and faithful laborers in the vineyard of our Lord. Nothing very expensive do I suggest but only a kind remembrancer of what he has done for you and your Leader.[37]

Her "token" was $1,000. The gift from the Church was a roll-top desk and chair.

After Mrs. Eddy's passing, Mr. Frye served as First Reader in First Church of Christ, Scientist, Concord, New Hampshire, and then in 1916 he was appointed to a term as President of The Mother Church.

Mary G. Gale The wife of a physician in Manchester, New Hampshire. Mrs. Gale's healing of pneumonia, consumption, and morphine addiction in 1868 was the first catalyst that eventually caused Mrs. Eddy (then Mrs. Glover) to write *Science and Health*. In appreciation for her healing, Mrs. Gale gave Mrs. Glover a copy of William Smith's *Dictionary of the Bible*. This was particularly valuable to Mrs. Glover at this period, as she was devoting her full time to studying the Bible.

Sarah (Sally) Knox Gault *(1784–1870)* Her farm abutted the Bakers' in Bow, New Hampshire. Sarah, a Methodist, was one of Mrs. Eddy's mother's closest friends. Her children were about the same age as the Baker children, and all were playmates. Sarah and Abigail often discussed Scriptural passages and prayed together about challenges that came up in their daily lives. Mrs. Eddy sent a copy of *Science and Health* to Mrs. Gault's son, Matthew, when it was first published.

Caroline Getty *(1864–1955)* A dressmaker from Great Britain, Mrs. Getty began studying Christian Science when her elder sister sent her a copy of *Science and Health* in 1903. Not long after, she received Primary class instruction from Lady Victoria Murray, and in 1908 she entered the full-time healing practice. In 1912 Mrs. Getty moved permanently to Paris, and the following year she was taught by Mrs. Eddy's student Laura Sargent in a Normal class. This resulted in her being the first Christian Science teacher in France. From 1914 to 1917, Mrs. Getty served on the three-member translation committee responsible for translating *Science and Health* into French. Later, she also worked on translating three other works of Mrs. Eddy's: the *Manual of The Mother Church*, *Rudimental Divine Science*, and *No and Yes*. In 1931 Mrs. Getty sent The Mother Church her account of Mrs. Eddy healing an actor of smoking (see p. 374).

William I. Gill Originally from England, William I. Gill was a Methodist minister with Unitarian ideas. At the time he became interested in Christian Science, he was pastor of a congregation in Lawrence, Massachusetts. Mrs. Eddy taught him in a March 1886 Primary class. In May of that year he was invited to serve on a trial basis as assistant pastor for the Church of Christ (Scientist) in Boston. In September he became Editor of *The Christian Science Journal* but held the position for only four months. His firmly held orthodox beliefs about the reality of evil so interfered with his understanding of Christian Science that his separation from the Church was inevitable, and he resigned as assistant pastor in January 1887. Over the next few years he aligned himself with the "mind-curists" in Boston and Chicago.

James F. Gilman *(1850–1929)* Primarily a landscape artist, James Gilman spent the first twenty years of his adulthood drawing and painting mostly Vermont farm scenes. He became interested in Christian Science in 1884 through friends in Barre. At the end of 1892 he moved from Montpelier, Vermont, to Concord, New Hampshire, and met Mrs. Eddy for the first time on December 20. In his reminiscences James describes his first interview with Mrs. Eddy, writing that

> most of what she said, and I do not know but all,
> seemed, by the occasional word or phrase, to have

an underlying spiritual meaning. But she seemed so much like a little child in it all that I found difficulty in realizing that I was in the presence of the noted personage who had become so much to me in my life.

I asked her a question when she had been saying that she loved *nature* in people as well as in scenery. I asked if it was not a law of Being, or nature, that we should advance by impulses like the waves of the sea or like the ebbing and flowing of the tides? She said that was the way while in our mortal thought, but that in the immortal Life it was all flowing, and no ebbing. "It [is] just action, action, action, always."[38]

In March 1893 Mrs. Eddy asked Mr. Gilman to work with her on illustrating a new poem she had written, "Christ and Christmas." They worked together throughout the spring and summer to get the pictures just as she wanted them. The book was published at the end of November with both Mrs. Eddy and Mr. Gilman listed as "Artists." The following year Mr. Gilman moved to Gardner, Massachusetts, and then in 1899 to Athol, where he was instrumental in organizing a Christian Science Society. From 1895 to 1905 he advertised in local newspapers as a "Christian Science Healer." After this he decided to devote himself to his artwork again and did so until his passing.

George Washington Glover (1811–1844) Mrs. Eddy's first husband. They met in 1832 at her brother Samuel's wedding to Eliza Glover, George's sister. He jokingly told Mary at that time he would come back and marry her when she had grown up. Eleven years later, on December 10, 1843, they married and moved first to Charleston, South Carolina, and then to Wilmington, North Carolina. Six months later he passed on from yellow fever. A construction contractor, he was preparing to go to a job in Haiti with Mary at the time of his passing. Mrs. Eddy wrote of him in her autobiography:

> ... He was highly esteemed and sincerely lamented by a large circle of friends and acquaintances, whose kindness and sympathy helped to support me in this terrible bereavement. ...
>
> Colonel Glover's tender devotion to his young bride was remarked by all observers. With his parting breath he gave pathetic directions to his brother masons about accompanying her on her sad journey to the North.[39]

George Washington Glover II (1844–1915) Mrs. Eddy's son George was born at the Bakers' home in Sanbornton Bridge, New Hampshire, three months after his father's passing. After his grandfather, Mark Baker, remarried, he was sent to live with a family friend. Mrs. Eddy told one of her secretaries about this in 1906:

> When my father married the second time, he refused to have George in the house any longer. After praying over him the whole night, I sent George to the old nurse, who had been called to the family for years in every case of sickness. Her name was Mary [Mahala]

Sanborn, and she was married to a man by the name
of Cheney. My agreement with them was that George
should go to school and receive a liberal education.

I married the second time, Dr. Patterson, for the
express purpose of having the boy with me, but my
husband thought that I cared more for George than I
did for him, and again I had to send my son away. The
last time I saw George [as a child], he was about ten
years old. The Cheneys then moved to the far West
[Minnesota].[40]

After a number of years George ran away and joined the
Union Army to fight in the Civil War. He was shot in the
neck during a battle and expected to die, when his mother
healed him (see p. 49). Mother and son did not meet again
until his visit to Lynn, Massachusetts, in November 1879. At
this time he was a gold prospector with a wife, Nellie, and two
children, Edward and Mary. He had just moved from a farm in
Fargo, North Dakota, to the Black Hills of Deadwood, South
Dakota. Mrs. Eddy tried to teach him Christian Science, but
he would not continue after the first lesson. In the winter of
1887–88 George brought his family (with another daughter,
seven-year-old Evelyn) east for a six-month visit to his mother
in Boston. In 1893 he brought his son, four-year-old George,
for a brief visit to Pleasant View in Concord, New Hampshire.
He visited his mother again in 1902, this time bringing his
daughter Mary with him.

In 1907 he and the same daughter were plaintiffs, along
with other relatives, in the "Next Friends" suit against Calvin Frye

and Church officers, claiming his mother to be mentally incompetent. After the suit was dismissed, he agreed to a $245,000 settlement from her estate with the condition that he not contest her will after her passing. He did not keep his promise.

Mary Baker Glover (Billings) (1877–1968) Mrs. Eddy's granddaughter was born in Fargo, North Dakota. She was healed by her grandmother of crossed eyes at the time her father was visiting his mother in 1879 (see p. 117). Mary met her grandmother for the first time in November 1887. In 1907 she was one of the plaintiffs in the "Next Friends" suit, along with her father and a few other relatives. Fortunately, her estrangement from the Church did not endure, despite the family's decision to contest Mrs. Eddy's will. Mary and her two sons, Harry and Marion Billings, enjoyed a warm relationship with Christian Scientists and Mrs. Eddy's Church. All three joined The Mother Church in 1936.

Mary Crane Gray After doctors advised Mrs. Gray to commit her husband to a sanitarium because of insanity, which she refused to do, a neighbor gave her *Science and Health*. Describing her early encounter with the book, she said, "I was drawn to the statement on page 10 [x] of the Preface ... 'The divine Principle of healing is proved in the personal experience of any sincere seeker of Truth.'" She then went to the Rector of the Episcopal church of which she was a member and asked him to heal her husband. He was not encouraging, as she explains:

> ... His reply was: "My dear child. If I should start doing that work, I wouldn't have any time for the regular church work. Take your physicians' advice, and place him where he can have proper care."

As I left the Rectory, I thought, what is the regular church work, if it isn't healing the sick? It is one of our Lord's commandments. Then the "still small voice" said, "Why don't you try Christian Science?" It is our God-given right to think and act rightly for ourselves, was my answer, and I wrote at once to Mrs. Eddy, asking her to heal my husband, explaining that I had confidence in her because of what I had just been reading of her writings.[41]

Mrs. Eddy healed her husband in 1905. Mrs. Gray wrote all of this in a letter to The Mother Church in 1935.

Charles E. L. Green Mrs. Eddy (then Mrs. Glover) healed Charles Green's four-year-old daughter, Josephine, of brain fever in 1873 (see pp. 302–303). Around 1907 Mr. Green gave Alfred Farlow a statement about this incident. In that statement he said, "Nobody took any stock in it [Josephine's healing], and the event was forgotten." Mr. Green included at the end of his statement a testimony of his own recent healing:

Two years ago when I turned to Christian Science, I was a wreck from rheumatism, nervous prostration, and was in hell from fear of the insane asylum. The doctors could do me no good. I went to a C. S. practitioner for two weeks, with no perceptible benefit; then I went to work for myself with the aid of the book [*Science and Health*]. I was healed of the rheumatism, nervous troubles, and eczema of 16 years standing. When my son came home and I showed him my arm that had been so disagreeable before and which was so completely healed, he would not credit it as the work of Christian Science. Rheumatism so completely gone that I can now run like a boy, at the age of 63 years, where before I had to slide down stairs because my knees refused to bear my weight, and when I moved them they squeaked like a rusty hinge. This summer I took a walk of 11 miles in one stretch.[42]

Helen M. Grenier Mrs. Eddy healed her around 1880 when Helen was a little girl in Lynn, Massachusetts. Her statement of this healing was given to The Mother Church in 1917. At the end of her statement, Mrs. Grenier writes:

Though I have passed through many trials and afflictions which might have been averted had I known and understood her [Mrs. Eddy's] teachings then, I am convinced that the benediction of that hour has at last brought me to the Truth.

I have had many demonstrations of Divine Love in my own body. One—an instantaneous healing after being deformed for four years and pronounced incurable by physicians. The deformity was caused by a shock to the nerves of the spine. Another—the healing of a crushed finger which was caught in a cog wheel; the healing was marvelous, to sense, but under treatment I suffered no pain or loss of finger, although loss of arm—blood poison—etc. was predicted. The bone grew in and the flesh filled in where it had been torn away, healing rapidly.[43]

Septimus J. Hanna *(1844–1921)* Judge Hanna is best known as the Editor of the Christian Science periodicals from November 1892 to June 1902. His wife, Camilla, served as Assistant Editor. They were both in Mrs. Eddy's last class, which she conducted in November 1898. In December 1886 he had gone through a Primary class taught by the Rev. J. S. Norvell, a student of Mrs. Eddy's, who had previously been a Baptist minister.

Septimus Hanna was admitted to the Illinois bar in 1867 and then moved to Council Bluffs, Iowa, where he held the office of judge of the county court. In 1871 he moved to Chicago, Illinois, to practice law, remaining there until 1879, when he moved to Leadville, Colorado, for his health. Judge Hanna became interested in Christian Science in 1886 because of the healing Camilla experienced from reading *Science and Health*.

A year and a half after Mrs. Eddy first met Judge Hanna in 1891, she asked him to become the Editor of *The Christian Science Journal*. In March 1894 she appointed him to the pastorate of The Mother Church. When she ordained the Bible and *Science and Health* as the Pastor of her Church at the end of 1894, Judge Hanna became the First Reader in the Church. He served on the Christian Science Board of Directors in October 1895, but had to withdraw from this after a month because his other official responsibilities, Editor and First Reader, were all he could effectively handle. (See Mrs. Eddy's August 5, 1897, letter to Judge Hanna on pp. 399–401.) He was elected President of the Church in October 1896 and served for two years. In 1902 he retired from his positions of Editor and Reader and was appointed to the Church's Board of Lectureship. He served as a Christian Science lecturer until 1914. In 1898 Judge Hanna was elected vice-president of the Church's Board of Education, and taught the Normal class in 1907. Upon Mrs. Eddy's passing, he succeeded her as president of that Board, serving in this office until his own passing in 1921.

Margaret E. Harding Mrs. Harding's account of Mrs. Eddy's (then Mrs. Patterson's) healing of George Norton's club feet was sent to The Mother Church in 1929. The incident was told to Mrs. Harding by George's mother, "Mrs. James Norton, the wife of a well-known musician of the old school, some time before 1900—while all three members of the Norton family were alive."[44] Mrs. Harding's daughter, Elizabeth, became interested in Christian Science after hearing about this healing.

Frances Thompson Hill (1886–1979) Her parents were pupils of Augusta Stetson, a student of Mrs. Eddy's. When she was twenty, Frances came to Boston to study music. Three years earlier she had been among the ten thousand Christian Scientists who were attending the Annual Meeting of The Mother Church and were invited to visit Pleasant View. She heard Mrs. Eddy speak from the second-floor balcony. Later Frances also had a private visit with Mrs. Eddy and at that time played for her the hymn "'Feed My Sheep'" which begins with the words "Shepherd, show me how to go." In 1911 Frances married Calvin C. Hill, who had worked for Mrs. Eddy for a number of years. A portion of his reminiscences appears in the biography *We Knew Mary Baker Eddy*. Mrs. Hill became active in gathering the reminiscences of others who had had contact with Mrs. Eddy and gave these to The Mother Church in 1946. She served on the *Christian Science Hymnal* revision committee that produced the Church's current hymnal, published in 1932. She also wrote the text of the "Easter

Hymn," No. 413. In 1944 Mrs. Hill advertised in *The Christian Science Journal* as a Christian Science healer, devoting the rest of her life to the full-time healing practice.

Emma C. Hopkins *(1849–1925)* Formerly a member of the Congregational church, Emma Hopkins was taught by Mrs. Eddy in an 1883 Primary class and the following year was appointed Editor of the precursor to *The Christian Science Journal*. She lasted only seven months in this position before Mrs. Eddy had to remove her because of the influence over her of Mary Plunkett, another student, who led her into the "mind-cure" school of healing. Mrs. Hopkins then became editor of the *Mind Cure Journal* (later renamed the *Mental Science Journal*). In 1886 she and Mrs. Plunkett went into partnership, forming unauthorized "Christian Science institutes" in Chicago, Detroit, St. Paul, and other cities in the midwestern United States. Mrs. Hopkins, who was especially interested in mysticism and theosophy, served as teacher and Mrs. Plunkett, as business manager. In the 1890s Emma Hopkins became a leader in the New Thought movement. She taught Ernest Holmes, the founder of the Church of Religious Science, as well as Charles and Myrtle Fillmore, who founded the Unity School of Christianity.

Charles Carroll Howe Curiosity rather than interest in Christian Science motivated Charles Howe to attend the first service held in the Original Edifice of The Mother Church on Sunday, December 30, 1894. He saw Mrs. Eddy on a number of public occasions between 1895 and 1900. Mr. Howe actually met her when she was entering the Church on January 5, 1896, to deliver a Communion address. At that point he was healed of disabilities caused by typhoid fever. While he read *Science and Health* and other Christian Science literature, he never joined the Church. He sent his reminiscences to the Church in 1932.

Emilie B. Hulin   Originally a member of the Congregational church, Mrs. Hulin attended Mrs. Eddy's Primary class in November 1888. Referring to that class in her reminiscences, she wrote:

> Mrs. Eddy was showing in class the definition of God . . . and showing that "Mind" is the "all seeing."
>
> She said that through the understanding of this she had healed a man of blindness whose eyeballs had been destroyed, and the eyeballs were restored whole. Someone in the class asked, "Well, if Mind is all that sees, why was it necessary for the eyeballs to be restored?"
>
> Mrs. Eddy replied: "Ah, I anticipated that you would ask that question. The effect of Christian Science is this. Science restores that standard of perfection which mortal mind calls for. If the eyeballs had not been restored, no one would have believed him when he said he could see."[45]

The previous year, Emilie had been taught Christian Science by Pamelia J. Leonard, a student of Mrs. Eddy's. Emilie served in Mrs. Eddy's household a number of times, first in the spring of 1895, then from the following winter for almost a year, and after that as the need arose. In her reminiscences she wrote:

...I saw [Mrs. Eddy] in her own home life and in various conditions of belief calling for demonstration, and I never saw her fail, but she adhered to what she taught and lived. Many were the lessons I learned at this time and which I have been most grateful for throughout the subsequent years, and never have I lost faith in Christian Science or its Discoverer, because I have seen her many wonderful demonstrations over the claims of the deceitful senses....

At one time the "First Members" were called to Concord to receive a lesson from her. It was a hot season in July. Twenty-five responded to her call. I was seated in the bay window of her home when I noticed the appearance of a storm gathering, and it was very violent and cyclonic in its appearance. Mrs. Eddy's attention was drawn to it by the flapping of the window curtains. She ceased talking for a few minutes and was perfectly silent. The clouds came to a sudden stop and then disappeared, and the sun was shining again. The Concord paper the next day spoke of it as a wonderful phenomenon.[46]

Mrs. Hulin advertised as a practitioner and teacher in *The Christian Science Journal* from 1890 to 1931. She lived in Brooklyn, New York, until 1924, and then moved to Brookline, Massachusetts. From 1923 to 1926 she was vice-president of The Mother Church's Board of Education, and she taught the Normal class in 1925.

Mary Ann Jarvis Originally a patient of Phineas Quimby's, she was healed by Mrs. Eddy (then Patterson) of consumption (see pp. 53–54) while spending two months in Miss Jarvis's home in Warren, Maine, in the spring of 1864. This healing appears in *Science and Health* on pages 184 and 185. During her stay in Warren, Mrs. Patterson gave two public lectures on the falsity of spiritualism. She began her first address, "To correct any misconceived ideas upon the subject, we would first say—that a belief in spiritualism, as defined by rappings, trances, or any agency in healing the sick coming from the dead, we wholly disclaim."[47]

William B. Johnson *(1839–1911)* Born in England, William Johnson came to the United States with his parents when he was a child. During the Civil War, he served three years in General Joseph Hooker's brigade. He became interested in Christian Science in 1882 after being healed of disabilities caused by injuries received in the war. Taught by Mrs. Eddy in one of her 1884 Primary classes, he then joined the Church of Christ (Scientist) in Boston. Mr. Johnson became Clerk of the Church in 1887 and held that position continuously until 1909. Mrs. Eddy appointed him to the Christian Science Board of Directors when she created that Board in her September 1, 1892, Deed of Trust, which served to reorganize the Boston congregation into The Mother Church, The First Church of Christ, Scientist. He remained on the Board through May 1909.

Several weeks after his retirement, Mr. Johnson wrote Mrs. Eddy,

Beloved Teacher:

What a contrast between the time when I retired from the clerkship of your dear Church and when I entered upon the duties of that office.

I recognize in the action of the Directors in voting me a salary [pension] that it was your love for me as always, that was the cause of this action: for this additional token please accept my thanks and gratitude once more.

What a contrast. When I began, I was struggling with poverty. My dear wife and I walked from South Boston in biting cold weather to save the five cent fare (if we had it) so that we might drop it into the contribution box.

My office for clerk work was my attic bedroom. Office supplies consisted of paper bags cut up and used to send out application blanks secured with paste made from a scanty store of flour. Stamps were obtained by asking teachers, when they sent for blanks, please send stamps, which they did generously.

Applications of those who had been admitted to membership with the Church were kept between pieces of cardboard marked alphabetically and tied with such bits of cord as I could pick up.

At that time there were no printed instructions nor By-Laws setting forth the requirements for uniting with the Church; it all had to be done with the pen, and as there were many mistakes made in filling out the blanks, the amount of writing to be done to have the mistakes corrected was great, and I had to work early and late. But I loved the work, I loved it and did not get tired. My wife and my son, only a youth then, encouraged and helped me.

He ends his letter telling Mrs. Eddy that he is devoting his full time to the study and practice of Christian Science healing.[48]

Julia Michael Johnston (1882–1965) Her mother, Annie R. Michael, was a student of Mrs. Eddy's, having taken a Normal class in 1887. Julia received her Primary class instruction in Christian Science from her mother. She first advertised as a full-time Christian Science practitioner in *The Christian Science Journal* in 1913. She became a teacher of Christian Science after attending The Mother Church's Normal class taught by Clifford P. Smith in 1916. Mrs. Johnston herself taught the Normal class in 1940. After this she wrote the biography *Mary Baker Eddy: Her Mission and Triumph*, which was published in 1946. Over the years, from the 1930s through the 1950s, Mrs. Johnston wrote a series of articles about two children growing up in Christian Science at the turn of the century. These were gathered together and published in 1959 as a booklet entitled *Elizabeth and Andy*.

Elizabeth Earl Jones (1881–1963) Though they never personally met, Miss Jones saw Mrs. Eddy three times when she was visiting Concord, New Hampshire, in 1902 and 1903. The two corresponded briefly in the years following. Miss Jones became interested in Christian Science when she was healed by it in 1898 of chronic headaches, dyspepsia, and neuralgia, which she had suffered from since childhood. She was taught Christian Science by one of Mrs. Eddy's students, Sue Harper Mims. After that she decided to devote her full time to Christian Science healing. In 1940 she became a Christian Science teacher when she went through the Church's Normal class taught by Julia M. Johnston.

Richard Kennedy (1849–1921) Born in Barnet, Vermont, Richard Kennedy first met Mrs. Eddy (then Mrs. Glover) in Amesbury, Massachusetts, in 1868, when he was nineteen years old and boarding at the Websters' home. He became Mrs. Glover's second student that same year. This was during the period when she was devoting most of her time to Bible study. In February 1870 the two moved to Lynn and formed a legal partnership, wherein she was to guide his healing practice, and he would pay her a portion of his earnings. He was unwilling to stop physically rubbing and manipulating patients—even though Mrs. Eddy had parted with that early practice. During the latter half of 1871, Mrs. Eddy discovered Richard Kennedy's immorality with one or more patients, and their partnership was dissolved in May 1872. After this Mr. Kennedy did whatever he could through mental and verbal manipulation to turn Mrs. Eddy's students away from her. Mrs. Eddy's perspicacity in discerning Kennedy's efforts to hinder her Cause is evident in this example of his mesmeric influence on one of her students:

> A young lady from Boston, who was suffering from ill health and a peculiar grief, became our student, and recovered her health and happiness. Our friendship flowed smoothly; nothing ever occurred to interrupt it, but the argus eye of the mesmerist was on her. He inquired her out thoroughly, and learned that we were strongly attached to her; that was enough. One evening she called on us to present us with a beautiful pair of vases. On leaving she startled us with the remark, "I shall probably never come to see you again, but shall always love you the same as now." We replied, "That will be a poor proof of it, when we reside so near you." She had

no reason for her remark, and claimed none, and we concluded it was merely mirthfulness. We parted with the usual affection, but have never seen her since, and certain unmistakable proofs have convinced us that the aforesaid mesmerist influenced her feelings and action.[49]

Richard Kennedy was committed to an insane asylum in Vermont in 1918 and passed away three years later from an unsuccessful operation for intestinal trouble.

***Edward A. Kimball** (1845–1909)* With only an eighth-grade education, Edward Kimball became a successful Chicago businessman, working twenty years in lumber and manufacturing before becoming interested in Christian Science in 1887. He learned of Christian Science from his sister after he had spent more than twelve months in a sanatorium, barely able to digest the simplest of foods. Healed, he attended two of Mrs. Eddy's Primary classes in 1888 and 1889. He was also a member of her last class in 1898. In 1893, at Mrs. Eddy's request, Mr. Kimball coordinated the Christian Science activities at the Chicago World's Fair and World's Parliament of Religions. Mrs. Eddy appointed Edward Kimball to the original Christian Science Board of Lectureship in 1898. Considered one of the ablest lecturers of Mrs. Eddy's day, he served as chairman of the Board of Lectureship and went on to deliver more than eighteen hundred lectures during the next twelve years. In 1898 Mrs. Eddy also asked him to serve as teacher in the Church's new Board of Education. He taught four Normal classes to prepare new teachers of Christian Science. In January 1901 Mrs. Eddy asked him to oversee her defense in the libel suit that had been brought by Josephine Woodbury in 1899. Six months later the suit was decided in Mrs. Eddy's favor. In September 1901 she chose Mr. Kimball, along with William McKenzie, to act as editorial assistants to her when she was working on her final major revision of *Science and Health with Key to the Scriptures*, which was published at the beginning of 1902 in its 226th edition.

George Kinter After years of struggling with ill health, George Kinter became interested in Christian Science when his mother-in-law was healed and she loaned him *Science and Health*. He regained his health in 1888 while reading this book. Later that same year he was taught Christian Science by Annie V. C. Leavitt, a student of Mrs. Eddy's. In 1890 he decided to devote his full time to Christian healing and advertised as a practitioner in *The Christian Science Journal*. Mr. Kinter became a teacher of Christian Science upon completion of the Normal class taught by Edward Kimball in 1901.

Mrs. Eddy called Mr. Kinter to serve in her household as a secretary and metaphysical worker in December 1903. When he came to Pleasant View Mrs. Eddy told him:

> Your principal duties at first will be to assist Mr. Frye; he has too much to do, and I will want you, among other things, to look after my mail. You will receive, open, read, and assort it, bringing to me only such letters and telegrams as I should see, and this will require you to be very wise....

> We have breakfast at 7.00 A.M., dinner at 12.00 noon, and our supper at six o'clock in the evening. Will that suit you? Do you drink coffee and tea? Because if

you do, you won't get any here. We don't have either. We drink cocoa shells,—it is a real nice drink and our faithful cook serves it good and hot.

Now you may go to your room. I want to write Mrs. Kinter. She has made it easy for me to keep you here, and I want to write her my thanks. I wish you would write her, too, how pleased I am with her letter. My, how it relieves me to have such friends.[50]

This first time in Mrs. Eddy's household, Mr. Kinter remained for one year. After that she asked him to work in her home for shorter periods during 1905, 1907, 1909, and 1910. After Mrs. Eddy's passing, he devoted the rest of his life to teaching and practicing Christian Science in Chicago, Illinois.

Flavia S. Knapp (1849–1898) After 13 years of ill health, Flavia had become an invalid, the doctors pronouncing her case incurable. In 1884, upon hearing about Christian Science, her husband, Ira O. Knapp, wrote Mrs. Eddy asking her to treat his wife. Mrs. Eddy referred the letter to a practitioner in Boston requesting that she take the case. In three weeks Flavia was healed and went on to take several classes from Mrs. Eddy. In July 1888, Flavia invited Mrs. Eddy to visit their farm in Lyman, New Hampshire. She came on August 20 and stayed six days. At Mrs. Eddy's request, Mrs. Knapp started teaching in 1892.

Upon Flavia's passing in March 1898, Mrs. Eddy told Irving Tomlinson, "Your dear teacher, Mrs. Knapp, was one of my best students, and had she remained with us, it was my intention to make her the teacher of the Massachusetts Metaphysical College."[51]

Ira O. Knapp *(1839–1910)* A schoolteacher, farmer, and local politician, who held virtually every office in the town of Lyman, New Hampshire, Ira Knapp felt most comfortable with Universalism as a faith before he became interested in Christian Science through his sister-in-law. Both he and his wife, Flavia, were healed by it in 1884, and that same year they attended one of Mrs. Eddy's Primary classes. They also went through another of her Primary classes the following year. In 1887 and 1888 Ira Knapp again had classes with Mrs. Eddy, the last, a Normal class. Mr. Knapp was one of the original Directors of The Mother Church appointed by Mrs. Eddy in 1892. He served as chairman of the Christian Science Board of Directors from the time he was appointed until 1903, and he remained a member of the Board up to the time of his passing. One of the Knapps' sons, Bliss, wrote a book about his parents' dedication to serving Mrs. Eddy and her Church. The book, *The Destiny of The Mother Church*, was published by the Christian Science Board of Directors in 1991.

Annie M. Knott *(1850–1941)* Born in Scotland and raised a strict Presbyterian, Annie Macmillan came to North America with her parents when she was twelve. (Her cousins founded Macmillan Publishers Ltd.) After her marriage, Annie Knott lived in London, England, from 1877 to 1882. She first heard of Christian Science when she moved to Chicago, Illinois, and was told about healings that had been accomplished through this new faith. But she didn't consider turning to it until after her young son, not expected to live after swallowing much of a bottle of carbolic acid, was quickly healed in Christian Science.

After witnessing this healing, Mrs. Knott studied Christian Science with Bradford Sherman, one of Mrs. Eddy's students in

Chicago. She moved to Detroit, Michigan, in 1885 and began a public practice of Christian healing. In 1887 she was taught by Mrs. Eddy in a February Normal class, and the following year attended another class with her. In 1898 Mrs. Eddy appointed her to The Mother Church's Board of Lectureship, where she served until 1903 when she became an Associate Editor of the Christian Science periodicals. Mrs. Knott was the first woman to be elected to the Church's Board of Directors. She served from 1919 to 1934, when she retired to devote her full time to healing and to teaching Christian Science.

John Lathrop *(1871–1941)* Raised in the Presbyterian church, John Lathrop became devoted to Christian Science after his mother, Laura, was healed by it in 1885 of a chronic illness that had left her an invalid. Several years after Mrs. Lathrop was taught by Mrs. Eddy, he went through one of his mother's Primary classes. In 1898 he was taught by Mrs. Eddy in her last class. At her request, he came to Boston from September to December 1899 to help with her defense during Josephine Woodbury's libel suit. He was also called to serve as a member of Mrs. Eddy's household from May to November 1903 and from September 1907 to February 1908. When Mr. Lathrop was about to return to his home in New York City this last time, Mrs. Eddy told him to devote himself to becoming the best Christian healer he could be (see p. 266). In 1911 Mr. Lathrop was elected to serve as First Reader in The Mother Church and then as President of the Church from 1914–1915. He was appointed to the Church's Board of Lectureship in 1918 and served as a lecturer for seven years. After that, he devoted his full time to Christian healing and the teaching of Christian Science.

Laura Lathrop *(1843–1922)* The daughter of a Methodist minister, Laura Lathrop became an invalid at seventeen due to several physical ailments that doctors would eventually pronounce incurable. After her husband's passing in 1884, and at the urging of friends, she traveled to Chicago, Illinois, in January 1885 to have Christian Science treatment, though she was highly skeptical of it. After nine weeks of treatment by Caroline Noyes, a student of Mrs. Eddy's, Mrs. Lathrop was so improved that she decided to attend Mrs. Noyes' Primary class in April. Four months later she was a pupil in one of Mrs. Eddy's Primary classes in the Massachusetts Metaphysical College, though she was not yet completely convinced of the truth of Christian Science. She recalls:

> I went to the College believing in a way in C.S. but
> so filled with egotism and innate skepticism of most
> religious statements that I was constantly on the *qui vive*
> [French for "on the alert"] to find a weak spot in Mrs.
> Eddy's armor. . . .
>
> Of course I do not pretend to remember all that
> Mother [Mrs. Eddy] said in her first lessons to me, but I
> *do* remember writing to my own mother, a minister's wife,
> that I had never heard any Christian teachings equal to
> Mrs. Eddy's.[52]

After that class Mrs. Eddy asked Mrs. Lathrop to go to New York City to help establish a Christian Science church there. In 1886 and 1887 Mrs. Lathrop again had class with Mrs. Eddy, and Mrs. Eddy healed her of heart disease when the latter was invited to visit in the winter of 1886–87 (see pp. 349–350). In 1891, again at her teacher's request, she organized Second Church of Christ, Scientist, New York City. Mrs. Lathrop devoted her life to the practice and teaching of Christian Science.

Ellen Brown Linscott Ellen Brown was a young woman when she was first taught Christian Science by Mrs. Eddy in 1883, and she was one of four students who lived at the Massachusetts Metaphysical College for several months during that year. In 1885 and in 1887 she attended class with Mrs. Eddy. Ellen Brown married John Linscott in 1887, and together they worked to establish Christian Science in Chicago, Denver, Washington, D.C., and other cities. Ellen Linscott devoted her entire adult life to the full-time public practice of Christian healing and to teaching Christian Science.

John Freeman Linscott *(1837–1931)* At the age of fourteen John Linscott went to work on a whaling ship. After four years at sea, he worked for a time in a law office until the Civil War broke out and he joined the Massachusetts cavalry, serving throughout the conflict. In the years following the war, he entered the United States Secret Service, where he worked to uncover and apprehend counterfeiters. He also learned quite a bit about liquor and drugs from his work, which led to a very successful career in lecturing for the temperance movement. During this period of his life, he first heard about Christian Science. In 1887 Captain Linscott was taught by Mrs. Eddy in both a Primary and a Normal class. After this he devoted himself to Christian healing and the teaching of Christian Science. He also worked with his wife, Ellen, to establish Christian Science churches in a number of cities around the country. He was appointed to The Mother Church's Board of Lectureship in 1900 and served in this capacity until 1904. Three years later the Board of Directors placed Captain Linscott on probation as a Christian Science teacher and Church member. He remained on probation for the rest of his life.

Delia S. Manley (1850–1919) Raised in the Baptist church, Delia Manley was in poor health until she turned to Christian Science in the early 1880s. When she was thirteen she had typhoid fever which left her with consumption. As an adult she was diagnosed and treated by numerous physicians, but all of them said her case was hopeless. When one of the doctors advised Mrs. Manley to try Christian Science, her husband contacted Mrs. Eddy's student Clara Choate to treat her. After her healing, she was taught by Mrs. Eddy in an 1882 Primary class.

When Gilbert Eddy passed away, Mrs. Manley stayed several days with her teacher. She recalled one time when Mrs. Eddy came to her: "She put her head on my shoulder and, weeping, said (I can see it all so plainly now as I recall it), 'I would be willing to live in a hut in the woods with him if I could only have the dear one back.'"[53] Mrs. Manley went through class again with Mrs. Eddy in 1884 and in 1887. She lived in Fall River, Massachusetts, and devoted the rest of her life to the public healing practice and to teaching Christian Science.

Arthur A. Maxfield Recalling the Christian Science treatment his father received, Arthur wrote: "In the spring of 1891 my father, a Civil War veteran, came under treatment by Captain J. S. Eastaman, C.S.D. of Boston, Massachusetts. He, the Captain, visited my father twice a week. I used to meet him at the depot with a horse and carriage, take him to see my father, then back to the depot in time for him to take the train back to Boston. On one of these trips he told me of a healing by Mrs. Eddy which he had witnessed that happened a day or two previously."[54] This healing appears on p. 168. Mr. Maxfield joined The Mother Church in 1895 and sent his reminiscences to the Church in 1934.

William P. McKenzie *(1861–1942)* The son of a Presbyterian minister, William McKenzie himself became one, graduating in 1889 from Knox Theological College, Toronto, Ontario, Canada. After attending the Auburn Theological Seminary in New York, he was ordained by the Presbytery of Rochester, New York, in 1890 and served as pastor to a small church for four years. During this period he also taught English literature and rhetoric at the University of Rochester. He first heard of Christian Science in 1891 at the home of a friend who had invited Daisette Stocking, a Christian Scientist from Cleveland, Ohio, to explain her new faith to afternoon guests. He immediately bought a copy of *Science and Health* and began to study it. He also began a correspondence with Miss Stocking, asking her many questions. He was taught Christian Science by Daisette's teacher, Pamelia Leonard, one of Mrs. Eddy's students. Mr. McKenzie was also a member of Mrs. Eddy's last class in 1898. Mr. McKenzie married Daisette Stocking in 1901.

Mr. McKenzie first met Mrs. Eddy when she invited him to visit her on Christmas Day, 1894, and by the following September he advertised in *The Christian Science Journal* as a practitioner, devoting his full time to the practice of Christian healing. In 1896 Mrs. Eddy appointed him to The Mother Church's Bible Lesson Committee, which prepares the weekly Lesson Sermons used in all Christian Science church services on Sunday. He remained on this committee for twenty-one years. On January 25, 1898, Mrs.

Eddy reorganized The Christian Science Publishing Society and appointed Mr. McKenzie to the three-man Board of Trustees. He served as a Trustee until 1917, when he was elected Editor of the Christian Science periodicals. In 1922, he was again made a Trustee and held the position until elected to the Christian Science Board of Directors ten years later. He served as a Church Director for the rest of his life.

Archibald McLellan *(1857–1917)* A successful businessman who also earned a degree from Kent College of Law in Chicago, Illinois, Mr. McLellan became interested in Christian Science after seeing its benefit on his wife's health. He was so impressed by what he heard when Mrs. Eddy spoke in Chicago in 1888[55] that he began to study Christian Science in earnest and received Primary class instruction, along with his wife, from Ruth B. Ewing, a student of Mrs. Eddy's. He became very involved with Christian Science church work in Chicago, and was appointed Committee on Publication for Illinois in 1900. Though Mr. McLellan never advertised in the *Journal* as a Christian Science practitioner or teacher, he did attend a Board of Education Primary class taught by Edward Kimball in 1903.

Mrs. Eddy appointed Mr. McLellan Editor of the Christian Science periodicals in 1902, and a year later she put him on the Christian Science Board of Directors, where he served as its chairman. He continued in both positions up to the time of his passing. He was a frequent visitor both to Pleasant View and Chestnut Hill, and Mrs. Eddy described him as "one of Nature's noblemen."[56] In 1913 he wrote to a friend, "It is for me to fulfill the trust reposed in me by our Leader as I see it, and leave the results with divine Love."[57]

Adelaide Morrison Mooney Adelaide's father, Henry H. Morrison, was the Western Union manager in Concord, New Hampshire. She wrote of her experience working for her father:

> I was employed as a Western Union operator in
> my father's office at this time. While Mrs. Eddy lived at
> Pleasant View, it was her custom to take daily drives to
> the city. At one time no one was permitted to stop her
> carriage except our Western Union Messengers. They
> always spoke of her genial smile and generosity to them.
> Many times my father would go out to her carriage, when
> she would stop at the office for telegrams, and sometimes
> [she] would ask his advice.[58]

In her reminiscences, which she sent to The Mother Church in 1943, Mrs. Mooney recounts her father's healing by Mrs. Eddy: "At the time of the 'Next Friends' suit, father and I worked from ten to fifteen hours daily sending newspaper copy. This was done without any sense of fatigue.... Mrs. Eddy presented autographed copies of *Science and Health* and *Miscellaneous Writings* to my father."[59]

Dr. Alpheus Morrill (1808–1874) Dr. Morrill was related to Mrs. Eddy through his marriage to Hannah Baker, a first cousin. He graduated from Dartmouth Medical College, afterward settling in Columbus, Ohio, where he became one of the leading physicians in the state. By 1847, when he returned to New Hampshire and opened his office in Concord, he had become a homeopath. The first president of the New Hampshire Homeopathic Medical Society, Dr. Morrill introduced Mrs. Eddy (then Mrs. Glover) to the practice around

1848. She wrote that, "homœopathy came like blessed relief to me."[60] After she had studied homeopathy in order to treat not only herself but others, he counseled her in her practice. They maintained a warm relationship throughout his lifetime. She eventually turned from homeopathy when she discovered Christian Science.

Henry Morrison See Adelaide Morrison Mooney.

Minnie Ford Mortlock As a teenager, Minnie Ford came to know Mrs. Eddy after her family emigrated from England in 1893, settling on a small farm near Pleasant View. Minnie later described how she met Mrs. Eddy, who expressed an interest in her:

> ... One day as Mrs. Eddy was driving by our house, our guinea hens made such a noise that they scared her horses, and that evening she sent word over to ask my father if he would loan her two of them to put into her stable so that her horses could get used to them, which he did. That is how she came to hear about us. She became quite interested in us and especially in me. I was then about 16 years old [in 1896].
>
> Miss Shannon, Mrs. Eddy's maid, would occasionally take me for a drive, and that is really how I came to go into Mrs. Eddy's home. Her household consisted of Mr. Calvin Frye, secretary, Miss Shannon, maid, and Miss Morgan, cook. I became quite useful to both Miss Shannon and Miss Morgan.
>
> The daily routine in the home began with Mrs. Eddy's breakfast, served in her room; at eleven o'clock, the

quiet hour when she would take her daily exercise on
the back porch, which went the length of the house
on the second floor. Dinner served promptly at twelve
o'clock in the dining room, Miss Shannon and Mr.
Frye dining with her. At three o'clock her daily drive
regardless of the weather. Supper at six o'clock and at
seven another quiet hour when she would sit in her
swing in a closed porch on the front of the house, after
which she would retire to her room. Her meals were
of the simplest, but she was very exacting, her motto
being, "with exactness grind ye all." One of her favorite
dinners was New England boiled dinner with a Bartlett
pear boiled with it; she was also fond of broiled squab
[pigeon], which were raised on the farm.[61]

Of her healing of tuberculosis after a visit with Mrs. Eddy,
Mrs. Mortlock wrote, "The healing must have taken place
immediately as I don't recall of any illness after that. And today
I am in perfect health. Thanks to dear Mrs. Eddy and Christian
Science."[62] Though never a member, Mrs. Mortlock gave her
reminiscences to The Mother Church in 1937.

Lady Victoria Murray *(1877–1926)* The daughter of the Earl
and Countess of Dunmore and a godchild of Queen Victoria,
she became a student of Christian Science after her mother's
healing in 1892 of spinal problems that doctors had diagnosed
as incurable. Lady Victoria received Primary class instruction
from a student of Mrs. Eddy's, Julia Field-King. After that she
entered the full-time public practice of Christian Science healing,
advertising in the *Journal* in 1900.

The following year, at Mrs. Eddy's invitation, she and her sister and parents attended the Normal class of The Mother Church's Board of Education taught by Edward Kimball. Immediately after that class, Mrs. Eddy called them to Pleasant View, where she gave them

> a beautiful and inspiring talk on the application of Christian Science, being informed at the same time that we were now teachers. Seeing that none of us had anticipated for a moment such a calling, we probably seemed hesitant, but Mrs. Eddy was firm and gave us additional counsel, expressing the while much satisfaction with the healing we had already done. It was evident to us that everyone was expected to be at work and that, whatever our seeming lack, Mrs. Eddy knew we could reflect the one [divine] Mind,— the only Teacher and Healer.[63]

After returning to England, Lady Victoria decided to live in Manchester. Her work to establish Christian Science in that city was instrumental in a branch of The Mother Church being dedicated there in 1908. Her remaining years were devoted to healing and to teaching Christian Science.

James Neal (1866–1930) James Neal was introduced to Christian Science while working as a cashier in Joseph Armstrong's bank in Irving, Kansas. He was first taught this Science in December 1887 by Mr. Armstrong, who had just returned from one of Mrs. Eddy's Primary classes. Immediately after this, Mr. Neal left his bank job and began working full time as a Christian Science healer. In May 1888 he went through another Christian Science class, this time taught by another of Mrs. Eddy's students, Janet Colman. Nine months later he took Mrs. Eddy's Primary class. In 1898 he attended Mrs. Eddy's last class, and thereby became a Christian Science teacher.

Mr. Neal had come to Boston at the end of 1892 to work as a Christian Science healer. At Mrs. Eddy's request he also worked in The Mother Church's publishing activities. In January 1897 he wrote to her of his desire to devote his full time to the healing practice. She gladly agreed, writing him an eloquent letter on the vital significance of healing to the Cause of Christian Science (see pp. 189–191). One year later she appointed him to the three-man Board of Trustees of the newly reorganized Christian Science Publishing Society. Ten months after that, Mrs. Eddy wrote Joseph Armstrong, the Manager of the Publishing Society, who was also a Director of the Church:

> I feel and discern the *need* of Mr. Neal giving his whole attention to healing the sick. No man can serve in C.S. two masters and do his duty to both. Mr. Neal consents to this change, and he thinks it will not interfere with Mr. Joseph Clark's work for the Pub. So. to have him take his [Neal's] place on the Board of Trustees. Have you any objection?
>
> I have named Mr. Clark to the Board and called for Mr. Neal's discharge on the grounds that he is needed to devote himself to healing. It is not right that he should lose aught of his spiritual power by so much material thought. Hence my duty and his in the case.[64]

In 1911 Mr. Neal was again made a Publishing Society Trustee. He served a little more than a year. In June of the following year he was elected President of the Church but resigned a month later when he was elected to the Christian Science Board of Directors. He remained a Director for seventeen years before retiring "to have more time for my practice and teaching work."[65]

Carol Norton *(1869–1904)* A cousin of Henry Wadsworth Longfellow, he was born on Christmas Day in Maine and reared as a Unitarian. Carol Norton lost his parents while still a boy and was raised in New York City by an aunt and uncle. He became interested in Christian Science when he turned to it because of a physical ailment that had plagued him for some time and that his doctors had been unable to cure. The healing so impressed him that he decided to devote his life to this new faith, leaving a promising business career behind. Augusta Stetson, a student of Mrs. Eddy's, taught him in one of her Primary classes, and it was not long before he became her assistant at the New York City Christian Science Institute. Through Mrs. Stetson, Mr. Norton came to know Mrs. Eddy personally, as they were both invited to Pleasant View a few times, and a regular correspondence grew between him and Mrs. Eddy. In 1893 Mrs. Eddy revised a poem he had written, "The New World," and asked the Christian Science Publishing Society to publish it as a booklet, which she wanted to have available at the Christian Science exhibit at the Chicago World's Fair.

At her invitation, Carol Norton attended Mrs. Eddy's last class in 1898, the same year she appointed him to The Mother Church's Board of Lectureship. He devoted himself to this work until his death in a trolley accident in 1904. Mrs. Eddy considered Carol Norton one of her most promising students, and especially appreciated his understanding of true womanhood. In one of his lectures he said: "The present age witnesses woman's ascension to her rightful place as man's equal. . . . Woman's spiritual leadership will not supersede that of man, because man will rise to the possession of a spirituality and love that is ideal. Then there will be fulfilled the vision of genuine sex co-operation."[66]

Elizabeth Norton She and Carol Norton were married in April 1901. Elizabeth had previously received Primary class instruction in Christian Science from Augusta Stetson, a student of Mrs. Eddy's. Upon reading a letter to her husband from Mrs. Eddy, Elizabeth was healed of a severe ankle injury (see pp. 371–372). Then, not long after her husband's accident and subsequent passing, she visited Mrs. Eddy:

> I shall never forget the first time I talked with [Mrs. Eddy]. She had sent for me to call upon her. On entering the room she extended her hand and asked me to be seated. I walked across the room and sat down in a chair. Mrs. Eddy very deliberately arranged her dress and sat down on a sofa. She looked at me so tenderly, and patting the sofa beside herself, she said, "You are too far away from Mother, darling." I immediately went to her. She took me in her arms and kissed me. She was not afraid to express her love humanly, and I did not mistake it, for I learned then and there, that divine Love must be expressed humanly in order to heal the broken hearted. [67]

Mrs. Norton attended the Normal class of The Mother Church's Board of Education in 1910, taught by Bicknell Young, a student of Edward Kimball. She lived in Boston, devoting the rest of her life to Christian healing and the teaching of Christian Science.

Edward E. Norwood (1868–1940) Raised in the Methodist church, Edward Norwood early on desired to become a minister, but chronic ill-health interfered with his college training. In the spring of 1893, at the suggestion of a friend, he contacted a Christian Science practitioner to treat his mother, who had been diagnosed as having an incurable disease, and he also began reading *Science and Health* to her. What he read so amazed him, he couldn't put the book down. After three weeks he was completely healed of his ailments, and his mother was much improved. He wrote to Mrs. Eddy in great gratitude for what had happened. In her reply she asked him, "Are you thinking of making Christian Science a study and practice? The spirit of love you manifest inclines me to ask this."[68] Two years later his advertisement as a full-time practitioner appeared in *The Christian Science Journal*.

Edward was taught Christian Science in an 1895 Primary class by Carol Norton. In 1898 he attended Mrs. Eddy's last class at her invitation. In 1902 Mrs. Eddy wrote Mr. Norwood a letter of deep gratitude for his search and discovery of evidence that her first husband, George W. Glover, had been a member of the St. Andrew's Masonic Lodge in Charleston, South Carolina. He had taken on this investigation in order to counteract a newspaper article that had attacked Mrs. Eddy's character and that of Colonel Glover's. In the latter half of 1906, Mrs. Eddy requested him to oversee in Washington, D.C., the production of new printing plates for *Science and Health*. Mr. Norwood devoted his adult life to Christian Science healing and teaching in Washington, D.C. His testimony of being healed when first reading *Science and Health* appears in that book's last chapter, "Fruitage," on pp. 694–695.

Harriet O'Brien After being healed through Christian Science, Miss O'Brien became a Christian healer herself. Her reminiscences include this account:

> In August, 1910, it was my inspiring privilege to see Mary Baker Eddy on her daily drive just as she was leaving her Chestnut Hill home. . . . As her carriage came out the gate, her love drew me right over to the carriage wheels. Mrs. Eddy, who was occupying the seat on the farther side of the carriage, turned her small, black parasol aside, leaned forward in her seat, turned toward me, and looked straight into my eyes, while her face was illumined with a wondrous smile. Although she did not speak to me audibly, these words from Scripture came distinctly to me three times, every word clearly, "Man shall not live by bread alone, but by every word that proceedeth out of the mouth of God." It seemed to me the carriage stopped, but that evidently was due to my losing, for a moment, the thought of time and being wholly absorbed in spiritual unfoldment and a newborn love for her whose teachings had raised me from a deathbed and healed me from wheelchair invalidism; a condition due to the teaching of old theology and a major surgical operation in which the ligaments controlling the limbs had been severed by mistake.

"Transparency" is the word that best expresses my impression of Mrs. Eddy from this experience. Instinctively I felt her great love, and I was conscious that no one I had ever seen loved me as much as she did. My entire thought was filled with a spiritual illumination, and there was a glory in the sunshine and landscape, as though a breath of heaven had swept earth and enveloped me, while tears of gratitude rained down my cheeks unheeded. I had caught a glimpse of the great difference between a mortal and spiritual man in God's image and likeness.

My trip to Boston was for the purpose of determining whether the time had come for me to open a practitioner's office. After seeing Mrs. Eddy all my questions were fully answered, and I returned to Kansas City and opened my office at once, healing desperate illnesses and sometimes raising the dying in one or two visits. . . .

This experience helped me see how inseparable and how much alike Mrs. Eddy and her writings are. [69]

Less than a year later, in 1911, Miss O'Brien's advertisement as a Christian Science healer appeared in *The Christian Science Journal* and remained there until March 1964. Mrs. Mary E. Dunbar personally told Miss O'Brien about the healing of her little daughter Ethel, which Miss O'Brien recounted for The Mother Church's archives in 1935 (see p. 148).

Mary Godfrey Parker (1868–1945) Mrs. Eddy (then Mrs. Glover) healed Mary Godfrey of membranous croup when she was a little girl in Lynn, Massachusetts (see p. 311). Before that she had healed Mary's mother of a badly infected finger, which the doctors had said would need to be amputated.[70] Her mother was responsible for introducing Asa Gilbert Eddy to Mrs. Glover.

Mary Godfrey Parker was raised in the Universalist church and was teaching in a Universalist Sunday school at the time she became interested in Christian Science. Her interest stemmed from two events: in 1898 her husband was healed of the after-effects of pneumonia, and at the same time Joseph Armstrong, the Manager of The Christian Science Publishing Society, called her to help in putting out the new *Christian Science Weekly* (later renamed the *Christian Science Sentinel*). She joined The Mother Church three years later and continued her work in the Publishing Society.

In 1902 Mrs. Parker wrote Mrs. Eddy:

> For the many, many blessings that have come to me through Science, I feel that I must express my gratitude to you. My childhood recollections of you in the Lynn house, when I was there with my cousin, Mr. Nash, and my mother, Mrs. Christiana Godfrey, are so full of love for you, that since becoming interested in Christian Science within the last few years, I have felt that I must tell you. When I look at the first edition of *Science & Health*, which you gave mamma so many years ago, I feel that I wish you knew how I appreciate it, and the great blessings that have come to me through it.[71]

Daniel Patterson (1818–1896) Daniel Patterson, an itinerant dentist with an interest in homeopathy, was a nephew of Mrs. Eddy's stepmother, Elizabeth. Mrs. Eddy married him in June 1853, not only out of love, but also in the hope that she could regain custody of her son George Glover II. But Daniel did not keep his promise to reunite her with her son, partly out of fear that the young boy's rambunctious behavior would adversely affect her health.

While on a commission from the governor of New Hampshire to deliver funds to Southerners loyal to the Union during the Civil War, Daniel was captured by Southern forces and placed in a prisoner of war camp. He escaped and rejoined his wife in Portland, Maine, where she was being treated by Phineas Quimby. In the fall of 1865, they moved to Lynn, Massachusetts, where he reestablished his dental practice. Mrs. Eddy would sometimes help his patients, through prayer, when they were in pain.

The following spring Daniel ran off with one of his female patients, but her husband tracked them down and retrieved his wife. Mrs. Eddy forgave Daniel, but when he did the same thing a few months later, she would not take him back. Mrs. Eddy (still Mrs. Patterson at the time) was granted a divorce in November 1873. Unbeknownst to her, Daniel passed away impoverished in Maine in 1896. In the mid-1880s Mrs. Eddy talked about her former husband with one of her students who had met Dr. Patterson previously without knowing his relation to her teacher. Mrs. Eddy spoke kindly but insightfully of him, saying, ". . . he treated me with the utmost consideration and delicacy, until the time when my little son came to be with me. Then our troubles began, for

Dr. Patterson's jealousy of my child was in proportion to his great love for me."[72]

Dorr Phillips Mrs. Eddy (then Mrs. Patterson) healed Dorr Phillips of a badly infected finger when he was a boy in Lynn. This was one of the first healings she accomplished after she discovered Christian Science. Mrs. Eddy stayed with his family twice for brief periods in 1866. Dorr helped her when she was exposing spiritualists as frauds:

> Mr. Dorr Phillips of Lynn, Mass., will tell you that at my request he invented a light that could be turned on instantaneously and took it into a séance, where he put on the light and exposed the medium outside of his ropes that they had tied him with doing the things that spirits were claimed to be doing, and [a notable citizen] of the city, Jonathan Buffum, who was present told the [medium] unless he left Lynn that night he would [be] put out of that city. In the morning he had disappeared.[73]

At one point a little later on, Mrs. Patterson wrote up an agreement to teach Dorr the "art" of healing,[74] but for reasons unknown this never came about.

Ellen Pilsbury (Philbrook) (1844–c1905) Mrs. Eddy's niece, the daughter of her sister Martha. In 1867 Mrs. Eddy (then Mrs. Patterson) healed Ellen, who was dying from enteritis (see pp. 285–286), and again several years later when she was not expected to live through childbirth (see p. 418). After her first healing, Ellen accompanied her aunt back to the home of Mr. and Mrs. Crafts in Taunton, Massachusetts, where Mrs. Patterson was living. The austerity of their house and her aunt's work regimen proved too severe for Ellen's sensibilities, and she returned to New Hampshire in a short time.

In 1899 Henry H. Goddard, a psychologist from Clark University, Worcester, Massachusetts, wrote to Ellen Pilsbury Philbrook in preparation for a book he was thinking of writing. She responded, "In reply to your letter asking for information in regard to Mrs. Eddy, I would say I have none to give you along the desired lines. In my childhood I was taught to regard my 'Aunt Mary' as a suffering saint. I removed west before Christian Science became the *Science* it is."[75]

***Lyman P. Powell** (1866–1946)* Raised in the Methodist church, Lyman Powell graduated from Johns Hopkins University in 1890. From 1892 to 1895 he was a Fellow at the Wharton School of Finance of the University of Pennsylvania. Then his life took a very different direction when he entered the Episcopal Divinity School in Philadelphia. He graduated in 1897 and was ordained to the ministry. After serving as pastor to two congregations in Pennsylvania, he became Rector of St. John's Church in Northampton, Massachusetts, in 1904. His interest in Christian Science around this time appears to have come from its effect on his own congregation and his involvement with the Emmanuel Movement, which also promoted spiritual healing. In 1907 he wrote a highly critical book, *Christian Science, the Faith and its Founder*. Of this, his biographer, Charles MacFarland, wrote, "I read the book which, it was clear, had been written in a spirit of extreme irritation. I remember my own observation that it was neither judicial nor judicious."[76]

Over the next twenty years, Dr. Powell's opinion of the religion and its founder would radically change. Beginning in 1918, and for the next seven years, he went on the lecture circuit, speaking primarily about education and the United States as a world influence. One of his lectures, "America's Greatest Woman," was about Mrs. Eddy. Dr. Powell returned to the ministry in 1926, becoming Rector of St. Margaret's Church in the Bronx, New York. He served for ten years before retiring as one of the more well-known clergymen, lecturers, and authors in America. Over his lifetime he wrote more than twenty books and booklets. In 1930 Dr. Powell published his biography of Mrs. Eddy, *Mary Baker Eddy: A Life Size Portrait*. In contrast with his previous critical book on the subject, his deep appreciation of her and his kind consideration of her Church are evident throughout. He followed the publication with a series of lectures on the subject, "Mary Baker Eddy, Educator," where he especially shone light on her humility and tolerance.

Julia E. Prescott *(1849–1924)* Raised in the Free-Will Baptist church, Julia Prescott first heard of Christian Science from a relative in 1885. She was healed of curvature of the spine while reading *Science and Health* and receiving treatment from a Christian Science healer. Not long after this she healed her own young son, who was suffering greatly from a severe attack of the croup. Julia Prescott was taught by Mrs. Eddy in a Primary class in 1886. Soon after her instruction, she started the Christian Science church in Reading, Massachusetts, with the help of another Christian Scientist. She first advertised as a practitioner in *The Christian Science Journal* in 1895, and four years later began teaching. One of Mrs. Prescott's students had known Phineas

Quimby at the time Mrs. Eddy (then Mrs. Patterson) was consulting with him. Mrs. Prescott asked this student, "Was Dr. Quimby's treatment anything like Christian Science?" Her pupil replied, "Oh no, it seemed like clairvoyance."[77]

Mrs. Prescott served in Mrs. Eddy's home from August 1905 to February 1906, and again for a number of weeks throughout 1907. In her reminiscences she wrote that one day while at Pleasant View Mrs. Eddy called her into her study

> and the sense of God was so great that tears came into my eyes. [Mrs. Eddy] noticed that I was affected, and she asked: "Why those tears, dear? Are you homesick?"
>
> "Oh, no," I responded, "but I feel that you are an angel."
>
> She asked: "You don't mean my personality?"
>
> "Oh, no," I answered. "I mean that you give us messages from God."
>
> She concluded: "You mean that I am the window. We are right under the focus of divine Love." I went to my room, feeling that all the world was filled with God, good.[78]

When Mrs. Eddy moved to Chestnut Hill, Massachusetts, in 1908, she asked Julia to come with her as a regular member of the household, but Mr. Prescott wrote to Mrs. Eddy and explained "that it seemed more of a sacrifice than he could make to have [her] go."[79] Mrs. Prescott lived in Reading, Massachusetts, and devoted her remaining years to Christian Science healing and teaching.

Lewis Prescott After reading Lyman Powell's biography of Mrs. Eddy (*Mary Baker Eddy: A Life Size Portrait*) in 1931, Mr. Prescott wrote to thank him and also told him about his own contact with Mrs. Eddy:

> In 1882 I was healed in Christian Science of consumption after eight years of invalidism. Preceding my full healing I met Mrs. Eddy and heard her lecture a few times [in Lawrence, Massachusetts, in the autumn of 1882]. After this healing I went to Boston to hear Mrs. Eddy preach, whenever she addressed her church. In those early days of Christian Science Mrs. Eddy preached on Sunday afternoons. Sunday mornings I went to Trinity Church and listened to Bishop [Phillips] Brooks. He was a gifted preacher, a fine man. A very whole man!...
>
> One Easter I heard Bishop Brooks preach on the "Resurrection." A splendid discourse. After luncheon I listened to Mrs. Eddy preach on the *same subject* in Chickering Hall, Tremont St.... I would like to tell you one impression Mrs. Eddy's sermon made upon me. As I listened, her words seemed to cause me to actually see Jesus stepping forth from the tomb, a victor over the "last enemy," and his body so glorified that he could pass through closed doors into his disciples' presence, proving, as Christian Science teaches, that matter is not substance. No longer was the resurrection a beautiful Bible-story to be believed in blind faith. It was an actual fact. What power gave Mrs. Eddy ability to show forth the living Christ? It was something more than a beautiful word-

picture. And the spirit of that sermon healed. The power was divine. And it set forth not only Mrs. Eddy's great spiritual discovery—Christian Science, but also showed what Mrs. Eddy had suffered and experienced.[80]

Mr. Prescott was taught Christian Science by Susie M. Lang, a student of Mrs. Eddy's. He first advertised as a healer in *The Christian Science Journal* in 1895. He lived in Lawrence, Massachusetts, devoting the rest of his life to this work till his passing in 1944.

Phineas P. Quimby *(1802–1866)* A clockmaker by profession, Phineas Quimby first became interested in mesmerism in 1838 when he heard a professional mesmerist lecture and demonstrate his skill. Literature and lecturers on mesmerism were not uncommon at this period in New England. Through further investigation, Mr. Quimby found he had a special talent for "magnetizing" others, putting them into a mesmeric sleep. For a period of time he toured Maine and New Brunswick, Canada, giving exhibitions, placing an assistant in a somnambulistic state and, through him, diagnosing illnesses and prescribing cures. Eventually he saw he did not need a middleman, and in the 1840s he returned to his home in Maine, beginning a regular therapeutic practice as a "magnetic doctor," first in Belfast, then Bangor, and finally in Portland. He encountered Mrs. Eddy (then Mrs. Patterson) in Portland in 1862.

Dr. Quimby's mesmeric treatment was based primarily on clairvoyance. He would first talk with his patients, discuss their problems, tell them what he perceived to be the source of their trouble, and then vigorously rub their heads or stomachs depending on where he saw the illness to be centered. The theory behind his practice was that man has two identities: one, the fleshly mind, which receives information through the material senses; the other, the clairvoyant mind, which is completely mental in nature, untouched by the senses. He believed that he could mentally influence or manipulate the clairvoyant mind in a patient, which would affect the fleshly, or "natural" mind, which would in turn affect the physical body for good or ill. Not until Mrs. Eddy suggested to him that there was a "science" behind his practice did Dr. Quimby first start referring to it with that term. After a while he received so many insights from their many discussions about his work and her "views of mental therapeutics" that he began to praise her to others.

As to his "manuscripts," which created quite a stir a number of years after Mrs. Eddy discovered Christian Science, it is highly unlikely that the bulk of these writings could be his own. Phineas Quimby was barely literate and found it difficult to write an articulate sentence. While he wrote simple notes to himself about specific cases he treated, it is not conceivable that he could have been the author of what has been published as *The Quimby Manuscripts*. While his concepts are woven throughout, it is obvious that others have rewritten and added much to his notes in an attempt to make his ideas comprehensible to readers and to insinuate that they are the source of Christian Science.[81]

The vast majority of the original notes in Dr. Quimby's hand were destroyed by his son George, who refused to let anyone inspect them after Mrs. Eddy had become well-known in Boston. When quotations from some of the doctor's alleged writings were published in 1887, Mrs. Eddy responded, "Some words in these quotations certainly read like words that I said to him, and which I, at his request, had added to his copy when I corrected it."[82] Considering all the evidence, one is left to conclude that Mrs. Patterson's influence on Dr. Quimby was far greater than any lasting effect he might possibly have had on her. (See Emma A. Thompson entry, pp. 522–524.)

William R. Rathvon *(1854–1939)* As a boy of nine, William heard Abraham Lincoln deliver his Gettysburg Address: "I was within a few feet of the President as he stood upon the rough board platform over which Old Glory was draped, and as I looked into his face he seemed even to my boyish imagination to be a prophet and seer as he uttered the closing words of his address."[83]

Raised in the Lutheran church, Mr. Rathvon became interested in Christian Science in 1893:

> I became very successful in business, but my wealth, mostly in silver mines, was wiped away in the panic of '93, and we were left practically penniless. While sojourning temporarily in Chicago, through association with friends of former years, we learned of Christian Science, and without resistance it entered our lives, ever to remain.

> Before leaving Chicago we were taught by Mrs. Mary W. Adams, an early student of Mrs. Eddy's and the following year (1894) left for Colorado, to begin pioneer work in Christian Science in the little town of Florence, the center of the oil district.[84]

In 1902 he and his wife, Ella, moved to Boulder, Colorado, where he divided his time between a job at an oil refinery and the public practice of Christian healing. The following year he was taught by Edward Kimball in a Primary class of The Mother Church's Board of Education. Then in 1907 he attended that Board's Normal class instruction taught by Septimus J. Hanna.

Mr. Rathvon was called to serve in Mrs. Eddy's household in 1908. Not long after joining her household, he asked Mrs. Eddy:

> ... Mother, would you object if I were to impart to my dear wife at times some of the good and helpful things you are constantly giving us? She is working bravely in Colorado to overcome the claim of separation and is making it much easier for me here than if her work was not so well done. I know some things I could tell her would help us both.

Mrs. Eddy replied,

> By all means, tell her such things and give her my love this night. And you must both know that what you are doing and giving is not a *sacrifice*, but an *offering*.[85]

Ella Rathvon was called to serve in Mrs. Eddy's home nine months later.

Another noteworthy exchange occurred a few months after Mr. Rathvon arrived. Mrs. Eddy asked her staff, "What is the highest attainment one can cherish?" Several answers were offered, but then she said,

> … Healing the sick. That requires the
> abandonment of everything. Away go automobiles and
> all else material. I gave up everything and I healed the
> sick. I saw a man crippled so that when he moved he
> was almost doubled up and had his hands on the ground
> to assist locomotion. I saw him seated on the curb with
> his head between his knees, on my way to a patient. As I
> passed I placed my hand on his head and said, "Do you
> know that God loves you?" At once he straightened up,
> erect as he ever had been.[86]

In 1911 Mr. Rathvon was elected to The Mother Church's Board of Lectureship and over the next seven years gave lectures in Europe, Asia, and Australia. He retired from this work when he was appointed Treasurer of The Mother Church in June 1918. Four months later he was elected to the Christian Science Board of Directors and remained on that Board until his passing.

Bertha S. Reinke (1859–1939) Else Buchenberger wrote The Mother Church that Bertha Reinke

> was born in Camionken, Kreis Loetzen, East Prussia, on
> 4 February 1859, where her father owned an estate.

> Her parents were Lutherans.…

> As a young girl, when she was to be confirmed, she
> rebelled against the strict doctrines of her church and
> refused to accept them; her pastor—so she often told us

—allowed her then to write her own confession of faith and accepted her in his congregation. Her governess had punished her severely for her apparent stubbornness, but bread and water and a locked room did not compel her to yield and give vows, which even as a child she knew she could not obey.

In 1888 an insatiable thirst for learning led her to Paris, where as lady companion to Countess Kessler and governess of their daughter, she had opportunity to study French and literature.

In Paris she met two German teachers, who were then living in U.S.A. and accompanied them to America in the hope of studying there psychology, theology, and especially medicine, which in those days was not open to women in Germany.

During this visit she heard Mrs. Eddy preach in Boston. Miss Reinke was taught Christian Science in the mid-1890s by Laura Lathrop, a student of Mrs. Eddy's.

Else Buchenberger's account continues:

In 1902 [Bertha] received word from her mother that she was seriously ill, given up by the physicians, and filled with longing to see her daughter once more. Miss Reinke took the first steamer, declared the truth as best she then understood it, and when she arrived in Berlin, where her mother lived, she had the joy of finding her well... .

Miss Reinke began the practice of Christian
Science in Berlin . . . and has been a practitioner in
Germany since 1902. In May 1913 at the call of a group
of Scientists in Hamburg, she moved to that city, to
help them organize as First Church of Christ, Scientist,
Hamburg, Deutschland.

From the time of her return to Germany, Miss Reinke
devoted her life to Christian Science healing. Else Buchenberger sent her account of Bertha Reinke's encounter with
Mrs. Eddy to The Mother Church in 1939. In her reminiscence
she wrote, "It has been my privilege to know Miss Reinke 22
years—as practitioner and truest friend in the highest sense of
the word."[87]

Miranda Rice When she became interested in Christian Science,
Miranda Rice was a homemaker and a Methodist. Even though
she was unable to pay, she was taught by Mrs. Eddy (then Mrs.
Glover) in her fourth class in 1872. Her sister, Dorcas Rawson,
had been taught two years earlier. In the beginning, Mrs. Rice
could not do enough for Mrs. Glover, due in part, perhaps, to
Mrs. Glover's metaphysical assistance at the birth of one of her
children (see pp. 304–305). For example, Mrs. Glover was helped
by her student at a time of physical distress: in 1874 Samuel
Bancroft notes in his diary that he had received a letter from
George Barry about "a strange experience my teacher passed
through." He goes on to relate that when Mr. Barry and a friend
entered Mrs. Glover's rooms,

> she arose to meet them, but fell back, lost consciousness,
> and, to their belief, was gathering herself on the other

side. George went after Mrs. R[ice], who came, and
immediately a change took place. George had called on
her mentally to come back, but Mrs. R[ice] called loudly,
as for someone afar off, and the answer came, faintly at
first, but stronger and stronger, till she was able to sit
up and have the Bible and manuscripts read to her, and,
finally, recovered.[88]

It came as a great shock to Mrs. Eddy when Mrs. Rice,
along with seven other students, deserted her at the end of
October 1881, signing a letter that accused their teacher of
unchristian behavior. As Mrs. Eddy understood it, these students
were victims of mesmerism and of the mental malpractice of
Richard Kennedy and Daniel Spofford. By 1884 Miranda Rice
had moved to San Francisco and was teaching unauthorized
classes in Christian Science, taking these occasions as opportunities to denounce Mrs. Eddy. Three years later Mrs. Rice studied
with Emma Hopkins, and not long after this became mentally
unbalanced. Upon her release from an asylum, she returned to
Massachusetts. In 1906 Mrs. Rice became a source for the *New
York World*'s muckraking attacks on Mrs. Eddy.

Nemi Robertson First taught by Mrs. Eddy in 1889, Nemi
Robertson entered the full-time healing practice in Orange, New
Jersey, in 1896. She also attended Mrs. Eddy's last class, held two
years later. She devoted her life to Christian Science healing and
teaching until her passing in 1926. Student and teacher corresponded with each other from time to time, and in 1891 Mrs.
Eddy wrote her pupil:

Your kind, sad, glad letter tells me quite a story of the cross.

But it is good to be afflicted, to drink in the experience by which we are made meet for the Master's crown. Love is in itself a purifier, and if we reach its glorious behests we must be purified in the process.

Wait patiently, dear one, on the Lord, and He will renew your strength—and "answer you out of the place of thunder and prove you at the waters of Meribah."[89]

Five years later Mrs. Eddy wrote Miss Robertson again along the same lines, right before the latter's advertisement as a Christian Science healer was to appear in *The Christian Science Journal*:

I am rejoiced over your sorrows and joys. They bring the fruits of Love, and patience has a rich reward. Thirty years I have been in the fiery furnace, and the dross has dropped away from the gold through agony. But "if we suffer with him we shall also reign with him." I am glad you are [working] patiently on and are reaping the reward of faith and understanding. Nothing but Christian growth can bring to you the experience you depict in your letter. May God be more and more understood and loved by you and your life be serene.[90]

Henry Robinson After beginning his law practice in Concord, New Hampshire, in 1875, Henry Robinson became interested in politics and served as a New Hampshire state senator from 1883 to 1885. He was elected mayor of Concord in 1895 for a two-year term. He also served as postmaster of the city from 1890 to 1894, and from 1898 to 1903. Mr. Robinson had the opportunity to be intimately involved in the evolution of the city during its transition from the nineteenth to the twentieth century, with the introduction of all the innovations and new technologies that attended that period. Though never a student of Christian Science, Mr. Robinson developed a friendly relationship with its Founder due to her prominence. In 1894 he wrote to her of his desire to prepare a biographical sketch of her for the local press. He interviewed her for this purpose in 1895, but due to his other duties was unable to complete his work on it at that time. In 1903 he finished the sketch, and Mrs. Eddy was very pleased with what he produced.

She wrote him:

> Your manuscript awes me, I wept as I read portions of it. It is a work of vast significance. Pardon my few erasures and please preserve them.
>
> Yes, yours is the truest trust well performed. God bless you in the good you have infused with the skill of Science and of art. You must have dipped your pen in the lore of ages and "the signs of the times." I feel very humble since reading it and only fear I am not worthy of all you have written.[91]

The "erasures" she referred to were the details of her physical healing in 1866 that prompted her divine discovery. She told him, "Narrating it now excites the enemy to either a sneer or to wholly discard Christian Science. That phenomenon is too transcendental to be told to-day."[92] The article was published by a local newspaper as a booklet entitled *A Biographical Sketch of Rev. Mary Baker G. Eddy.*

Adela Rogers St. Johns (1894–1988) A journalist who covered major stories for the William Randolph Hearst newspapers for more than sixty years, she became a well-known American personality. In the movie *His Girl Friday*, the character of Hildy Johnson was based in part on Adela St. Johns. Mrs. St. Johns studied Christian Science on her own. She wrote to Irving Tomlinson in 1926 the account of the newspaper reporter's healing that appears on pp. 378–383.

John Salchow (c1865–1945) John Salchow grew up on a farm in Kansas, his parents having emigrated from Germany. He gave this account of his introduction to Christian Science:

> I remember my folks had always felt very bitter towards religion when I was a boy. . . . We were, therefore, never allowed to go to church. As a young man I instinctively felt that there must be a God, and I remember asking others about their religion, hoping that they would be able to tell me the right way. But they always turned me off and never seemed to be able to offer anything that satisfied. Finally, I think sometime in 1883 or 1884, my sister Bertha secured a few copies of the first *Christian Science Journals* and passed them on to me to read. My curiosity was aroused, and just when I was wondering how I could find out more about this new religion, Mr. Joseph Mann came from the East to visit his brothers Christian

and Frederick at Junction City. I knew both brothers well.
... While Joseph was staying with his brothers, I went
down to see them all and then learned of his wonderful
healing from an almost fatal bullet wound.[93]

At once John ordered by mail a copy of *Science and Health*.
The book arrived while he was working in the fields:

> ... I was so anxious to see what it was all about that I
> immediately read a page or two. I had been suffering
> from an acute attack of stomach trouble that day, a
> condition which had been chronic for years, and after
> I read those few pages it entirely disappeared. In fact, I
> forgot the condition so completely that it was not until
> almost six months afterwards that I realized I had been
> free all that time.[94]

As a result of his interest, and their own reading of the
textbook, John Salchow's entire family embraced the new faith.
He, his father, mother, and one of his sisters were taught Christian
Science by Joseph Mann, a student of Mrs. Eddy's.

In January 1901, on the recommendation of Mr. Mann,
John Salchow was called to serve in Mrs. Eddy's household. He
described his work as a handyman in the house and around the
property:

> My day at Pleasant View usually started about 3:30
> to 4 o'clock in the morning in the summer and possibly
> an hour or half hour later in the winter. I would hoe the
> garden, milk the cows, feed the pigs, then August Mann

would give the horses their grain, and I would groom them down. By that time it would be nearly seven o'clock and I would stop for breakfast. After that there were the lawns and gardens to take care of, ice to take up to the house and cottage, or necessary repairs at the house, barn, or cottage such as plumbing, electric wiring, carpentering, etc. In the evening I milked the cows again and watered the lawn if necessary. It was not often in the summer that my day was over before ten at night.[95]

In addition, Mr. Salchow told of running errands for Mrs. Eddy, delivering messages in Concord or driving visitors from town:

I was frequently asked to drive down to the station to meet those who had been asked to come to serve Mrs. Eddy. I would always try to engage the person in conversation, and from the character of his remarks I could judge pretty well as to whether he could help Mrs. Eddy or not. If I sensed any personal pride or self-exaltation, when we arrived at Pleasant View I always left the horse hitched, for I knew it would not be long before that person would be starting back to the station—and there were quite a few who went back.[96]

Mr. Salchow was with Mrs. Eddy up to the time of her passing. After that he went to work for The Christian Science Publishing Society.

Laura E. Sargent *(1858–1915)* The daughter of a sea captain who had become a shipbuilder, Laura Sargent learned of Christian Science in 1882 from a friend who was then receiving treatment from a practitioner. She was also in need of help, having spent much on physicians without finding a permanent cure. After she was healed by a Christian Science practitioner, she began to study *Science and Health*. Laura was taught Christian Science in the class Mrs. Eddy conducted in Chicago in May 1884. She also attended another of Mrs. Eddy's Primary classes in December of the same year. In 1886 and 1887 she went through other classes with Mrs. Eddy.

Mrs. Eddy asked Laura Sargent to join her household staff in 1890. She would serve her teacher as a metaphysical worker for the next twenty years, off and on, for months or years at a time, depending on the need. From 1895 to 1899 Mrs. Eddy appointed her as custodian of the Mother's Room in The Mother Church. From 1903 to the time of Mrs. Eddy's passing, Mrs. Sargent lived continually in Mrs. Eddy's homes at Pleasant View and then Chestnut Hill. Laura Sargent was one of several workers in the home whom Mrs. Eddy especially depended on for prayerful support during challenging times.

Often Mrs. Eddy would call her staff together and give them instructions or lessons about a particular point in Christian Science. Mrs. Sargent would afterward write down some of these lessons. One time she wrote, "[Mrs. Eddy] said to ask ourself each day 'How do I know that I am a Christian Scientist?' The only answer must be by what we demonstrate of the healing power of Love and Truth." At another time she wrote, "Mother called us and told us the secret of Christian Science healing was in these words: 'All things are possible with God.'" And after Mrs. Eddy spoke of herself, Laura wrote,

"Mother said that she was simply the window that admitted the Light and that we must not mistake the window for the wall or spatter the window and thus dim the light to ourselves."[97] In 1913 Mrs. Sargent taught The Mother Church's Board of Education Normal class.

***Victoria H. Sargent** (1848–1930)* Victoria Sargent was Laura Sargent's sister. (The two had married brothers, thus the same last name.) Like her sister, Victoria Sargent was also healed in Christian Science. This occurred in the summer of 1884 from reading *Science and Health*. Victoria attended Mrs. Eddy's Primary class in December of the same year. In October 1886 she went through Mrs. Eddy's Normal class. After this she began to devote time to the practice of Christian Science healing, and in 1895 she taught her first class. From that point on she gave her full time to healing and teaching.

In 1907 Mrs. Eddy called Victoria Sargent to Concord, New Hampshire, to help in prayer about the "Next Friends" lawsuit. She was there for several weeks and visited Pleasant View a few times. On one of those occasions, Victoria told Mrs. Eddy:

> . . . My students recognize you to be God's witness and mouthpiece. They are convinced that God is guiding you in this work which you are carrying on for the cause of Christian Science. They feel that you fulfill the prophecies of the Scriptures—that you represent the God-crowned woman mentioned in the Apocalypse.[98]

In response Mrs. Eddy pointed a finger upward and said, "That is from above."[99]

In 1915 The Mother Church appointed Mrs. Sargent custodian of the Chestnut Hill home. Along with this responsibility, she devoted her time to Christian Science healing and teaching.

Amos Scribner Mrs. Eddy (then Mrs. Glover) boarded at Amos Scribner's home at 7 Broad Street, Lynn, Massachusetts, for a short time in 1874 and for the first three months of 1875. While living there she bought the house across the street, number 8 (now 12 Broad Street). Even though Mrs. Glover had healed Mrs. Scribner and her child of physical ailments and had cured one of Mr. Scribner's friends who was at the point of death (see pp. 103–104), Mrs. Scribner remained quite hostile toward Christian Science as a practical explanation of God and man. It's not surprising, therefore, that after Mrs. Glover moved, the Scribners disappear from the pages of her life story.

Clara Shannon (1858–1930) Born in England, Clara Shannon emigrated with her family to Montreal, Quebec, Canada, in 1873. Upon reaching adulthood she began a professional singing career, and was soloist at St. George's Anglican Church. She became interested in Christian Science after being healed of a severe physical ailment in 1887. The following year she attended one of Mrs. Eddy's Primary classes, and afterward she began a public healing practice in Montreal. In 1889 she took the Normal class at the Massachusetts Metaphysical College and began teaching Christian Science. She also established the Montreal Institute of Christian Science and helped organize what became First Church of Christ, Scientist, Montreal.

In 1894 Mrs. Eddy asked Miss Shannon to join her at

Pleasant View. She remained a member of the household as a metaphysical worker until 1903, when she went to live in London, England. There she devoted her full time to Christian Science healing. In 1907 she served again at Pleasant View for three weeks and upon her return to England began teaching Christian Science at Mrs. Eddy's request. During Clara's time at Pleasant View, Mrs. Eddy once told her and Calvin Frye that the *Manual of The Mother Church* "is God's Law as much as the Ten Commandments and the Sermon on the Mount. Well, the time will come when these By-Laws will be recognized and acknowledged as Law by law."[100] On another occasion, Clara recorded that "Mrs. Eddy showed us how it is *God* who heals and not the student and that we must have faith in God, in the allness of God, in the omnipotence of Truth, and know that God is *all*, and then we will see the healing."[101] Miss Shannon was preparing to return to her teacher's home at the beginning of December 1910, but Mrs. Eddy passed on before Miss Shannon left London. She remained there, healing and teaching for the rest of her life.

Emma C. Shipman (1871–1958) Reared in the Congregational church, Emma was healed of a physical ailment by reading *Science and Health* when she was fourteen. For a time she lived in Lisbon, New Hampshire, with close relatives who were Christian Scientists; two of her aunts had been taught by Mrs. Eddy. In 1893 Emma took the Primary class in Christian Science from Annie Louise Robertson. She went on to attend Boston University and after graduation became a schoolteacher in Brookline, Massachusetts. During her summer vacations, she helped organize the White Mountain church in Fabyans, New Hampshire. Miss Shipman was present when Mrs. Eddy delivered her first address in The Mother Church on May 26, 1895, and was present again when she gave the Communion sermon in January 1896.

Mrs. Eddy taught Emma Shipman in her last class in November 1898. Miss Shipman recalled that, in this last class, Mrs. Eddy told her students: "Think of the changeless nature of the Shepherd! You must get a more tender sense of the fatherliness of God. Your God is your life." Characterizing this class further, Miss Shipman wrote in her reminiscences, "Her teaching made me see what I had not grasped before, that Christian Science cannot be attained through the intellect, but that it must be interpreted through the purified affections and is learned only as we live it."[102] The year after this class, Miss Shipman began devoting her full time to the public practice of Christian Science healing.

In 1900 Miss Shipman was in the Obstetrics class taught by Alfred Baker of the Church's Board of Education, and the following year, at Mrs. Eddy's request, she attended the Normal class taught by Edward Kimball. Miss Shipman conducted her own first Primary class in 1905. The year before she had been invited for a week's visit to Pleasant View. Mrs. Eddy told her that she wanted to get to know some of her newer students better, and the two had daily conversations about Christian Science.

Miss Shipman was serving on the Church's Literature Distribution Committee when the committee received a large number of periodicals from Mrs. Eddy's home at Chestnut Hill. Among them was the *Christian Science Sentinel* for January 6, 1906, which included this quotation from Phillips Brooks, the Episcopal pastor of Trinity Church in Boston: "God has not given us vast learning to solve all the problems, or unfailing wisdom to direct all the wanderings of our brothers' lives; but He has given to every one of us the power to be spiritual, and by our spirituality to lift and enlarge and enlighten the lives we touch." Under this quotation Mrs. Eddy had written in pencil, "The secret of my life is in the above."[103]

From 1915 to 1922 Miss Shipman served on the Church's Bible Lesson Committee; in 1949 she was elected to a term as President of The Mother Church; and in 1952 she taught the Board of Education's Normal class. When not involved with church duties, Miss Shipman devoted her time to Christian healing and to teaching Christian Science.

***Alice M. Sibley** (1864–1939)* Lucretia Brown, one of Mrs. Eddy's students, first brought fifteen-year-old Alice to hear Mrs. Eddy deliver a Sunday sermon in 1879. It was not long before they were introduced and became quite fond of one another. Mrs. Eddy especially appreciated Alice's loving nature, innocence, and liveliness of thought. She gave Alice a copy of her newly published third edition of *Science and Health* as a birthday present. Several months before, Mrs. Eddy had written her, "My forthcoming book is like a meteor of light or a clear coin taken from the old mine of my other works."[104] In July 1882, after Asa Gilbert Eddy's passing, Alice accompanied Mrs. Eddy during her month-long stay in Barton, Vermont. When they returned to Boston in August, she went through Mrs. Eddy's Primary class. After 1883, however, they lost contact with each other. Alice Sibley went on to become a schoolteacher in Boston, where she taught for many years. She did not pursue her interest in Christian Science.

Hanover P. Smith Not long after Mrs. Eddy healed him of deafness and dumbness when he was nineteen, Hanover Smith went through one of her Primary classes in 1880. He was one of a small group of students that lived for a time at the Massachusetts Metaphysical College in Boston when Mrs. Eddy taught there in the 1880s. In 1887 he attended another one of her classes. That same year he published, with Mrs. Eddy's assistance, a fifty-two page pamphlet entitled *Writings and Genius of the Founder of Christian Science.* In it he writes of his teacher's conduct in the classroom:

> Her eloquence, good sense, and ready wit play spontaneously about her. Her mental products are rich with overflowing Soul, giving birth to ideas,—like springs gushing from the fountain-head. She has no poverty of thought or expression, no vague abstractions. A humorous remark sometimes bursts from her in a ludicrous image or a surprising illustration.

> She is the mistress of ridicule. Like Sydney Smith, she can see and expose the absurd, but always keeps her sarcasm in abeyance, until it is necessary for idol-breaking.

> There is no want of elevation of thought, or of dignity and grace of expression. She utters no naked truths, but clothes them with vestments of immortality. Her thoughts enter the inmost sanctuary of Mind, and lift the student above all that is sordid, giving him aspirations towards heavenly virtue.[105]

Mr. Smith advertised in *The Christian Science Journal* as a Christian Science healer from 1885 to 1893.

Daniel Spofford (1842–1924) A shoemaker in Lynn, Massachusetts, Daniel Spofford became interested in the teachings of Mrs. Eddy (then Mrs. Glover) at the time his wife, Addie, was studying with her in November 1870. After studying copies of Mrs. Glover's teaching manuscripts which his wife had, he began to practice healing a little. He himself studied with Mrs. Glover in April 1875 at her invitation. In April 1876, at Mrs. Glover's request, he took on the task of running the Christian Scientist Publishing Company, previously a two-man operation. It meant he was in charge of promoting and selling her new book *Science and Health*. Unfortunately, he was not successful in this position, and Mrs. Glover became very dissatisfied with his ineffectiveness. After Mrs. Glover married Asa Gilbert Eddy at the beginning of 1877, Mr. Spofford's relationship with his teacher fell apart. He came to feel that she was unworthy to carry on the mission of Christian Science and launched out on his own to practice healing.

In May 1878, Edward Arens, a student of Mrs. Eddy's, persuaded her to bring a lawsuit against Mr. Spofford for unpaid tuition. The case was dismissed the following month because of defects in the writ and insufficient service. Four months after that, at the end of October, Mr. Arens and Mr. Eddy were arrested for conspiracy to murder Mr. Spofford, who had gone into hiding as part of an elaborate hoax. By the time the case came to trial in January 1879, the deception had been exposed and it was dismissed. Much of the evidence points to Richard Kennedy as the instigator of this strange episode.

Mr. Spofford fades from the scene at this point until he reappears in 1904 as one of Georgine Milmine's sources for her muckraking articles about Mrs. Eddy, which appeared in 1907 in *McClure's Magazine*. Mr. Spofford's appreciation for his former mentor and teacher shines through his misconceptions of her, however, as can be seen in these comments from a September 18, 1904, letter he wrote to Miss Milmine:

> ... my opinion of [Mrs. Eddy] as a teacher is that the lessons were beyond any equivalent of gold or silver, and notwithstanding from [a] cause to me unknown, I incurred the enmity of what I might term the *personal* Mrs. Glover and for a quarter of a century have been the victim of a relentless persecution, I have always considered her as my spiritual mother and the only teacher of Moral Science.[106]

In that same letter, he acknowledged the significance of Mrs. Eddy's contribution to the world:

> You ask "what was the power she evidently possessed by which she attracted and held her followers?" To me it was that she had come with the Truth for which the Christian world had been looking for lo these eighteen centuries, and my opinion has not changed although I had a struggle to separate Principle from person. So long as she has brought to the world that good

which the world without her would not have received, thus much give her credit.[107]

***Augusta Stetson** (1841–1928)* In her book of reminiscences and writings, Augusta Stetson states:

> During the spring of 1884, I heard of several cases of Christian Science healing in Boston and was invited to attend a lecture which was to be given by Mrs. Eddy, in a handsome home on Monument Hill, Charlestown, Massachusetts. I went to the lecture weighted with care and nearly prostrated from the effects of watching for one year in the room of an invalid husband. During this lecture I lost all sense of grief, physical weakness, and prostration.[108]

In November of that year Mrs. Stetson attended Mrs. Eddy's Primary class in the Massachusetts Metaphysical College at the latter's suggestion. After the class Mrs. Stetson encountered a number of opportunities to test her new learning through healing and soon found herself with a public practice that took all her time. In 1885 Mrs. Stetson would substitute when needed for Mrs. Eddy in the pulpit, conducting the Sunday services in the Church of Christ (Scientist) in Boston. The following year, in February, she attended Mrs. Eddy's Normal class and then went to New York in November at Mrs. Eddy's request to help Laura Lathrop and Pamelia Leonard establish Christian Science there through healing and teaching. She was a charter member of First Church of Christ, Scientist,

New York City, which was organized in 1887. Augusta Stetson regularly preached for this church and was appointed its pastor in 1888. In 1889 she took the Primary class again with Mrs. Eddy. And the following year she formed the New York City Christian Science Institute.

Mrs. Eddy was more patient and long-suffering with Mrs. Stetson than any other of her students. She saw such potential in her that time and again she strove to help her overcome worldliness, ambition, and ego. Unfortunately, this effort was in vain. Mrs. Stetson let these malignant qualities erode her Christianity to such a degree that she actively tried to ruin anyone in New York City whom she considered a rival. In 1909 the Christian Science Board of Directors revoked her status as a practitioner and teacher, and removed her from membership in The Mother Church. Her remaining years were spent in explaining herself and her actions and attempting to continue teaching.

In one of Mrs. Eddy's many Bibles, she noted that Romans 8:5–8 pertained to "Augusta":

> For if men are controlled by their earthly natures, they give their minds to earthly things; if they are controlled by their spiritual natures, they give their minds to spiritual things.

> Because for the mind to be given up to earthly things means death; but for it to be given up to spiritual things means Life and peace.

> Abandonment to earthly things is a state of enmity to God. Such a mind does not submit to God's Law, and

indeed cannot do so. And they whose hearts are absorbed in earthly things cannot please God.[109]

M. Adelaide Still *(1873–1964)* In her reminiscences Adelaide Still writes, "I started the earthly dream in Banwell, a village of Somersetshire, England. My parents belonged to the working class. They were good, honest persons, Nonconformists; my father being of the Puritan type and very strict." When Adelaide was fifteen, she joined the Congregational church. She continues her recollection: "In 1900 Christian Science was introduced by a teacher of a Bible Class which my sister and I attended in this church. I was very much interested and in November of that year bought the textbook [*Science and Health*]."[110] She took the Primary class in Christian Science in 1901 from E. Blanche Ward, a Christian Science teacher.

Miss Still came to the United States in 1906, and the following year was invited to join Mrs. Eddy's Pleasant View household. She began as a housekeeper, but after a few months Mrs. Eddy asked Adelaide to become her personal maid, a position she held up to the time of Mrs. Eddy's passing. In her reminiscences, Miss Still described Mrs. Eddy's daily routine:

> Mrs. Eddy retained the customs of her New England training .... For many years her breakfast, consisting of cornmeal mush and milk, was served in her bedroom at six o'clock punctually, but the last year or two she allowed me to bring it an hour later. About the same time, she also changed the cornmeal mush for breakfast, to a glass of milk, fresh from the cow....

As soon as Mrs. Eddy was dressed, she went to her chair in the study and opened, first her Bible, and then her *Science and Health*, and read whatever verse or paragraph her eyes first rested upon. She usually read these aloud to whomever was in the room with her, sometimes calling the [metaphysical] workers and giving them a lesson from them.

Miss Still records this example of a morning lesson:

July 15, 1907. Opened to Romans 14:22, "Hast thou faith? have it to thyself before God. Happy is [he] that condemneth not himself in that thing which he alloweth."

Mrs. Eddy said, "We should allow nothing which we cannot justify. He who sees sin and condemns it not will suffer for it. Can we work out a problem correctly if one figure is not in accord with the principle of mathematics? Can I enter the kingdom of heaven if I allow one sin? Will not that destroy the whole problem?"

Miss Still continues her description of Mrs. Eddy's routine:

After reading the selections and explaining them, she would sit in her chair thinking and praying until nine-thirty, when she went downstairs .... At eleven or eleven-thirty, she read her morning mail which the secretary had placed on the desk for her. Her instructions were to bring to her attention only such letters as were necessary or of special interest. From these she selected those which she wished to have published in the *Sentinel*.

At twelve I brought her dinner tray to her and got her out-of-door clothes ready for the drive which started at one o'clock .... At two o'clock the secretary ... brought her business mail to her, except when she had appointments; then they were kept first. She usually lay on her couch for a while, but she often spent the time meditating or working on problems of the day, and it was not unusual for her to call the students and give them instructions ....

At six o'clock she had her supper .... She did not drink either tea or coffee, and did not expect the students in the house to drink it, but if there were workmen who were non-Scientists on the place, she would send word to the cook to make them some coffee, especially if the weather was cold. She ate simple food, never seeming to tire of home-made ice cream and custard pudding, which were served twice a day; also, she had a cup of soup both for dinner and supper, cream of tomato being her favorite for some years. Sometimes a little meat for dinner, such as liver or squab; for supper fish hash, creamed toast or cereal.

She took the time after supper for a little social relaxation. Mr. Frye would sit with her while Mrs. Sargent and I had our supper. . . . When I returned from supper, I often found Mr. Frye chatting with her about events or news of the day. At Chestnut Hill Mr.

Dickey sometimes took turns with Mr. Frye in sitting
with her. She was usually in bed by nine-thirty. Always
her *Science and Health* and a pad and pencil were placed
on the small marble-topped table at the head of her
bed, and occasionally she would call us all in after she
had retired, and give instructions for handling certain
phases of error or some special problem which needed
solving.[111]

For several years after Mrs. Eddy's passing, Miss Still
remained in the Chestnut Hill home as a caretaker and
companion to Laura Sargent. After that she worked for a
period in the Treasurer's Office of The Mother Church. William
Rathvon, one of Mrs. Eddy's secretaries, wrote of Adelaide:
"… her understanding of Christian Science has been clear,
and from the first she has been an invaluable member of the
household. Being trained as a personal maid before coming to
this country, she understands the technical part of her duties
thoroughly, and is proving herself true as steel and loyal as the
most faithful of the old or new."[112]

Marguerite F. Sym Originally a Presbyterian, Marguerite Sym
was taught Christian Science in Mrs. Eddy's Primary class in
1889, and the following year began to devote her full time to
the public practice of Christian Science healing. She had met
Mrs. Eddy prior to the class: "While on a visit to Boston in the
autumn of 1888, I was taken by a student of Mrs. Eddy's to call
upon her and we spent the evening at her house.… On taking
leave of me that evening she took my hand in hers and said,
'put your hand in God's hand, let Him lead you.'"[113]

In June 1895, Marguerite again visited Mrs. Eddy and provided this account:

> ...I had the honor of taking supper with Mrs. Eddy in
> company with Mrs. Julia Field-King. Mrs. Eddy talked
> throughout the whole meal, ate a good supper herself,
> and rebuked me for eating so little, but I was so interested
> in her conversation that I forgot to eat. She looked
> beautiful that evening, radiant, her glowing face slightly
> flushed; her flesh had a quality almost of transparency
> that I have never seen in any individual—with her dark
> blue eyes and silver hair, she was a picture of loveliness.[114]

Abigail Dyer Thompson (c1878–1957) Christian Science was introduced into Abigail Thompson's home in 1884, when she was a little girl. At that time her mother, Emma, was healed of neuralgia by studying *Science and Health*. Abigail met Mrs. Eddy two years later: "My first impression of Mary Baker Eddy was gained in early childhood, in August 1886, at the time my mother received her Primary class of instruction in the Massachusetts Metaphysical College."[115] A few months after their first meeting, upon a return visit to Boston, Mrs. Eddy instantly healed Abigail of an inherited "lung trouble" that doctors had diagnosed as terminal:

> ...One morning as I stood looking over the mail, Mrs.
> Eddy passed through the hall on her way to hold a
> few moments' consultation with a student....Almost
> instantly after our Leader began her conference with him,
> the sound of my prolonged rasping cough attracted their
> attention, and finally when I leaned on the banister for

support, Mrs. Eddy held up her hand to stop the conversation and listened for a moment, then she said, "I do not like the sound of that child's cough." Closing her eyes for a short time she worked earnestly. The coughing ceased at once, and not only did the distressing phase of the condition yield, but the whole mortal law which lay back of the trouble was broken, and through the many years that have followed I have rejoiced in complete freedom from any return of this so-called family inheritance.[116]

A year or so after this Mrs. Eddy again healed her, this time of a severe hip ailment (see pp. 146–147).

When Abigail Thompson was about twenty she entered the full-time public practice of Christian healing. A year later, in 1898, she and her mother were students in Mrs. Eddy's last class. Miss Thompson devoted the rest of her life to healing and to teaching Christian Science. In her reminiscences she wrote, "Mrs. Eddy made very little of a diagnosis of disease. She often said, 'Let the patients talk freely at first, it is the way they lay their burdens down; mentally you must walk a short distance with them, but never permit people to indulge in daily descriptions of their feelings.'"[117] On another occasion Mrs. Eddy spoke to her "of the importance of more and better healing work in our Movement." Miss Thompson also recounts this exchange:

> . . . she asked if I had been careful to keep a record of my own cases of healing for future reference. I replied, "No, it had never occurred to me to take any particular note of them, even in thought, other than being grateful for the inspiration and growth they brought in awakening a

desire to make still better demonstrations in the future."

She said, with great earnestness, "You should, dear, be faithful to keep an exact record of them, for you never know when they might prove valuable to the Cause. I regret exceedingly that my own early healings were not recorded, because in the rush of a crowded life it is easy to forget even important experiences, and I am sorry to say that has been true of much of my best healing work."[118]

In 1929 Miss Thompson wrote the Christian Science Board of Directors:

I once heard our Leader describe how she had done her healing work, and I will give it to you as nearly as I can recall her words:

"I saw the love of God encircling the universe and man—filling all space—and that divine Love so permeated my own consciousness that I loved with Christ-like compassion everything I saw. This realization of divine Love called into expression 'the beauty of holiness, the perfection of being,' which healed, and regenerated, and saved all who turned to me for help."[119]

Emma A. Thompson (1842–1913) Growing up near Portland, Maine, Emma, an energetic child and a brilliant student, was afflicted with severe attacks of pain in the head that physicians pronounced an extremely acute form of neuralgia. No method of medical treatment brought relief. In a notarized affidavit, Emma Thompson related what happened when she was twenty:

I became acquainted with Dr. P. P. Quimby for the first time late in the year 1862. As I recall it, his home was then in Belfast, Me [Maine]. He traveled about the country giving a form of treatment similar to magnetic healing. At this time I was at the home of my father, Pitman Morgan, near Portland, Me. I had been very ill with severe neuralgic pains in the head and Dr. Quimby was called to give me treatments.

After several paragraphs, she continued:

...I then tried other courses of treatments and remedies, without success, until 1884, when I was finally and permanently healed through the reading of "Science and Health with Key to the Scriptures," by Mary Baker G. Eddy.

Upon my first visit to Dr. Quimby, I saw Mrs. Eddy in his office in Portland, as a patient. He had cited my case to her, and she remained in the room during my treatment.

There was nothing in Dr. Quimby's method of treating disease which bears any resemblance to the teachings or methods of Christian Science. He never spoke of God to me, or referred to any other power or person but himself. (As far as I know he had no manuscripts or books relating to his subject.) He gave me nothing to read and no explanation of his treatment. In fact he had no explanation. I distinctly recall that before he left our home [the morning of my first treatment], my father offered him a check for one thousand dollars if he would impart to him or any member of his family his method of treating disease, to which the doctor replied, "I cannot. I don't understand it myself."

> I have been through three classes under Mrs. Eddy's teaching; have been in active practice of Christian Science for over twenty years, and can testify that the instruction and methods of healing disease are in no way similar to those employed by Dr. Quimby,—but on the contrary are diametrically opposed thereto.[120]

Emma Thompson began her public practice of Christian Science healing soon after her own healing occurred from reading the Christian Science textbook. She devoted the rest of her life to this healing work.

Irving C. Tomlinson (c1860–1944) The son of a minister, Irving Tomlinson became one himself. After graduating from Akron University in Ohio with a bachelor's degree from the Classical Department in 1880 and a master's in 1884, he attended the Theological Department of Tufts College in Medford, Massachusetts, and graduated as a Bachelor of Divinity in 1888. He immediately entered the ministry and became pastor of the First Universalist Church of Arlington, Massachusetts. In investigating the role of healing in the Christian church, the Rev. Tomlinson attended a Sunday service of The Mother Church in Boston in 1894. After going to a number of weekly testimony meetings, he became convinced "that there was at least one church carrying out the Master's injunction to heal the sick."[121]

He attended Primary class with Flavia S. Knapp, one of Mrs. Eddy's students. Soon after this he resigned from the

Universalist church, and in 1897 entered the public practice of Christian healing. In 1898 Irving Tomlinson was one of the five members appointed to the newly created Board of Lectureship. Mrs. Eddy also placed him on the Bible Lesson Committee, where he served for over twenty years. And in November 1898 she invited him to her last class. The following year, 1899, Mrs. Eddy called him to Concord, New Hampshire, to be First Reader of the Christian Science church in that city. He held this position until 1906. While living in Concord, especially after 1900, Mr. Tomlinson was in almost daily contact with Mrs. Eddy, carrying out the assignments she gave him. When she moved to Chestnut Hill, he joined her household and became one of her secretaries. Irving Tomlinson is perhaps best known for his biography, *Twelve Years with Mary Baker Eddy*, which he began in the early 1930s as an effort to write out his reminiscences. It was published posthumously in 1945.

In writing his reminiscences, Tomlinson used notes he had made in calendar notebooks while working with Mrs. Eddy. In the opening pages of those reminiscences, he wrote:

> As one intimately acquainted with our Leader, the writer knows full well that her life was dedicated to God; for he knows that with her, every waking hour of every day of every year was given to the worship of God and the service of man. In her calendar there were no days of respite from active duty. The dials of the time-pieces at Pleasant View and Chestnut Hill had no hours for leisure. Those were days of unremitting toil, whose only rest was in the sustaining presence of divine Love and in hours of holy prayer. In the years the writer knew

Mrs. Eddy, there was not a single moment given to idleness—the welfare of mankind and their highest good was always her constant care.[122]

William Bradford Turner *(c1870–1937)* After being healed through Christian Science treatment, Mr. Turner eventually became a healer himself. He writes of that journey:

> My earliest recollections of Christian Science carry me back to the city of Minneapolis, Minnesota, as a lad of fourteen. From infancy I had never known what it was to be well, never known what it meant to feel strong.

> Nervous disorders racked me physically, and frightened me mentally. A wonderfully sweet mother and a devoted father did all they could to put me in the way of health. Relief would come, temporarily; but I heard it whispered that probably I would not live long. Organic difficulties of a serious nature developed, from which, also, I obtained, now and again, relief, but only temporarily.

Around 1884 William Turner's father introduced him to Emma Thompson, who had been healed that year by reading *Science and Health*. "I received help through Mrs. Thompson's Christian Science treatment, but it was not until eleven years later that I was impelled to an earnest study of the subject."[123]

In the latter part of the 1890s he was taught the Primary class in Christian Science by Flavia Knapp, a student of Mrs.

Eddy's. He appreciated hearing Mrs. Eddy speak on several occasions:

> Mrs. Eddy herself I never came personally in
> contact with, though it was my rare privilege to hear her
> speak a number of times, twice in the original edifice of
> The Mother Church, once in Tremont Temple, Boston,
> and each time, besides, that she spoke to the Annual
> Meeting visitors invited to her home at Pleasant View, in
> Concord, New Hampshire.[124]

Mr. Turner served on the Bible Lesson Committee at the same time as Julia Bartlett. He first advertised as a full-time Christian Science healer in *The Christian Science Journal* in 1903. He devoted himself to this practice for the rest of his life.

Ludie M. Waldron Formerly a Baptist, Ludie Waldron wrote The Mother Church in 1946:

> I should like to mention, before closing, that Mr.
> Waldron as a young student of preparatory school for
> Yale University, enjoyed a most unique and beneficial
> acquaintance with our Leader, Mary Baker Eddy. It was
> in Concord, [New Hampshire], and he was working his
> way through this school. It happened that Mrs. Eddy
> needed some one to translate her foreign letters. As
> my husband speaks several languages, he was fortunate
> in getting this work to help him with his expenses of
> schooling.

My husband is not a student of Christian Science, but he cherishes many beautiful memories of our Leader, and it is a privilege to listen to his reminiscences of those times. Such as the loving gifts she gave him; the various events connected with those of her household. He often had the privilege of occupying a room at Pleasant View; and was well acquainted with the coachman, the cook, etc., and loved Mrs. Eddy with his boyish enthusiasm.

He recalls the healing of a young lineman, who was working in front of her home, and was hit in the eye by a wire; someone ran into the house to ask the owner to send for a doctor; the young man was brought into the house, and our Leader talked with him; also had him put to rest in a quiet room. The next day Mr. Waldron saw the same young lineman; and he was healed.[125]

Mary Webster A spiritualist, "Mother" Webster was the wife of Nathaniel Webster, a retired sea captain, who was superintendent of cotton mills in Manchester, New Hampshire. A young neighbor wrote in later years, "The Websters were loved by all, and she did many loving acts of kindness. No one called on her in vain, she was always ready to go."[126] A "healing medium," Mother Webster would prescribe various remedies for boarders and friends in need. Mrs. Eddy (then Mrs. Glover) stayed in the Websters' Amesbury, Massachusetts, home for ten months, beginning in the autumn of 1867. She devoted most of her time there to writing out her notes on the first book of the Bible, Genesis. The young neighbor in Amesbury wrote:

I saw Mrs. Glover when she first came to
"Grandma" Webster, and I have always remembered her
eyes, just so full of love and tenderness. I often saw her
and Mrs. Webster when they went to walk the first of the
evening; they went across a little bridge over the Powow
(a branch of the Merrimac) and stood on the bank of the
Merrimac. The view was beautiful at sunset.[127]

Janette E. Weller *(1840–1925)* As a young woman, Mrs. Weller
was a schoolteacher in Littleton, New Hampshire. In her reminiscences she wrote of her introduction to Christian Science:

In March 1884, I first heard of Christian Science
and its healing work. I immediately purchased a copy
of the seventh edition of *Science and Health with Key to
the Scriptures* by Mary B. G. Eddy, and read it through
carefully, giving most of my time for three weeks to its
study. I had not heard that the reading of the book healed
the sick, but before those three weeks had passed, I awoke
to find that all the claims of disease and pain from which
I had suffered for more than twenty years had vanished
and that I was free as a bird.[128]

That same year Mrs. Weller attended one of Mrs. Eddy's
Primary classes in the Massachusetts Metaphysical College. Five
years later, in 1889, she was in the last Normal class Mrs. Eddy
taught in Boston.

According to her reminiscences, Mrs. Weller devoted the
ten years after her Primary class to Christian Science healing

work in Littleton, New Hampshire; Binghamton, New York; Philadelphia, Pennsylvania; and Spokane, Washington, before settling in Boston, Massachusetts. She worked for a few months in Mrs. Eddy's home at the end of 1896 and the beginning of 1897. After this Mrs. Weller devoted the rest of her life to the practice of Christian Science healing.

Sally Wentworth *(1818–1883)* In September 1868 Mrs. Eddy (then Mrs. Patterson) went to live in the Wentworths' home on a farm in East Stoughton, Massachusetts. A Universalist at the time, Sally Wentworth became Mrs. Eddy's third student. On August 11, 1869, she wrote out the following contract:

> For value received in instruction which enables me to heal the sick and to teach others the science whereby I have learned to heal, I hereby agree to give Mrs. M. M. Patterson board free from expense so long as, and whenever she requires it; and when she is absent from my home to pay her the sum of two dollars per week. This sum to be paid her on condition that I am practicing or teaching this science.[129]

Mrs. Eddy lived with the Wentworths for a year and a half, but she never received the weekly sum stated in the contract.

Parsons Whidden *(1801–1869)* Parsons Whidden received his M.D. degree from Dartmouth Medical College in 1836. Over his lifetime he practiced in the New Hampshire towns of Danbury, Alexandria, Pembroke, Warner, and Northfield. He married Mary P. Tilton of Sanbornton Bridge in 1832, and in this way became distantly related to Mrs. Eddy through her sister Abigail Baker Tilton. In the summer of 1849, Mrs. Glover went to Warner for two months to be treated by Dr. Whidden for what had been diagnosed by her regular physician as dyspepsia caused by a disease of the spinal nerves.[130] She took advantage of her time in Warner to study allopathy with Dr. Whidden because she needed this knowledge in order to better understand homeopathy, which was her prime interest at that time.[131] In later years she wrote of this pursuit: "I returned [from the South] to my Father's at Tilton, New Hampshire. Read Allopathy and qualified myself for a Homeopathic student and afterwards in Homeopathy for a physician. Studied Graham's system of dietetics and qualified myself for an Homeopathic physician only to abandon that practice for Metaphysics."[132]

Lilian Whiting (1847–1942) American journalist, essayist, and poet. Two of her articles on Margaret Fuller were published in the *Cincinnati Commercial*, which led to her being employed by that paper. That experience enabled Lilian Whiting to become a reporter for the *Boston Traveller*. She later became the paper's literary editor, holding that position until 1890. She wrote a weekly feature called "Boston Letters" for western newspapers, and became editor in chief of the *Boston Budget*. Miss Whiting interviewed Mrs. Eddy in 1885 and at one point asked about entering her September Primary class that year. Due to an overly full schedule, she did not go through with this.

In the interview published in the *Ohio Leader*, Miss Whiting wrote:

> Mrs. Eddy impressed me as a woman who is—in the language of our Methodist friends—"filled with the

spirit." It seems to be a merely natural gift with her. She
is, by nature, a harmonizer. My own personal experience
in that call was so singular that I will venture to relate
it. I went, as I have already said, in a journalistic spirit.
I had no belief, or disbelief, and the idea of getting any
personal benefit from the call, save matter for press use,
never occurred to me. But I remembered afterward
how extremely tired I was as I walked rather wearily
and languidly up the steps to Mrs. Eddy's door. I came
away, as a little child friend of mine expressively says,
"skipping." I was at least a mile from the Vendome
[hotel], and I walked home feeling as if I were treading
on air. My sleep that night was the rest of elysium. If I
had been caught up into paradise it could hardly have
been a more wonderful renewal. All the next day this
exalted state continued. I can hardly describe it; it was
simply the most marvelous elasticity of mind and body.[133]
(See also pp. 339–340.)

The Rev. James Henry Wiggin (1836–1900) After graduating
from the Meadville Theological Seminary in 1861, James
Wiggin became a Unitarian clergyman. He retired from
the active ministry in 1875 to devote himself to writing and
editing. A friend of John Wilson, the owner of the University
Press (printers of *Science and Health* from the third edition
until 1930), James Wiggin became engaged in proofreading,
revising, and editing manuscripts. In an article in the December
1906 issue of *The Christian Science Journal,* Mrs. Eddy wrote of
her past relationship with her editorial assistant, which had
begun in 1885:

… I engaged Mr. Wiggin so as to avail myself of his criticisms of my statement of Christian Science, which criticisms would enable me to explain more clearly the points that might seem ambiguous to the reader.… .

My diction, as used in explaining Christian Science, has been called original. The liberty that I have taken with capitalization, in order to express the "new tongue," has well-nigh constituted a new style of language. In almost every case where Mr. Wiggin added words, I have erased them in my revisions.[134]

Mrs. Eddy asked James Wiggin to become editor of the *Journal* in 1886. He served in this capacity from January to August, and again from January 1887 to January 1889. While he never became a student of Christian Science, the Rev. Wiggin did accept Mrs. Eddy's offer to sit through one of her Primary classes in 1886. The sixteenth edition of *Science and Health*, published that year, included an index for the first time, which James Wiggin prepared.

At one time when he was not feeling well, Mrs. Eddy wrote Mr. Wiggin the following letter:

My dear Mr. Wiggin:

Mr. Frye told me yesterday you were not as well as usual. I have taken the liberty to send a team to your door with your drive prepaid to take you out in the cool of the day. Now step right into it and leave all cares behind, and tell the driver to take you into pleasant places as long as you care to drive.

Most truly,
M. B. G. Eddy.

P.S. Remember the City lieth four square and every side is *safe, harmonious.* This City is the kingdom of Heaven already within your grasp. Open your spiritual gaze to see this and you are well in a moment.[135]

Unfortunately, in his last years James Wiggin became critical of his former employer and benefactor, and of her discovery.

Sibyl Wilbur *(1871–1946)* An American journalist and an organizer of the Woman's Suffrage Party in New York City, Sybil Wilbur wrote a series of articles about Mrs. Eddy for the magazine *Human Life* that appeared from the December 1906 through December 1907 issues. She used these as the basis for her 1908 biography, *The Life of Mary Baker Eddy.* What is especially significant about this biography is that Miss Wilbur was able to personally interview people in Mrs. Eddy's past who had known the religious leader before she became famous. Irving Tomlinson read Miss Wilbur's book to Mrs. Eddy in 1909, and he wrote to the Christian Science Board of Directors about this in 1929. In his letter he stated, "When the account of the cures recorded on pages [140] to [144] was read to Mrs. Eddy, she remarked, 'The account of cures told is told just as they occurred.'"[136]

Sibyl Wilbur began her journalistic career as a society reporter for the *Minneapolis Journal*, which three years later sent her to report from Europe. As a national reporter for the *Minneapolis Times*, she toured the West and also reported on Southern interests. In 1896 she wrote a series of articles exposing governmental fraud and graft for the *Washington Times*. In order to write a series for the *New York World* on the conditions of working women in America, Miss Wilbur took jobs as a waitress, hospital nurse, office stenographer, and a telephone operator. As labor editor for the *Chicago Journal*, she scooped all other reporters with her account of the Virden riot in Illinois.

In 1904 Sybil Wilbur became a reporter for the *Boston Herald*. Miss Wilbur first interviewed Mrs. Eddy in May 1905; her story about the interview sold 60,000 extra copies of the *Herald*. What she was learning of Christian Science prompted her the following year to take Primary class instruction with Alfred Farlow, but she never became a member of The Mother Church. After finishing her biography of Mrs. Eddy, she became deeply involved with the women's suffrage movement.

Cordelia Willey A Presbyterian, Cordelia Willey had been an invalid for ten years when her doctors told her family to prepare for her passing. One of Mrs. Eddy's students, Ellen Brown (Linscott), healed her in April 1887 after being contacted by the family. Miss Willey first met Mrs. Eddy in June 1888 at the reception held after the latter had given her address "Science and the Senses" in Central Music Hall in Chicago. Three months later she was taught by Mrs. Eddy in a Primary class. During one of the lessons, Mrs. Eddy healed her of an overwhelming fear (see p. 352). After this Miss Willey devoted her life to the practice of Christian Science healing, advertising in *The Christian Science Journal* from 1891 until her passing in 1943.

Abigail Winslow Well-to-do Quakers, Abigail and her husband, Charles, were close friends of Mrs. Eddy's (then Mrs. Patterson) in Lynn, Massachusetts, in 1866. Mrs. Eddy had met them previously while living with the Thomas Phillips family. (Abigail Winslow was Mr. Phillips's sister.) Mrs. Eddy stayed with the Winslows briefly in the autumn of 1866 and kept in touch with them over the next few years. Even though she healed Abigail of hip disease during a visit in 1868 (see pp. 287–288), the Winslows tried to dissuade Mrs. Eddy from continuing her efforts to promote divine Science because they felt the world would say she was mad if she continued to preach divine healing.

Josephine Curtis Woodbury (c1850–1930) In a booklet she published, Josephine Woodbury wrote that her parents "were numbered among progressive Unitarians and prominent Abolitionists."[137] She grew up in Milford, Massachusetts, and first became interested in Christian Science when she was about thirty; in 1880 her son was healed of membranous croup, and she was restored to health with the help of a Christian Science healer. In 1884 Mrs. Woodbury took Mrs. Eddy's Primary class, and followed this by going through two other classes in 1886 and 1888. In the latter half of the 1880s, she was quite involved in church work in Boston, assisting for a time in editing *The Christian Science Journal*, and in 1886 establishing, as an "institute" for teaching, the Academy of Christian Science.

At the beginning of December 1889, Mrs. Woodbury withdrew her membership from the Boston Church of Christ

(Scientist), explaining she was simply following Mrs. Eddy's lead in disassociating herself from organizations. More likely her withdrawal was prompted by the embarrassing condition she found herself in. In June 1890, she bore a child and declared she had been unaware of the pregnancy. Having told her students that she had abstained from marital relations with her husband for some years prior to this event, she explained that the baby was the result of an immaculate conception. In actuality she had been having an affair with a man in Montreal, Quebec, Canada. After Josephine Woodbury visited Pleasant View in 1894, Mrs. Eddy wrote her:

> ... You seemed deeply penitent and I pitied you
> sincerely.... I forgave you then and there and told you
> I would try to have you admitted to our Church if you
> so desired....
>
> I have asked the Church to reconsider and restore
> you not at all because you deserved this at my hand but
> because it is doing as I would be done by and gives you
> one more chance for repentance and reformation under
> the teachings of the Bible and my book.[138]

Notwithstanding Mrs. Eddy's attempts to save her, Josephine Woodbury began an all-out attack on her teacher in 1899, first through an article in *Arena* magazine and then in a libel suit seeking $150,000 in damages. The suit was dismissed in 1901. By 1909 Mrs. Woodbury had moved to England; she devoted the rest of her life to vilifying Mrs. Eddy through private lectures and teaching.

Alice Swasey Wool While living in Beverly, Massachusetts, Alice Swasey Wool went to be treated by Mrs. Eddy sometime during the summer of 1876 or 1877 and was healed of an abdominal pain that doctors had been unable to relieve (see pp. 310–311). This experience did not cause her to become interested in Christian Science at that time, but about fifty years later she began its study and then joined The Mother Church in 1928. Mrs. Wool sent her reminiscences to the Church in 1932. Not long after, a friend of hers wrote that Mrs. Wool remembered from her youth

> that in appearance Mrs. Eddy was slender, had dark hair parted in the middle and waved on the side & that she wore a dark dress. She was principally impressed with [Mrs. Eddy's] eyes—which she said "looked right through her, and that it would be impossible to lie to those eyes." [Mrs. Wool] never saw her again. She felt that this healing influenced her life, though she did not come into Christian Science until many years later.[139]

Wallace W. Wright The son of a Universalist minister in Amesbury, Massachusetts, Wallace Wright was twenty-five years old when he wrote to Mrs. Eddy (then Mrs. Glover) on March 10, 1871, asking nine questions about Moral Science, her teaching of it, and the results therefrom. He was considering taking her class at the time. Mrs. Glover's answers prompted him to join her April class. Not long after this he moved to Knoxville, Tennessee, and began a successful healing practice. This success, however, was short-lived as he was unable to maintain the discipline of living in the "strait" and "narrow way" that Jesus requires of his followers.[140]

By August of that year Mr. Wright was demanding back the money he had paid for tuition plus two hundred dollars. Mrs. Eddy refused, but she offered him this advice:

> The happiness of life is in doing right, and in holding the consciousness of this and of having filled our short page of existence with worthy examples and worthy lessons for our fellow man. To be happy and useful is in your power, and the Science I have taught you enables you to be this, and to do great good to the world if you practice this Science as laid down in your Mss [manuscripts]. Time alone can perfect us in all great undertakings, and as "Rome was not built in a day," so you cannot be perfect nor I cannot be perfect until we have passed through the furnace and are purified .... .

> ... I shall never pay you a cent of your demand. I have fulfilled all obligations I am under to you aside from those I owe to humanity. I have done my duty to you—do yours to others.[141]

Unfortunately Mr. Wright did not heed her counsel. Instead he wasted the next few years of his life trying to ruin her by alleging publicly that Moral Science was mesmerism. To Mrs. Eddy, that was no different than claiming that white was black, and she responded to that effect in the *Lynn Transcript* during the first months of 1872.

This conflict served to focus Mrs. Eddy's thought on the importance of presenting to the public a clear statement of the divine Science she had discovered and was then teaching. God's direction for her was exceedingly clear when, one day in February 1872, she opened her Bible to Isaiah 30:8: "Now go, write it before them in a table, and note it in a book, that it may be for the time to come for ever and ever."[142] That month she began writing *Science and Health*.

NOTES

NOTES

UNLESS OTHERWISE SPECIFIED, ALL DOCUMENTS are included courtesy of The Mary Baker Eddy Library in Boston, Massachusetts, USA, and many of these documents are under the copyright of The Mary Baker Eddy Collection. These documents are indicated by an alphanumeric notation, and can be accessed with assistance from the Library's research staff. Minor changes in spelling and punctuation have been made to these materials when necessary for clarity; insertions and deletions are noted with brackets and ellipses, respectively.

Title Page
1. Emma Shipman reminiscences. See Biographical Glossary, pp. 508–510.

Preface
1. Mary Baker Eddy, *The First Church of Christ, Scientist, and Miscellany*, p. 111.
2. Mary Baker Eddy, *Science and Health with Key to the Scriptures*, p. 109.
3. John 8:58.

4. *Science and Health*, p. x.

5. A10234b.

Part One—A LIFETIME OF HEALING

Prelude: MARY BAKER EDDY'S PURITAN HERITAGE

1. *Science and Health*, p. 359.

2. Richard Sibbes, *Saints Cordialls*, 1637, pp. 383–384, quoted in William Haller, *The Rise of Puritanism* (Philadelphia: University of Pennsylvania Press, 1938, 1972 reprint), p. 161.

3. *Miscellany*, pp. 128–129. [Note: Throughout this book, the authors use Mary Baker Eddy's unique capitalization of certain words that she considered synonymous with God: Principle, Mind, Soul, Spirit, Life, Truth, and Love.]

4. I John 4:16.

5. I Thessalonians 1:2, 4.

6. Romans 8:28, 29.

7. Mark 16:16.

8. John 5:24.

9. Acts 16:30, 31.

10. *Science and Health*, p. 582.

11. Ibid., p. 24.

12. Haller, p. 89.

13. In *Science and Health*, p. 593, Mrs. Eddy defines *salvation* as "Life, Truth, and Love understood and demonstrated as supreme over all; sin, sickness, and death destroyed."

14. See Matthew 7:14.

15. Mary Baker Eddy, *Rudimental Divine Science*, p. 2.

16. Mary Baker Eddy, *Manual of The Mother Church*, p. 15.

17. Ibid., p. 41.

18. *Science and Health*, p. 447.

19. L02619 and *Miscellany*, p. 174.
20. *Miscellany*, p. 311. Mrs. Eddy was actually seventeen.
21. In 1892 Mrs. Eddy reorganized her Church, which eventually resulted in the removal of the Congregational style of democratic government from The Mother Church. She did, however, retain this form of government in Christian Science branch churches, local churches outside of Boston.
22. V00805. Mrs. Eddy's paraphrase of the first and third tenets draws on the multiple versions of the tenets in print at that time.
23. Matthew 10:8; Luke 9:2 and 10:9.
24. John Bunyan, *Grace Abounding to the Chief of Sinners*, 1666 (Springdale, Pa.: Whitaker House, 1993), p. 139.
25. Ibid., pp. 150–151. The parable was from Luke 16:19–31. The Bible verse was I Corinthians 15:55.
26. John Bunyan, *The Pilgrim's Progress*, 1678 (London: Penguin Books, 1987), p. 127.
27. *The Pilgrim's Progress* resonates in the following references from *Science and Health*: 21:15–2; 360:4–12; 378:14–16; 380:15–17; 404:15–16; and pp. 430–442.
28. *Science and Health*, p. 418.
29. Ibid., p. 149.
30. John 5:19; 14:10.
31. John C. Lathrop reminiscences; *We Knew Mary Baker Eddy* (Boston: The Christian Science Publishing Society, 1979), p. 118.
32. Haller, p. 362.
33. A12030.
34. Proverbs 22:6.

Chapter 1: THE GIFTS OF CHILDHOOD

1. Clara Shannon reminiscences.

2. Abigail Baker was 37 when Mary was born. Adam Dickey recounted in his *Memoirs* (p. 132) that Mrs. Eddy told her household she felt the circumstances of her birth were similar to Isaac's birth in the Bible, referring them to Hebrews 11:11. To another, Mrs. Eddy wrote about an exchange between her mother and Sarah Gault, her mother's close friend: "When Mother was pregnant with me, she heard voices and said [to] Sister Gault, 'I wish you would help me on a thing that troubles me. When I am about my work I am stopped and troubled with a voice "What shall be born of you shall be born of God."'" (L15725)

3. Irving C. Tomlinson notes. Jotted down at the time or soon after Mrs. Eddy spoke, Irving C. Tomlinson's notes were the basis for his book, *Twelve Years with Mary Baker Eddy.*

   Even after Mary was born, Abigail Baker continued to ponder the thoughts that had come to her during the pregnancy. She told Sarah Gault, "...I don't know what is to become of this child. While I bore her I had such sinful thoughts. ... a voice seemed to say to me, 'that which shall be born of thee shall bring about a great revolution.'"

   In addition, while she was pregnant with Mary, a conviction had come over Abigail that the child she was carrying was holy and consecrated. Also a recurring voice insisted throughout the nine months, "You can heal the sick." A11923; A11917; see also the Clara Shannon and Janette Weller reminiscences.

4. *The Christian Science Journal,* April 1889, p. 4. The *Journal* is an official organ of The First Church of Christ, Scientist. This article was written by Joshua F. Bailey. (See p. 413.)

5. Quoted in a pamphlet by Septimus J. Hanna, *Christian Science History*, 1899.

6. A11809.

7. Ibid. Another example of Mary's "dominion" with animals can be seen with the family's pet dog. Adam Dickey related in his *Memoirs*: "The family had a dog in the house named 'Ben,' and when they were assembled in the sitting room the dog was made to understand that he must always lie under the table. Sometimes he would disregard this injunction and would come out and sit before the fire with the family. Mrs. Eddy said she found out that by mentally addressing the dog he would obey her without her speaking a word aloud. When she saw that Ben was in for trouble, because of his presence in the room, she would mentally say, 'Ben, go under the table and lie down,' and immediately the dog would rise and walk under the table and lie down. This, she said, occurred many, many times, and was one of the incidents of her childhood which she always kept to herself." (pp. 136–137) Mrs. Eddy told Irving Tomlinson, "This I thought about and thus was working my way toward the light." (A11909)

In the manuscript "Historical Facts Concerning Mary Baker Eddy and Christian Science," Alfred Farlow recorded: "When she was well along in her teens Mrs. Eddy was one day with her books under a shade tree near where a farm hand was plowing. His horse balked and he was unable to make him pull either by coaxing or driving. Mary left her books and came to the rescue. She patted the horse and quieted him with kind words. Then she said she thought he would go all right, and this he did at once.

"On another occasion, on the event of an approaching storm the men were trying to get into the barn with a load of hay. In the haste and excitement the horses had become frightened and refused to move. Mary insisted upon having a ladder placed at the rear of the wagon, climbed to the top of the load with the agility of a squirrel, calmly took the lines, spoke to the horses and they immediately pulled the load into the barn" (pp. 21–22).

8. Harriet Betts reminiscences.

9. Irving Tomlinson reminiscences. Mrs. Eddy actually moved from Bow when she was fourteen and a half.

10. Alfred Farlow notes.

11. Irving Tomlinson, *Twelve Years with Mary Baker Eddy: Amplified Edition* (Boston: The Christian Science Publishing Society, 1996), p. 5.

12. Tomlinson notes. In *The Life of Mary Baker Eddy* (Boston: The Christian Science Publishing Society, 1907, 1976, pp. 33–34), Sybil Wilbur recounts how this man appeared during a Sunday church service and stood beside Mary during hymn singing. Afterward, he allowed himself to be taken away without any resistance.

13. Mary Baker Eddy, *Retrospection and Introspection*, pp. 8–9. See also I Samuel, chapter 3. In an interview she gave to the *New York World*, published April 17, 1898, Mrs. Eddy recounted this experience: "Even when I was a child my life was different. There were strange things in it; strange things happened to my mother before my birth. Once a minister, a good old soul, held me to his side and told my mother she ought to consecrate me to God.

"When I was very little I used to hear voices. They called me. They spoke my name, 'Mary! Mary!' I used to go to my mother and say: 'Mother, did you call me? What do you want?' And she would say: 'No, child, I didn't call you.' Then I'd go away to play, but the voices would call again distinctly.

"There was a day when my cousin [23-year-old Mehitable Huntoon], whom I dearly loved, was playing with me when she too heard the voices. She said: 'Your mother's calling you, Mary,' and when I didn't go I could hear them again. But I knew it wasn't mother. My cousin didn't know what to make of my behavior, because I was always an obedient child. 'Why, Mary,' she repeated, 'what do you mean by not going?'

"When she heard it again we went to my mother and my cousin said: 'Didn't you call Mary?' My mother asked if I had heard voices and I said I did. Then she asked my cousin if she had heard them, and when she said 'yes' my mother cried. She talked to me that night, and told me when I heard them again—no matter where I was—to say: 'What wouldst Thou, Lord? Here am I.' That is what Samuel said, you know, when the Lord called him. She told me not to be afraid, but surely answer.

"The next day I heard voices again, but I was too frightened to speak. I felt badly. Mother noticed it and asked me if I had heard the call again. When I said I was too frightened to say what she had told me to, she talked with me and told me that the next time I must surely answer and not fear.

"When the voice came again I was in bed. I answered as quickly as I could, as she had told me to do, and when I had spoken a curious lightness came over me. I remember so well. It seemed to me I was being lifted off my little bed, and I put out my hands and caught its sides. From that time I never heard the voices. They ceased."

In his *Memoirs*, Adam Dickey recorded Mrs. Eddy's description of this "lightness": "Her body was lifted entirely from the bed on which she lay, to a height, it seemed to her, of about one foot. Then it was laid gently back on the bed. This was repeated three times. As a child she was afraid to tell the circumstances to anybody, but she pondered it deeply in her heart and thought of it many years afterward, when she was demonstrating the nothingness of matter and that the claim of the human body was a myth." (pp. 140–141)

In later years, after talking to one of her students, Janette Weller, about this incident, Mrs. Eddy said, "I have no *words* to describe *what* I saw, but I saw Heaven." (Weller reminiscences)

Perhaps it is possible Mrs. Eddy was also thinking of this experience when she wrote, "The effects of Christian Science are not so much seen as felt. It is the 'still, small voice' of Truth uttering itself. We are either turning away from this utterance, or we are listening to it and going up higher. Willingness to become as a little child and to leave the old for the new, renders thought receptive of the advanced idea." (*Science and Health*, pp. 323–324)

14. See *Science and Health*, p. 40.
15. A10134.
16. *Retrospection*, pp. 13–14.
17. Ibid.

Chapter 2: God's gracious preparation

1. L02682.
2. *Christian History*, vol. VII, no. 4, p. 35. This is an excerpt from Finney's *Lectures on Systematic Theology*, 1846–1847. His ideas of "Christian Perfection" came to him in the late 1830s.
3. A11134. This document is an early draft of *Retrospection and Introspection*.
4. *Retrospection*, p. 21.

5. A11431.

6. Mary Baker Glover, *Science and Health*, first edition (Boston: The Christian Scientist Publishing Company, 1875), p. 315.

7. A11031.

8. *Retrospection*, p. 20.

9. Ibid. The details of the "plot" are given in the May 1983 *Journal* article "An important historical discovery" by Jewel Spangler Smaus, p. 284.

10. *Miscellany*, p. 345; see also Norman Beasley, *Mary Baker Eddy* (New York: Duell, Sloan and Pearce, 1963), p. 346.

11. To prepare herself for instruction in homeopathy, Mrs. Patterson first studied allopathy with Dr. Parsons Whidden for two months in the summer of 1849. See Parsons Whidden entry, pp. 530–531.

12. *Science and Health*, p. 156.

13. *Mary Baker Eddy*, p. 347.

14. A11887.

15. Mary Baker Eddy, *Miscellaneous Writings 1883–1896*, p. 355.

16. L10106.

17. A10402.

18. I John 4:19.

19. *Retrospection*, p. 24.

20. Published in *The Covenant*, October 1846. This periodical was published by the Odd Fellows, a fraternal organization.

21. F. B. Eastman affidavit.

22. *Science and Health*, p. viii.

23. Ibid.

Chapter 3: WAITING AND WATCHING ... THE DAYSTAR APPEARS

1. II Corinthians 10:4.
2. A10222.
3. A11805.
4. A11765; Alfred Farlow notes.
5. Frances Thompson Hill reminiscences.
6. *The Independent Democrat* (newspaper), July 3, 1862.
7. Quoted in *Christian Science History* by Septimus J. Hanna, first printing, p. 36.
8. *The Quimby Manuscripts*, ed. Horatio W. Dresser (New York: University Books, 1961), pp. 230–232.
9. A11043.
10. A10342.
11. A11446.
12. A11950.
13. *Science and Health*, pp. 184–185.
14. A11764.
15. *Science and Health*, first edition (1875), p. 351.
16. Mrs. Patterson accompanied her husband to his dental office on occasion when they were living in New Hampshire. More than forty years later, Mrs. Eddy received a letter from a Lucy W. Bancker recalling one such occasion: "When I was a girl of twelve years, I sat in Dr. Patterson's dental chair in Franklin N.H. (my name was Lucy W. Clark, and my father was Chas. Clark) and, listening to your reading Ossian's poems, I was nearly oblivious to the pain. The memory of that reading has always lingered with me, and as I look back upon my past life, it seems as though a change came over me. I knew it at the time. I was conscious of a power protecting me, a power outside of

myself." (*The Christian Science Journal*, February 1896, p. 480)

The following incident occurred just before the discovery of Christian Science. Elizabeth J. Moulton recalled this eyewitness account of Mrs. Patterson's assistance with patients: "In the winter of 1866, in company with my school-mate, I visited a dental office. My friend was to have a number of teeth extracted. I remained in the parlor while my friend was in the dental chair. You could look from the parlor directly to where she was sitting. The dentist, who was in attendance, I think was Dr. Patterson, gave the gas, but my friend took it, the tube, and threw it down and exclaimed, I can't take it. Immediately a door opened into the office, and a lady appeared with uplifted hands and advanced to the chair where my friend was sitting and said, 'I will take all your pain.' I will add the figure of the lady was small and delicate, her complexion fair as a babe and cheeks rosy . . . ."

At the end of her letter, Moulton wrote, "I never knew how I knew it was Mrs. Eddy, for no one ever told me, and I never saw her again until I heard her preach Sundays in Hawthorne Hall, Park St., Boston, and I never knew she married a Patterson until I came into C.S. in 1885." (Elizabeth J. Moulton letter, April 1, 1904)

17. *Science and Health*, p. 573.
18. Psalms 46:1.
19. *Science and Health*, third edition (1881), p. 156. Mary Baker Eddy, the sole author of *Science and Health with Key to the Scriptures*, uses *we* here to refer to herself in conformity with the literary conventions of her time.
20. Subject File: Henry Robinson. Owned by Longyear Museum; used with permission.
21. *Miscellaneous Writings*, p. 24.

22. A11887.

23. John 16:7–14.

24. *Science and Health*, p. 295; A11047.

25. *Science and Health*, p. 455.

Chapter 4: THE PIONEER ALONE: A MISSION REVEALED

1. A11824.

2. *Miscellaneous Writings*, p. ix.

3. Luke 9:58. In November 1868 Mary wrote to her friend Sarah Bagley, "if you . . . could understand the spiritual or rather scientific sense of the 9th Chapter of Luke you would see my life in its truer meaning." (L08307)

4. Luke 9:62.

5. See *Miscellaneous Writings*, p. 370.

6. *The Life of Mary Baker Eddy*, p. 134.

7. *Miscellaneous Writings*, p. 24.

8. *Science and Health*, first edition (1875), pp. 189–190.

9. Ibid., third edition (1881), p. 101. See page 221 in current edition.

10. *Miscellaneous Writings*, p. 380.

11. "My first writings on Christian Science began with notes on the Scriptures. I consulted no other authors and read no other book but the Bible for about three years. What I wrote had a strange coincidence or relationship with the light of revelation and solar light. I could not write these notes after sunset. All thoughts in the line of Scriptural interpretation would leave me until the rising of the sun. Then the influx of divine interpretation would pour in upon my spiritual sense as gloriously as the sunlight on the material senses." (*Miscellany*, p. 114)

12. *Miscellaneous Writings*, p. 380.

13. *The Life of Mary Baker Eddy*, pp. 140–141.

14. Abigail Dyer Thompson reminiscences.

15. Margaret E. Harding reminiscences. At the time of this healing, Mrs. Glover told Mrs. Norton of a store in Boston "where straps might be adjusted to brace the feet and legs of the boy until they were stronger. These were later secured and were afterwards found to be unnecessary, since strength came rapidly to the legs and feet of the boy, who afterwards became a mechanical engineer and lived a useful and happy life."

16. A11070.

17. *The Life of Mary Baker Eddy*, pp. 142–143.

18. A10224.

19. A11949.

20. A10062b.

21. *Science and Health*, first edition (1875), p. 338.

22. Hiram Crafts letter to Calvin Frye, February 23, 1902, Subject File: Hiram S. Crafts.

23. *The Life of Mary Baker Eddy*, p. 165; Irving Tomlinson notes.

24. A09000.

25. Notation in Mrs. Eddy's handwriting in the margin next to Psalm 103: "My brother, Albert raised me up from a sick bed by reading to me this Psalm." The Book of Psalms (New York: American Bible Society, 1879). B00016, Bible Collection. (See pp. 75–76.)

Chapter 5: MORAL SCIENCE

1. See *Miscellany*, p. 105. Very soon after the healing, one of the doctors told Mrs. Glover that Mrs. Gale was addicted to morphine, taken for relief from consumption, which had been healed at the same time as the pneumonia. Mrs. Glover then felt the need to pray day and night about the addiction. In three days

it was cured. (Subject File: Henry Robinson. Longyear Museum, used by permission; see also *Miscellaneous Writings*, p. 242.)

2. Clara Shannon reminiscences.

3. Abigail Dyer Thompson reminiscence file; Mary Baker Eddy, *Pulpit and Press*, p. 54; Robert Peel, *Mary Baker Eddy: The Years of Discovery* (Boston: The Christian Science Publishing Society, originally published by Holt, Rinehart and Winston, 1966), pp. 223–224.

4. A11065.

5. *Miscellaneous Writings*, pp. 69–70. *Boston Traveller* newspaper supplement, Communion season, 1900; Tomlinson, *Twelve Years*, p. 56.

6. A11351.

7. D. Lee Slataper letter, June 17, 1938. In *Mary Baker Eddy: The Years of Discovery* p. 228, Robert Peel writes that Mrs. Glover "asked Slataper about [Oscar], and he told her that at the doctor's orders he was giving the sick boy aconite. After the lecture she went back to their lodgings. The lad responded to her few words immediately, and next day when the doctor arrived he was back at his studies, perfectly well."

8. A10088.

9. Stephen Babcock letter, May 19, 1929. In his letter Mr. Babcock referred to "Mrs." Bagley, not knowing she wasn't married.

10. *The Life of Mary Baker Eddy*, pp. 186–187.

11. L03919.

12. Subject File: Alfred Farlow, Elizabeth Moulton statement.

13. L11061.

14. A11950.

15. A11071.

16. Samuel P. Bancroft, *Mrs. Eddy As I Knew Her in 1870* (Boston:

Press of Geo. H. Ellis Co., 1923), p. viii.

17. F00362.

18. *Mrs. Eddy As I Knew Her In 1870*, p. 119.

19. Emma Shipman reminiscences.

20. Lida W. Fitzpatrick reminiscences.

21. *Science and Health*, p. 458.

Chapter 6: TEACHER, COUNSELOR, AUTHOR

1. A10328. There are several other accounts of Mrs. Eddy healing girls of dumbness during her early years of practice:

"Soon after the discovery of Christian Science, while Mrs. Eddy lived in Lynn, a lady brought her twelve-year-old daughter to see if anything could be done for her. The child had been deaf and dumb from birth and was then attending a deaf and dumb school which was in the same building where Mrs. Eddy was living.

"The child was of sweet, gentle character, and Mrs. Eddy saw the only way to heal her was to rouse her; so she said, 'It is well you have never heard or spoken to give voice to your wicked thoughts.' Whereupon the child stamped her foot and spoke,—her first words—'You lie!' She returned to the schoolroom and spoke to the teacher, who fainted, and Mrs. Eddy was called to help her, also." (Grace Greene [Felch] reminiscences)

"A lady brought her daughter to Mrs. Eddy one day and asked to leave her with her as she could not speak. After doing all she could to help the girl, with apparently little effect, it occurred to her to test her in another way, and she said to her, 'Well, I suppose the reason you do not talk is because you cannot talk.' At once the girl answered her, 'I *can* talk and I do talk,

and I *will* talk, as much as I like and you can't stop me!' So Mrs.
Eddy was able to send her home to her parents cured of the
devil of dumbness." (Clara Shannon reminiscences)

A Mrs. Mosher who had come to Richard Kennedy's
office in Lynn for treatment witnessed a similar healing: "She
saw there a girl afflicted with dumbness whom the student
[Kennedy] had not been able to heal. At last he asked Mrs. Eddy
to help. Mrs. Mosher was present when Mrs. Eddy walked up
to the dumb girl and said, 'God did not send this upon you. You
can speak. In the name of Jesus Christ of Nazareth, I command
you to speak!' The girl shrank back, cried out, 'I can't, and I won't!'
and fled out of the room. But she was able to speak ever after."
(*The Christian Science Monitor*, May 9, 1914)

In the case of a grown woman: "A man brought his wife to
Mrs. Eddy for treatment for dumbness. Mrs. Eddy looking at
her, detected the devil of stubbornness. She said, severely, 'It is
well, madam, that you have not been talking these years'—and
the woman opened her mouth and began to defend herself!"
(Edward E. Norwood reminiscences)

2. Matthew 13:46.
3. *Manual*, p. 83.
4. L09662.
5. Lida Fitzpatrick reminiscences.
6. Ibid. See also *Miscellany* 105:7–10. At that time it was believed
   that spiritualists were able to heal others.
7. *Science and Health*, third edition, vol. II, pp. 13–16. (Once again
   here, Mrs. Eddy refers to herself as *we*, following the conventions of the day.) Mrs. Eddy wrote: "We doctored [Barry]
   gratuitously, and his friends when he requested it, gave him
   business chances that others coveted, etc. . . . For his sake we

taught the lady whom he wished to marry gratuitously, and endeavored to realize the obligations of the word mother that he had asked permission to call us." At the time, Mrs. Eddy also bequeathed to him $5,000 in her will.

Because of Kennedy's efforts to turn Barry against her, Barry ended up suing Mrs. Eddy, attaching her real estate for more than $20,000, all for carrying out household duties and business assignments he did voluntarily, and originally told her he wanted to do without pay. The court awarded him $350.

Mrs. Eddy wrote further about Kennedy, "From the time we dissolved partnership with the aforesaid mesmerist, because of his depravity, he avowed his intention to injure us, and we have the testimony who have heard him say that he would follow us to the grave for that purpose." (Ibid.)

Mrs. Eddy also healed Barry's sister, Annie, of acute rheumatism. (Transcript of testimony: George W. Barry vs. Mrs. Mary G. Eddy in Subject File: Alfred Farlow)

One can see that a change took place in Mrs. Eddy's thought regarding handling mental malpractice between the 3rd edition of *Science and Health* (1881) and the 6th edition (1883). In the 3rd edition, 46 pages were devoted to the subject and a good deal of it focused on Kennedy's activities, whereas in the 6th edition the issue takes up only 12 pages and Kennedy disappears from the chapter completely. Two specific examples of her change in thought can be seen, first in Mrs. Eddy's 1884 letter to Caroline Noyes: "It is time for you now to handle the malicious [mesmerism] or belief just as you do sickness. Declare for God as *all* and that there is nothing beside Him. Don't take up a personality, but class it all in one lump of error." And in her 1889 letter to Caroline Frame: "Let our finite judgment never settle on *who* is troubling us, and never defend ourselves against a person. Rather ask *what* is troubling, and then meet the *what*."

8. *Lynn Transcript*, February 3, 1872.

9. B00009, Bible Collection.

10. L10106. Here, the word *epoch* signifies a memorable date, not a distinctive or lengthy period of time.

11. *Science and Health*, first edition (1875), p. 5.

12. Ibid.

13. *Lynn Transcript*, January 13, 1872.

14. John 17:11–21.

15. *Science and Health*, first edition, p. 352.

16. Ibid., p. 353.

17. Helen A. Nixon reminiscences.

18. John Randall Dunn reminiscences.

Chapter 7: THE "CAUSE OF TRUTH"

1. Twenty years after the fact, Mrs. Eddy spoke of her experience of first writing *Science and Health* to a guest at her home: "I could not originate such a book. Why, I have to study it myself in order to understand it. When I came to the writing each day, I did not know what I should write until my pen was dipped in the ink and I was ready to begin." (James Gilman reminiscence) She also wrote of this in an article for the *Boston Herald* (December 3, 1900): "It was not myself, but the divine power of Truth and Love, infinitely above me, which dictated 'Science and Health with Key to the Scriptures.' I have been learning the higher meaning of this book since writing it." (See also *Journal*, January 1901, p. 597; *Miscellany*, p. 114.)

2. Mary Baker Eddy, *Message to The Mother Church for 1902*, pp. 15–16.

3. A11060.
4. *Science and Health*, first edition (1875), p. 4.
5. *Retrospection*, p. 38.
6. L02043.
7. *Miscellany*, p. 105.
8. A10328.
9. EF074, October 9, 1901.
10. Matthew 5:6.
11. L12666.
12. It's interesting to note that most of the early editions of *Science and Health* were bound in vibrantly colored covers of blue, green, red, and purple.
13. L07808.
14. L07816.
15. *Retrospection*, p. 15.
16. Clara Choate reminiscences. These Sunday afternoon meetings continued for two months in this location, the last one being held February 2, 1879.
17. L08737.
18. Annie M. Knott reminiscences. Another healing involving a prenatal incident is recorded in Eloise Knapp's reminiscences. Mrs. Eddy was called to help a sick child: "Mrs. Eddy paid no attention to the discord or phase of sickness the child was manifesting, but turned to the mother of the child and said, 'You fell before this child was born.' The mother answered, 'No, I never fell while I was carrying the child.' Mrs. Eddy declared, 'There is no effect from prenatal shock or fear,' and the child was healed. Then the mother said, 'Yes, I do remember now; a few days before the child was born, I fell down two steps. I had forgotten all about it.'" (Victoria Sargent, as recorded in Eloise

Knapp's reminiscences)

19. Gilbert Eddy and Edward J. Arens (students of Mrs. Eddy's) were arrested and jailed on a charge of conspiracy to murder Daniel Spofford, a disaffected student. This was later changed to attempted murder, as Spofford showed up very much alive. He had been in hiding. Eventually the entire incident was exposed as a hoax, and as the true facts came to light they led Mrs. Eddy to believe that Richard Kennedy was behind it all.

20. L02051. Mrs. Eddy originally intended the second edition of *Science and Health* to be "a book of over five hundred pages" that would give a "fuller synopsis of our metaphysical system." (*Science and Health*, second edition, p. 5) The printer's proofs were so filled with typographical errors, however, that Mrs. Eddy could only salvage 167 pages and so had to publish a considerably smaller edition of her textbook. She labeled it "Vol. II" because she wanted the public to consider it in conjunction with the first edition/volume published three years earlier.

21. Minutes of the Church of Christ (Scientist), 1879–1889.

Chapter 8: PASTOR

1. Minutes of the Christian Scientist Association.

2. L02655. The church members called Mrs. Eddy to the pastorate of the Church on August 16, 1879, and she formally accepted on December 1. The charter for the Church of Christ (Scientist) was granted on August 23. Mrs. Eddy would preach for her Church for almost a decade. She was officially ordained as Pastor on November 9, 1881, and continued in this office until resigning on May 28, 1889.

3. Helen M. Grenier reminiscences.

4. L13362.

5. The first regular service of the Church was held in Charlestown (part of Boston) on October 19, 1879. Services were moved to Hawthorne Hall, 2 Park Street, Boston, on November 30. From October 1, 1882, to June 24, 1883, services were held at 569 Columbus Avenue, the Massachusetts Metaphysical College and Mrs. Eddy's home. After a summer break they returned to Hawthorne Hall on November 4, and continued there through October 18, 1885, except for summer recesses. To accommodate a growing attendance, services were moved to Chickering Hall in Boston. They continued there until December 30, 1894, when the first service was conducted in the newly constructed edifice of The First Church of Christ, Scientist, on Falmouth Street in Boston.

6. Mary B. G. Billings reminiscences.

7. Mary Baker Eddy, *Christian Healing*, p. 16. Prior to this statement in her sermon, Mrs. Eddy had told her listeners, "Christian Science repudiates the evidences of the senses and rests upon the supremacy of God. Christian healing, established upon this Principle, vindicates the omnipotence of the Supreme Being by employing no other remedy than Truth, Life, and Love, understood, to heal all ills that flesh is heir to" (p. 15). Mrs. E. L. Clark of Roxbury, Massachusetts, certainly experienced this when, a month later, she "was instantaneously healed by Mrs. Eddy in May 1880; she had suffered with chronic indigestion which occasioned severe headaches from her childhood." (Alfred Farlow manuscript, "Facts and Incidents Relating to Mrs. Eddy," p. 171)

8. L09676.

9. *Miscellaneous Writings*, p. 223.

10. Ibid.

11. Calvin Frye wrote in his diary on November 29, 1899: "This morning Mrs. Eddy told me her first experience with mental [poison]: She had healed the wife of Mayor Atkinson of N'p't, Mass." (EF074; the abbreviation stands for Newburyport.)

12. *Science and Health*, p. 451.

13. Julia S. Bartlett reminiscences and Subject File: Alfred Farlow. In her reminiscences, Bartlett also wrote of witnessing another healing: "I never saw a grander demonstration of Truth than I witnessed as a young student when I saw our Leader stand before one who had for a long time seemed to be held by a very stubborn error. When it did not yield, she gradually rose to a greater and greater power until she seemed a tower of strength, not sparing the error the sharp, cutting rebuke necessary for its destruction, until this woman whom Satan had bound was free, and she has since been a faithful worker in the cause of Christian Science."

14. *Science and Health*, third edition (1881), p. 167.

15. *Science and Health*, p. 361.

16. *Science and Health*, third edition (1881), p. 85.

17. *Science and Health*, p. 92.

18. Robert Peel, *Mary Baker Eddy: The Years of Trial* (Boston: The Christian Science Publishing Society, originally published by Holt, Rinehart and Winston, 1971), pp. 95–96.

19. The way Mrs. Eddy presented herself to the public may have contributed to this accusation of love of money and hypocrisy. She dressed "richly" when she preached on Sunday. At one service, during time set aside for questions from the congregation, an eyewitness reported that someone asked, "Do you think it Christian to wear purple velvet and diamonds?" She responded, "There are ladies here I presume with much more

expensive dresses on, as this is velveteen, thirty-six inches wide, and only one dollar per yard. The cross and ring were given me by those who had been healed in Christian Science with the request that I wear them." (Mary Harris Curtis letter, October 3, 1917)

Another account of this question and answer is recorded in Edward E. Norwood's reminiscences: "'How is it that Mrs. Eddy, a professed follower of the lowly Nazarene, wears diamonds and velvet?' Mrs. Eddy smiled and replied, 'I will say to the friend who asks this, that this diamond cross at my throat was given me by a gentleman whose wife was raised from a dying bed; and this dress, which he calls velvet, is velveteen, cost $1.75 a yard, and has been made over three times!'"

As to the diamond ring, a lady physician had given it to her out of gratitude for being healed. The problem had been "a chronic trouble of long standing that drugs had failed to heal, but that she had been entirely free from it from the day she first met Mrs. Eddy." She gave Mrs. Eddy the ring, described as an heirloom, "stating that it was the most valued thing she had in her possession." (Julia Bartlett reminiscences; Alfred Farlow manuscript, "Facts and Incidents Relating to Mrs. Eddy," p. 134)

20. Matthew 18:15.
21. Minutes of the Christian Scientist Association; Peel, *Years of Trial*, p. 99.
22. A11907.
23. "Christian Science," *Mind in Nature*, June 1885. Mrs. Eddy was responding to two previous articles by Bishop Samuel Fallows, who labeled Christian Science as "telepathic power" and "*un*-Christian." See also *Journal*, February 1885, p. 5.

Chapter 9: LAUNCHING OUT DEEPER

1. L02496.
2. L07689.
3. L10642.
4. L02499.
5. A11418.
6. L12626.
7. Mrs. Eddy and some of her students had established the College at the end of 1880, receiving a charter from the state in January 1881.
8. At the time of Gilbert Eddy's passing, Mrs. Eddy believed that mental poison, resulting from malicious mental malpractice, was the cause of his death.
9. B00002, Bible Collection.
10. L04885.
11. L04093.
12. See *Science and Health* 109:11–16.
13. A09000, 41:2–3. Compare with *Science and Health* 291:13–16 (to ,).
14. A09000, 593:9–14. Compare with *Science and Health* vii:13–15 *Truth,* and 224:22–27.
15. After much revision and expansion, *Historical Sketch of Metaphysical Healing* was published in 1891 as the book *Retrospection and Introspection.* The same treatment was given to *Defence of Christian Science,* which was later issued as *No and Yes.*
16. During Mrs. Eddy's instruction, healings were not uncommon. Of her August 1883 Primary class, she wrote in a letter: "I healed a gentleman of a chronic disease of twenty years' standing in my last class. It was done instantaneously." (L05619) In another class "a clergyman asked Mrs. Eddy if

he could be healed of 'a partial blindness.' 'Yes,' she replied, 'if you will only touch the hem of His garment.' The healing was instantaneous." (Beasley, *Mary Baker Eddy*, p. 308) And in her November 1884 class, Eugene H. Greene, of Portland, Maine, was healed. His wife, Grace, who was in the same class, reported: "During this class Mr. Greene was healed of a hernia he had had for many years, and other minor troubles. Mrs. Eddy had previously healed him of tuberculosis of ten years' standing." (Grace Greene [Felch] reminiscences)

In her book *Rudimental Divine Science* (pp. 14–15), Mrs. Eddy wrote, "People are being healed by means of my instructions, both in and out of class. Many students, who have passed through a regular course of instruction from me, have been invalids and were healed in the class; but experience has shown that this defrauds the scholar, though it heals the sick.

"It is seldom that a student, if healed in a class, has left it understanding sufficiently the Science of healing to immediately enter upon its practice. Why? Because the glad surprise of suddenly regained health is a shock to the mind; and this holds and satisfies the thought with exuberant joy.

"This renders the mind less inquisitive, plastic, and tractable; and deep systematic thinking is impracticable until this impulse subsides.

"This was the principal reason for advising diseased people not to enter a class. Few were taken besides invalids for students, until there were enough practitioners to fill in the best possible manner the department of healing. Teaching and healing should have separate departments, and these should be fortified on all sides with suitable and thorough guardianship and grace."

17. L02069. She lectured in Hershey Hall on the Bible text "Whom do men say that I am?"
18. *Miscellaneous Writings*, p. 54.
19. Delia S. Manley reminiscences.
20. Ibid.
21. Minutes of the Christian Scientist Association. See Luke 5:4.
22. V00915. "Softening of the brain" is a literal description of a degenerative disease sometimes connected to senile dementia or paralysis.
23. L02633.
24. Philippians 2:5.

Chapter 10: DEFENDER OF THE CAUSE

1. *Miscellaneous Writings*, p. 95.
2. Ibid., pp. 95–97.
3. Minutes of the Christian Scientist Association: May 6, 1885.
4. Ibid., February 4, 1885.
5. William B. Turner reminiscences.
6. Minutes of the Christian Scientist Association: January 7, 1885.
7. Revised and reprinted in *Miscellaneous Writings*, p. 242.
8. The Prospectus issued by the College stated that the Primary class was comprised of twelve lessons, spread over three weeks, the first six lessons taught on consecutive days. The Normal class, intended to train teachers, was open only to students who had taken the Primary class, and indicated that students needed "to practice [Christian healing] from one to two years before entering."
9. *Years of Trial*, p. 186.
10. L11013.
11. Luther Marston was one of those students. Mrs. Eddy had

healed him before he became disaffected from the Cause. She
refers to this in her article "Mind-Healing History," in the June
1887 issue of *The Christian Science Journal*. This article was in
response to a lecture about Phineas Quimby, "The True History
of Mental Science," given by Julius Dresser in Marston's Church
of the Divine Unity (Scientist) in Boston. Marston printed the
lecture in his *Mental Healing Monthly* along with comments of
his own. Mrs. Eddy wrote: ". . . Mr. J. A. Dresser has again 'let
loose the dogs of war.' In other words, he has loosed from the
leash his pet poodle, to alternately bark and whine at my heels.
In a peppery pamphlet, Mr. Dresser delivers a stupendous eulogy
over the late P. P. Quimby, as his healer, and exaggerates and
fabricates in Quimby's behalf; but all that is kind, and I wish it
was honest. I commend gratitude, even in a child who hates his
mother; and this gratitude should be a lesson to that suckling
littérateur, Mr. Marston, whom I taught, and whose life I
saved three years ago, but who now squeaks out an echo of
Mr. Dresser's abuse." (*Journal*, June 1887; see also *Years of Trial*,
pp. 225–230)

Another of the students Mrs. Eddy had healed before he
became disaffected was Dr. H. E. Stone of Springfield, Massachusetts. She refers to him in her article "Malicious Newspaper
Reports" in the June 1888 issue of the *Journal*. The article was
written to publicly refute the charge made in the *Springfield
Union* that she "habitually employs a physician in Boston, but
is not willing to have his name known." She wrote: "I have
neither called nor consulted a physician for myself for over
twenty years . . . .

"The doctor in Springfield, alluded to as one of my physicians,
has not the degree of M.D. He was a student of mine, but may at

present be figuring under one of the many cognomens belonging to the mind-traffic, which are obsolete in Christian Science. This item could be published with authority, namely, that I healed him instantaneously of a severe chronic bronchial affection, which he said had afflicted him for more than twenty years, and was growing rapidly worse. His expectoration was of such an alarming nature that he told me he emptied his spittoon daily, to prevent his daughter from seeing the discharge from his throat...."

There is a note in Calvin Frye's handwriting, probably dictated by Mrs. Eddy in preparation for this article, that says in part, "Relative to the falsehoods afloat about Christian Science, I have only this to say: Dr. H. E. Stone of Springfield, who boasts of what he should be ashamed of, had better tell the truth once about the priestess of C.S., namely that she healed him instantaneously of a severe cough and a chronic bronchial affection [sic] that he could do nothing for, and which must have proved fatal had it not been for her remarkable aid according to his own statement." (A11064)

12. Mrs. Eddy warned her followers of the mind-curists' mental malpractice in her remarks at the Sunday service on July 4, 1886: "Never was there a more solemn and imperious call than God makes on us all, right here, for fervent devotion, and an absolute consecration to the greatest and holiest of all causes. The hour is come. The great battle of Armageddon is upon us. The powers of evil are leagued together in secret conspiracy against the Lord and against His Christ, as expressed and operative in Christian Science. Large numbers, in desperate malice, are engaged day and night in organizing action against us. Their feeling and purpose are deadly, and they have sworn enmity against the lives of our standard-bearers.

"What will you do about it? Will you be equally in earnest for the Truth? Will you doff your lavender-kid zeal, and become real and consecrated warriors? Will you give yourselves wholly and irrevocably to the great work of establishing the Truth, the Gospel, and the Science which are necessary to the salvation of the world from error, sin, disease, and death? Answer at once and practically, and answer aright!" (*Journal*, August 1886, p. 116)

Calvin Frye referred to the mental attack in a July 14, 1888, letter he sent to the Christian Science field: "About two years ago, I was having much to contend with from the attacks of malicious mesmerism, by which the attempt was made to demoralize me, and through me to afflict Mrs. Eddy. While under one of those attacks, my mind became almost a total blank. Mrs. Eddy was alone with me at the time, and, calling to me loudly without a response, she saw the necessity for prompt action, and lifted my head by the forelock, and called aloud to rouse me from the paralyzed state into which I had fallen. This had the desired effect, and I wakened to a sense of where I was, my mind wandering, but I saw the danger from which she had delivered me and which can never be produced again. Their mental malpractice, alias demonology, I have found out, and know that God is my refuge.

" 'When ye shall see the abomination of desolation spoken of by Daniel the prophet, stand in the holy place, (whoso readeth, let him understand) then let them which be in Judea, flee to the mountain,' where I have found refuge." (L15943)

Emma E. Cooley, who served as Assistant Editor to the *Journal* from December 1890 through October 1892, recorded a similar incident in her reminiscence: "[Mrs. Eddy] told of going into Mr. Frye's room one night, and found him sinking.

She pulled him out of bed and onto his feet, holding him up, walked him around the room, audibly declaring life, until he was himself again."

13. L14725.

14. Lewis Prescott reminiscences.

15. H00042. In her reminiscences, Addie Towns Arnold tells of the time Mrs. Eddy healed William Gill: "When Mr. Gill lived in Lawrence he was a near neighbor of ours, and I remember his telling me about a wonderful healing he had when he first took over his duties as editor of the *Journal*—Mrs. Eddy being the practitioner. He said that one day in going to Boston (he commuted from Lawrence to Boston daily), he jumped off the train and injured his ankle very badly. He went on to the office, treating himself, but suffering intensely all day. Things went on this way for three or four days, growing worse and worse all the time. I remember seeing him and telling him he ought to have someone help him. Finally the condition got so bad that he had to telegraph Mrs. Eddy that he could not come in that day. She immediately wired to him that his duty was in Boston and that he should come down and go directly to her. He managed to come, but he was in such acute pain and misery that he was totally unfit for work. Mrs. Eddy entered the room where he was, stood beside him for a while and then briefly spoke to him. Turning her back on him she walked to the window and looked out. As she stood there his ankle snapped back into place. He said the snap was so loud you could hear it all over the room. I remember that night when he returned to Lawrence you would never have known that anything had ever happened to it—he walked so easily and naturally."

Chapter 11: "THOSE WHO WATCH AND LOVE"

1. Mrs. Eddy had renamed the *Journal of Christian Science* to this in 1885.

2. That Mrs. Eddy found joy in her work as Pastor can be seen in a letter she wrote to a student, Ellen Brown (Linscott), the previous summer: "I took into the Church last Sunday 28 members. I send you the order of Services. We had a solemn earnest assembly. Hall *full*, wonderful effects followed. I have had boxes of flowers and letters every day telling me about it. At my meeting Friday eve for examining Candidates, a deaf girl heard and answered me." (L07868)

3. *Journal,* March 1888, p. 629. Mrs. Eddy's definition of *baptism* in the Glossary of *Science and Health* (p. 581) is, "Purification by Spirit; submergence in Spirit."

4. *Journal,* May 1888, pp. 93–94. The questions the twelve girls answered are noted in the *Journal.* There is no record of the answers given.

5. L03470.

6. Abigail Dyer Thompson. See Biographical Glossary, pp. 520–522.

7. Abigail Dyer Thompson reminiscences. See also the *Christian Science Sentinel,* October 3, 1931, p. 94, and *We Knew Mary Baker Eddy,* pp. 67–68.

8. Harriet O'Brien reminiscences.

9. Bertha Reinke reminiscences.

10. The substance of this address can be found in *Miscellaneous Writings,* pp. 98–106. Susan B. Anthony, a leader in the women's suffrage movement in the United States, was in the audience.

11. *Boston Evening Traveller,* June 23, 1888.

12. Emilie B. Hulin reminiscences.

13. A10273.
14. L12804; *Journal*, July 1888, p. 201.
15. L13004. The parable Mrs. Eddy is referring to is in Luke 20.
16. V01069.
17. Mary Baker Eddy, *Poems*, pp. 6–7.
18. Clara Shannon reminiscences.
19. L04491.
20. *Science and Health*, p. 103.
21. Minutes of the Christian Scientist Association.
22. L08683.
23. L12782. *Years of Trial*, p. 252.
24. Minutes of the Christian Scientist Association.
25. L10677.
26. L11172.
27. L03502.
28. L13091.
29. L05956.
30. See Psalms 34:14 and I Corinthians 13:4–7.
31. *Science and Health*, Forty-fourth edition (1889), pp. 92–93: "As the crude footprints of the past lose themselves in the dissolving paths of the present, we should understand the Science that governs these results, and plant our footsteps on firmer ground. Every so-called pleasure of sense gains a higher or lower definition, with the lapse of time. This unfolding should be painless progress, attended by love and peace, instead of envy and pride."
32. L00008.
33. Mrs. Eddy made it clear that this applied only to the Boston church: "Be it understood that I do not require Christian Scientists to stop teaching, to dissolve their organizations, or to desist

from organizing churches and associations." (*Journal*, December 1889, p. 434)

34. *Journal*, June 1889, p. 156; July 1889, p. 204; January 1890, pp. 477–478: "The fact is, I withdraw from an overwhelming prosperity, and was never better satisfied with my own demonstration of *Christian Science*. My dear students never expressed such a grateful sense of my labors with them as now, and were never so capable of relieving my tasks as at present."

35. *Journal*, December 1889, p. 431. Also, *Miscellaneous Writings*, pp. 355–359.

Chapter 12: IMPELLED BY LOVE

1. L08229.
2. *Science and Health*, fiftieth edition (1891), pp. 55–56. See also the final edition, p. 162.
3. *Journal*, December 1905, p. 572.
4. L04139.
5. L08931.
6. *Years of Trial*, pp. 267–268.
7. Ellen Brown Linscott, C.S.D.
8. L11026.
9. L12650.
10. L08565. See *We Knew Mary Baker Eddy*, pp. 90–91.
11. Arthur A. Maxfield reminiscences. Eloise M. Knapp recorded in her reminiscences that Captain Eastaman gave this testimony a few years later in the Original Edifice of The Mother Church.
12. Incoming Correspondence: David Easton to Mary Baker Eddy, September 30, 1891.
13. L04680.
14. With the 1892 Deed of Trust, Mrs. Eddy began to drop the

Congregational model in favor of centralizing the authority for running the affairs of the Church, under the *Church Manual*, in the Christian Science Board of Directors. Thereafter, she reduced and ultimately eliminated the congregation as a decision-making body.

15. *Journal*, March 1892, p. 488. See also *Miscellaneous Writings*, p. 91.

16. In 1895, these Rules and By-Laws were compiled and published as the *Manual of The Mother Church*.

17. L01584; the student was Alfred Farlow. There is very likely a connection between Mrs. Eddy's use of the word *storm* in this letter to describe church organization difficulties and an incident she noted on a flyleaf in one of her Bibles (B00009): "Opened to Jeremiah 29th—7 to 20th ver. In my sweet home when I calmed the terrible storm that was coming (Concord N.H. June 25 1892)."

Chapter 13: THE DEMAND FOR MORE GRACE

1. Adelaide Morrison Mooney reminiscences.

2. Anna White Baker reminiscences.

3. Ludie M. Waldron reminiscences. For a fuller account of this healing, see the entry on Ludie Waldron in the Biographical Glossary.

4. L03485. See also Robert Peel, *Mary Baker Eddy: The Years of Authority* (Boston: The Christian Science Publishing Society, originally published by Holt, Rinehart and Winston, 1977), p. 41.

5. *Journal*, January 1894, p. 429. See also *Miscellaneous Writings*, p. 374.

6. L07433; Mrs. Eddy wrote this letter to Edward Kimball. See also *Years of Authority*, p. 60.

7. L05974. Another incident with runaway horses occurred in 1903. Samuel Ramseyer related the incident in the June 1925 issue of *The Christian Science Journal* (p. 148): "In June, 1903, I was obliged to spend a Sunday in Concord, New Hampshire, at that time the home of our beloved Leader, Mary Baker Eddy. Early in the morning I decided to take a drive, but was informed that apparently there was no conveyance available in the city. I evidently expressed much disappointment, for the hotel clerk tried again, and I was finally furnished with a western horse together with a native horse and a buckboard. When I left the hotel, the clerk informed me that if I drove down a certain road about half past twelve I would very likely meet the Discoverer and Founder of Christian Science. His remark meant nothing to me at the time, as I did not remember ever having heard of Christian Science or of Mrs. Eddy before.

"It took two men to hold the horses until my companion and I could get into the buckboard. The western horse was much larger than the native one. We started off at a rapid rate. We had been driving for about an hour and had reached the outskirts of the town, the horses seeming all the time to be getting more excitable and anxious to have their own way, when we turned into a road which led down a steep hill, and I almost lost control of the horses. We were going at a very high rate of speed when I noticed a victoria [carriage] turn out and come to a standstill ahead. As we went by very quickly I saw a lovely lady seated in the victoria, and what the clerk had said to me passed through my mind. Immediately the horses calmed down. I put the whip in the socket, relaxed the lines, and we drove for over an hour in perfect ease and comfort, enjoying the beautiful June morning. When we returned to the hotel, the attendants met us and frankly said they did not expect us to return safely."

8. L05458.

9. Clara Shannon reminiscences.

10. Mrs. Eddy would visit her Church only four times. On April 1, 1895, a Monday, she made a private visit and stayed overnight in the Mother's Room before returning to her home in Concord, New Hampshire, the next day. The following month, on May 25, a Saturday, she again spent the night in the Church. The next morning she addressed the congregation during the church service before returning home that day (see *Miscellaneous Writings*, p 106). On January 4, 1896, a Saturday, she made an overnight visit and then delivered an address at the Communion service the following day. All of these visits were unannounced to the public. On February 6, 1908, Mrs. Eddy drove slowly down Falmouth Street in order to see the Church's large Extension in person. She did not stop to go in. This was reported in the Boston newspapers the following day.

11. L02748. See also Julia Michael Johnston, *Mary Baker Eddy: Her Mission and Triumph* (Boston: The Christian Science Publishing Society, 1976), pp. 134–135.

12. Emilie B. Hulin reminiscences.

13. L05082.

14. *Sentinel*, September 12, 1903, p. 24. See also *Miscellany*, p. 230.

15. Evening meetings were changed from Friday to Wednesday in 1898.

16. L05043. See also *Journal*, April 1895, pp. 40–42, and December 1939, p. 469; and *Christian Science Weekly* [*Sentinel*], October 6, 1898, p. 4.

17. John 16:7–14.

18. August 1888. Emma C. Shipman reminiscences. Mrs. Eddy's statement recalls these Scriptures: "... God hath chosen the weak things of the world to confound the things which are mighty" (I Corinthians 1:27); "And [the Lord] said unto me, My grace is sufficient for thee: for my strength is made perfect in weakness. Most gladly therefore will I rather glory in my infirmities, that the power of Christ may rest upon me. Therefore I take pleasure in infirmities, in reproaches, in necessities, in persecutions, in distresses for Christ's sake: for when I am weak, then am I strong" (II Corinthians 12:9, 10).

Chapter 14: THE FOUNDER AT WORK

1. *Miscellaneous Writings*, pp. 120–125.

2. *Journal*, February 1897, p. 550.

3. L03453.

4. Charles Carroll Howe reminiscences.

5. L05911; *Sentinel*, April 4, 1936, p. 610.

6. L05459; *Sentinel*, March 28, 1936, p. 590.

7. *Journal*, February 1896, p. 445. See also *Miscellaneous Writings*, p. 317.

8. Minnie Ford Mortlock reminiscences. See also *Miscellany* 247:13–18.

9. Minnie Ford Mortlock reminiscences.

10. *Journal*, March 1897, p. 575.

11. L03524.

12. L03528.

13. See "Dedicatory message," *Miscellany*, p. 183.

14. The months in this paragraph coincide with the dates of Mrs. Eddy's correspondence when she instituted these changes.

The notices of them in the Christian Science periodicals were
published at later dates.

15. L02402.

16. See chapter 15, pp. 203–204.

17. A10125. See also *Journal*, April 1898, p. 3.

18. A10125. Later, in November of that same year (1898), Mrs.
    Eddy again described the "secret place" in her letter of welcome
    to the Normal class she was about to teach: "The secret place,
    whereof David sang, is unquestionably man's spiritual state
    in God's own image and likeness, even the inner sanctuary of
    Divine Science, wherein mortals enter not without a struggle or
    sharp experience, and wherefore they put off the human for the
    Divine." (*Journal*, December 1898, p. 588)

19. Mary E. Dunbar reminiscences.

20. Genesis 1:26.

21. Revelation 22:2.

Chapter 15: THE "WEDDING GARMENT" OF DIVINE LOVE

1. Incoming Correspondence: G. A. Walther letter to Mary Baker
   Eddy, January 11, 1899.

2. L07610.

3. Matthew 22:1–14.

4. Mary Baker Eddy, *Message to The Mother Church for 1900*, p. 15.

5. EOR10.01. See also Clifford P. Smith, *Historical Sketches*
   (Boston: The Christian Science Publishing Society, 1992),
   p. 166.

6. Clara Shannon reminiscences. See also EF071.

7. L11198.

8. L09748.

9. Marie Chalmers Ford reminiscences.

10. *Miscellany*, pp. 131–133.

11. Annie Louise Robertson reminiscences in *We Knew Mary Baker Eddy*, p. 105. Mrs. Robertson originally gave her account as an address to those gathered in Boston to attend an Annual Meeting, and this was published in the July 10, 1937, issue of the *Sentinel*, pp. 901–902.

12. *Sentinel*, January 16, 1902, p. 321.

13. L04317.

14. *Journal*, February 1900, p. 735. See also *Poems*, p. 79.

15. L14525.

16. L00155.

17. L08043.

18. L03744.

19. Joseph I. C. Clarke, *My Life and Memories* (New York: Dodd, Mead, & Co., 1925), p. 337.

Chapter 16: "The Cause needs healers"

1. *Miscellany*, p. 111.

2. For the origin and further background of the marginal headings, see the editorial *"Science and Health:* textbook for self-improvement" in the September 1993 issue of the *Journal* (pp. 39–42).

3. Whereas the 1902 reading was for the purpose of making corrections, *Science and Health* xii:20–22 refers to her reading the textbook in 1907 specifically for the purpose of "elucidat[ing] her idealism."

4. L08403.

5. L14299.

6. F00246. See also *Message for 1902*, p. 16. Wycliffe's translates Luke 1:77, "for to give science and health to his people . . ."

7. V00274.

8. L03057.

9. L15516.

10. L08352.

11. H00071.

12. Clara Shannon reminiscences.

13. Theresa M. Hayward to Bureau of History and Records, November 1934, reminiscence files.

14. Lottie Clark reminiscences.

15. L04273.

16. *Sentinel*, September 12, 1903, p. 24. Reprinted in *Miscellany*, pp. 229–230.

17. L00383.

18. L01365.

Interlude: ADVICE FOR HEALERS

1. Acts 10:34.

2. *Journal*, October 1888, p. 375.

3. *Journal*, April 1889, pp. 19–21; *Miscellaneous Writings*, pp. 279–282.

4. *We Knew Mary Baker Eddy*, p. 56.

5. Ibid., pp. 56–57.

6. *Manual*, p. 83.

7. L04080.

8. L04081.

9. L04074.

10. V00865.

11. L07907.

12. L07823.

13. L07882.

14. L05911.
15. A11409.
16. A11445.
17. L13426.
18. L03980.
19. A11410.
20. A11413; John 4:35.
21. L02167.
22. L12629.
23. L05468.
24. L07766.
25. L01953.
26. L11242.
27. L04096.
28. L10478.
29. L03374.
30. L02044.
31. L06047.
32. L07455.
33. L05195. The Scriptural reference is to Psalms 91:7, with emphasis added.
34. L07594.
35. L04428.
36. L04440.
37. L04448. The phrase "scalding tear" comes from Mrs. Eddy's poem "The Mother's Evening Prayer" (*Poems*, p. 4). The Scriptural reference is to the story of Jesus' resurrection; see Mark 16:1–6.
38. L04450; see John 8:31, 32 and Revelation 21:4, 25.
39. L10705; see *Christian Science Hymnal*, No. 335.

40. L03524; see Matthew 6:13.
41. L02421.
42. L09957.
43. A10312.
44. L04529; II Corinthians 2:16. Also see II Timothy 4:7.
45. L03474; see Mark 2:22 and Luke 12:27.
46. L03406.
47. L09924.
48. L14405; see Matthew 25:14–29.
49. L05459.
50. L04262.
51. A12030.
52. A11442; Mark 13:15.
53. L04284.
54. L05413.
55. L07847.
56. L05563.
57. L08114.
58. L12805.
59. L04349.
60. L01813.
61. L04460; see Joshua 24:15.
62. L13116.
63. A11958.
64. L04415; see Mark 13:37.
65. L13040; see Mark 3:27.
66. L04864.
67. F00147.
68. L09622; see Psalms 91:4.
69. L04285.

70. L04546.

71. L05517.

72. A11886.

73. A11921.

74. A11973.

75. L13339.

76. L02891; see Deuteronomy 6:4 and Mark 12:29.

77. L02897.

78. L03333B; see Romans 8:28.

79. *Science and Health*, p. 427.

Chapter 17: THE CROSS

1. H00094.

2. George Kinter reminiscences.

3. Mary Crane Gray reminiscences.

4. *Boston Herald*, June 11, 1905.

5. Matthew 10:38.

6. *Miscellany*, p. 4.

7. L10930.

8. L08548.

9. L14627. On one occasion a different horse than usual was harnessed to her carriage. "'Where is Jerry?' asked Mrs. Eddy. 'Jerry is lame,' was the reply. 'Put Jerry in the harness,' said Mrs. Eddy. The coachman obeyed, and soon the carriage came up the driveway, with Jerry in the harness, limping at each step. 'Jerry,' said Mrs. Eddy, 'mind your *own* business,' and Jerry stopped limping." (Edith L. Woodmansee reminiscences.)

10. V00698. See also Lyman P. Powell, *Mary Baker Eddy: A Life Size Portrait* (Boston: The Christian Science Publishing Society, 1991), p. 234; *Twelve Years*, p. 269.

11. L15400.
12. V03226.
13. *Science and Health*, p. xii. The dictionaries of Mrs. Eddy's day defined *idealism* as a term applied to metaphysical systems. See also *Science and Health* 132:20–27, where she equates *idealism* with the "true idea of God," the Christ.
14. Ibid., p. xii.
15. L13998. General Booth lived to be 85, passing away in 1912.
16. *We Knew Mary Baker Eddy*, p. 182.
17. The "Masters" consisted of a judge, a psychiatrist (then known as an alienist), and an unbiased attorney. They were to determine Mrs. Eddy's competence to conduct her own financial affairs.
18. *Twelve Years*, p. 71. See also Part Two, pp. 378–384.
19. Lady Victoria Murray reminiscences.

Chapter 18: CROWNED BY LOVE

1. John Lathrop diary. Mr. Lathrop was one of Mrs. Eddy's secretaries at the time. See p. 469.
2. Ibid.
3. *Sentinel*, January 18, 1908, p. 391.
4. *Science and Health*, p. 107.
5. Ibid., p. 455.
6. *Memoirs*, p. 68.
7. This statement also appeared in the *Journal*, May 1908, p. 65, and was reprinted in *Miscellany*, p. 286.
8. L09772.
9. L08756. Psalms 46:10. See also *Miscellany*, p. 275.
10. *Science and Health*, second edition (1878), p. 166.
11. *Miscellany*, p. 353.
12. Alexander Pope, "An Essay on Man" (1733), epistle I, line 274.

13. *Miscellaneous Writings*, p. 4.

14. L03466. Two weeks after this, Mrs. Eddy abolished the Communion service in The Mother Church to stop the annual pilgrimage of multitudes of Christian Scientists from outside the Boston area.

15. A11333.

16. *Manual*, p. 49.

17. L13481.

18. Incoming Correspondence: Alfred Farlow to Mary Baker Eddy, July 20, 1909.

19. L01572.

20. See *Science and Health*, p. 269.

21. William Rathvon reminiscences. See Luke 12:7.

22. L10416.

23. L01775. Ephesians 5:14.

24. Helena Hoftyzer reminiscences.

25. A10347 and the September 1, 1917, *Sentinel*, where "Principle and Practice" was published posthumously. The Scriptural references are from Mark 16:15 and Matthew 10:8.

26. L01953.

27. Elsie Bergquist reminiscences.

28. Elizabeth Earl Jones reminiscences.

29. William Rathvon reminiscences.

30. L13841.

31. L04726.

Part Two—More Healing Works of Mary Baker Eddy

1. A more extensive account of this healing can be found in *We Knew Mary Baker Eddy*, pp. 4–6.

2. A more extensive account of this healing can be found in *We Knew Mary Baker Eddy*, p. 9.

3. Isaiah 55:1.

4. Mark 16:17, 18.

5. See II Corinthians 5:17.

6. A more extensive account of this healing can be found in *We Knew Mary Baker Eddy*, pp. 70–71. In that account Knott states: "Here I ought to say that I had scarcely left [Mrs. Eddy's] presence to ascend the stairs when I was aware of a warm glow in my hands, and all sense of chilliness and discomfort had gone. Not only was this true, but in the classroom I could not help observing that my hands seemed to be changed, and the redness and roughness due to the cold outside had entirely vanished, nor did it ever return."

7. In her reminiscence Caroline Bates writes of her healing: "My father was in the practice of medicine at New Haven, Connecticut, for nearly fifty years. I went down under laws of the doctors when quite young; was a constant sufferer from many ills.

   "July fourth, 1885, I went to a neighboring city to have a crayon picture made to leave with my husband. I did not think he would have me with him long. While there, a friend gave me *Science and Health*, saying, 'I think it will help you.' She opened a door to another room and said: 'Go in there where it is quiet and read.' She said, 'I cannot tell you anything about it.' After reading two or three pages, I was healed, and perfectly healed. I was free from pain. I caught the idea of non-intelligent matter. I began reading at page forty-four of the fourteenth edition. From that time on I went to the book for my healing.... .

   "Ten years after I was healed my attention was called to the fact that I could not remember the uses of medicine, although I had been educated in it up to the time of my healing."

8. The Rev. Phalen was the minister of the Unitarian Church in Concord, New Hampshire, from 1892 to 1899, and Chaplain of the First New Hampshire Volunteer Infantry in the Spanish-American War. He interviewed Mrs. Eddy on November 30, 1897. He begins his reminiscence: "It has been my good fortune to know in the United States and England some of the outstanding men and women of the nineteenth and twentieth centuries.... I have known brilliant and distinguished American and European women—but among all the people I have known Mrs. Eddy, the Discoverer and Founder of Christian Science, stands forth as the most remarkable."

After relating the healing of the woman with the mental breakdown, the Rev. Phalen went on to say, "I have read and heard very often that Mrs. Eddy was an errant egotist and that she was continually intruding her personality. I desire to say that I felt no such thing in my interview with her, nor do I find it in her letters. On the contrary, my impression was that she felt she was the channel of the divine grace, the woman chosen by the Eternal to show new light and truth on the path of life. She made no claims whatever, and instead of appearing puffed up with a consciousness of power, she appeared to me a rare example of humility. There was an atmosphere of gracious gentleness and mysterious charm about her I have never been able to analyze. It could be felt and I felt it, but I cannot adequately portray my impression in words. Her voice was low and sweet, and I was struck at once by her choice of words and the way she used them, in a rather unusual way putting into them a wealth and weight of meaning all her own."

9. The event at Pleasant View in Concord, New Hampshire, actually took place on July 5, when the holiday was observed. July 4 was a Sunday.

10. "Miss Bartlett said that while Mrs. Eddy was living at 385 Commonwealth Avenue, Boston, Mr. Calvin Frye suddenly passed on, and Mrs. Eddy raised him from the dead." (Lottie Clark reminiscences)

11. Mrs. Eddy was never a member of the Methodist Episcopal Church. According to the letter the Rev. Larmour sent Mrs. Eddy, he found her name on Bow's town records, "and thinking [he] would not slight any of the older members of the town, [he] ask[ed] them to contribute . . . ." (E. N. Larmour letter, December 7, 1903, in Larmour reminiscence file)

12. *Manual*, p. 42.

13. *Miscellany*, pp. 355–356.

Appendix A: More Advice for Healers

1. L07393.

2. See Mark 3:27.

3. V04759.

4. L08565. For the parable of the tares and wheat, see Matthew 13:24–30. For the quoted Scriptural references, see Proverbs 3:5, 6 and John 16:33.

5. A11179.

6. L08893.

7. L14478.

8. L05197.

9. L04434.

10. The next sentence was written overleaf, and both sentences were marked with orange crosses. Most likely, the second sentence

was meant to take the place of the first.

11. A12003.

Appendix B: BIOGRAPHICAL GLOSSARY

1. L02912.
2. Addie Towns Arnold reminiscences; for the Biblical allusion, see Matthew 16:5–12.
3. L08307. Mrs. Eddy changed her mind about moving west and instead stayed with the Wentworths for a year and a half.
4. L10710.
5. A11923.
6. Irving C. Tomlinson reminiscences; Mary Baker Eddy, Scrapbook SB001, p. 7.
7. Georgine Milmine, *The Life of Mary Baker G. Eddy*, p. 108.
8. Subject File: Eddy—Family—Abigail Tilton.
9. *Retrospection*, p. 10.
10. V01939. In Mrs. Eddy's day influenza was called "la grippe," and she used this name in her reference to healing Alfred.
11. Anna Baker reminiscences.
12. F00182. See Mark 8:18.
13. Subject File: Eddy—Family—Elizabeth Baker.
14. A11437.
15. A11025. English philosophers John Locke and Francis Bacon, French philosopher and writer François de Voltaire, and Scottish philosopher David Hume.
16. A11763.
17. *Mrs. Eddy As I Knew Her in 1870*, p. 8.
18. Julia Bartlett reminiscences; *We Knew Mary Baker Eddy*, pp. 40–41. The Bible passage recalled here is a paraphrase of Luke 10:7.

19. William Bradford Turner reminiscences.

20. Harriet Betts reminiscences. Irving Tomlinson also relates this healing in his book, *Twelve Years with Mary Baker Eddy: Amplified Edition*, pp. 54–55. He indicates that, along with being restored to life, the child's ill temper was healed as well. In Clifford Smith's account of this healing in *Historical Sketches* (p. 71), he refers to the little boy as "Stanley." Both of these accounts say this healing took place in Lynn.

21. Clara Brady reminiscences.

22. James Brierly reminiscences. Mark 5:26.

23. Ibid.

24. Clara Choate reminiscences.

25. *Memoirs*, p. 140.

26. Mary Dunbar reminiscences.

27. Incoming Correspondence: Joseph Eastaman to Mary Baker Eddy, 1910.

28. *Journal*, May 1889, pp. 88–89; see also *Miscellaneous Writings*, pp. 177–180.

29. L16187.

30. Ruth Ewing reminiscences.

31. Alfred Farlow, "Historical Facts Concerning Mary Baker Eddy," pp. 51–52; see also *The Years of Discovery*, p. 212.

32. Incoming Correspondence: Alfred Farlow to Mary Baker Eddy, June 24, 1909.

33. Lida W. Fitzpatrick reminiscences. See Acts 17:28.

34. Marie Chalmers Ford reminiscences.

35. L02011.

36. Alice French reminiscences.

37. L00352.

38. James F. Gilman to Carrie Huse, December 18 and 20, 1892, in

James F. Gilman reminiscence file. See also his draft reminiscences in the same file and *Painting a Poem: Mary Baker Eddy and James F. Gilman Illustrate "Christ and Christmas"* (Boston: The Christian Science Publishing Society, 1998), pp. 21–22.

39. *Retrospection*, p. 19.
40. L15722.
41. Mary Crane Gray reminiscences.
42. Subject File: Alfred Farlow, C.E.L. Green statement.
43. Helen Grenier reminiscences.
44. Margaret E. Harding reminiscences.
45. Emilie B. Hulin reminiscences. A similar healing was recorded in Mary E. Eaton's reminiscences: "Mr. Frank Gale told me that Mrs. Eddy said a patient came to her with the eyes running out, and one declaration she made was: 'Sight is ever present,' and the sight was restored and new eyeballs formed."
46. Emilie B. Hulin reminiscences.
47. V03349.
48. Incoming Correspondence: William B. Johnson to Mary Baker Eddy, June 17, 1909.
49. *Science and Health*, third edition (1881), vol. II, pp. 16–17.
50. George Kinter reminiscence file.
51. Bliss Knapp, *The Destiny of The Mother Church* (Boston: The Christian Science Publishing Society, 1991), p. 125.
52. Laura Lathrop to Alfred Farlow, February 8, 1901, in Subject File: Alfred Farlow, Research by, 1862–1906.
53. Delia S. Manley reminiscences, in the Frances Thompson Hill reminiscence file.
54. Arthur Maxfield reminiscences.
55. *Miscellaneous Writings*, pp. 98–106.
56. Subject File: Archibald McLellan.

57. Ibid.

58. Adelaide Mooney reminiscences.

59. Ibid.

60. *Miscellany*, p. 345.

61. Minnie Ford Mortlock reminiscences.

62. Ibid.

63. Lady Victoria Murray reminiscences.

64. L02865.

65. *Journal*, December 1929, p. 506.

66. *Journal*, March 1902, p. 739.

67. Elizabeth Norton reminiscences.

68. L11127.

69. Harriet O'Brien reminiscences. Matthew 4:4.

70. Mary Godfrey Parker reminiscences. See also *We Knew Mary Baker Eddy*, pp. 4–6 and 9–10.

71. Subject File: Mary Godfrey Parker.

72. Janette E. Weller reminiscences.

73. A11006. Jonathan Buffum, a well-known spiritualist, was very active in Lynn civic affairs.

74. L14551.

75. This letter was sent to Mrs. Eddy by her cousin and legal counselor, Henry M. Baker, May 3, 1899. For the story of Goddard's interest in Mrs. Eddy, see Judge Septimus J. Hanna's reminiscences, pp. 66–68.

76. Charles MacFarland, *Lyman Pierson Powell, Pathfinder in Education and Religion* (New York: Philosophical Library, 1947), p. 215.

77. Julia Prescott reminiscences.

78. Ibid.

79. Ibid.

80. Subject File: Lyman Powell—Correspondence—January 13, 1931.

81. The published *Manuscripts* were edited by Horatio Dresser, who had previously written of them: "One searches his manuscripts in vain for a clear explanation of his method of silent cure." *A Message to the Well* (New York: Putnam, 1910), p. 88.

82. *Miscellany*, pp. 306–307.

83. William Rathvon reminiscences.

84. Ibid.

85. Ibid.

86. Ibid.

87. Else Buchenberger account in Bertha Reinke reminiscences.

88. *Mrs. Eddy As I Knew Her in 1870*, p. 10.

89. L05918.

90. L05924.

91. L13317.

92. L13318.

93. John Salchow reminiscences. Joseph Mann's healing is related in *We Knew Mary Baker Eddy*, pp. 167–170.

94. John Salchow reminiscences.

95. Ibid.

96. Ibid.

97. Laura Sargent reminiscences.

98. Victoria Sargent reminiscence file. See Revelation 12.

99. Victoria Sargent reminiscence file.

100. Clara Shannon letter to the Christian Science Board of Directors, August 16, 1927, in the Clara Shannon reminiscence file.

101. Ibid.

102. Emma C. Shipman reminiscences.

103. Ibid.

104. L13357.

105. Hanover P. Smith, *Writings and Genius of the Founder of Christian Science* (Boston: Hanover P. Smith, 1886), pp. 38–39.

106. Daniel Spofford letter to Georgine Milmine, September 18, 1904, private collection, used by permission. The references to incurring Mrs. Glover's "enmity" and being "the victim of a relentless persecution" can be seen as examples of the effect of Richard Kennedy's efforts (through mesmeric manipulation) to turn Mrs. Eddy's students away from her.

107. Ibid.

108. Augusta Stetson, *Reminiscences, Sermons, and Correspondence, 1884–1913* (New York: G. P. Putnam's Sons, 1926), pp. xi–xii.

109. B00027, Bible Collection; R. F. Weymouth, *The New Testament in Modern Speech* (London: James Clarke and Co., 1903).

110. Adelaide Still reminiscences.

111. Ibid.

112. William Rathvon reminiscences.

113. Marguerite F. Sym reminiscences.

114. Ibid.

115. Abigail Dyer Thompson reminiscences.

116. Ibid. See also *We Knew Mary Baker Eddy*, pp. 66–67.

117. Abigail Dyer Thompson reminiscence file.

118. Ibid.

119. Ibid.

120. Subject File: Alfred Farlow—Affidavits.

121. *Twelve Years*, p. xvii.

122. Irving Tomlinson reminiscences.

123. William B. Turner reminiscences.

124. Ibid.

125. Ludie Waldron reminiscences.

126. Annah E. Davis reminiscences.

127. Ibid.

128. Janette E. Weller reminiscence file.

129. Subject File: Wentworth Family.

130. *Years of Discovery*, p. 95.

131. L13931.

132. A10994.

133. Robert Peel, *Christian Science: Its Encounter with American Culture* (New York: Henry Holt and Company, 1958), p. 112.

134. *Miscellany*, pp. 317–319; see also pp. 319–325.

135. L02164.

136. Irving Tomlinson reminiscences.

137. Josephine Woodbury, *War in Heaven: Sixteen Years' Experience in Christian Science mind-healing* (Boston: Press of Samuel Usher, 1897), p. 5.

138. L02652. Mrs. Woodbury was admitted to The Mother Church on two years' probation in 1895, but she was expelled one year later for continuing misbehavior.

139. Alice Wool reminiscences.

140. Matthew 7:14.

141. L09012.

142. B00009, Bible Collection.

INDEX

INDEX

A

Adams, Mary W., 226, 361, 494
Albion, Maine, 54, 432
Allan, Charlotte, 228
Amesbury, Mass., 75, 78, 84, 85, 412, 464, 528, 538
animal magnetism, 141, 155–157, 244, 245, 247, 257, 377, 399
Anthony, Susan B., 573n10
Arens, Edward, 438, 512, 562n19
Armstrong, Joseph, 176, 253, 410, 478, 479, 485
Arnold, Addie Towns, 411

B

Babcock, Mrs. 223
Babcock, Stephen, 84, 556n9
Badgely, R. O., 298
Bagley, Sarah, 78, 84–86, 412, 554n3
Bailey, Joshua F., 237–238, 413, 546n4
Baker, Abigail Ambrose (mother), 18, 27–30, 33–34, 38, 414, 448, 546n2, 548–549n13
Baker, Abigail Barnard (sister) (Mrs. Alexander Tilton), 27, 36, 62, 74, 411, 414, 417, 418, 531
Baker, Albert (brother), 27, 75–76, 415, 555n25
Baker, Alfred E., 209, 231–232, 249, 415, 509, 591n10
Baker, Anna B. White, 415–416
Baker, Elizabeth P. (stepmother), 416, 486
Baker, George Sullivan (brother), 27, 31–32, 74–76, 416–417
Baker, Henry M. (cousin), 594n75
Baker, Mark (father), 27, 31, 33, 34, 416, 417, 418, 451, 531
Baker, Martha Rand (sister-in-law), 417–418
Baker, Martha Smith (sister) (Mrs. Luther Pilsbury), 27, 418, 487
Baker, Mary (see Mary Baker Eddy)

YVONNE CACHÉ VON FETTWEIS, a native of California, grew up in New York City. A published writer at sixteen, her poetry has appeared in national anthologies. She attended Wagner College, majoring in English literature, and has done graduate work that included a stint at American University. She worked at The First Church of Christ, Scientist, in Boston, Massachusetts, for more than 30 years, most of which she spent working with the Church's historical collections. She became Manager of the Church History department in 1991, and was appointed Church Historian in 1995, a position she held for five years. She's also been a member of the Organization of American Historians. Yvonne advertised in *The Christian Science Journal* as a Christian Science practitioner for more than 20 years. She was also a member of the Church's Board of Lectureship for a year, specifically assigned to lecturing about Mary Baker Eddy. She lives in Ormond Beach, Florida.

ROBERT TOWNSEND WARNECK, a Christian Science practitioner and teacher, has lived in Pennsylvania, Ohio, New York, Massachusetts, and Vermont. He graduated from Syracuse University with a degree in British literature. Upon graduation, Rob moved to Boston to work for The Mother Church, The First Church of Christ, Scientist. In more than 25 years of employment (1973–1999) he worked in the office of the Manager, Committees on Publication; in Branch Church Activities; in the office of the Board of Directors; as a research assistant to the Clerk; and as the senior researcher in the Church History department, the collections of which are now in The Mary Baker Eddy Library. In 1999 Rob entered the full-time healing practice of Christian Science. In 2003 he became an authorized Christian Science teacher. His poems and articles have appeared in *The Christian Science Journal* and the *Christian Science Sentinel*. He happily resides in Burlington, Vermont, with his wife and two cats.